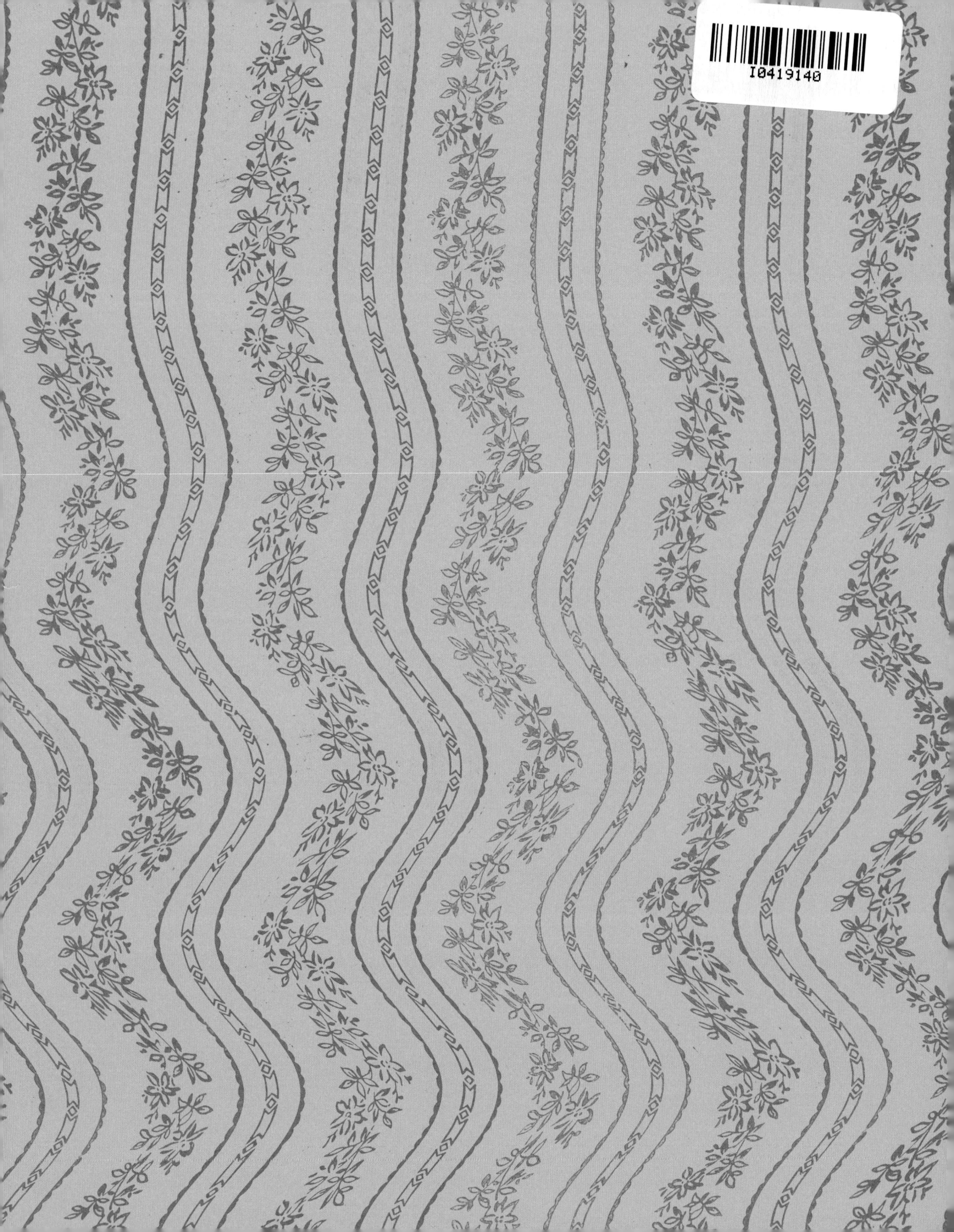

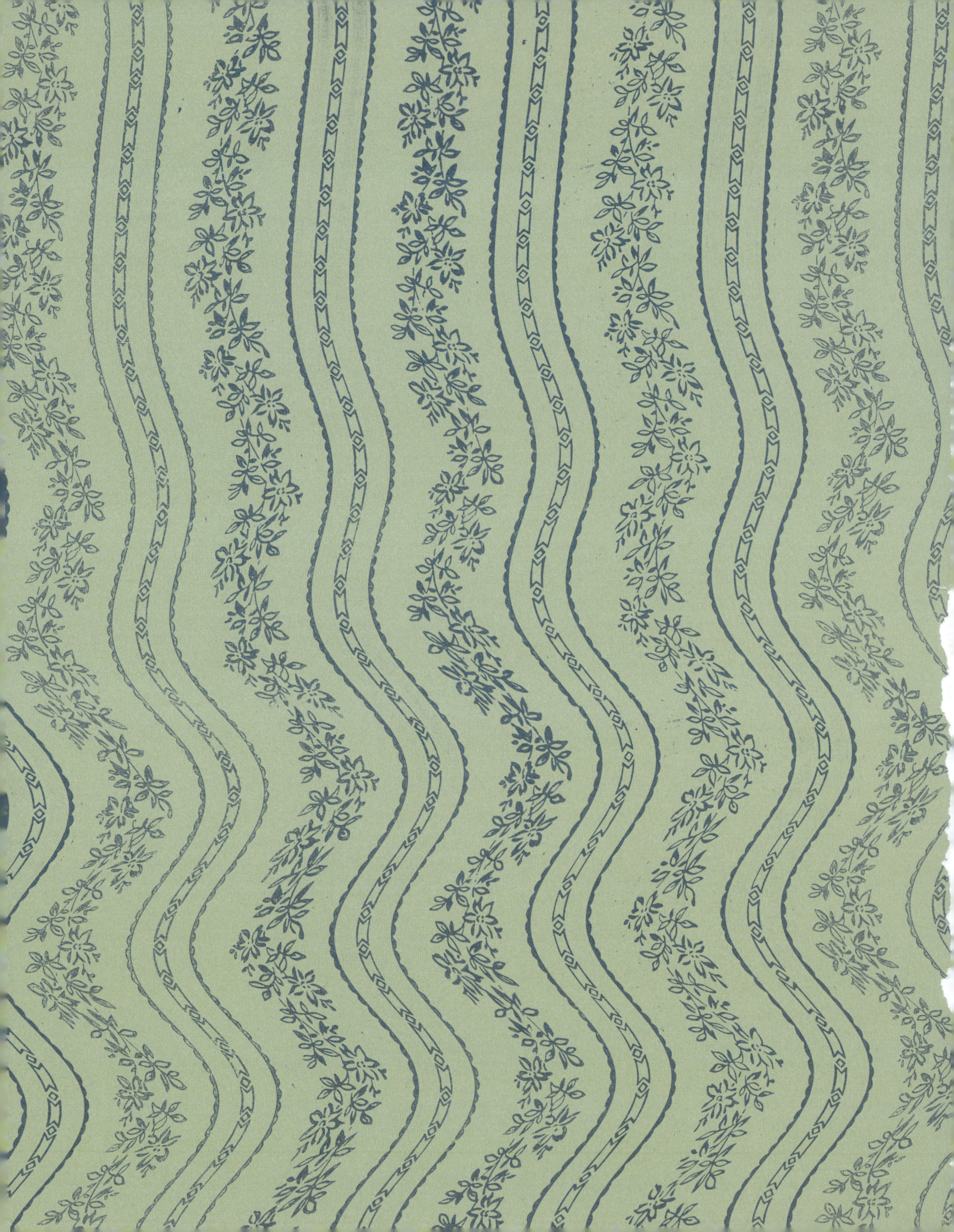

Bodies & Souls

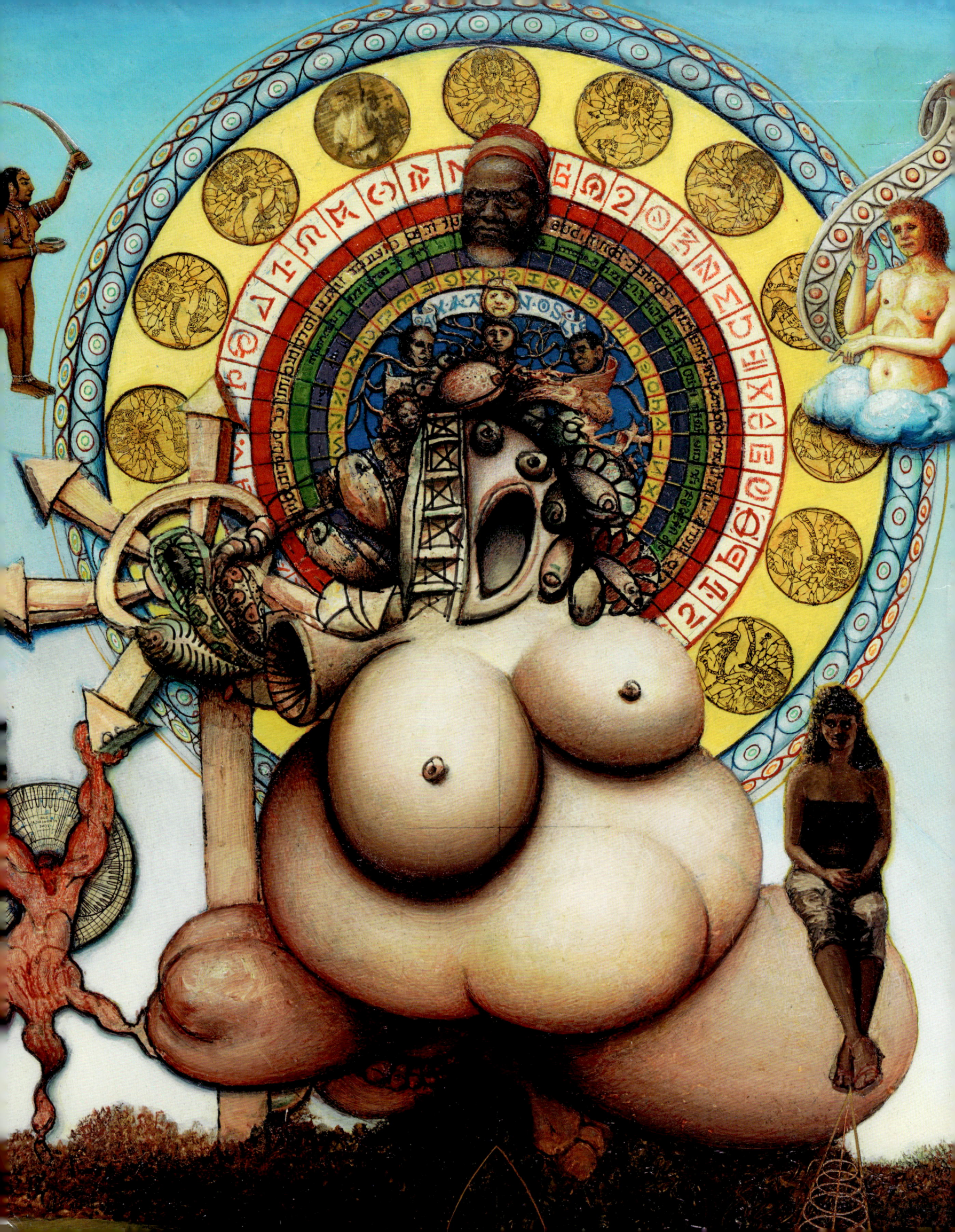

Bodies & Souls

Robert Cozzolino
Robert Kohler
William R. Valerio

Pennsylvania Academy of the Fine Arts
Woodmere Art Museum
Distributed by the University of Pennsylvania Press
Philadelphia

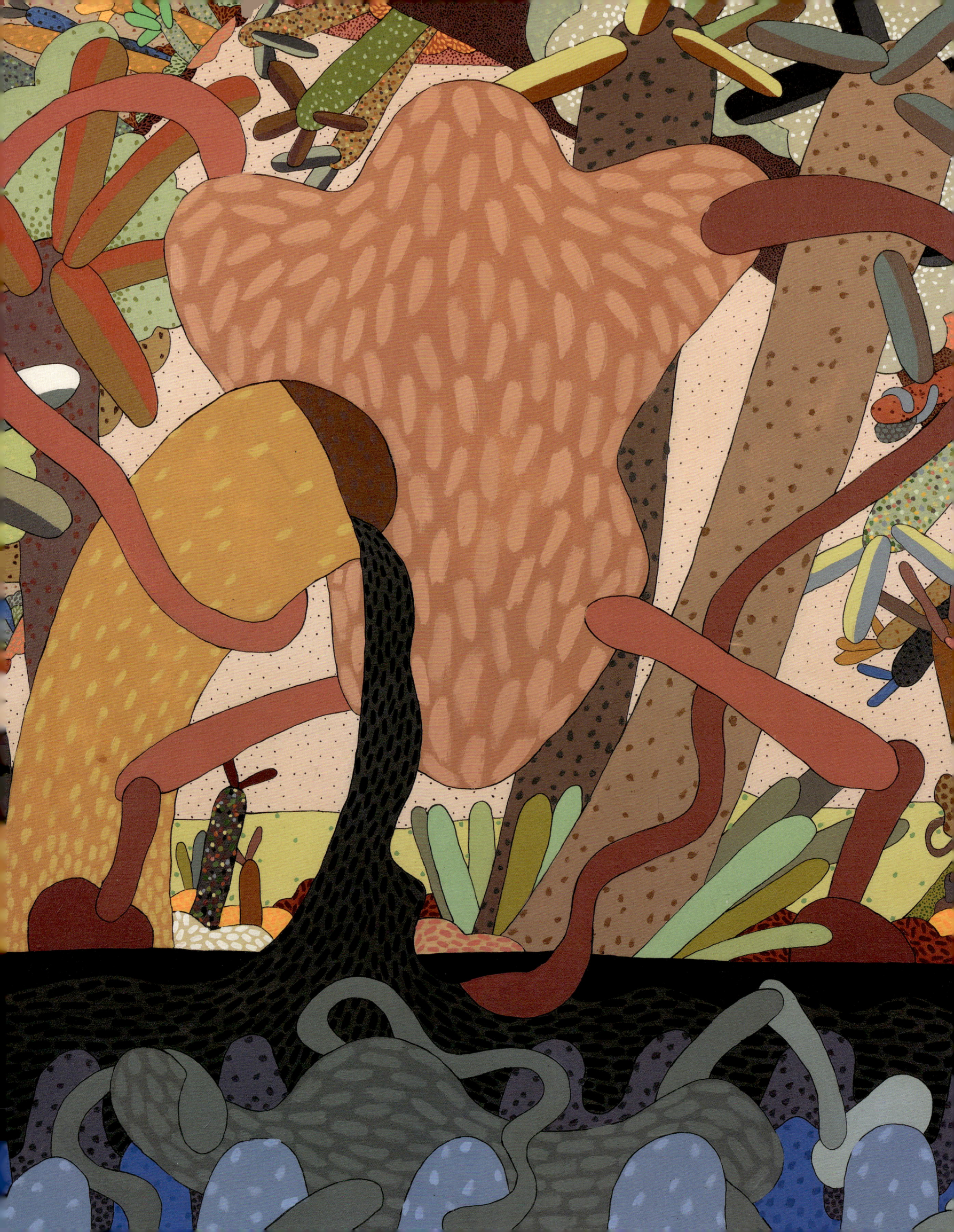

Contents

Directors' Foreword   7

Judith Thomas and
William R. Valerio

Partners in Science and Art

Reflections on Robert Kohler's
Artistic and Scientific Visions and
the Transformation of
Woodmere's Collection   11

William R. Valerio

Passionate Figuration   19

Robert Kohler

Bodies and Souls   45

Robert Cozzolino

Plates 73

Robert and Frances Coulborn
Kohler Collection   195
Contributors   207
Acknowledgments   209
Index of Works Illustrated   213

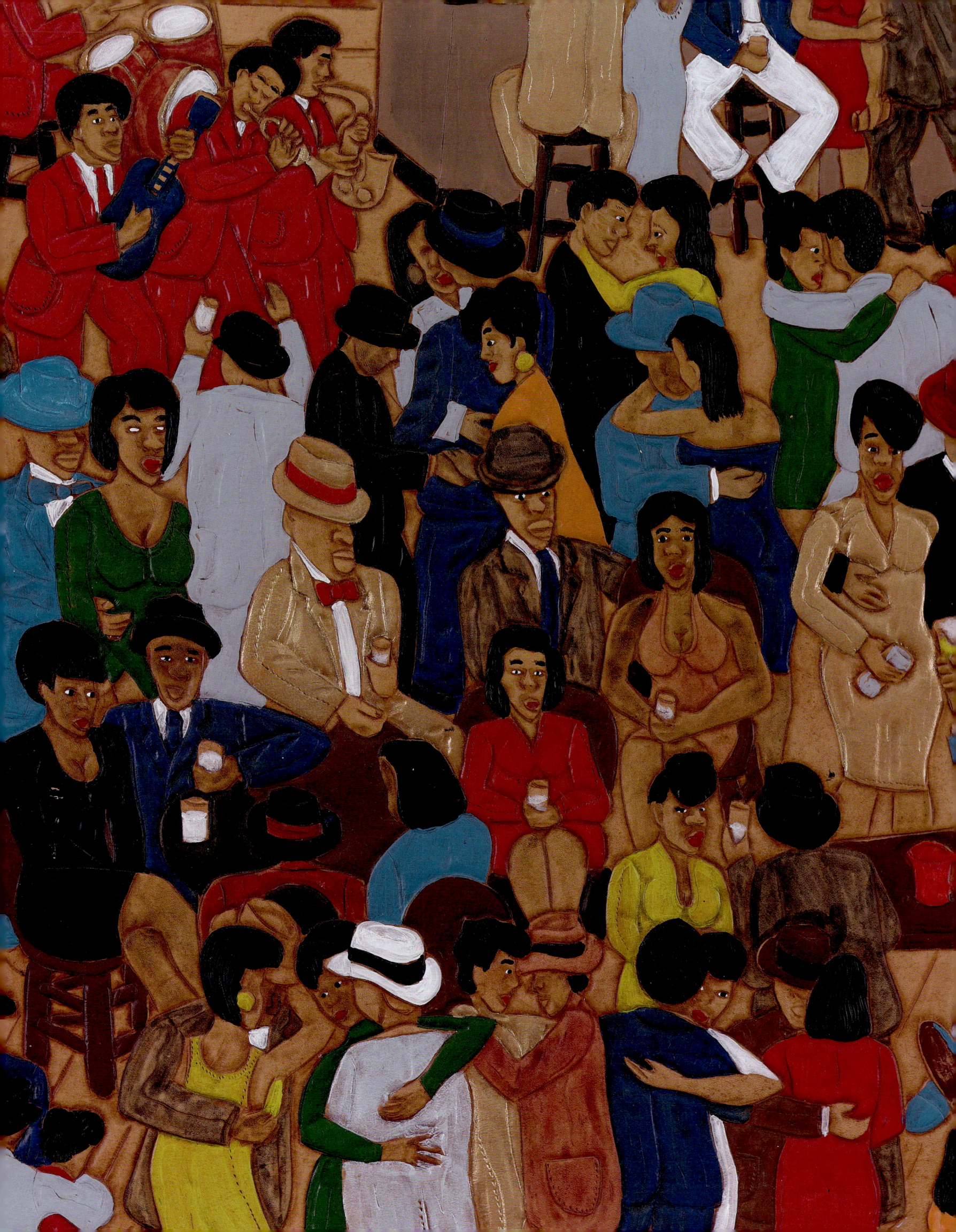

Museums are living, breathing institutions, continually evolving with the passions of the individuals who sustain them. Robert (born 1937) and Frances Coulborn Kohler (1938–2021) are collectors of American art who, over the last two decades, have been transformative supporters and donors of art to both the Pennsylvania Academy of the Fine Arts (PAFA) and Woodmere. For both institutions, the Kohlers' gifts have been of a scale and importance that creates forward momentum and widens our views to the future.

PAFA traces its origin to 1805 and the vision of a group of prominent Philadelphians—including artists and naturalists Charles Willson Peale and William Rush—who envisioned the arts at the center of the civic and educational life of their young country. Since that time, PAFA has served as our country's first art museum and academy of artists, especially important in shaping the figurative tradition and realist tendencies in American art. Rob and Frances began collecting art with serious intent in the 1980s, and in 2013 they made a commitment to bequeath much of their collection to PAFA. Primarily interested in the figurative arts and deeply rooted in the quirks, sensuality, and emotive jolts of the Chicago imagists, the Kohlers focused on the twists and turns of realist figuration in American art, its profundity in humanistic thought, and many permutations of spiritual consciousness. Their collecting, like that of PAFA, spans the broad geographic field of American art, with its diverse equilibria of artists working in regional communities. The Kohlers' collection offers a particularly compelling answer to the question of how PAFA's history in the figurative arts finds meaning today and a significant place in American culture in the future.

The nature of the Kohlers' involvement with Woodmere has been different. Dedicated to constructing a history of the visual arts in Philadelphia's cultural milieu, the museum's holdings reflect the achievements of the city's artists, and their contributions to American art are the main storyline in the museum's programs. At Woodmere, the Kohlers' first gifts came in 2004 with donations of works by Philadelphia artists from their collection. Over time the relationship deepened, and the Kohlers became partners to Woodmere's curatorial staff. In large part, they have underwritten the institution's ability to purchase modern and contemporary work—some by artists whose families have lived in the city for generations, some by artists whose families arrived more recently, and some by artists who are immigrants themselves. When Woodmere opens its new collection galleries in Frances M. Maguire Hall this fall, the Kohlers' presence will be felt throughout.

This catalogue and the associated exhibitions at PAFA and Woodmere are organized by Robert Cozzolino, a curator of American art, who, alongside and sometimes together with the Kohlers, has contributed tangibly to the vitality of both PAFA and Woodmere. A curator at PAFA from 2004 to 2016, Cozzolino conceived and implemented some of the museum's most important exhibitions. He is also singularly responsible at PAFA for having built the relationship with the Kohlers that led them to select the institution as the right place to steward their collection in perpetuity. Given Cozzolino's bent to become involved in the local art scene in Philadelphia (or wherever he may be living), and the intensity of his interest in the regional permutations of American art most broadly, he has also served Woodmere as a frequent guest curator, lecturer, and program participant. Bob's work on these exhibitions illuminates the significance of the Kohlers' collecting vision as a contribution to American art. He also helps us articulate the many ways their involvement at both museums has made each a stronger platform for sharing the beauty, ideas, and inspiration of the arts with our communities. From a very deep place, PAFA and Woodmere express gratitude to Cozzolino and to the Kohlers for their extraordinary contributions that have shaped our ability to thrive and grow as institutions of American art.

The staffs of both institutions shine as always in undertaking the professional activities associated with organizing our two exhibitions and this catalogue. Working together is always more complex than stewarding a project at one's own institution, and both staffs rose to the occasion. At PAFA, special mention goes to Brittany Webb, formerly the Evelyn and Will Kaplan Curator of Twentieth Century Art and the John Rhoden Collection; Harry Philbrick, former Interim Director of the Museum and Jennifer Johns, Museum Registrar. At Woodmere, we extend thanks to Rick Ortwein, Deputy Director of Exhibitions and Collections; Amy Gillette, Associate Curator; Laura Heemer, Registrar; Juliana Liska, Associate Registrar; and Hildy Tow, The Robert McNeil Jr. Director of Education. We also thank our trustees, particularly Jamie Biddle, chair of PAFA's Museum Committee, and Elie-Anne Chevrier Lewis, chair of Woodmere's Collections Committee, who have encouraged us to nurture the Kohlers' vision and generosity.

Finally, we are happy to acknowledge each other in this catalogue and the associated exhibitions. Having collaborated on numerous professional endeavors for over a decade and developed a special bond as mutually supporting institutional leaders during the COVID-19 pandemic, we have found it an easy pleasure to work together.

Thank you, one and all.

Judith Thomas
Deputy Director and Interim
Director of the Museum
Pennsylvania Academy of the Fine Arts

William R. Valerio, PhD
The Patricia Van Burgh Allison
Director and CEO
Woodmere

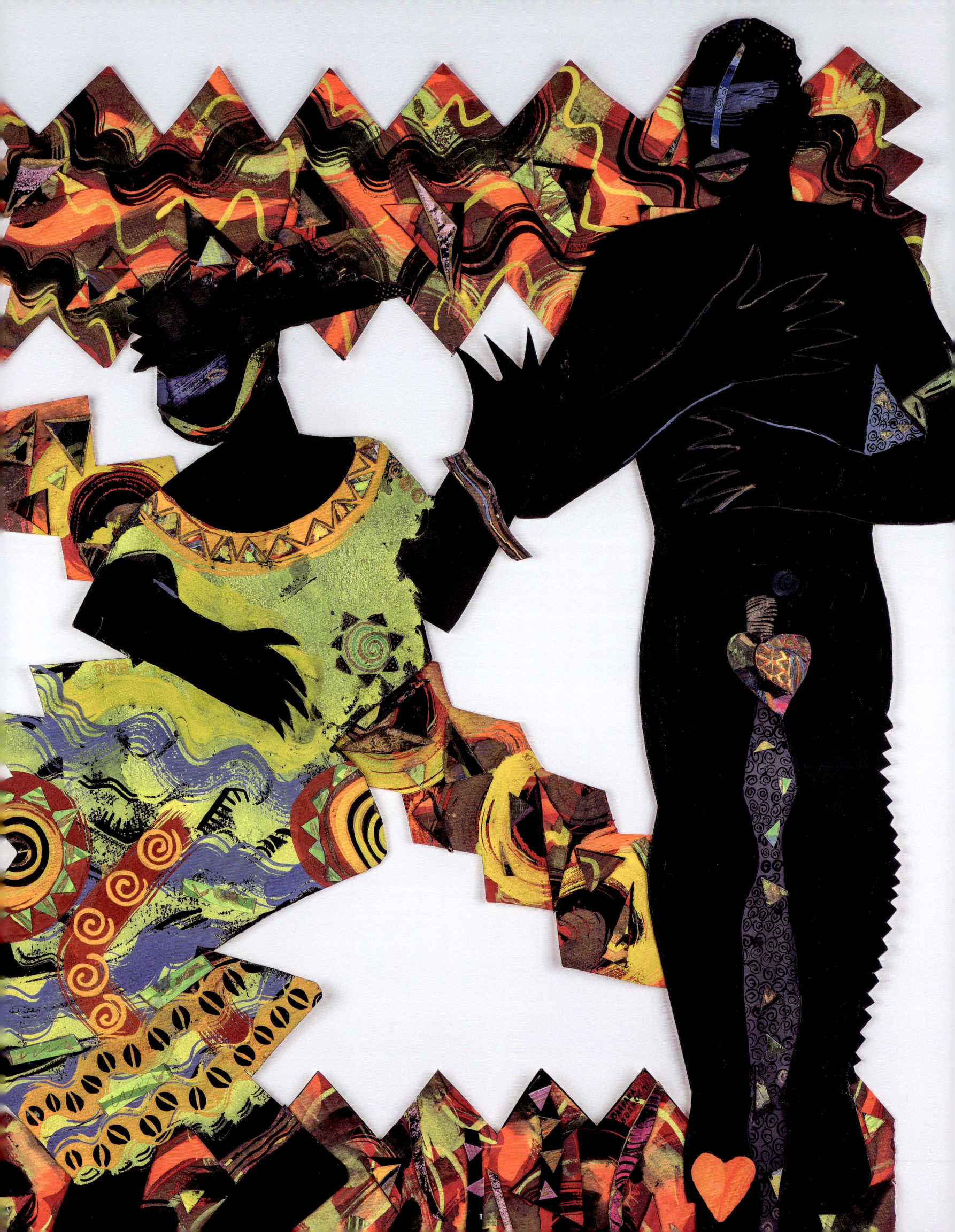

Partners in Science and Art Reflections on Robert Kohler's Artistic and Scientific Visions and the Transformation of Woodmere's Collection

William R. Valerio

Among the greatest privileges of my now fifteen years as director of Woodmere has been collecting art for the museum with my friend and philanthropic supporter Robert Kohler and his late wife Frances Coulborn Kohler. Together, we have come to realize—from the perspective of the rearview mirror—that our work has transformed the museum's collection, especially (but not exclusively) in the area of contemporary art. We have filled gaps and connected the dots to demonstrate aspects of the historical trajectory and distinct parts of the evolution in Philadelphia's many communities of artists. Woodmere's mission is to collect the arts of Philadelphia. With the Kohlers' underwriting of acquisitions, we have broadened the "conversations" that take place on our gallery walls, bringing new voices into a more inclusive dialogue, while also adding richness, going deep in some areas and collecting some artists' work extensively. A museum must be an enjoyable place, but also an interesting one in order to meaningfully engage its communities.

In preparing to describe what we have done, and to better understand the often-unspoken drivers of our partnership, I started reading Rob's books, written during his distinguished three-decade career as a University of Pennsylvania professor, scholar, and thought leader in the history of science. I was drawn to two books in particular—*Lords of the Fly* (1994) and *Partners in Science* (1991)—which explore the broader social context behind the evolution of modern genetics, pulling back the curtain on scientists as people with subjective points of view and on scientific institutions as organizations with complex power structures. Of relevance to our project at Woodmere, *Partners in Science* also describes the complicated yet foundational role of philanthropy in steering advancements in science. Frances had been editor for her husband and managing editor for other historians of science at the *Isis* journal at the University of Pennsylvania,[1] and went on to work as an editor and writer at the Chemical Heritage Foundation. It struck me that the Kohlers had studied and been immersed in organizational histories in which individual philanthropic entities— funders and foundations—shaped the findings of science, often facilitating

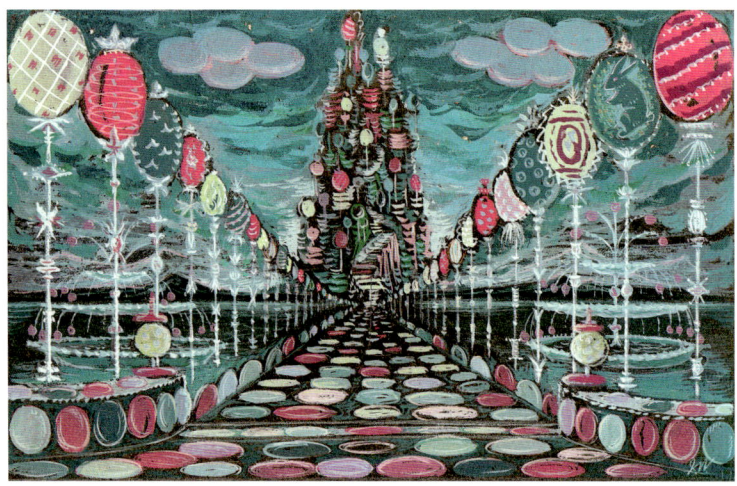

Fig. 1 John Winters, *Untitled (Easter Eggs)*, Wanamaker's display design, c. 1965. Gouache on paperboard, 5 × 7 in.

Fig. 2 Joan Wadleigh Curran, *Fish on a Plate*, 1982. Gouache on paper, 20¼ × 29¾ in.

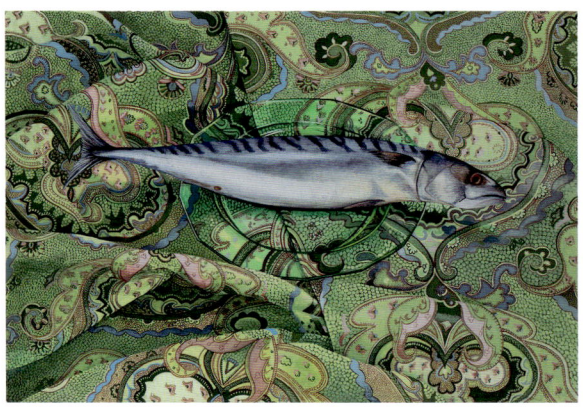

new discoveries, but sometimes hampering or even diverting the stream. Positive and negative, it was affirmation that they approached our partnership with remarkable awareness and sensitivity. Our work together deepened over time, and without pressure or a sense of indulgence, we acquired 148 works of art, bidding at auctions or buying from galleries and directly from artists' studios. Our conversations were about familiar artists and aesthetics, new and overlooked figures, and interpretations of contemporary art as a social force. To be clear, the actual science of genetics and fruit flies was not the model for the art we collected. However, it was more that the humanistic grounding in their discipline, with its twists and turns, made the Kohlers open to the complicated process of collecting art at an institution. A museum must be truthful to its mission, interpreting it to some extent dispassionately, regardless of personal taste. At the same time, it is impossible for any director, curator, or funder, being human, to completely escape personal biases and assumptions.

There are many Philadelphia symbols, tropes, and conventions, and the Kohlers and I talked about many of them as they pertain to the arts: "brotherly love" as a component of our city's Quaker heritage, or the impact of artists like Cézanne, Brancusi, and Duchamp, whose legacies veritably flow down the great steps of the Philadelphia Museum of Art. We also discussed another, more unfortunate aspect of the cultural life of Philadelphia, that being its supposed secondary status in relation to the art of New York. In conventional American art history, Philadelphia is important in the eighteenth and nineteenth centuries, but come the twentieth century, New York seized the leading edge with the Armory Show, the New York School, Pop, Minimalism, and Conceptualism. Artists and collectors in Philadelphia and other American cities followed suit.

The Kohlers, however, rejected the idea of Philadelphia's dependency on New York early on. It is an easy parallelism to see that in Rob's various explorations of the history of science, the scientists who follow the lead of others rarely move the needle in advancing their field. In *Lords of the Fly*, new discoveries are made when scientists ask hard questions and push beyond accepted understandings and norms. Many assumptions encumber the collecting of museums, among them a bias for studio-made work over art produced in commercial contexts, often framed in art history as the difference between "high" and "low." One of my favorite acquisitions of recent years was one Rob spotted at auction: a portfolio of works on paper by John Winters (1904–1983), by night a modern artist and by day the chief display designer at Wanamaker's department store in Center City Philadelphia (fig. 1). From New Year's Eve to Christmas, the experience of the holiday displays at Wanamaker's was thrilling, and Winters, we learned, was largely responsible for the visual pleasures of the great hall and the store windows that became nationally famous. When we show Winters in our galleries, he draws visitors in, as intended.

Original thinking drives science forward and original thinking was what the Kohlers sought in their first forays in collecting art and giving to Woodmere. This was in the mid-2000s, prior to my arrival at the museum

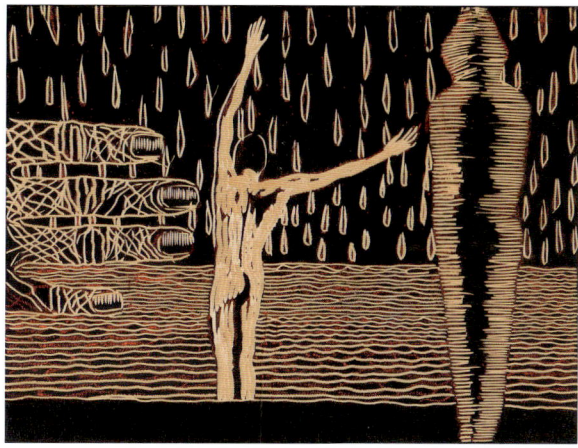

Fig. 3 Frank Hyder, *The Dance,* 1987. Oil on plywood, 15 × 19½ in.

in 2010, and their first major gift was a coherent group of paintings and works on paper by the artists Frank Hyder, Sidney Goodman, Frank Galuszka (plate 42), Tina Newberry, Joan Wadleigh Curran (fig. 2), and Martha Mayer Erlebacher, who were mostly associated with the Charles More Gallery in Philadelphia. They were part of the "new" figurative realism of the time and of the veiled, sometimes odd sensibility with the figure that descends from Philadelphia's great Thomas Eakins in the nineteenth century but then explodes in the twentieth century in the work of other artists that now feature in Woodmere's collection, in part thanks to the Kohlers' generosity: Walter Stuempfig, Leon Kelly, Ben Kamihira, and George Biddle.[2] All of this reflects the uniquely dark side of our city's metropolitan culture in the middle and late twentieth century, described as "Philadelphia Noir" in the literary realm by Carlin Romano, who writes about the psychological impact of an urban architecture that had once been the outward expression of America's industrial strength, but had been crumbling for decades.[3] Everything about Hyder's blackened, carved-wood *Dance* (1987; fig. 3), with its monstrous hand and mummy-like totem, captures the city's disturbing noir spirit. So does the work of Goodman, who in the 1980s and 1990s built dramatic, sometimes violent tableaus, pieced together from photographs he took on his urban sojourns. In *A Waste* (1984–86; fig. 4), the artist appears in the lower margins, camera in hand, shooting an industrial catastrophe.

A notable, large painting among the Kohlers' first gifts to Woodmere, Erlebacher's *In a Garden* (1976; plate 46) is a haunting image of three women in a rocky landscape, gesturing in distress. The title references the biblical garden of Gethsemane, the site of Christ's spiritual agony prior

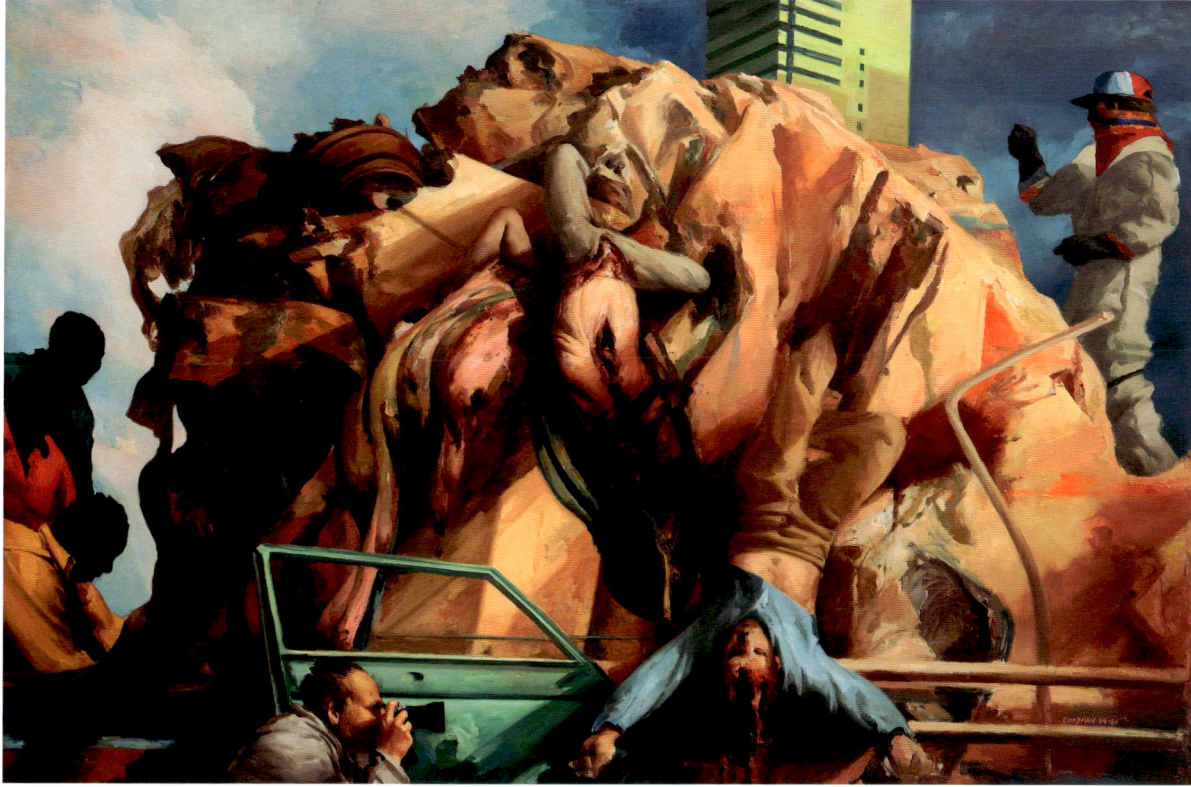

Fig. 4 Sidney Goodman, *A Waste,* 1984–86. Oil on canvas, 89 × 128⅝ in.

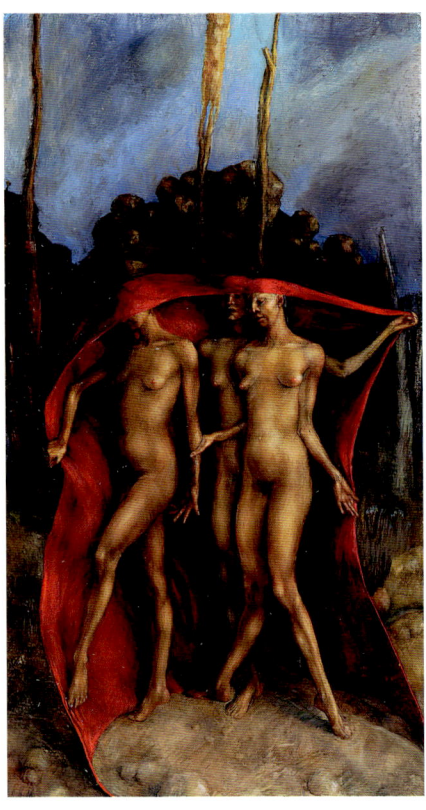

Fig. 5 Tina Newberry, *The Three Graces*, 1987. Oil on Masonite, 22 × 11¾ in.

to his crucifixion. Rob and I shared the privilege of knowing the artist personally, and we admired her commitment to a figurative realism built on an empirical study of the body; the biological specificity of its elements in various stages of growth, maturity, and decline; and the physics of its interaction with its context. Erlebacher concerned herself, for example, with the degree to which the flesh of a depicted foot interacts with the pressure of the body's weight against its ground, the shapes of teeth, and the character of sexual parts as they develop over a lifetime (in this last matter she was inspired by Michelangelo's depiction of the nude Adam in his different life stages). However, the Kohlers and I agreed that what makes *In a Garden* exceptional is that it pushes beyond the limits of observation. The biblical Gethsemane embodies the tension between the physicality of life itself (Christ's presence on earth) and the spiritual unknown in death, that elusive boundary between what we know and what will always exist beyond our grasp.

Among the common threads that unite the Kohlers' dedication to the history of science and their passion for the arts is a belief that achievement requires long-term commitment. Processes in art and science are often slow, and this pace allows for the development of greater depth. In assessing an artist's work, there is always a consideration of evolution over time. For example, in 2019, we felt compelled to reach out to Tina Newberry, who had relocated to Bloomington, Indiana, for a teaching position (she has since returned to Philadelphia). The Kohlers' 2004 gift to Woodmere of *The Three Graces* (1987; fig. 5) from the More Gallery staked out a position in Philadelphia noir with a strange, dreamlike take on the mythological trio of graces. Now we wanted to know about Newberry's new work. Inserting her self-portrait into layered tableaus built on well-known photographs of American history, she was asking: How does a woman find herself in the narratives of "great men"? Similarly, Rob has followed the progress of Ashley Flynn since her time at Moore College of Art and Design. When visiting her studio, we went big and purchased a monumental construction that portrays, at mural scale, the Kensington neighborhood and the tragedies of America's opioid epidemic, as centered there. In addition, it is not always about the size of the work; it can be about purposeful selection or quantity. When we recently became aware of a major auction at Material Culture of the work of Andrew Turner, and an exhibition of works by Marta Sanchez at the Brandywine Workshop and Archives, we were thrilled to purchase a group of paintings that trace the evolution of the artists' careers.

Beyond a curiosity about an artist's or scientist's trajectory over time, Rob asserts that true understanding, in either field, requires an element of unconventional thinking. This led us to practitioners who at first might seem weird but then demonstrate a fearless willingness to stand out in the advancement of unusual ideas or even resolved ones. Rob's deep passion for the work of Anne Minich came to mind several times when I was reading about unconventional scientists in *Lords of the Fly*. Thanks to the Kohlers, both Woodmere and PAFA will steward Minich's legacy into the future with large collections of her work (figs. 6 and 7). Minich, in her nineties at the time of this writing, draws her aging body with an unflinching combination of toughness and virtuosity. She also remains driven by her passion to grasp the inexplicable magic of the seashells, driftwood, animal bones,

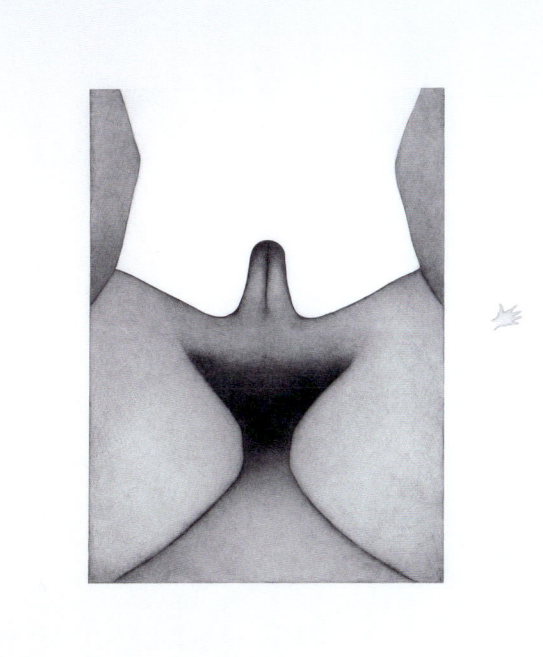
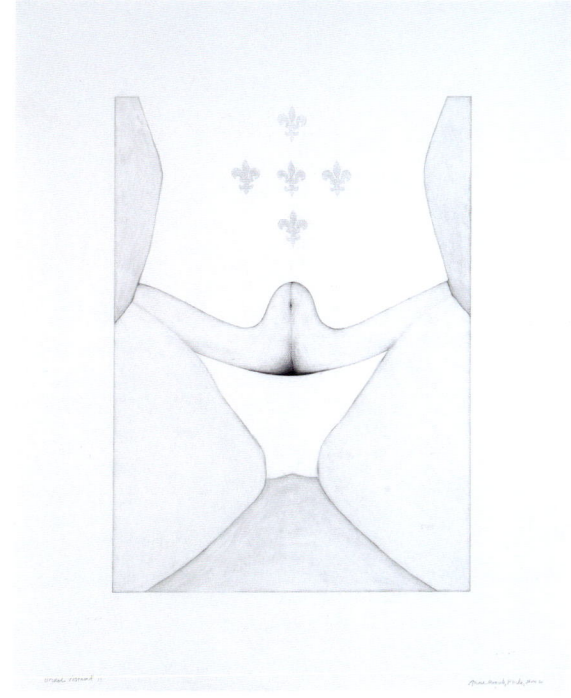

fossils, and rocks that she integrates into her work and orchestrates as remarkable harmonies. There is an attempt in Minich's oeuvre at arranging the universe: she often poses in relation to her mysterious array of found objects, and together they achieve a certain sense of order and sometimes even tranquility. In *Lords of the Fly*, Rob movingly describes how scientists, being human, assert illusionary structures of order and invent rules-based relationships as the only path toward understanding the overwhelming randomness that governs populations of fruit flies, and the universe itself.

Science and humanity: If a single overarching statement can be made about the history of science in Rob's writings, it would be that science is a construct built by organized collectives of people. Again and again, the humanity and essence of a scientific discovery derive from many people's unique contributions. The individual scientists are imperfect humans across a great range of personality types, some able to be lead or raise the large sums required for major scientific undertakings. Others by their nature are better suited to hands-on, meticulous work alone in the laboratory, and many are flawed individuals when judged by today's ethical standards. Nonetheless, respect for each person's contribution is important to the history.

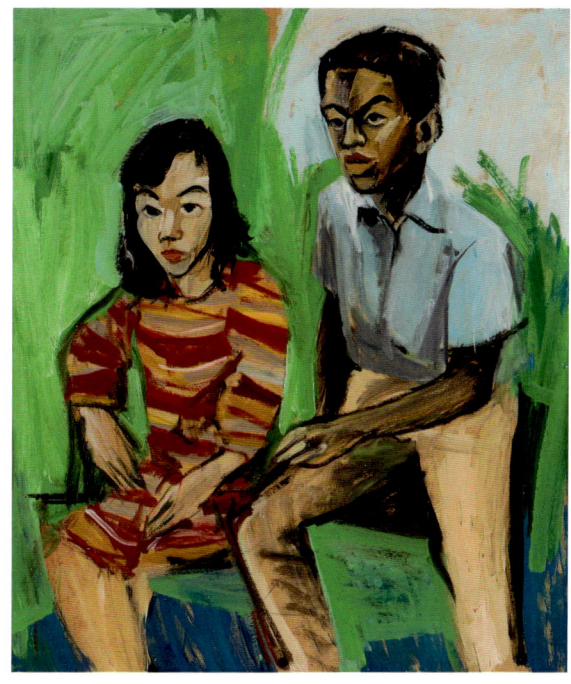

In collecting art, this approach translates to an active interest in artists across the spectrum of diversity in age, gender, and ethnicity, with an extra dimension of curiosity for those who may not have landed in positions of validation, as on the roster of a successful gallery or an appointment in a college department. The artist Bernard Harmon, for example, was a teacher in West Philadelphia high schools, not only a consuming profession but also one that doesn't afford the institutional support for an artist's career. On attending an exhibition of his work at Gratz Gallery, Rob proposed Woodmere's acquisition of *Striped Dress* (c. 1970; fig. 8) together with his son, the artist Willie Kohler, in honor of the artist's dedication to his students.

On another level, Rob's professional and personal humility spurred one of the most significant aspects of our partnership: assembling a collection that strives to reflect the racial diversity of our city. From the outset, we determined that we could not merely acquire a few trophy examples by Black artists, but rather we must collect deeply, to represent a range of

Fig. 6 Anne Minich, *Bridal Vestment I*, 2016. Graphite on rag paper, 30 × 24 in.

Fig. 7 Anne Minich, *Bridal Vestment II*, 2016. Graphite on rag paper, 30 × 24 in.

Fig. 8 Bernard Harmon, *Striped Dress*, c. 1970. Oil on board, 42 × 36 in.

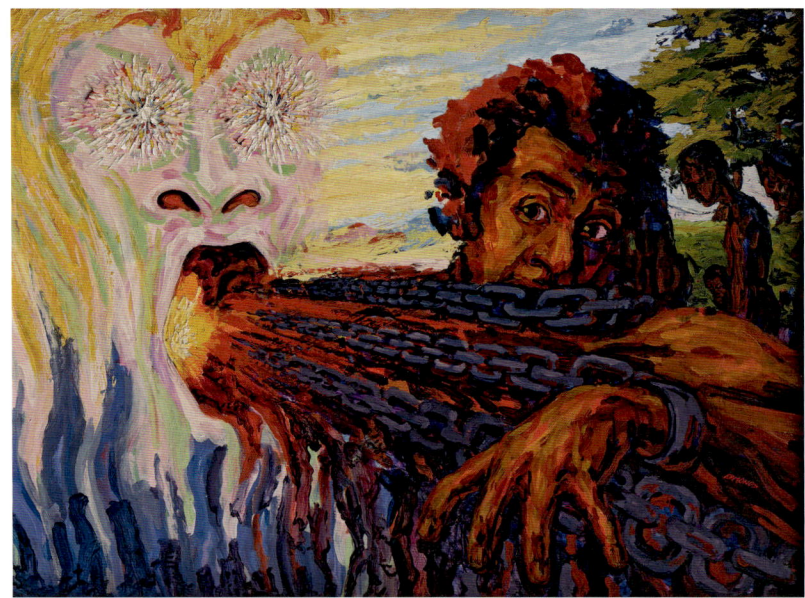

Fig. 9 Walter Edmonds,
Sold into Bondage, 1974. Oil
on board, 32 × 42 in.

Fig. 10 Barbara Bullock,
Healing Feeling, 1998. Acrylic,
matte medium, and gold
leaf on watercolor paper,
50 × 41 in.

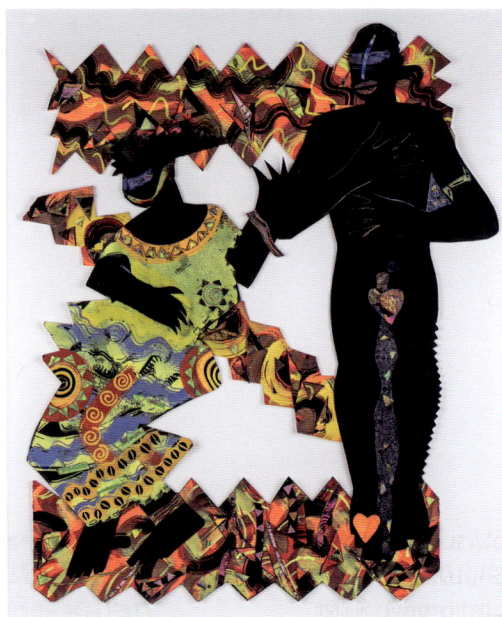

voices and—to the extent possible—the broad trajectories of artists. An exhibition we organized at Woodmere in 2015, *We Speak: Black Artists in Philadelphia, 1920s–1970s*, was our guide. The show was based on almost one hundred oral histories, and it not only gave shape to the specific exhibition's checklist, but it also served as a foundation for our further interests and activities. *We Speak* demonstrated that despite several remarkable exceptions (such as the support for Henry Ossawa Tanner at PAFA, or for Paul Keene at the Philadelphia College of Art), Black and Brown artists, like their counterparts in the realm of science, were excluded from the platforms that create the history of art and the larger dialogues of their respective fields.[4] They had to build their own communities.

A revelation to both Rob and me in *We Speak*, for example, was the work of Roland Ayers. In our oral histories, he was singled out as a key figure by Allan Edmunds of the Brandywine Workshop and Archives, and separately by my colleague Nancy Goldenberg, who had been a neighbor of the artist in Mount Airy. Ayers primarily worked in ink and watercolor on paper, and his intricate, dreamlike tableaus blended the historical past and the lived present with an intensity of observed detail, social acuity, an insatiable curiosity about the universe, and a firm understanding that all of this is grounded in the empirical study of nature and human sexuality. I will never forget standing in front of Ayers's *Cataclysm, Rebirth New World* (1968) with Rob and Frances, and the decision we made there and then that this was an artist to know. To date we have collected twenty-one works by Ayers as well as significant archival materials, from which Woodmere organized *Roland Ayers: Calligraphy of Dreams* (2021), an exhibition largely underwritten by the Kohlers. Since that time, Woodmere has shown and acquired works by Selma Burke, Paul Keene, Didier William, Andrew Turner, Kukuli Velarde, Twins Seven-Seven, Dindga McCannon, Dara Haskins, Rafael Ferrer, Walter Edmonds (fig. 9), Danny Simmons, Ed Bing Lee, Alex Queral, Charles Searles, Ellen Powell Tiberino, Barbara Bullock (fig. 10), and Henry Bermudez (plate 22). These artists are outstanding figures in Philadelphia's creative community, and they represent our larger goal to acquire works that offer a more complete vision of our city's culture.

An important accomplishment in our efforts has been to acquire the work of Barbara Bullock. I had known her through a long-standing partnership with Lewis Tanner Moore and his collection, which had been shown at Woodmere. It became a top priority for the Kohlers after they saw *We Speak*. Bullock's work straddles paintings and sculpture in unique ways, expressing a powerfully felt spiritual vision through forms of vibrant painted paper that she twists, curls, and generally manipulates into three-dimensional wall reliefs. The work has nothing to do with Western ideas about science, and in fact it grows from convictions that extend back to the 1960s, when the artist made extended trips to the African continent and immersed herself in non-Western cultural sensibilities, visual strategies, and powerfully encompassing ideas about the disposition of life. Bullock would probably reject the relevance of genetic science as the carrier of humanity's truth. This is to say that while the Kohlers spent their life as historians of science, the art they (and I) love the most represents something more than scientific knowledge and quest for proofs, facts, and certainty.

Twins Seven-Seven (plate 126) holds a special place in our collecting history, and his legacy needs to be reckoned with in American art more broadly. Like Bullock, who knew him well and brought him into the circle of artists at the Ile-Ife Black Humanitarian Center,[5] he asserts a spirituality in his depictions of the figure that contradicts the Western understanding the human body as a physical entity. For Twins, it is all about the spirit, and, living his professional life as an artist between Osogbo, Nigeria (where he was born), and Philadelphia, he asserted over and again the Yoruba belief that many lives exist within each individual one. The central narrative of his career and of his name itself was that his seven sets of twin siblings (thirteen deceased brothers and sisters) lived within him. He, the one, represented the fourteen, seven and seven. In the same way, the fish, once eaten, swims as a spirit in the eater's veins, and the spirits of ancestors are contained in the limbs and organs of one's body. Twins depicts this straightforwardly in his art. It's not that he proposed new theories we would consider "science." However, he contradicts all that we in the West consider scientific, and this makes for a compelling framework from which to embrace the unseen mysteries that give meaning to life. It is wonderful that when confronted with a pair of wood reliefs made by Twins, Rob felt compelled to purchase both, one for Woodmere and the other for PAFA.

As a final note, it is crucial to never forget that museums, like institutions of science, are shaped by people. In Woodmere's history there are many standout individuals. Charles Knox Smith achieved his dream of founding Woodmere, opening its doors to the public in 1913. Edith Emerson, who served as curator and director from the early 1940s through her retirement in 1978, established the museum's mission to focus on the artists of Philadelphia. When a future history of Woodmere is written, the Kohlers' legacy will be intertwined with my own, and for that I am grateful. We are committed to stewarding many artists' works into the future, and in so doing have made Woodmere a more interesting museum, with a collection that better reflects the spirited and audacious people who make up our wonderful city.

Notes

1. For more about *Isis*, see https://www.journals.uchicago.edu/journals/isis/about.

2. Filmmaker John Thornton offers an impressive history of the Charles More Gallery and its community of artists in this YouTube video: https://www.youtube.com/watch?v=mlW7nq4ijFY.

3. Carlin Romano, *Philadelphia Noir* (Akashic Books, 2010).

4. *We Speak: Black Artists in Philadelphia, 1920s–1970s* (September 26, 2015–January 24, 2016) was guest curated by Susanna W. Gold, PhD, with Woodmere assistant curator Rachel Hruszkewycz.

5. *Africa in the Arts of Philadelphia: Bullock, Searles, and Twins Seven-Seven* (February 8–September 7, 2020) was guest curated by Susanna W. Gold, PhD, with Woodmere assistant curator Rachel Hruszkewycz.

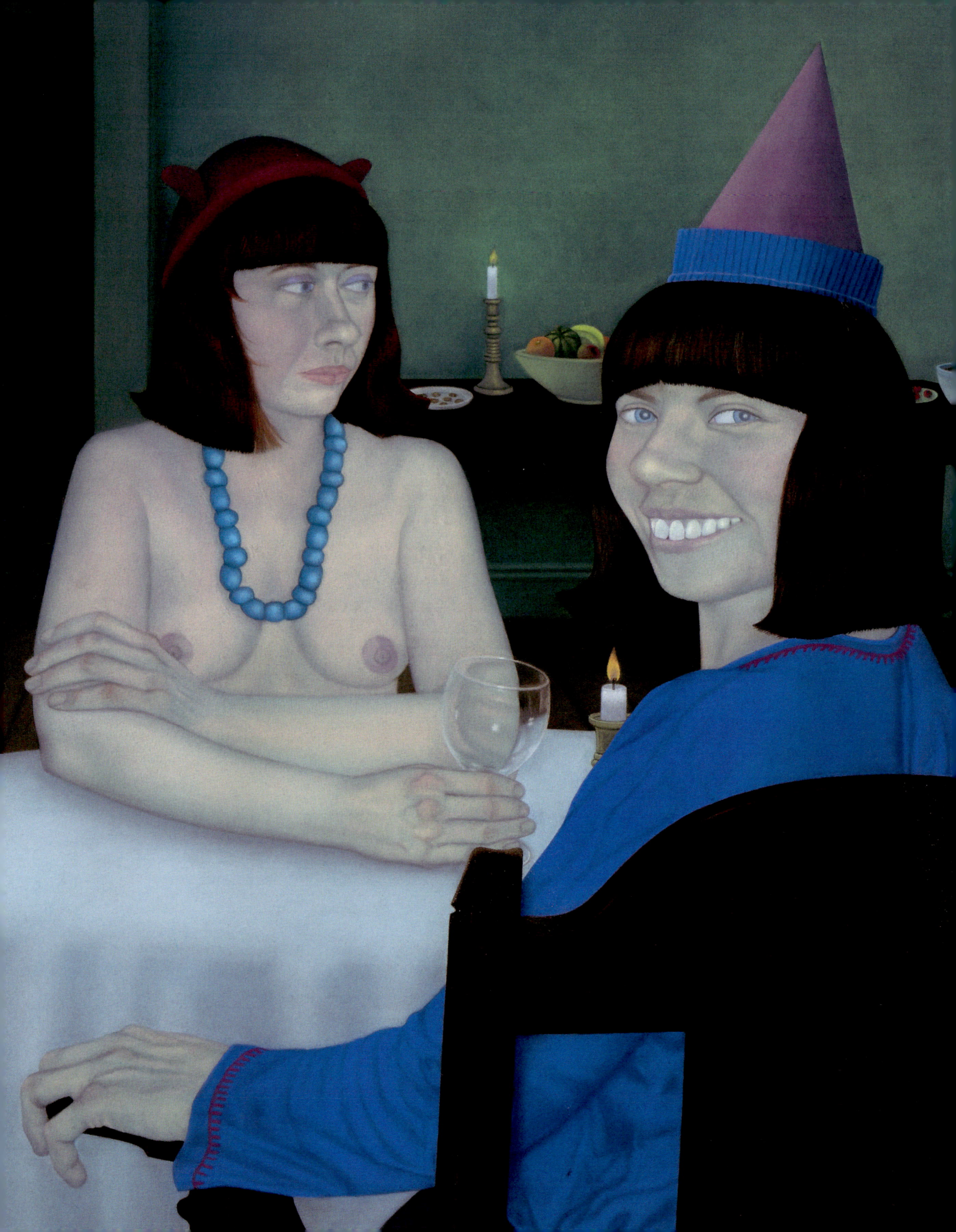

Passionate Figuration

Robert Kohler

My wife, Frances, and I devoted half a century to creating this collection, and it was one of the most enjoyable and rewarding activities of our lives. So, what is it all about? Visitors have often remarked on its distinctive qualities: visual exuberance, a range of artists from celebrated to unknown, and subjects that are intense, personal, and sometimes pretty strange. It's not merely an accumulation of things that happened to strike our fancy. Nor is it an assortment of signature works by artists anointed by critics or market makers as significant and collectible. We collected thoughtfully and with purpose, trusting our own instincts. Avoiding the art world's mainstream for its byways and edges, we sought out artists who don't fit conventional categories. We favored work that came from and spoke to artists' lives and our own.

The collection was for us a work of art in itself, with a guiding vision that took shape in its making. We called that vision "expressive figuration," until Harry Philbrick, then museum director at the Pennsylvania Academy of the Fine Arts (PAFA), remarked after a visit that "passionate figuration" might more aptly describe what he saw. It was a good suggestion. *Passionate* figuration embraces a range of expressive styles, from loosely gestural to smoothly precise. And it puts the emphasis where it belongs: on the experience of making and enjoying art. This essay describes how our collecting began and evolved, and how it acquired its distinctive personality.

With a few exceptions, we acquired the works that make up this collection starting in the early 1980s. We had been collectors since the late 1960s: not of fine art, but of art crafts—artisanal objects made or viewed as art. Persian village rugs were our first serious love, then Inuit sculptures in stone and bone, and, in the late 1970s, art glass. Art crafts were at the time expanding and beginning to be recognized as art, and it was exciting to be in the thick of it. It was the early years of the Canadian government's project to create a cottage industry of quality Inuit art in the far North, and there was a tide of fresh and vigorous work by Native peoples, whose way of life gave them a deep material understanding of a harshly beautiful environment and their place in it. At the same time, a lively revival of art glass

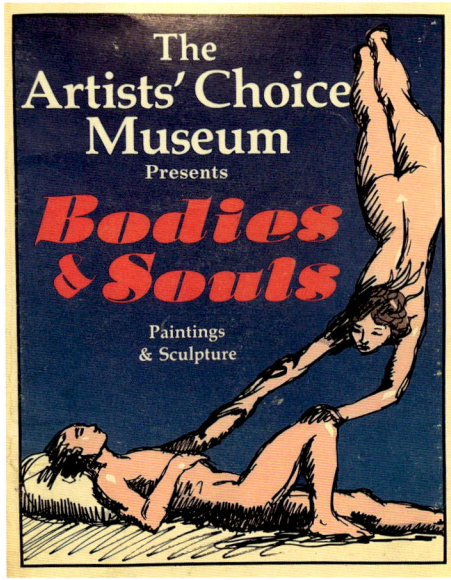

Fig. 1 Cover of the catalogue for *Bodies & Souls*, 1983, design and drawing by C. Leopardo.

was taking shape in the US, inspired by Art Nouveau, a style we had always loved. The point of collecting was not only for us to acquire things for our own pleasure but also to participate in significant cultural movements.

In contrast, contemporary fine art—minimalism, conceptualism, postmodern, ironic Pop—had no appeal. These seemed to us to be products of clubby art world coteries, designed to be esoteric and to elevate fine art above the lesser concerns of everyday life. Our few purchases of fine art were sporadic and limited to inexpensive Japanese and other prints. We bought art as beginners typically do: buying what we liked with no thought of making a coherent collection. Thus, it was not in fine art, but in the more open and down-to-earth art crafts that we first experienced the lasting pleasures of deliberate collecting. We read and studied, visited craft galleries and fairs, asked questions, and informed ourselves about who was who, what was being made, and what it all might signify. We were developing our particular eye. And while we did not continue to collect crafts, our early engagement with them powerfully affected our subsequent purchases of fine art. A taste for strong color, design, and materiality as well as craftsmanship and connection to everyday experience—the defining elements of art crafts—are visibly present in the fine art we acquired.

How, then, did we go from a casual interest in fine art to serious and informed collecting? One event especially transformed our disapproving—and ill-informed, it turned out—view of current fine art. That was Frank Goodyear's landmark 1981 exhibition *Contemporary American Realism Since 1960* at PAFA.[1] The culmination of a series of smaller shows in the late 1970s, it revealed that a broad revival of figuration had been underway for some time in the world of fine art. There was much we liked, and *Contemporary American Realism* became our guide to a whole world of art we hadn't seen, because we didn't know where or how to look for it. The exhibition was by later or even by current standards rather tamely realist. But that suited us well enough, as our own taste at the time was on the realist side.

Another influential overview was the exhibition *Bodies & Souls*, organized by the Artists' Choice Museum in 1983, which displayed the work of 156 artists in eleven galleries along Fifty-Seventh Street in New York (fig. 1).[2] The last of six surveys of current figurative art by this short-lived artists' collective, it was more diverse and adventurous than *Contemporary American Realism*, including much that was expressionist, fantastic, raunchy, or all-out weird—a visual cornucopia. Here were artists established and unknown exploring all sorts of figuration and energized by a sense of escaping or subverting mainstream orthodoxies. The sense of participating in a significant cultural movement, which we had enjoyed with the art crafts, we felt again as we found our way into the expanding world of fine art.

Commercial galleries were from the outset our portals into this unfamiliar world. Guided by *Contemporary American Realism* and *Bodies & Souls*, we found the gallerists who handled art we liked and who welcomed novice collectors like us. From them we learned how to look and what to collect. Our chief entry point in Boston, where we lived in the 1960s, was Bernie Pucker's Pucker Safrai Gallery. And in Philadelphia, our home since 1973, we took to hanging out in the Charles More Gallery. In the larger world of New York, we were drawn especially to Robert and Jane Schoelkopf's eponymous gallery, Bella Fishko's Forum, and the Allan Frumkin Gallery (later, with George Adams, the Frumkin-Adams and then the Adams Gallery), as well as the DC Moore, Nancy Hoffman, and Terry Dintenfass Galleries. Later, in Chicago, John Corbett and Jim Dempsey's newly opened Corbett vs. Dempsey Gallery, which then specialized in underappreciated Chicago artists, became a favorite place to look and learn.

At the same time, we formed a habit of random exploring: vertically, in the gallery condominiums of Fifty-Seventh Street, and horizontally in the scattered galleries of upper Madison Avenue and SoHo. We thus became foragers in the groves and thickets of contemporary figurative art, combining unplanned wandering with patient watching and waiting in favored spots, as foragers have always done. We steered clear of auctions, deterred by the hazards of buying (or not) quickly and sight unseen without the guidance of those who know how to safely navigate that world. We greatly enjoyed and valued our relationships with gallerists. They were our trusted teachers and partners in collecting, and some became lifelong friends.

Although we did not realize it at the time, we had found our way into a rather special neighborhood of the art world, where gallerists happily engage with collectors like us. We knew from experience that high-end galleries did not as a rule welcome conversation with visitors who clearly were not insiders or deep-pocketed buyers. So we stayed away from them and formed relationships with gallerists who favored marginalized art styles and welcomed collectors of modest means who look long and hard, ask questions, and make up their own minds to buy or not. That meant giving up on celebrity artists whose work we liked. But in the booming market of the 1980s and 1990s, they were already out of our reach. The art world's margins were for us always more congenial than its inner sanctums.

As we became aware of just how many opportunities there were to spend limited funds, we developed guidelines to focus and concentrate our buying. Our first principle was to collect only figurative works. Landscapes and still lifes can be expressive and passionate, of course, but depictions of human figures are generally the most engaging. Self-portraits were from the start our favorites, and portraits of people close to the artists: spouses, family, fellow artists. We were drawn especially to depictions of couples and groups going about their daily lives—vignettes of human relationships and life stories (fig. 2). The walls of our house are covered with faces: not generic ones, but particular people inviting us into their personal lives. How could we live with all these insistent strangers, visitors often asked. And our answer was always the same: How could we live without them?

Our second rule of collecting was to favor living artists. Lives in progress rewarded us with surprises and discoveries, and we enjoyed giving artists we value little boosts in their careers. Besides, the work of living artists is generally more available and affordable than the work of "deadies" (as Bob and Jane Schoelkopf fondly called them). We never privileged "emerging" artists, though. Artists so designated are too often pawns in marketing games, and artists' early work is often not their most accomplished. Instead, we looked for artists in mid-career—as a rule the most experienced and assured time of life—or in later life, when some bloom late or

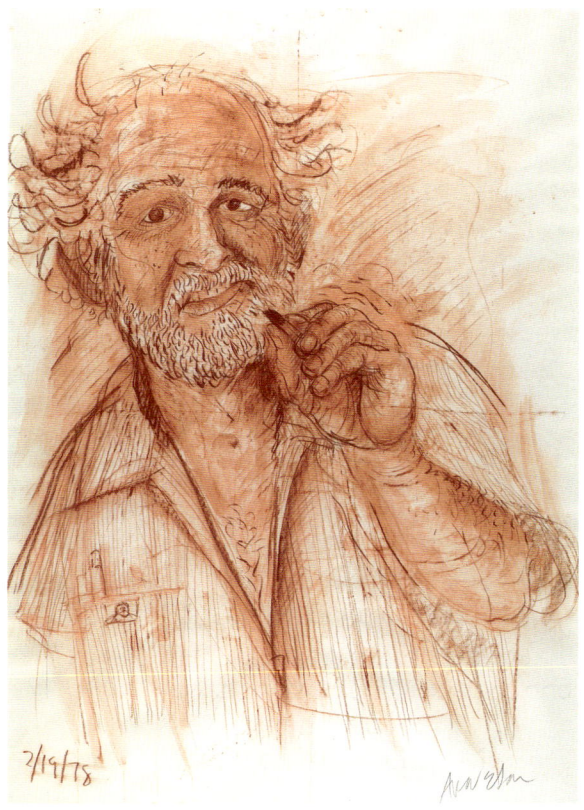

Fig. 2 Robert Arneson, *Self-Portrait Drawing*, 1978. Conté crayon on paper, 40 × 30 in.

for a second time. This practice meant that we collected mainly artists of our own generation. But that's not a bad thing. As it happened, ours was an exceptionally good vintage for passionate figuration, the core decades of the figurative revival. We could not do now what we did then with ease.

A third guideline was to collect in depth the work of artists we especially liked. That wasn't always feasible, of course, given the unavoidable limits of availability and affordability. Collecting in depth is hard with artists whose work is well known and sells fast and for keeps. It's more likely to succeed with those who are not constrained by early celebrity but can instead develop slowly and freely. Their earlier work may remain unsold and available to collectors who come in late but with hindsight know what to look for. With artists who make art we like only briefly or sporadically, windows of access may be brief, depending on how their life paths and ours do or do not cross in opportune ways. Collecting in depth thus contains an inherent element of contingency and luck. But that's fine. It's an adventure and a rewarding way to share and steward artists' aspirations and achievements. That for us was always what mattered.

Our fourth rule of collecting was to acquire only what we considered to be an artist's most accomplished or significant works. If these were not to be had, we did not buy token placeholders, but moved on to artists whose finest work was available and affordable. Although this discipline was sometimes painful, it had real benefits. It made us seek out artists who for no good reason (e.g., age, social identity, temperament, bad luck) had been undervalued by critics and market makers, as well as works by recognized artists that were excellent yet for some reason hadn't easily sold, often because of subject matter that was atypical or unpalatable. We did well buying what others didn't care or dare to buy. This strategy requires a connoisseur's knowing eye, rather than the easier knowledge of art world brands and fashions, and that's a good thing. Of all the pleasures of collecting, exercising connoisseurship is one of the greatest.[3]

Within these general guidelines, how did we go about deciding what specifically to acquire? What were our touchstones of quality? One was craft: not just in the narrow sense of technique, but in the deeper sense of a tactile understanding of materials and materiality (*craeft* it was once called).[4] In whatever medium artists make their own—drawing, painting, sculpting, sewing, assembling—we looked for material know-how and flair in color, design, and expression. Craftsmanship has not been universally honored in the high-art culture of our day. It was our good fortune to have acquired an informed appreciation for it in the art crafts. Craft is, however, not a sufficient reason to buy. A work of art must also be passionate. We would typically ask ourselves if a work was a bit tame for us, a bit lacking in strong feeling, and if it was, we passed. "Buy the toughest work you can stand," Allan Frumkin once counseled us, and we never went wrong following that advice. Art that is intense and passionate never ceases to challenge and engage. It doesn't fade into invisibility like knickknacks or wallpaper. However, we stayed away from art that consciously aims to shock or disrupt. That sort of thing is too often shallow or designed merely to get attention, and it needs no encouragement. We favored art that insinuates itself assertively but nonviolently into our lives.

Although we agreed in principle about the kinds of things to acquire, we didn't always see eye to eye on particular pieces. Yet that was seldom a problem. Having lived our entire adult lives together, we knew how to keep disagreements from becoming existential struggles, rather than just issues to think and talk through together. And so it was, too, with art collecting. Neither of us ever wanted to veto or dictate, only to be heard and taken seriously. I'm generally more inclined to buy strategically to extend and shape the collection, while Frances liked to buy what appealed personally. But I didn't push limits too hard, and she wasn't too strict in reining me in. Our principle of concord on occasion caused us to miss opportunities on the margins of our understanding. But more often it saved us from mistakes that come from buying too much with the head and not enough from the heart, or vice versa.

In practice it wasn't hard to know our shared mind and eye: the signs are visceral. If, when standing before a work of art, we felt that fluttering in the midsection that is the unfailing symptom of love, no discussion was needed. With art that's familiar, a glance is often enough to know if it's right, and we would signal agreement by a quiet word or covert look or nod. This quick and bodily sense of loving a work of art isn't some mysterious instinct or intuition. It's the accumulated knowledge and experience of connoisseurship. With art that was new to us, we would take the time to look and feel our way into it together. But when looking and thinking became dithering indecision, we took it as a sign that we shouldn't buy, at least not yet.

The distinctive "eye" of the collection thus grew out of the activities and habits of our life together, including our professional lives as editor and historian—our shared word craft. Knowing good visual art is not so very different from knowing good prose. Good writing states ideas clearly and supports them with apposite empirical evidence. Good art uses strong material depictions to embody the unseen feelings and meanings of visual experience. No piece of writing left my desk until Frances laid her unfailing editorial hand upon it. No work of art entered our collection without her stamp of approbation. In life we decided and did everything together, and so it was in art collecting. Decisions about whether or not to buy were a double pleasure: personal and aesthetic. An artist friend saw us, she said, as two people joined at the hip, and that's how it felt. Our collection has a distinctive personality because it is deeply us.

How we came to love art that is edgy and unconventional, yet not radical or revolutionary, is harder to say. It was no doubt rooted in accidents of personality and our coming of age in the 1950s. Neither of us was particularly at ease with the orthodoxies of that decade. But we were too set in our ways and preoccupied with our young family to be drawn into the cultural revolutions of the 1960s and 1970s. As in life we were between conventional and radical cultures—*in* both, but *of* neither—so too in art we were in between. It was our conscious choice to collect weird figuration, but what that was in practice took shape in the process of collecting. Commitments to particular artists became precedents—permissions, in a way—for committing to others who worked in congruent styles.

The first fine art we bought and kept was Jane Lund's pastel *Party for Myself* (c. 1974–75; see p. 52), a quadruple self-portrait of the artist as goody-goody, sexpot, fiend, and fool. It's a vivid memory. There it was, over a doorway in the Pucker Safrai Gallery—and we hated it! How could anyone choose to live with such a thing, we asked ourselves. But later that day, driving home to Philadelphia, it stuck in our minds, and we independently realized that our strong feelings were a good sign—not of dislike, but of love. We called the gallery the minute we arrived home, and soon after returned to buy more of Lund's odd work: a funny ceramic sculpture of a woman and her dog dreaming, respectively, of sanctity and a bone, as well as a suite of disturbing lithographs of Jane and her family in bad-dream dramas. (They were, in fact, from dreams, she told us.) These were followed later by pastels exploring the uneasy adjustments of individual identity in marriage. High points are her loving yet slightly uneasy picture of herself with her husband, Thomas, in blue-face (*Anniversary*, c. 1975; fig. 3); the scene of three nude masked Janes tossing about Tom's blue head (*Ancient Rite*, c. 1974–75; fig. 4); and her extraordinary nude self-portrait, heavily and uncomfortably pregnant. These formative acquisitions opened the way to acquiring equally weird work by other artists.

The even weirder art of Boston-based artist Deborah Kravitz was another early surprise in the Pucker Safrai Gallery (fig. 5). We were immediately taken by their painterly beauty and fantastic subjects: lizard-people embracing and having sex, a newborn human-animal creature spilling eggs of artistic creativity (herself, Kravitz explained), and a three-clawed Cyclopean monster (actually, a favorite childhood doll) navigating threatening dreamscapes (fig. 6). Here was an artist dealing with urgent matters of life and holding nothing back. We bought a group of these powerful little paintings on the spot. As Bernie Pucker wryly observed, we were now committed collectors of weird stuff, and he was right. Much later we acquired a large group of Kravitz's most personal works that she had kept for herself, so that in one place at least her singular art would be preserved in depth. (She

Fig. 3 Jane Lund, *Anniversary*, c. 1975. Pastel on paper, 28 × 31 in.

Fig. 4 Jane Lund, *Ancient Rite*, c. 1974–75. Pastel on paper, 34 × 29 in.

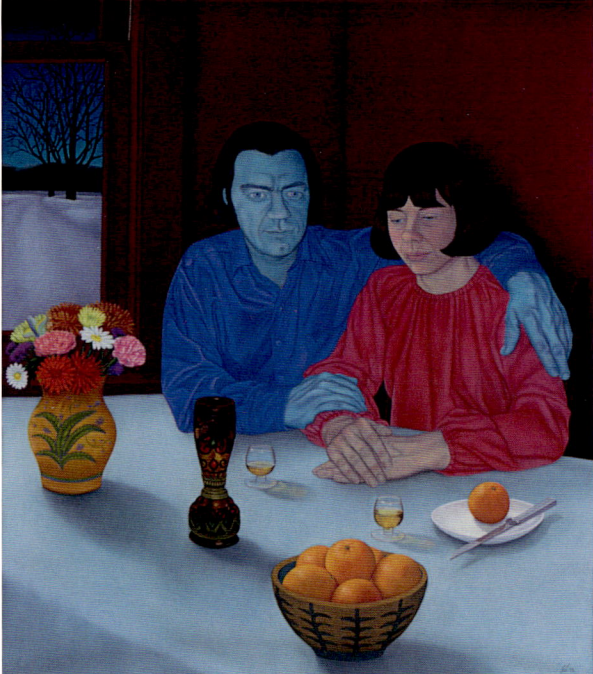

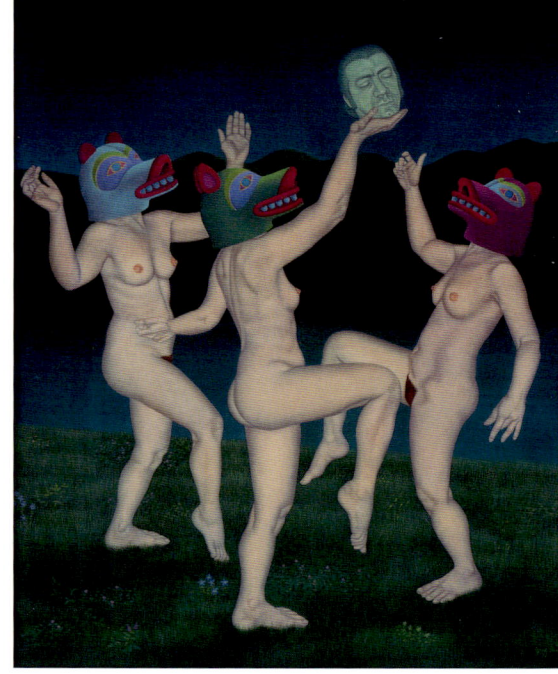

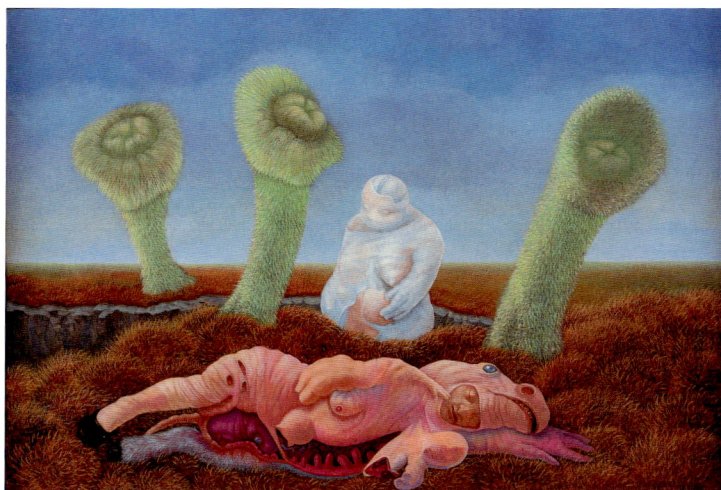

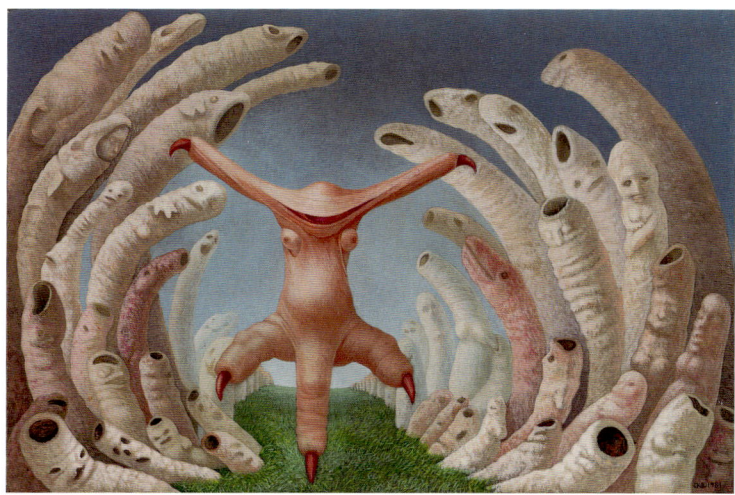

has always worked for a living, so has had an uneven art career.) Standouts include a children's crucifixion and a domestic scene of three sisters playing with dolls—one tearing them apart, one making and repairing, one vainly seeking love—based partly, Kravitz told us, on her own family life.

Gregory Gillespie was our third formative artist, and the first who wasn't a chance discovery. He was already well known, and his work fetched high prices in regular shows at the Forum Gallery. His great self-portrait from the Hirshhorn Museum was the standout in PAFA's *Contemporary American Realism*, and the catalogue of his 1977 retrospective opened his life's work to in-depth study (fig. 7). Getting access as buyers wasn't as easy. Collectors lined up to buy his new work, and it sold fast. We spent several years looking for works that were affordable and available, and making ourselves visible as serious collectors—getting a place in line. Our first purchase, in 1983, was *Beetle and Frog* (1972), a work that unsurprisingly hadn't sold (a dead frog being devoured by a flesh-eating beetle is not everyone's cup of tea). To us it was beautiful, evocative of life and death, and affordable. Two years later our persistence and evident knowledge of Greg's oeuvre led Bella Fishko to offer us first crack at a superb 1985 portrait, *Rita* (fig. 8). It would cost a good part of a year's art budget, but we knew we would never regret going all out. ("He's a genius," Bella liked to say, "a *genius!*") And that dual commitment—ours to Greg and Bella's to us—opened the door to collecting in depth. High points include a soulful early self-portrait with shaved head (an homage to Van Gogh); a forceful painting of his first wife, artist Frances Cohen Gillespie (*Dark Painter*, 1982–83; fig. 9), a work we had long desired; and a life-size picture of his friend and friendly rival, William Beckman, that mischievously combines Bill's face and Greg's hands. As fine small works from the 1960s—the artist's formative decade in Italy—surfaced on the secondary market, a collection in depth slowly took shape.

A signature large self-portrait from Greg's mid-career unfortunately eluded us. (We once watched helplessly and in pain as one of his best was sold in Bella's back room.) In hindsight, though, there is no cause for regret. In the artist's last decade, inward-looking portraiture became a less favored vehicle for his deep dives into selfhood than pictures of people who mattered in his life, especially women. And it was precisely these works that were available and relatively affordable at the time we were collecting most actively—our good fortune. His portrait of Fran as a Renaissance artist from the year of their divorce attests to his respect for her art and her role in his own artistic career. (She may look angry but is, in fact, just steely—it's how Greg painted himself.) And his enigmatic *Self-Portrait with Mother and Son* (1991–92; plate 21) probably draws on his own experience of

Fig. 5   Deborah Kravitz, *Rebirth of the Discarded Ones*, 1980. Acrylic on panel, 7¼ × 10¼ in.

Fig. 6   Deborah Kravitz, *The Path*, 1981. Acrylic on panel, 5¼ × 7¾ in.

Fig. 7   Gregory Gillespie at the opening of *Contemporary American Realism Since 1960* at the Pennsylvania Academy of the Fine Arts, Philadelphia, September 1981. Photograph by Rosemary Ranck courtesy of PAFA.

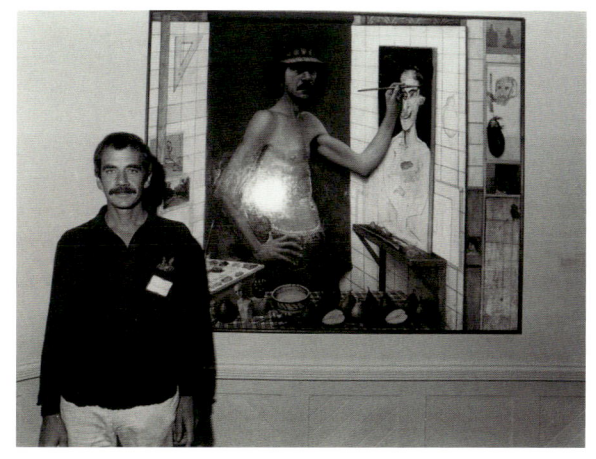

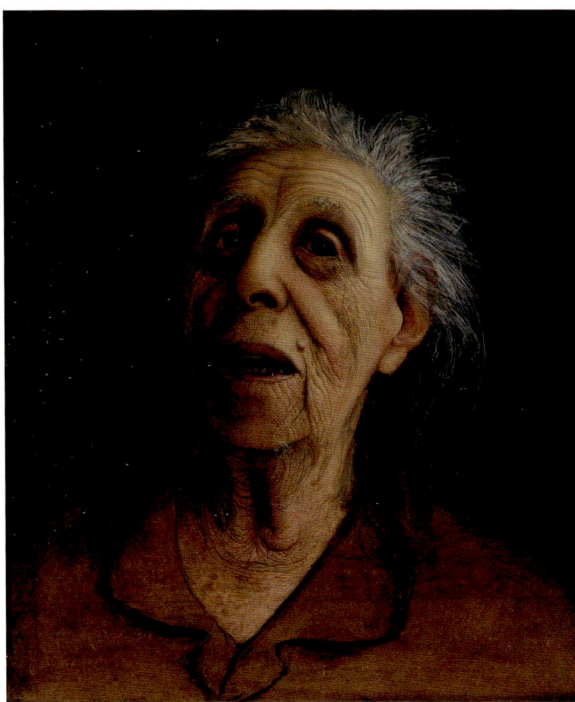

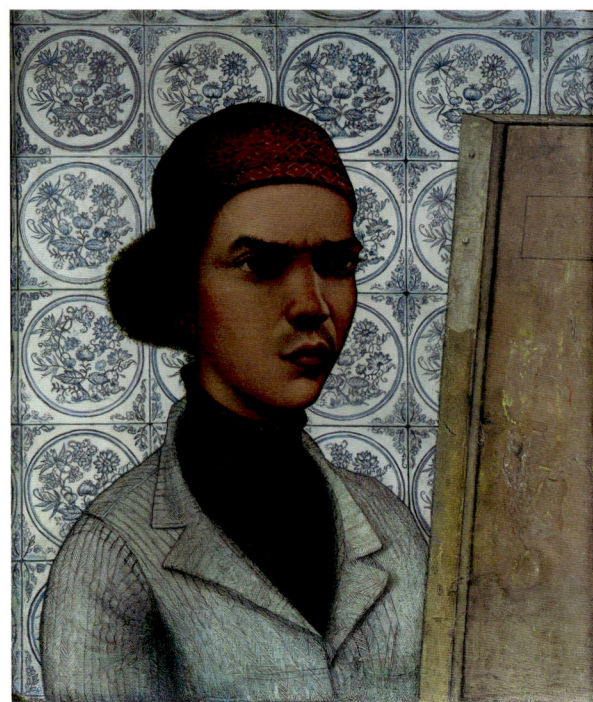

Fig. 8 Gregory Gillespie, *Rita*, 1985. Oil on panel, 19½ × 15¾ in.

Fig. 9 Gregory Gillespie, *Dark Painter (Portrait of a Renaissance Painter)*, 1982–83. Oil on panel, 23 × 20 in.

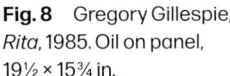

maternal relationship, or lack of it. (His unstable mother had been mostly absent, in a psychiatric hospital.) To these anchoring works we added a portrait of his troubled daughter Lydia with her demon, and two late paintings of his second wife, Peggy—one softly ambivalent, the other sharply so. Greg told us more than once that we were his ideal collectors, because we did not confine ourselves to the large, mid-career set pieces that everyone wanted, but acquired works in a range of sizes, styles, and subjects from all periods of his life. We treasured his endorsement. His art shaped our taste, and it remains the heart and soul of our collection.

What drew us so strongly to Greg's art was the way he unites the physical and the metaphysical aspects of the world we live in. He is sometimes mistaken for a realist. But, as he was always quick to point out, he never confined himself to realistic portrayal. He created images by free association and used precise depiction to enable viewers to make his feelings real.[5] He saw no sharp line between seen and imagined: "I enjoy both approaches and I enjoy mixing them up so that the 'realist' paintings have elements of the bizarre, the fantastic, and (I hope) an almost hallucinatory, iconographic quality about them; and I work on the more imaginary pieces for months to make them as specific and tangible as I can." The visible world was to him unaccountably strange, and the products of his mind, mysteriously real. "Thoughts are alive," he wrote, "they live, they pulse with life!"[6] Although he had mystic inclinations in midlife, Greg was always a man of the material world—a man of paint. As he put it: "I just want to look at paintings that are sensuous, delicious, and possess visual powers as tremendous as the greatest of the past."[7]

Passion in figurative art need not be weird and tough, of course; it can also be joyful, or just obsessive. Much of the work in our collection is not particularly weird, or at least no longer seems so in a world that gets weirder by the day, but it's all in one way or another intense. Take, for example, the work of William Beckman, who caught our eye in *Contemporary American Realism* with his great double portrait of himself and his wife, sculptor Diana Moore. Our first acquisitions came a few years later with a drawing of Diana, followed by a lovely little oil painting (*Diana #7*, 1985; fig. 10) that has all the visual presence of his large showcase portraits. We knew at first glance it was the right one for us.

These were followed by a youthful and atypically soulful self-portrait (it's the one the artist wishes he had kept for himself, he told us): a penetrating small portrait of Greg, and an uneasy portrait of Beckman's daughter Deidre against a backdrop of the artist's Minnesota family farm. Beckman's portraits are not deliberately strange, but in their obsession with personhood and paint they are passionate.

On the joyful side is Puerto Rican–born artist Rafael Ferrer, whose colorful and spirited paintings we admired early on in the Nancy Hoffman Gallery. We began modestly with several small portraits, selecting for juicy paint and striking personality. A high point is the uneasily sexy portrait of a topless woman in slatted sunlight (*Untitled*, 1988). The model, we later learned, was very nervous about posing nude, and Ferrer deftly captured the conflicting emotions of painting and being painted. We followed these with larger works from the first years of the artist's transition, in the early 1980s, from postmodern assemblage and performance to narrative figure painting. A large naked Venus rising from a tropical sea (*Encuentro*, 1983; fig. 11) was a formative commitment. And it was followed by an unsettling scene of a mother and child, both nude and on separate chairs and paths, unaware of or indifferent to each other (*La Espera*, 1983). This acquisition was a memorable experience. We had long been mooning over an image of the work in an art magazine, knowing that it would be just the one for us and lamenting that it could never be ours. And then one day we ventured to ask our friends in the Hoffman Gallery if it might one day come loose and learned that just days before it had come in for resale! Ferrer's lively and affectionate depictions of Dominican people and village life, which fortuitously he was making in the years of our most active collecting, have been a special pleasure. This happy conjuncture of the artist's life with our lives as collectors enabled us to acquire his best new work affordably and in depth.

In the 1990s and 2000s we began deliberately to expand the range of our collecting, especially to the art of Chicago and the San Francisco Bay Area. Midwestern and West Coast artists were at the time not well exhibited in New York. Critics and curators were mostly dismissive, and galleries, with few exceptions, were uninterested. The most significant exception was Allan Frumkin's gallery, which he opened in Chicago in 1952 and took to New York in 1959. There, within easy reach from home, we could explore the varied work of these wildly inventive artists. Bay Area and Chicago art were not homogeneous schools, but diverse hot spots in the revival of figuration. If we found one artist we admired, we had only to look around to see others we might like as well. The gallery was an ideal place to learn and a one-stop shop. Collecting regionally was not something we planned, or for a time were even consciously aware of doing. We were just in the right place at the right time, and the idea took shape in the doing. As a practice of foraging and buying, it worked.

We came first to the Californians, in 1987, acquiring a bronze wall sculpture by Robert Arneson (*Head Skinned and Dyed*, 1986). It's the skin of the artist's face and scalp nailed up as an art hunter's trophy (Arneson was famously fond of art jokes). More followed, especially wall masks, which were more home sized and affordable than the life-size sculptures for which the artist is best known. Favorites include one of

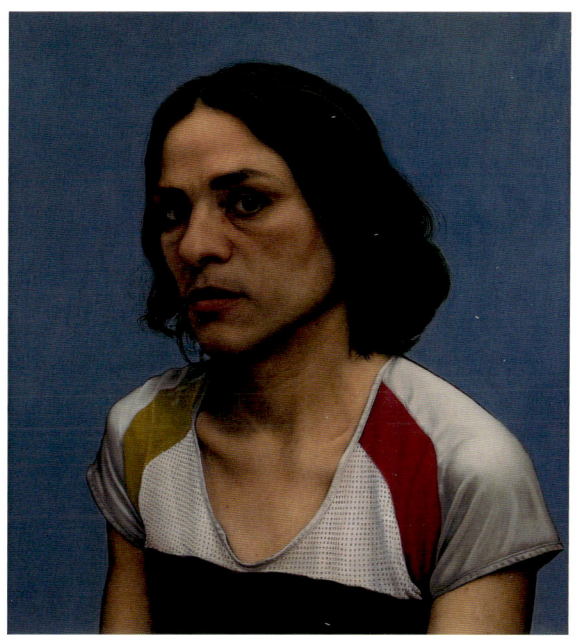

Fig. 10 William Beckman, *Diana #7*, 1985. Oil on panel, 22¾ × 20 in.

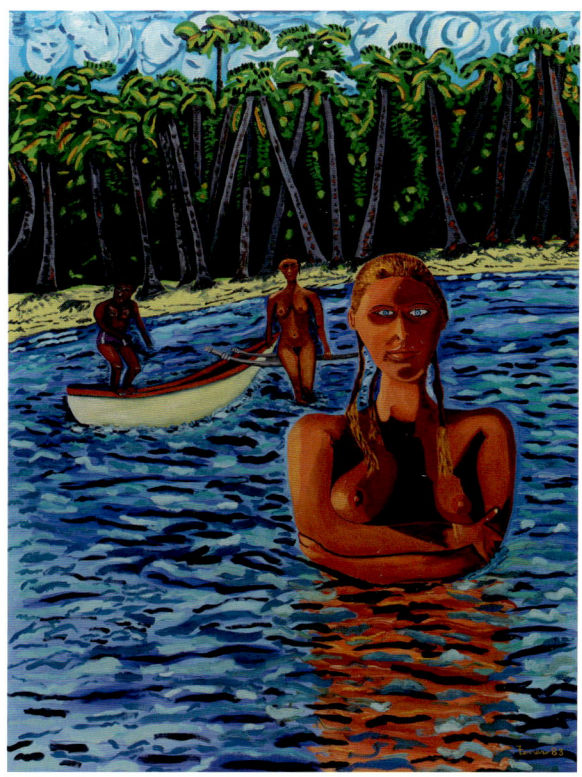

Fig. 11 Rafael Ferrer, *Encuentro*, 1983. Oil on canvas, 80 × 60 in.

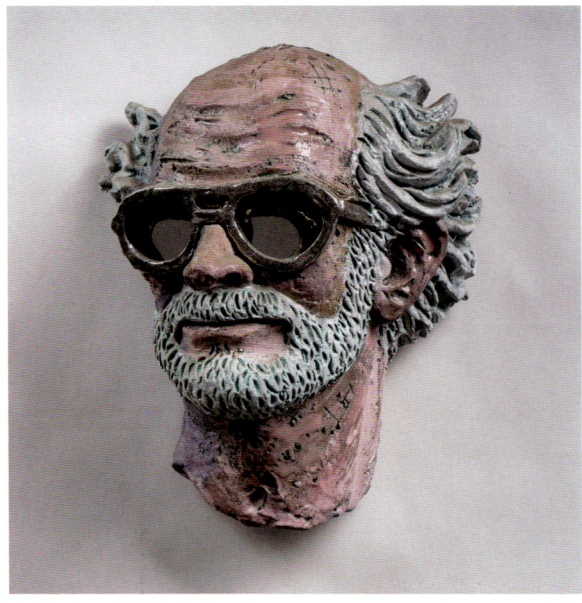

Fig. 12 Robert Arneson, *Reflections with Pink and Silver*, 1990. Glazed ceramic, glass, 16 × 12 × 6 in.

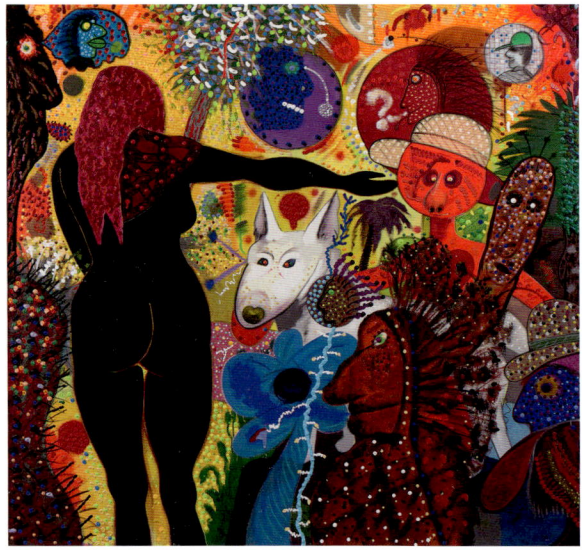

Fig. 13 Roy De Forest, *Savage Echoes*, 1982–83. Acrylic on canvas, 74½ × 78 in.

Kohler

Jackson Pollock—Arneson's ideal of the artist he hoped to become—with his nose bloodied in a drunken fight, and the mask version (fig. 12) of his famous standing self-portrait *California Artist* (1986), lampooning a New York critic's dismissive jibe at California artists as pot-addled airheads. An early self-portrait with his shadow imposed may refer to the initial diagnosis of what would be terminal cancer. And a double self-portrait mask depicting one head devouring the other in a bloody cannibal kiss (*Head Eater*, 1991; plate 10) may represent the disease that was in effect eating him alive, or perhaps just the human capacity for self-destruction. Either way it was the toughest work there was on offer. We've also done well with Arneson's less well known but no less powerful works on paper: jokey self-portraits in various moods, and—a favorite of ours—the affectionate painting of his fellow artist Roy De Forest. It's expressive figuration California style: humorously serious, wildly inventive, and unguardedly personal.

Joan Brown was our other California favorite. Our first acquisitions, in 1993, were a pair of small but iconic self-portraits from 1972: one brashly self-confident, the other uncharacteristically humble and unsure. These were followed by more works from the 1960s and 1970s—our favorite period—as they came back for resale. A special one is the large double portrait from 1961 of Brown and her then-husband Manuel Neri in Moroccan costumes. (She loved to dress up and try on borrowed personae for size.) It's a signature work in her impasto early style and arguably one of the best (plate 19). Works in her flatter 1970s style include our Munchian dance of death with her phobic (and, here, victorious) rats, and her construction of a hip "love" rat leaning on his vintage guitar (*Rock 'n' Roll Rat*, 1967). Brown identified with animals, and this one looks benign, but a rat may suggest mixed feelings about California's happy hippy pop culture. We were looking to buy more, but a collection in depth was not in the cards. Most of her best and most personal work was either too large for us or not available. Brown and Arneson both died young (she in 1990, he in 1992), just about the time we were becoming seriously interested in Bay Area art. Our lives did not align.

We also developed an abiding affection for the art of Roy De Forest, Arneson's best friend and co-conspirator in the Bay Area's Junk or Funk art, or (their preferred term) Nut art scene. Unlike Arneson and Brown, De Forest was never drawn to portraiture. His subjects were imagined scenes of cartoony humans and animals enacting enigmatic dramas (he was devoted especially to his beloved pet dogs). Our first acquisition, in 2001, was a large and typically crowded scene of a shapely Gauguin nude in a diverse crowd of admiring males and a white dog (*Savage Echoes*, 1982–83; fig. 13). The next, a polychrome bronze sculpture (*Dog Bench #1*, 2001–3) was a memorable event. Entering the Adams Gallery, Frances made a beeline for the bench, planted herself firmly on it, and declared to all that it was hers! It's not strictly speaking figurative, but for De Forest dogs were human, so it is an allowable stretch of the category.

Because De Forest was productive and not (yet) widely appreciated outside the Bay Area, we were able to acquire fine works from the 1970s and 1980s (our favorite period) affordably and in some depth, as they turned up in George Adams's back room. Subjects include alert sentinel dogs watching for "outriders," a talking horse, a cow with windows in its middle and figures leaning through, and brick dogs and dog-shaped houses (plate 91). There are recurring scenes of voyaging and outdoor adventure in exotic places. What it all means exactly isn't clear and most likely wasn't meant to be. De Forest's sole aim was to create and then inhabit imagined worlds, which became real with being explored through art. The artist described himself as "an eccentric individual creating fantasy art with the amazing intention of totally building a miniature cosmos into which the artful alchemist could retire with all his friends, animals, and paraphernalia."[8] Nut art was, in his words, a "squirrel in the forest of visual delights."[9] So, too, is Nut art collecting.

Rounding out our collection of Californians is ceramist Viola Frey. Although she was not a member of the Arneson Nut art circle, her work has similar qualities of freewheeling fancy and humor. Our first purchase was her "portrait" of the author Edith Sitwell as an ear of corn. It took us by surprise in Nancy Hoffman's art fair booth. ("What's that?! No joke? It's available? We'll take it!") Other collectors had been admiring it but had moved on to make up their minds. Thinking it likely that we would have just this one chance, we didn't hesitate. Our next acquisition, a full decade later, was another enigmatic sculpture: an animated tureen in a top hat devouring a bird and doll baby (*The Dinner, also Junk Eating*, 1978–79; fig. 14). Whatever these odd things may mean, they're fun and irresistible. Frey's vigorous works on paper are equally engaging. Her warm domestic scene of a kissing couple and a benevolent dog, in impasto outlined in sgraffito—a ceramist's technique—was love at first sight. We did not buy Frey's art in depth, though not from lack of trying. She produced abundantly, recycling a repertoire of motifs drawn largely from her collection of flea-market knickknacks. But it was her more personal works that we really liked, and these came along less often—hence our sporadic and modest acquisition.

It was a few years later, in the early 2000s, that we took up with the Chicago Imagists, the young and diversely inventive artists who had burst on the scene in the late 1960s and 1970s. Their devotion to "low" pop culture (comics, advertisements, flea-market finds) has led some to see them as a Midwestern variant of ironic New York Pop, but they were never that. The Imagists painted low stuff because they lived and loved it. It was their world, their visual idiom. If they looked anywhere for inspiration, it was not east to New York, but west to California (where some of them lived and worked for a time). Imagism, like Nut art, was a nursery for varied modes of figuration, from emblematic abstraction to comic-book storytelling. It was that diversity that made both locales such rich and enjoyable hunting grounds for passionate figuration. We could see a family of related styles and select the ones we liked.

We were especially drawn to Gladys Nilsson's warm-hearted cartoony figures—think Popeye's rubber-limbed girlfriend Olive Oyl. The artist gets ideas from her own life and from sitting in public places and watching the nonstop carnival of humankind. Dancing, shopping, flirting, bathing, grooming, golfing, socializing, and just milling about are some favorite subjects. Our first, toe-in-the-water purchase was a small watercolor collage of a woman getting dolled up and going out (fig. 15). It was our second acquisition, four years later, that was the all-out commitment: a large and gently satiric self-portrait for her sixtieth birthday (plate 18). It was the standout

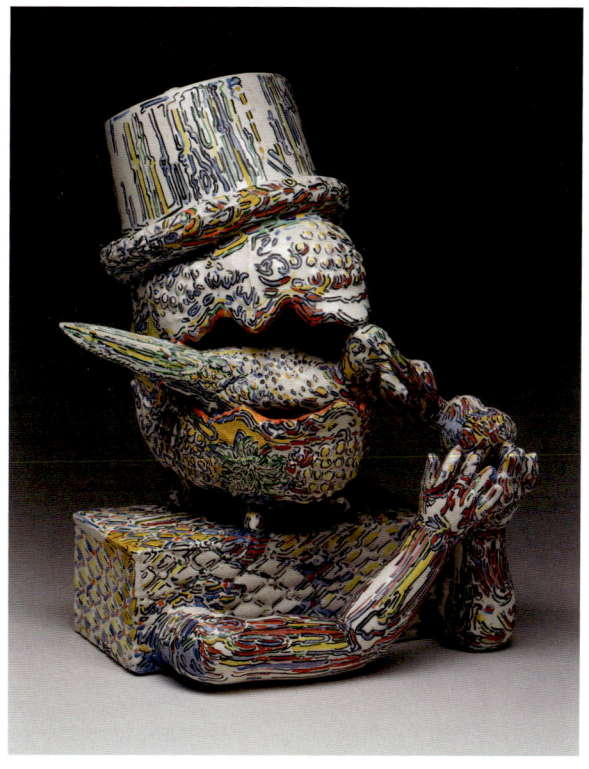

Fig. 14 Viola Frey, *The Dinner, also Junk Eating*, 1978–79. Glazed ceramic, 19 × 15 × 12 in.

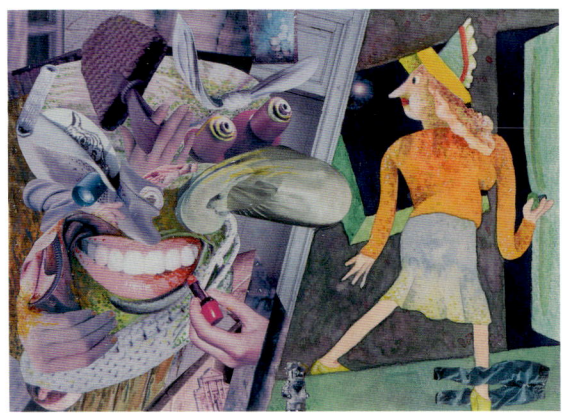

Fig. 15 Gladys Nilsson, *Going*, 1995. Watercolor, gouache, and collage on paper, 5½ × 7½ in.

piece in a show at the Jean Albano Gallery in Chicago. We were in town at just the right moment, and it was so obviously a major work that we had to take the plunge. It was our good luck to be on the spot, but we were well prepared to see and understand.

With that bold plunge, how could we not go on to collect work from every period of Nilsson's life? And so we did: from her late 1960s explorations of materials and narrative styles, to the gently unsettling oil paintings from her years in the Bay Area in the 1970s with her husband Jim Nutt—beach scenes of blobby figures hinting at trouble in paradise—and on to her signature everyday dramas in gorgeous watercolor. A second large work depicts the artist stepping into an afterlife filled with embracing and welcoming couples (*Checking Out the Other Side*, 1987; plate 120). As critic John Yau wrote: "Through the medium of watercolor she has singlehandedly created a world based on close observation, but which is, as she says of [the artist, John] Graham, 'not of this world.'"[10] Her varied subjects and unfailing craft made each new acquisition a distinctive addition to a collection in depth. So, when exceptional works came along at affordable prices—which they routinely did, thanks to Nilsson's unlimited creativity and the art world's irrational undervaluing of works on paper—there was nothing to hold us back. Our Chicago gallerists alerted us to things they thought we would like, so we could buy with confidence in absentia and sight unseen.

The other Chicagoan on whom we focused is Robert Lostutter. Also supremely skilled in watercolor, as well as in oil and graphite, he is artistically akin to the Imagists but less well known. He has always worked more for himself than for the market and did not take part in Imagists' group exhibitions. He created his distinctive visual world in intense explorations of human passions and relationships. Bizarre images of immensely thighed women and fiercely predatory birdmen—male heads with exotic plumage and savage demeanors—are his preferred subjects, as well as impassioned and sparring couples, and armed or costumed warriors bound and masked, with points and edges compressing soft flesh (plate 53). Thanks (once more) to our Chicago gallerists, we were able to collect this weird and strangely beautiful art affordably and in depth. A special late addition was the large and disturbing graphite drawing of an entwined couple enraged and biting (*A Sign of My Time*, 1977; fig. 16). It's one of the artist's greatest and toughest works, from his personal collection—almost scary in its intensity. John Corbett and Jim Dempsey knew we would love it and called us straightaway when the artist decided to let it go.

Some Imagists whose work we liked and desired were for various reasons hard to buy. Christina Ramberg's fragmented and disintegrating female bodies are frighteningly weird. (As an exceptionally tall woman, she was obsessed with the conventions that made women womanly—or not.) But she worked slowly and died in her prime, in 1995, so her singular paintings were always in short supply and eagerly sought after. We were fortunate to secure two fine, small works just before the New York art world finally woke up to Chicago art ("Hey, look what we've discovered! Who knew?!") and quickly drove her prices out of reach. The art of Ed Paschke and Karl Wirsum is likewise flamboyantly and beautifully weird. But the works we liked best date from just a few years, in the late 1960s and 1970s, and came back for resale only as they became too pricey for us, especially

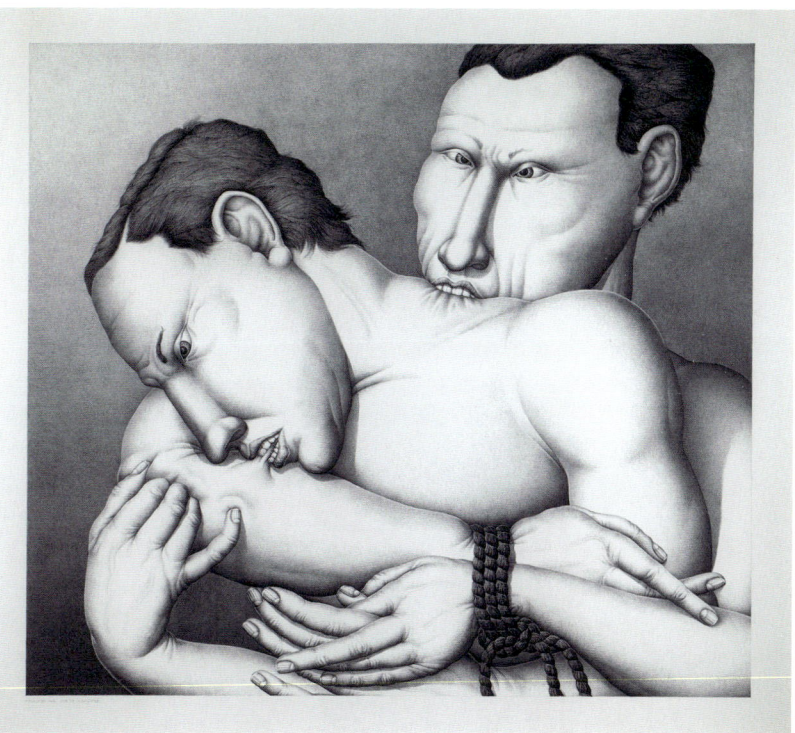

the oil paintings. We did belatedly acquire some fine works on paper by both artists, thanks to gallerists who knew what we wanted and kept us in mind. Wirsum's large ink drawing of a wildly kinetic chorus girl (fig. 17) and Paschke's arresting drawings of bizarrely distorted and costumed denizens of Chicago's gritty cultural byways—paintings in graphite—are no less fine than these artists' more valued oils (plates 34 and 35).

In expanding our collecting horizons, we were at first somewhat cautious, and sometimes too cautious. We were uncertain of our first Arneson: it wasn't clay and it wasn't in the round—was it really the right one to start with? (We were reassured to learn that if we didn't buy it, Allan Frumkin would.) We almost didn't purchase our first work by Red Grooms—one of his early homages to favorite artists. We liked it a lot, but it wasn't his signature New York subject: hit pause. Luckily, we realized as we were walking out the gallery door that it would be a mistake to wait. With such a rare and lovable painting, it was now or never. So we turned around and bought *Gauguin* (1963) then and there. We weren't always so bold. We should have gone all out at auction for a juicy early street scene by Grooms. It went high but was a great one, and a rarity. And we dithered too long about Joan Brown's affectionate early painting of her pet dog Bob. We liked it, but at the time it seemed too casually painted for us, and it was not a human figure. (There we were wrong: Brown's animals are typically stand-ins for herself.) We likewise came to regret not saying yes right away to Greg Gillespie's portrait of Bella Fishko with the artist's hands and a brush—a sly acknowledgment of the gallerist's formative role in his art and life. Bella put us first in line for it, but the price was high, and we let the opportunity slip away. These are painful memories. But on the bright side, we have bought very few things that we came to regret. We always bought to keep, and that required a degree of caution that is unavoidably sometimes overdone.

With some artists it just wasn't easy to know our minds. For years we blew hot and cold about paintings by Bob Thompson, looking hard yet never buying. As marvelous in design and color as many are, they always seemed too formalist for us and too rooted in modernist art history—art more from other art than from life. And though he was enormously productive, the competition for his best small and affordable works was discouraging. The last straw for us was spotting just the right one at a fair only hours after it had been sold. The struggle was just too painful; we stopped looking. We did buy three very good drawings that chanced to come our way, including the tender portrait of his wife, Carol, reading (*Artaud*, 1964; fig. 18) and a pensive self-portrait recording a mellow evening with art friends (*High Night #2*, c. 1963). Thompson's drawings are generally more spontaneous and personal than his paintings and, perhaps for that reason, were not (yet) expensive. We should have made them a priority and been more proactive in seeking them out.

As the collection grew and took on a distinctive character, our purchases became more directed and methodical. With our favorite artists we took care to keep gallerists in mind of what we wanted, and we began to

Fig. 16   Robert Lostutter, *A Sign of My Time*, 1977. Graphite on canvas, 44 × 48 in.

Fig. 17   Karl Wirsum, *Untitled* (Study for *Show Girl Series*), 1969. Ink on paper, 36 × 24 in.

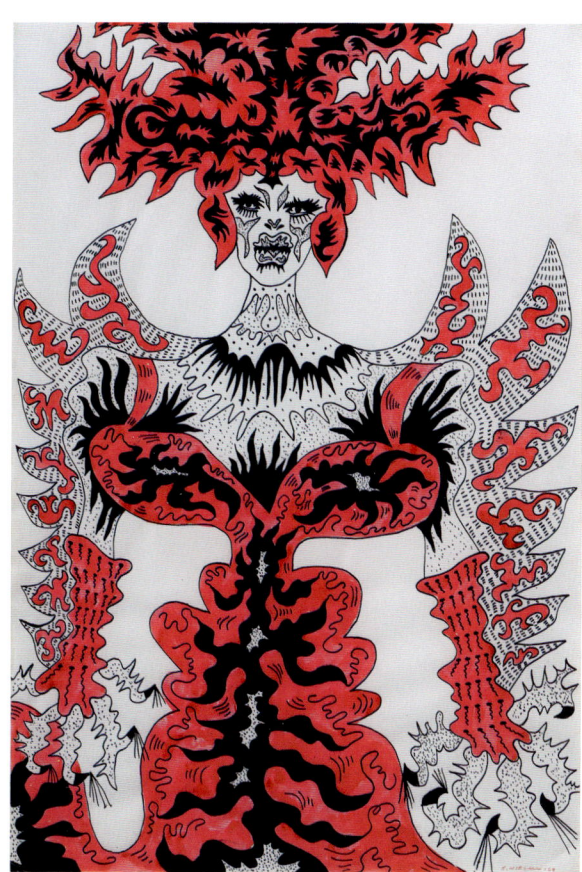

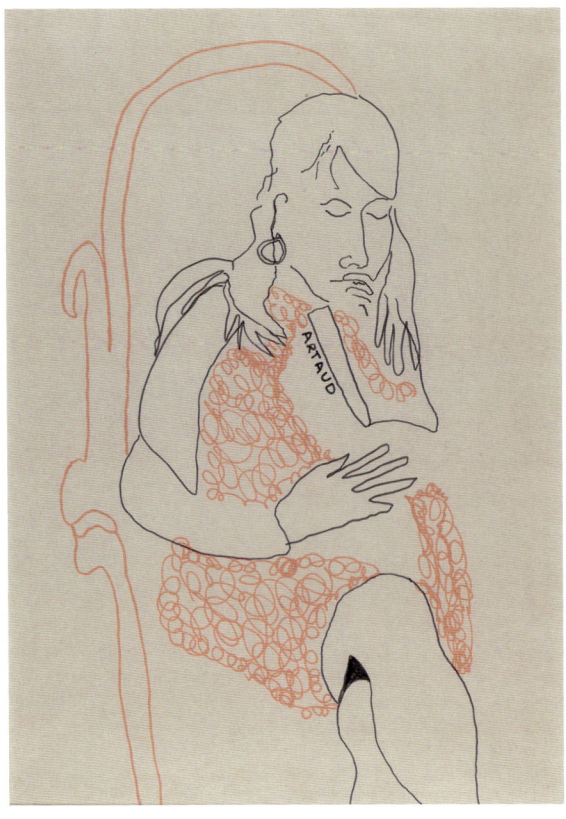

Fig. 18 Bob Thompson, *Artaud*, 1964. Marker on paper, 19½ × 13¾ in.

Fig. 19 Rafael Ferrer, *La Pintura: Descarga del Monte*, 1995. Oil on canvas; 96 × 72 in.

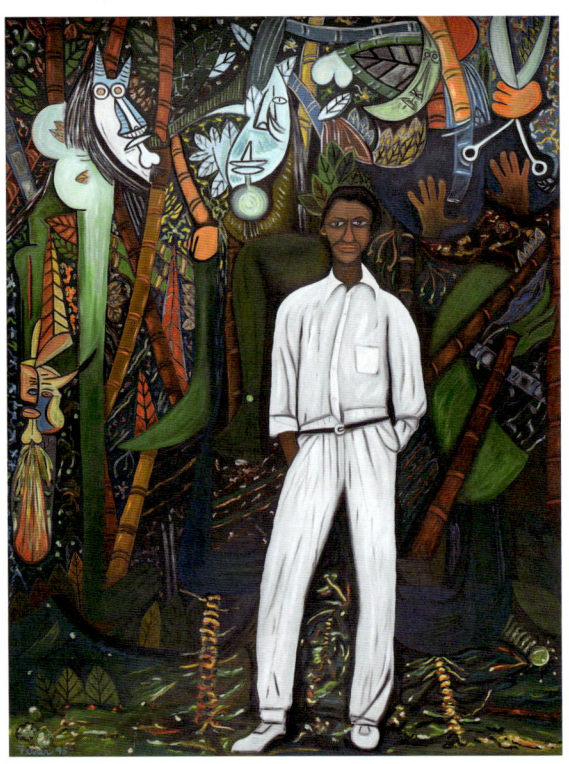

browse gallery exhibitions and back rooms—and auctions—online. It was a way of getting in first for the best. And exceptional pieces did unexpectedly turn up: like Jane Lund's sly double portrait of herself and her eighteenth-century Swiss avatar, the mischievous virtuoso pastelist Jean-Étienne Liotard (*Artists of a Certain Age*, 2016; plate 20). It's a playful reflection on Jane's own mischievous artistic persona—a masterwork two years in the making. Knowing our long and active interest in Jane's work, Cheryl and Bob Fishko called us first when it came in. Another special piece is a magical and luminous little painting of the newly adopted daughter of Greg and his wife, Peggy, showing Julianna as a diminutive woodland sprite, in the manner of the Victorian fairy artist Richard Dadd. It was a family heirloom, but Peggy and Julianna let it go to us—an appropriate second home.

We likewise secured a couple of Rafael Ferrer's large masterworks. These turned up unexpectedly on the website of the artist's gallery, Adam Baumgold, which I was by then routinely browsing. The first was the portrait of his idol, Cuban modernist Wifredo Lam (*La Pintura*, 1995; fig. 19). We had lusted after the work when it first entered Nancy Hoffman's gallery, though at the time it was way too big ever to be ours. And then, twenty years later, there it was again, back for resale and now with a place we could keep it, at PAFA as a promised gift. The second surprise, a year later and again on Baumgold's website (back from the same collector), was a warm-hearted scene of village musicians (*El Bolero*, 1983–84; plate 84). Music making was a favorite subject of this musician-artist, and we had long been uncomfortably aware of its absence in our collection. We had tried. One brand-new one in the Hoffman Gallery was too big, and another got away at auction in competitive bidding. But the one that went public discreetly online was the best of the lot. It was luck, but not blind luck. Prepared and persistent foraging greatly improves the odds of capture.

We also unexpectedly acquired pieces by artists whose work we knew and loved but had given up hope of ever owning. Among these was the rare figurative painting by Frances Cohen Gillespie that took us by surprise in Rich Michelson's Northampton gallery. We had come in to inspect some youthful works by Greg, her then-husband, but there facing us as we entered was Frances's large nude self-portrait (plate 2). Fran was almost wholly devoted to intricate and luscious floral still lifes, and her early figurative works were few and never came up for sale. Yet there it was: one of her most personal and best. We knew at once it was the one we would buy. Such surprises are a joy of regular gallery going: you go in to buy a Greg and come out with a Fran. And then not long after—mirabile dictu—along came a second great one: Fran's striking large portrait of their young daughter (*Leila*, 1972–73; fig. 20). It felt miraculous but wasn't quite that. When the work was unexpectedly offered for sale (by Fran and Greg's son Vincent), Michelson knew we were the most appropriate new home for this family treasure and arranged a sale.

Another happy surprise was the Cuban American Juan Gonzalez. We had long wanted to include him in our collection but had never even gotten close. New work was avidly sought and sold out before his openings and once sold never reappeared—not *ever*. Yet there in Nancy Hoffman's basement storage were two wonderful little works back for resale. It took a few moments for our minds to process what our eyes were seeing: two of this artist's most personal and emotional paintings—in fact, the two we would have chosen of all he ever made. A time-lapse scene recalls his early family life in Cuba, from birth—with an angelic annunciation, no less—to his coming out as a gay man in midlife (*Nacimiento*, 1979; p. 64). And in a darkly luminous self-portrait, he faces a certain death, from AIDS, with a mix of apprehension and hope of a Christian rebirth into life eternal (*Jardin Gris*, 1989; plate 23). These small but powerful paintings could serve as bookends to a life that was all too short yet passionately lived. Whoever had first acquired them had collected thoughtfully and well. And we were at the right place at the right time to keep them paired. It was a stroke of luck, though sadly one that was not repeated.

In this concentrated phase of our collecting, we were also able to play catch-up with artists whose work we admired early on and could have bought, but had not. With these we didn't wait for the goddess Fortuna to take us in hand but took action to make up for past neglect. Tabitha Vevers was one of these. We had been visiting her early gallery installations for several years with interest but no urgency to buy, until her sold-out show of her new series of flying dreams. These we would have acquired had we been paying attention. So we came early to her next exhibition and secured the one we liked best, and the next year got an online preview and bought several more. It was also at this show that we met the artist. She noticed us looking long and hard at her most challenging and slightly naughty painting (*Anonymous*, 2003; p. 66) and, curious, introduced herself. It was the start of a lasting friendship. As her range of subjects expanded—to sex and procreation, the death and rebirth of nature, human feelings—there were pieces in each new show that spoke to us, and we made it our business to be always first in line. There's a climate apocalypse of fire and ice, an expulsion from a climate-flooded Eden, and a multibreasted marsupial Eve repopulating a post-deluge world (fig. 21). A group of early personal works that she had kept for herself filled in a collection in real depth of an artist who paints beautifully and from the heart about things that matter.

It was a similar story with Anne Kraus. Trained as a painter, Kraus had fallen in love with Victorian painted ceramics and retrained as a ceramist. Shunning conventional craft shapes and subjects, she made artful forms decorated with images from her own emotional life. Although we had liked and followed her work for years, we had been slow to buy. The small functional forms she then favored (cups, saucers, teapots, plates) had limited space for narrative, which was what we liked best. Then, in the late 1990s, larger works began to appear in her gallery shows: double flat-sided pots and large wall tiles, covered with elaborate dream stories of being lost in alien and threatening places and times (e.g., *The Dormant Garden*, 2001; plate 81). In these, drama got the upper hand over form, and we loved them.[11] But they sold fast to her devoted buyers, and we seemed always to be just too late. The distress of seeing all those nasty little red dots (meaning, *sold!*) spurred us to get in first for a change. This we did successfully for a few years, until the artist's life was cut tragically short in 2003. She was just forty-seven.

With Eric Stotik the interval between our first interest and first buy was very long indeed. We bought an intriguing youthful work at a

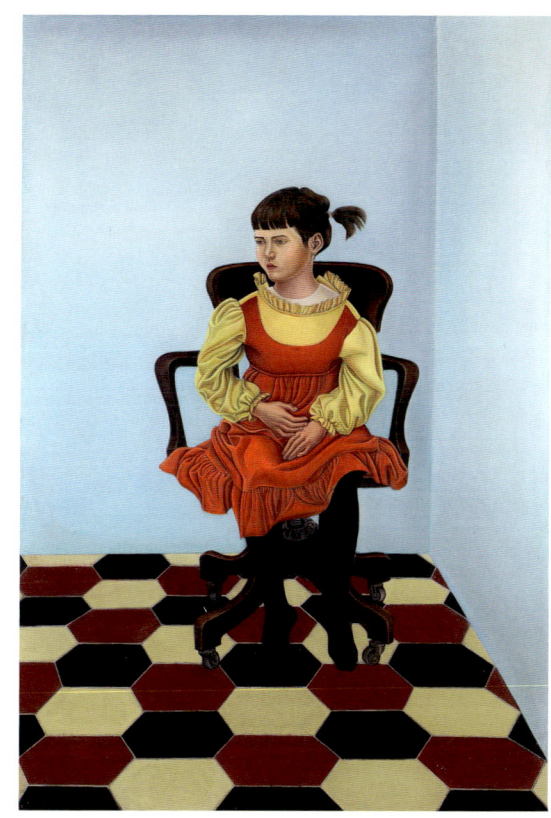

Fig. 20 Frances Cohen Gillespie, *Leila*, 1972-73. Oil on panel, 72 × 48 in.

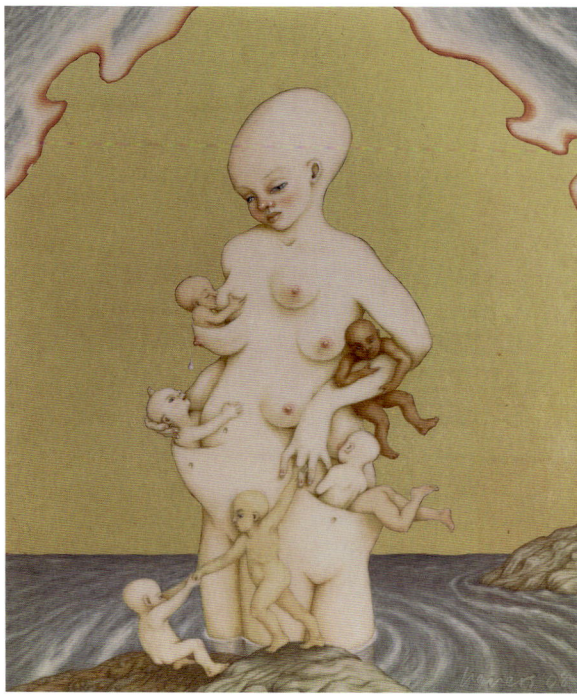

Fig. 21 Tabitha Vevers,
Eden: Marsupedonna, 2008.
Oil and gold leaf on ivorine,
9⅝ × 8 in.

New York art fair, but failed to follow up with the artist's Portland, Oregon, gallery. Then, twenty years later we somehow became aware that the artist in mid-career was turning out a lot of beautifully painted and weird—*very* weird—work (plates 100, 111, and 112). It was time to pay attention, and we did, getting email previews of each new show and selecting the toughest and most enigmatic and evocative to buy. These were scenes of troubled human relationships, dystopian phantasms of machine society, a packed crowd of threatening political zealots, and Goyaesque intimations of violence and war. Though the strange imagery resists precise interpretation, it is likely rooted in Stotik's experience of growing up as a missionary child in New Guinea. His imagery is redolent of culture shock, whether of leaving industrial modernity or of reentering is hard to say—maybe both.

Darrel Morris was another long-deferred commitment. We first saw his singular and deeply personal embroideries in his MFA show at the School of the Art Institute of Chicago, where he and our painter son Willie were classmates. We were intrigued by the medium and the craft, but it seemed too early then to commit, and we neglected to stay in touch. Then, fifteen years later, Willie alerted us that Morris had a large accumulation of excellent work from his life to date, and for very reasonable prices. These were memories of a shy gay boy who liked stitchery and was growing up an outsider in an oppressively conventional Appalachian town. There seemed to be no form of humiliation he did not suffer. Here he is: a three-legged chick pecked bloody by "normal" birds, a boy outfielder inevitably dropping the ball, a diminutive bellhop forever holding the door for oversized alpha males, a son scorned by the macho men in his family (*More Like Your Brother*, 2013; fig. 22). He is abandoned by a lover leaving the room and pushed away even by his pet cat. It's art that's painfully personal, ruefully humorous, and beautifully made.

Last but not least of our catch-up artists was John Wilde, a leading member of the circle of Surrealist-inspired artists in southeastern Wisconsin. He was one of the very first artists we followed closely, in the 1980s, in regular visits to his New York gallery. A superb draftsman and painter, Wilde captures the metaphysical oddity of the physical world by exhaustively depicting how it looks and feels to him. As he wrote in a youthful diary: "I want little more than to record, through the facet of my oft-miraculous sensitivity, the actuality of these things."[12] Yet, oddly, we failed to see a work that seemed just right for us. Well, there was one: a striking painting of a smiling nude woman hugging a giant desiccated mouse (*Portrait of D*, 1988, Madison Museum of Contemporary Art). We looked and looked some more, but it seemed too big in size and price to be the first step with an artist who was new to us and like nothing else we knew, so we passed. It was a beginner's mistake, not trusting our eye. What kept us from buying other pieces is less clear. Were his tougher and more personal works shown in New York less than his easier and more saleable still lifes and landscapes? Or were we just too picky, or not paying attention?

Then, almost thirty years later, the kind of works we had given up hope of ever acquiring suddenly began to surface, from the artist's family and estate, and from his early collectors: special pieces exploring his intimate relationships. These range from a warm home scene with family and friends, to a stagey Surrealist scene of sex and mayhem (*Love After Murder*, 1989;

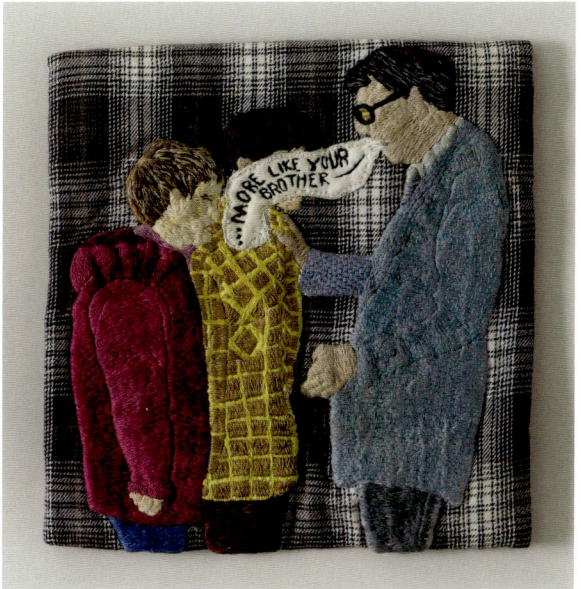

plate 99). In a late-life view of his young self, he looks forward in disbelief at his long life's varied achievements (*Myself in 1944 Contemplating the Following 60 Years*, 2004; plate 38). In short order we assembled a substantive collection of his most personal work. A particular favorite is the frontal nude portrait from 1968 of Shirley Grilley, who would become his second wife the following year, in the provocative style of German Neue Sachlichkeit.[13] Many of Wilde's paintings feature generic "naked ladies." They were his favorite subject, he liked to say, along with fruits and vegetables: all symbols of life. But no other depiction is as boldly individualized as this one, and we may hazard a guess why. The untimely death of his first wife, Helen, in 1966 had for a time left Wilde bereft and unable to paint (see our *H. and Death #2*, 1968; fig. 23). *The Chair* (1968; fig. 24) may thus represent both an artistic and a personal return to life. No Surrealist symbol, this one: The lady's real!

In addition to filling in and catching up, we also began, in the 2010s, to think about art locales and circles that we sensed would suit us yet we had made no effort to explore, like New York. Could the contemporary art world's capital city really be as poor in passionate figuration as its poverty in our collection would suggest? Or had our dislike of the city's hegemonic mainstream art deterred us from looking? We knew from exhibitions like *Bodies & Souls* and critical writing on New Humanism that all kinds of representational art were made in New York between the 1970s and the 1990s. We knew as well of artists' efforts at the time to give figurative expressionism an organized presence in the city of Abstract Expressionism: notably the Artists' Choice and Rhino Horn groups.[14] So we began to look with open minds and, no surprise, found much to like. New York thus belatedly became our third regional cluster—or fourth, if we take our New England group to be a third.[15] It was the first time we collected a regional art circle in a planned, proactive way, rather than by just venturing in and looking around. George Adams was once again our guide. He knew where good things were, because he and Allan Frumkin had shown and sold them the first time around.

Fig. 22 Darrel Morris, *More Like Your Brother*, 2013. Embroidery appliqué on fabric, 7⅜ × 7⅜ in.

Fig. 23 John Wilde, *H. and Death #2*, 1968. Oil on panel, 6¾ × 8¼ in.

Fig. 24 John Wilde, *The Chair*, 1968. Oil on canvas, 40 × 30 in.

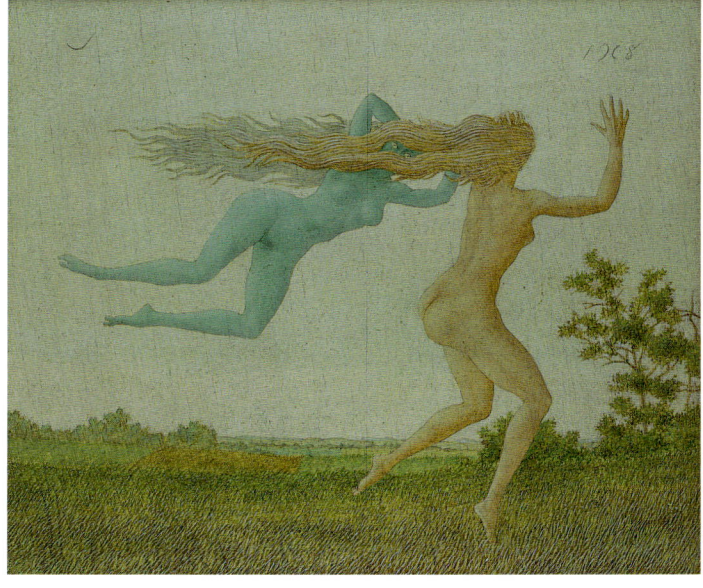

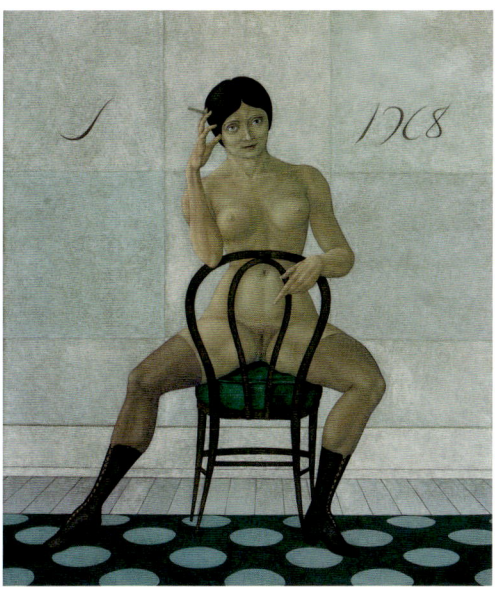

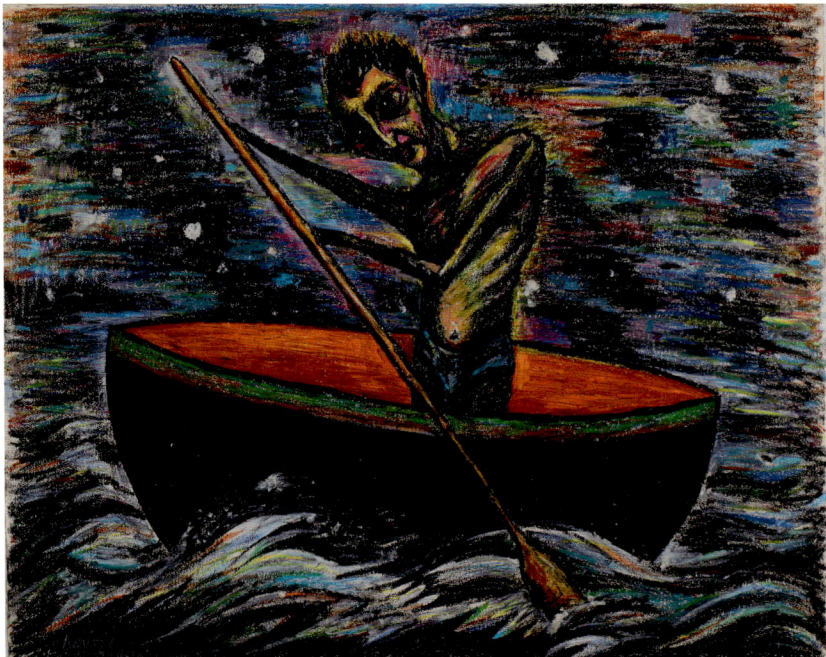

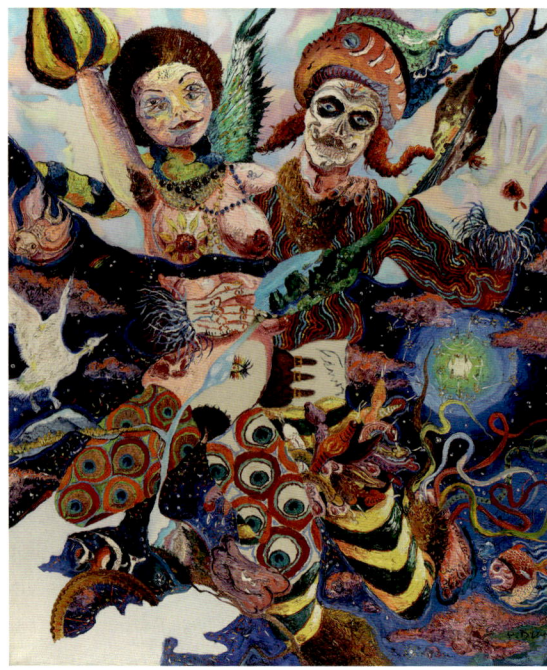

Fig. 25 Luis Cruz Azaceta, Study for *The Journey*, 1986. Oil pastel on paper, 35½ × 44½ in.

Fig. 26 Peter Dean, *Crazy Dance at the Crack of Reality*, 1976. Oil on canvas, 75 × 62 in.

Luis Azaceta, we agreed, was a priority. A Cuban American of the Castro diaspora, he painted vigorously—violently—of the fear and deracination he experienced as a young refugee in a strange city at its 1970s nadir of urban violence and disorder. And because his kind of art was at the time very out of fashion in New York, excellent early works were available at affordable prices. We began cautiously with small self-portraits, and these were soon followed by the weird and funny *Self-Portrait as Cockroach* (1981; plate 26). Then fortune smiled, as two of the artist's earlier signature works unexpectedly surfaced in George's back room. The huge and overwhelming self-portrait as a horseman of the apocalypse in a burning city was a once-in-a-lifetime acquisition (*Self-Portrait: Apocalypse Now—or Later?*, 1981; plate 118). And this was followed by his oil pastel of a lone and terrified *balsero* adrift on the waves of the Florida straits (Study for *The Journey*, 1986; fig. 25). We thus acquired, with surprising ease, a group of the artist's most powerful figurative works. And just in time: we were just one step ahead of a market revival.

Peter Dean was another out-of-fashion figurative expressionist who caught our eye. The standout member of the Rhino Horn circle, he was a double immigrant to New York: as a child in the late 1930s from Anschluss Vienna, and as an aspiring painter from a brief career as a field geologist. He, too, found compelling subjects in New York's Bohemian street culture, not as apocalypse but as carnival, which he captured in high-color impasto paintings of its people and public happenings. Subjects include parades (a pope on Broadway seeming to give him a benediction), assassinations (John Lennon, Malcolm X), and protests against oppression (of women, of Native Americans). Expressive self-portraits in various moods and disguises were another favorite mode (exalted, downcast; hero, hipster), as well as allegorical ventures into untamed edges of human consciousness (*Crazy Dance at the Crack of Reality*, 1976; fig. 26). In his own words: "I am a magician who transforms the images of our times into painting. I interpret reality into fantasy and back again. I'm a juggler of color and textures. I'm a seer of the past and a prophet of the future. I ride the hurricane. I walk on the tightrope of sanity. I live on the edge of the world."[16] Dean was prolific and always in top form, and died in his prime (in 1993, at age fifty-eight), so his estate was full of excellent works at accessible prices. In a visit with George Adams to Dean's family home and studio, we selected a group of his finest paintings. It was once more a fleeting opportunity: not long after, his entire estate was sold to a private collector.

Red Grooms was yet another late 1950s immigrant to the city (from middle-class Nashville), who reveled in the street life of Lower Manhattan. We had long admired his works and had two, acquired serendipitously at an interval of ten years. The first was *Gauguin* (1963), as I've mentioned, and *P'town Bicycle* (1971–74; plate 27) was another nice surprise. We knew the latter well from the catalogue of PAFA's 1985 retrospective; it was the work we most longed to have. Then one day browsing George Adams's website, there it was, back for resale and all ours. That, and a spate of good early work in auctions, suggested that the time was right to collect more aggressively. And we did acquire some exceptional pieces: a narrative scene of the escape of a prison trusty down Grooms's home street in Chinatown, sunny watercolor portraits of himself and vacation friends (*Self-Portrait, Summer*, 1980; fig. 27), and a set of his spirited and funny lithographs of raffish city life (*No Gas*, 1971). We were looking to acquire more, but market prices revived, and auction listings thinned, dashing any such hopes.

Rounding out our New York group is Philip Sherrod, yet another art refugee (from Oklahoma) reacting in his own way—with affection—to 1970s New York. Sherrod took on the role of urban recorder and celebrant. He loved walking the city streets looking for interesting happenings, which he painted on the spot in a loose style expressive of the unruly exuberance of urban life. Our blimp-sized baby hovering over Lower Broadway is a characteristically odd and endearing Sherrodic scene (*Bar, Baby, and 6th Avenue*, 1977; fig. 28). The artist is an insatiable observer of people, and he loved them all. We narrowly missed a spirited self-portrait at auction but were compensated with a striking impasto portrait of an androgynous young person (*Untitled*, 1970) and a sexy double portrait of women friends (*Doris and Helena [as Two Sisters]*, n.d.).

New York's homegrown figurative expressionists were eclipsed in the 1990s when blue-chip galleries began to import the tonier (and more

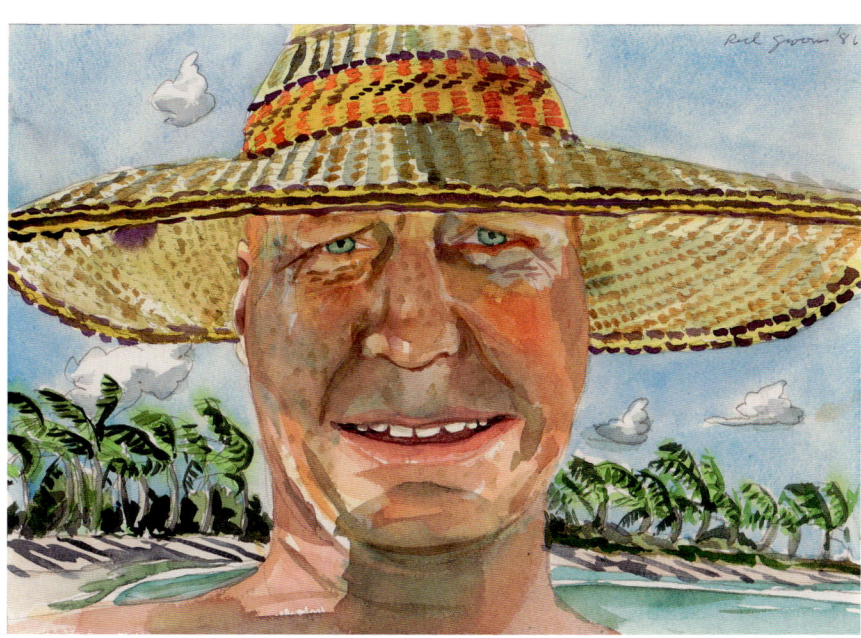

Fig. 27 Red Grooms, *Self-Portrait, Summer*, 1980. Watercolor on paper, 10 × 14 in.

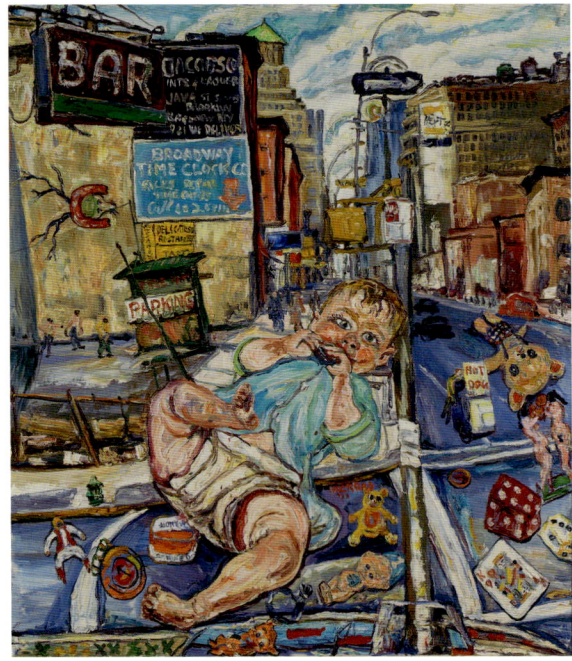

Fig. 28 Philip Sherrod, *Bar, Baby, and 6th Avenue*, 1977. Oil on canvas, 54 × 46 in.

Fig. 29 Sam Messer, *New York Harbor*, 2006. Oil on canvas, 17 × 13 in.

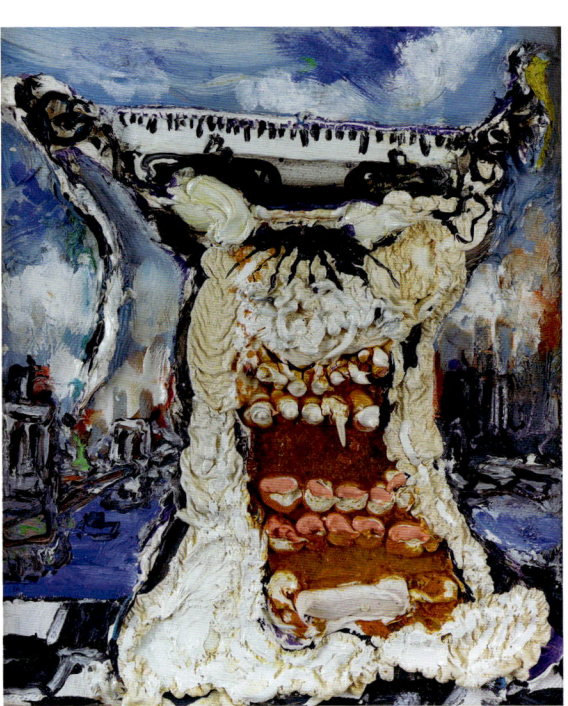

profitable) German expressionists. But their spirit lives on in the work of younger artists like Sam Messer, whose spirited, juicy paintings took us by surprise in a Boston gallery. It was love at first sight, and we went all out for three, including a large painting of his author wife, Eleanor Gaver, at work in Brooklyn, with a view of the Manhattan skyline. That was it, we thought. But six years later our interest was rekindled when we began to collect New York art systematically and in depth. Messer fit, and in visits to his studio we acquired some fine early works: a tender portrait of his daughter, and vigorous portrayals of the ancient and irascible outsider artist Jon Serl, whom Messer had befriended in California in the 1990s. Portraits of an author friend's manual typewriter, from a large series of this emotional machine in varied moods, are a comical and oddly effective expansion of what counts as figurative (e.g., *New York Harbor*, 2006; fig. 29). It's all vintage New York.

Of course, many accomplished artists are not members of an art circle. For some, a degree of isolation enabled them to remain steadfastly themselves: not outsiders, but *outliers*, neither alienated from the art world nor its captives, but drawing idiosyncratically on subjects and styles. In our late collecting we acquired outliers almost exclusively, especially women. Anne Minich is exemplary. Brought up to be a proper Philadelphian, she left the settled life of a clerical marriage to pursue a Bohemian life on the move and on the edge. (A stint in art school mainly taught her what she did *not* want to do or be.) Her art is all about sex and religion, she likes to say— bodies and souls. Her bold self-portraits were our favorites: from her first, made while still a housewife, which confirmed her feeling that she was meant to be an artist (*AEGM at 35*, c. late 1960s; fig. 30), to her most recent, of an aging body balding and undergoing chemo (*Feral Nun*, 2012–13; p. 47). She knows the art world but has always kept a healthy distance and gone her own singular way. Whatever catches her eye she makes her own, from Christian altars and icons to found objects, abstracted forms, and expressive single lines.

Irene Olivieri is similarly nourished by a rich and varied life, in a range of natural environments with distinctive animal denizens: ocean shore (harbor seals), mountain forest (catamounts), high desert (lizards, pack rats). Human-animal hybrids capture her bodily sense of kinship (e.g., *Papachongo*, 2024). Bones for her also have a special significance, not as grim reminders of mortality, but as bearers of the memories that outlive mortal flesh. Bones of mice and voles gathered from owl pellets form a sensuous nude woman (*Paleo Girl*, 2006). And in a striking tableau the artist's own skeleton appears, to quiz her and make sure she's living her life fully and responsibly. It's a cliché of death repurposed to expand and enrich life.

Some of our outliers find inspiration in the written word. Gina Litherland's theatrical scenes of human and animal lives draw on classic European literature and fairy tales, and the scary stories of the Brothers Grimm, as well as Surrealist and occult texts. She identifies especially with Red Riding Hood and wolves. Two luminous portraits (presumably herself) bring to life the competing demands and rewards of domesticity and art. A Cinderella artist sweeps up as a domestic mouse looks on from her nest (*Housekeeping*, 2015). And a determined artist adventurer strides boldly forth with companion animals into a winter landscape

(*Queen of an Uncharted Territory*, 2008; fig. 31). In *Lupercalia* (2011), a cat, horse, goat, and wolf guide a sleeping girl's dreams or memories of life's stages.

Kyle Staver likewise finds subjects in the meeting of eternal myth and homely everyday life. In warmly sensual scenes, couples enjoy leisurely mornings together in bed and bath (*Feeding the Cockatoo*, 2009). Epic dramas from humanist and Christian literature bring the universality of art to what's most personal and transitory. And art forms devised to transcend ordinary lived experience are made down-to-earth real.[17] Staver has an uncanny way of giving her figures, and her viewers, a physical sensation of flying: in air (*Trapeze*, 2012), underwater (*Groupers*, 2013), and on waves (*Dolphins*, 2021; fig. 32). Art lookers thus become part of the art.

In a category all to themselves are Winfred Rembert's scenes of his early life in the Jim Crow South, richly fashioned in tooled and dyed leather. He learned his craft from a fellow inmate in Georgia prisons, where he spent seven years after a near-fatal run-in with police and a lynch mob in the aftermath of a (peaceful) civil rights protest.[18] His work took us by surprise in a West Philadelphia art and antiques fair, and we hastened to learn and follow up with gallery visits. Rembert was at the time not widely known in the world of fine art, so we were able to acquire a group of his best and most personal pieces. These include a scene of the artist-to-be in prison stripes digging a ditch, and another of him watching longingly through prison bars the man who taught him the leather craft that years later, in New Haven, would give him a second life, in art (*T. J. the Tooler*, 1998; fig. 33). His works are unpretentious miracles of color, design, materiality, and emotional punch. An unforgettable portrait of his formidable mother-in-law (*Sugar Cane*, 2009; plate 33) is another. We were looking to acquire more of his affectionate memories of Black community life, when his death and the publication of his Pulitzer Prize–winning memoir brought him instant celebrity, along with a tenfold increase in prices. That was it for us.

What, if anything, unites outliers and gives them the historical importance they deserve? There's no off-the-shelf art historiography that would serve. "Outsider" artists find kinship in borrowed folk idioms and populist alienation from the market world of schools and careers. For outliers no art is alien. Nor do modernist art histories have a place for those whose work does not inspire or feed a vanguard movement. Outliers, in Peter Schjeldahl's pregnant phrase, are "prepossessing misfits." As he wrote, in a review of the great yet not widely known Norwegian village artist Nikolai Astrup: "We are too habituated to the canonical march of modernist progress and a reflex of deeming anything marginal to it 'minor.' An exploration of hinterlands elsewhere might well foster a category of similarly prepossessing misfits."[19] I would add only that it's not just geographical edges and hinterlands that need to be explored, but also those of aesthetic style—for example, passionate figuration.

Collecting is commonly regarded as parasitic on creative art making. But if done with knowledge and purpose, it is very much a creative act. Like composing histories and curating museum exhibitions, collecting helps to winnow the uneven superabundance of all that's made and to give what's best a public presence. In hindsight, we were collecting as if for a museum

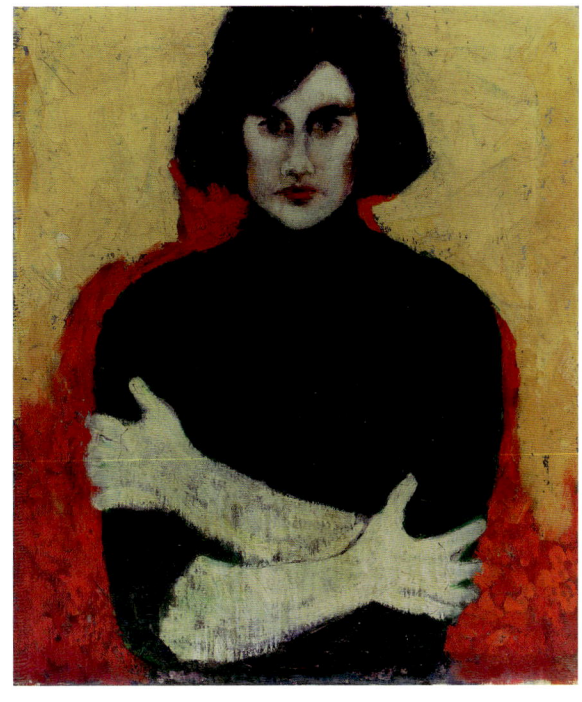

Fig. 30 Anne Minich, *AEGM at 35*, c. late 1960s. Oil on canvas, 24 × 20 in.

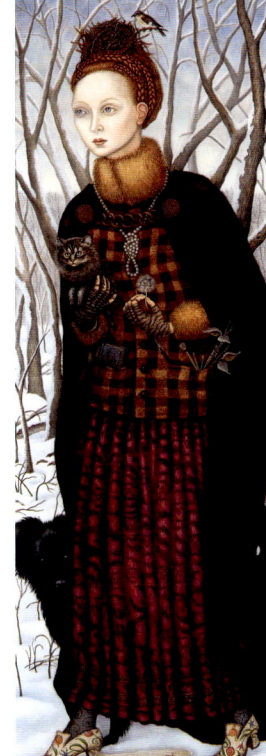

Fig. 31 Gina Litherland, *Queen of an Uncharted Territory*, 2008. Oil on Masonite, 30 × 10 in.

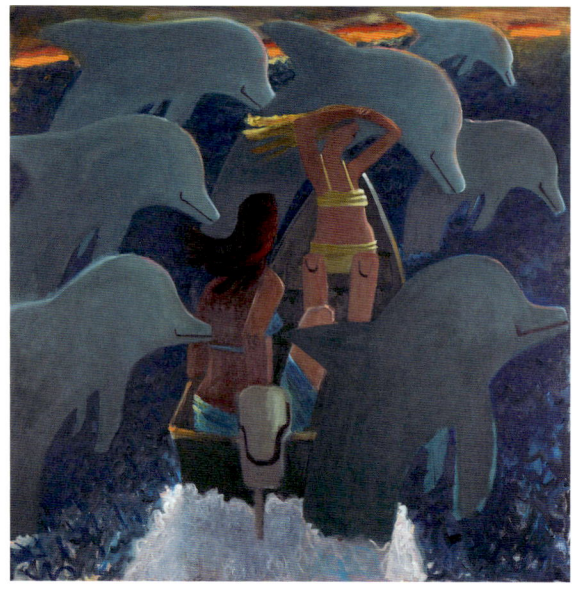

Fig. 32 Kyle Staver, *Dolphins*, 2021. Oil on canvas, 70 × 68 in.

Fig. 33 Winfred Rembert, *T. J. the Tooler*, 1998. Dye on tooled leather, 25¾ × 24¾ in.

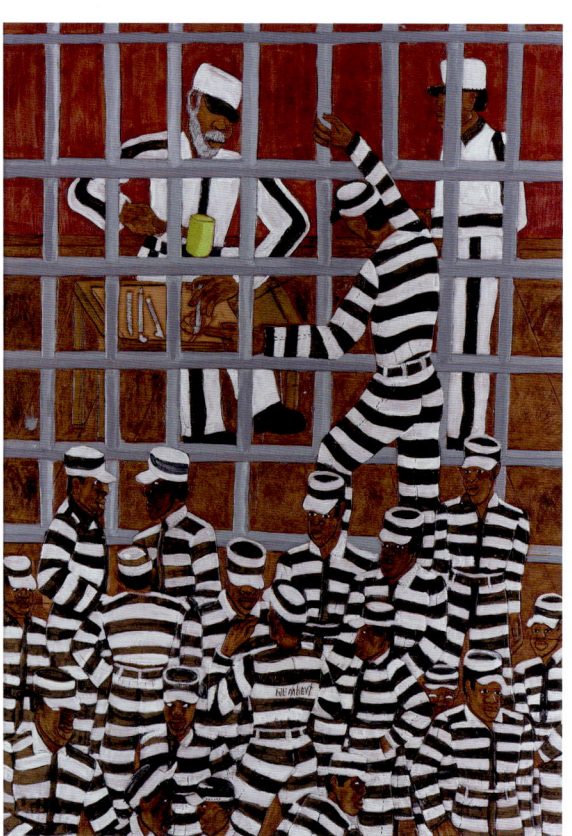

exhibition long before we had an inkling that such a thing might one day happen. We were unwittingly outliers: curators avant la lettre.

Our sense of the larger significance of our collecting grew in part out of our relationship with Robert Cozzolino and PAFA. We met in 2006, not long after Bob's arrival as PAFA's new curator of modern art. John Corbett, a mutual friend, was in town to see Bob's inaugural exhibition of Chicago art, and to visit our collection. Having seen both, he brought us down to PAFA posthaste to meet Bob and arrange for him to see how alike we were in our taste for weird or edgy figuration and artists of art world byways. Bob has described himself as a "curator of the dispossessed" (or, should we say, of the *pre*possessed). So, too, might we describe ourselves as collectors. Our relationship with Bob began with occasional small assists with acquisitions and gradually became a regular collaboration. It was understood that we would help out only with art that was more or less congruent with our own collecting tastes. Bob could feel free to ask for anything, and we were free to say no. Protected by these simple ground rules from the museum's limitless desires, we were able to take an active part in building PAFA's collection.

The expanding scale and range of our collecting made more urgent a concern that had long been in the back of our minds: what to do with our collection after our deaths. It was urgent especially for our sons, who groaned that each new acquisition was one more thing they would one day have to deal with. Selling it off was unthinkable. If a collection is thoughtfully and lovingly built only to be dismantled and dispersed, what's the point of creating it? A museum bequest was the obvious option. We had always regarded ourselves less as owners of art than as its temporary stewards. But we also knew that larger museums were likely to cherry-pick and to display little of what they did accept. (An offer to loan a large Greg Gillespie self-portrait to the Philadelphia Museum of Art had been dismissed as not in line with the museum's exhibition plans. We took note.)

However, our projects with Bob opened our eyes to the advantages of a smaller and more flexible museum like PAFA, which is restricted to American art and committed in both museum and school to a wide range of figurative modes. It was an auspicious moment, with Bob leading PAFA away from safely conventional lines and into more interesting byways, especially the art of Chicago and the Midwest. He was, in short, reshaping PAFA's collection in much the same way that we were shaping ours. And there was a precedent to guide us, in Linda Lee Alter's 2010 gift of her singular collection of art by women. PAFA, it was clear, would welcome a large and quirky collection that embraced outliers and misfits along with artists who had achieved a measure of celebrity (fig. 34). There was no cherry-picking of trendy names: A cross section of artists at all levels of reputation and achievement was precisely the point. So, when Bob gently broached the idea of a bequest, it was not an unfamiliar thought. We didn't need to weigh pros and cons or compare alternative venues. That groundwork had been done. We said yes in principle, with details to be worked out along the lines of the Alter gift. A contractual bequest simply made official and mutually binding the relationship that had taken shape in our informal collaborations with Bob. It is a happy thought that what has given us so much pleasure of mind and eye will remain a source of public enjoyment and understanding in years to come.

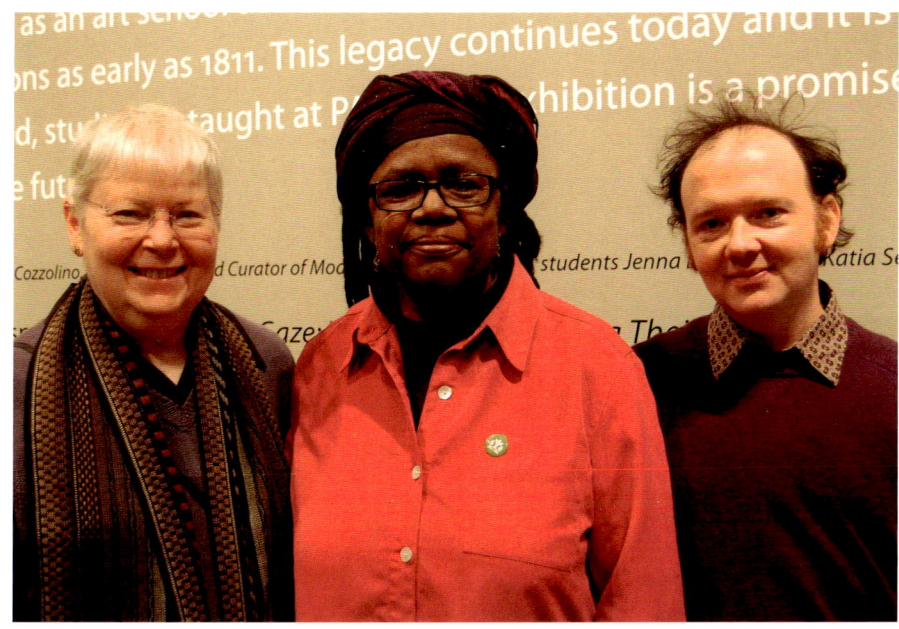

Fig. 34 L–R: Linda Lee Alter, artist Diane Edison, and Robert Cozzolino following Edison's artist talk during *The Female Gaze: Women Artists Making Their World* (2012).

Notes

1. Frank H. Goodyear Jr., *Contemporary American Realism since 1960* (Boston: New York Graphic Society, in association with the Pennsylvania Academy of the Fine Arts, 1981).

2. *Bodies & Souls* (New York: Artists' Choice Museum, 1983).

3. Connoisseurship is a powerful yet under-valued way of knowing the world. Carlo Ginsburg, "Morelli, Freud, and Sherlock Holmes: Clues and Scientific Method," *History Workshop Journal* 9, no. 1 (Spring 1980): 5–36, https://doi.org/10.1093/hwj/9.1.5; S. J. Freedberg, "Berenson, Connoisseurship, and the History of Art," *New Criterion* 7, no. 6 (February 1989): 7–16, https://newcriterion.com/article/berenson-connoisseurship-and-the-history-of-art/.

4. Alexander Langlands, *Craeft: An Inquiry into the Origins and True Meaning of Traditional Crafts* (New York: W. W. Norton, 2017).

5. Gillespie described (and illustrated) in a late drawing how he broke through the limits of the seen: "Expand the mind. How? Do something that is not familiar. Words are familiar. Draw. Observe the mind while drawing. The thought is, if I don't know what to do—make patterns, make eyes, legs, arms, bodies, repeat lines forms, feel mildly desperate like what is the point of anything." Every new start was thus a barely controlled trip to the brink of insanity and back. Untitled and undated drawing in the author's collection.

6. "Artist's statement," in *Gregory Gillespie Recent Paintings, The Real and the Imagined* (New York: Forum Gallery, 1986), 2–3.

7. Quoted in Theodore E. Stebbins Jr. and Susan Ricci Stebbins, *Life as Art: Paintings by Gregory Gillespie and Frances Cohen Gillespie* (Cambridge: Harvard University Art Museums, 2004), 16.

8. Quoted in Virginia M. Mecklenburg, *Modern American Realism, The Sara Roby Foundation Collection* (Washington, DC: Smithsonian Institution Press, 1987), 47.

9. Quoted in Scott A. Shields, *The Candy Store Gallery: Funk, Nut, and Other Art with a Kick* (Munich: Hirmer, 2022), 42.

10. John Yau, "Gladys Nilsson's Portraits of Everywoman," *Hyperallergic*, November 23, 2014, https://hyperallergic.com/164198 /gladys-nilssons-portraits-of-everywoman/.

11. Anne Kraus, "The Point of Function," *Studio Potter* 27, no. 2 (1999), 42–43, https://studio potter.org/digital-issue/137; Garth Clark, "Anne Kraus: A Survey," exhibition catalogue, Garth Clark Gallery, 1998. The tile pieces depict elaborately illustrated pots, a device that enabled Kraus to have flat surfaces for narratives without totally giving up on form.

12. Cited in Robert Cozzolino, "Myself Before the War: John Wilde's Early Work," in *John Wilde, The Early Work* (Milwaukee: Tory Folliard Gallery, 2016), 9–18, quote p. 15.

13. The chair that gives the painting its name, a bentwood Thonet, was a signature of the interwar German café society, in which the "new objectivity" flourished. It was a style that Wilde admired yet almost never used, reserving it, perhaps, for pieces with the most personal meaning for himself. Surrealist tropes of "naked ladies" would not have done for the lady in *The Chair*.

14. Barry Schwartz, *The New Humanism: Art in a Time of Change* (New York: Praeger, 1974); Adam Zucker, "Re-introducing the Rhino Horn Group," July 24, 2014, https://berkshirefinearts .com/07-24-2014_re-introducing-the-rhino-horn -group.htm.

15. Jane Lund and Gregory and Frances Gillespie were members of the self-styled "Valley Realists," a circle of ten or so mostly realist artists living around Northampton, Massachusetts. Without having the group's options comparatively in mind, we had simply chosen one by one the artists who were most to our edgy taste.

16. Quoted in Adam Zucker, "Peter Dean: Life on the Edge of the World," November 22, 2014, https://berkshirefinearts.com/11-22-2014_peter -dean-life-on-the-edge-of-the-world.htm.

17. "In Her Own Words: Kyle Staver," *Two Coats of Paint*, January 26, 2013; John Seed, "Kyle Staver: Into the Mythological Zone," *John Seed*, February 2, 2013, http://www.johnseed.com /2013/02/kyle-staver-into-mythological-zone .html.

18. Winfred Rembert, *Chasing Me to My Grave: An Artist's Memoir of the Jim Crow South* (New York: Bloomsbury, 2021).

19. Peter Schjeldahl, "A Great Unknown: Discovering the Norwegian Artist Nikolai Astrup," *New Yorker*, July 26, 2021, 64–66, quote p. 66; Schjeldahl, "Scaling Up: Early Modernism at the Whitney and a Show by Walter Price," *New Yorker*, June 13, 2022, 72–73.

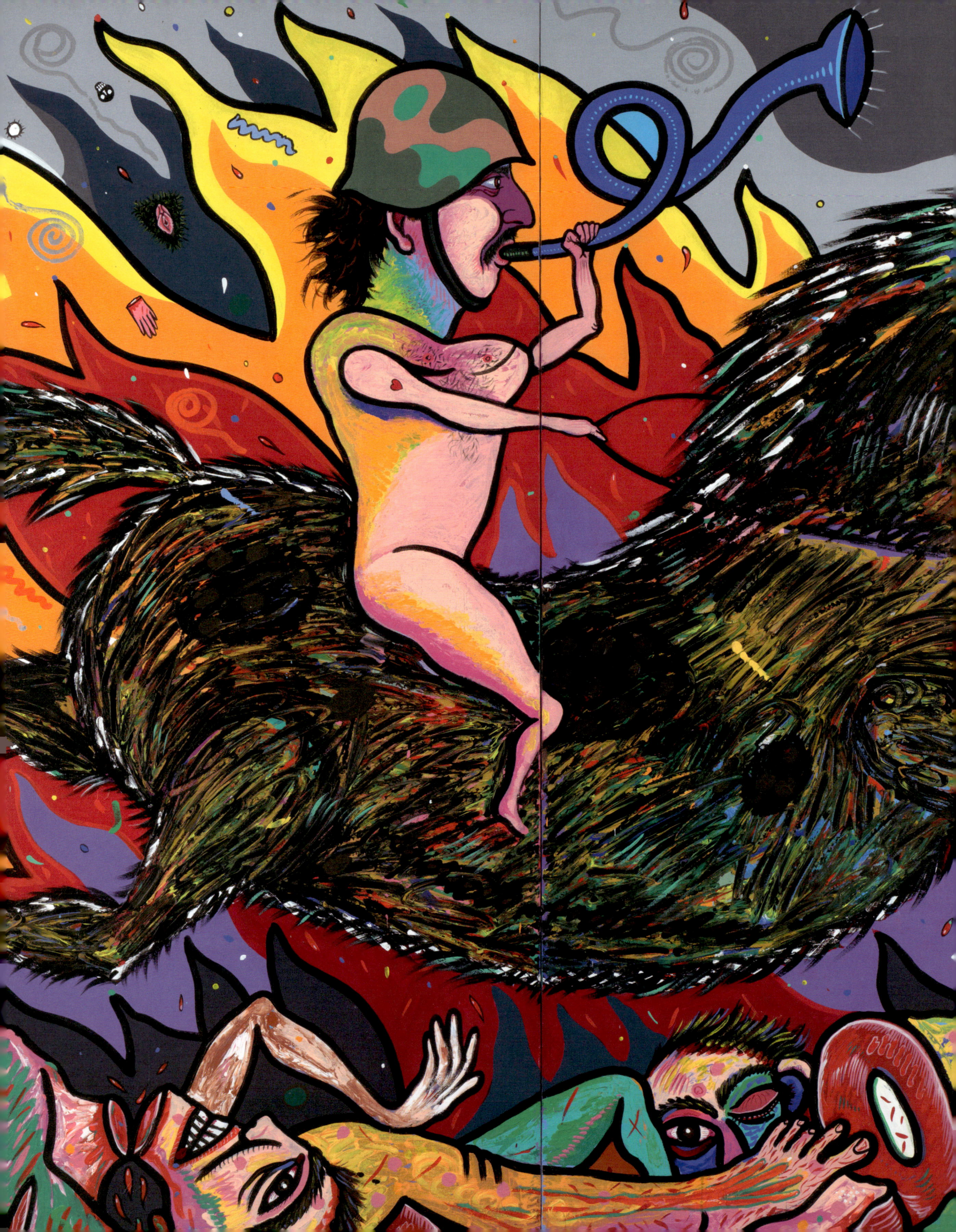

Bodies and Souls

Robert Cozzolino

When the hole appeared, it was the size of a fist. Fingers poked through, searched its edges, and began to pull, expanding it outward to become many feet high and wide (fig. 1). Pulsating waves defined its edge. In flux and pliable, it seemed capable of closing as suddenly as it appeared. The opening revealed a brightly lit world, with pale-yellow rolling hills decorated by a procession of trees swelling with green boughs. Dancers frolicked among them, arm in arm, hand in hand. A woman stood at the opening, wearing bloodred shorts and socks and a tangerine-colored top edged with dark orange frills at neck and cuffs. She appeared curious but pleased, delighted before the portal. Her hands tenderly held the edges as she stepped through to the other side.

Why would she leave her sunny, animated world to enter the shadows? Others from her realm might shun this place, turn away in fear, or deny its existence. As she passes through, the woman leaves behind people who go about their lives with eyes closed. None of them notice her slipping through the portal that will likely vanish afterward. She moves between worlds with confidence, knowing something else about the darkness. It is generative, full of possibility, offering a new path and fresh start. As Kerri ní Dochartaigh writes in *Thin Places*,

> The dark has been painted—over much time—as being a negative thing, a part of existence to be wary of, a bringer of fear and things best not to be thought of. Yet nature tells us of a different story. The earth tells us, over and over, as each year turns the circle of itself around, that it is in the dark where beginnings are found. Life first is dreamed, birthed and shaped in the absence of light. The seeds sown in autumn germinate underground through winter before appearing as shoots in spring.[1]

This transformation occurs at a sacred place, a thin space between worlds. Something enabled this person to see the passageway shimmering in the sunlight. It drew her in, knew she would be receptive, allowed her

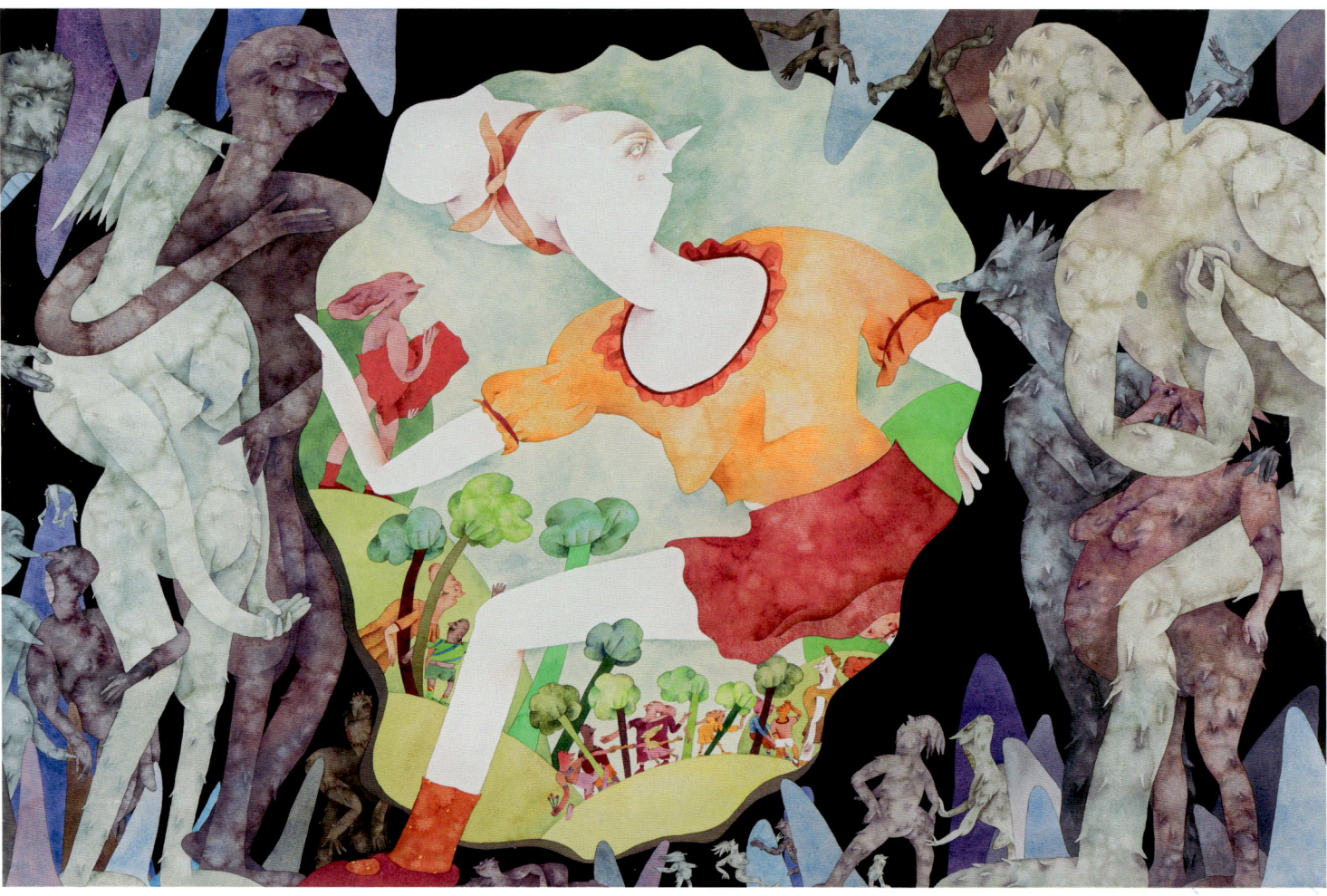

Fig. 1   Gladys Nilsson,
Checking Out the Other Side,
1987. Watercolor on paper,
40 × 60 in.

to see into the otherworld. Inside it is dim but colorful. Protruding stalactites and stalagmites glow purple, cobalt, cerulean. The interior teems with life, small and large creatures sprouting spiky tendrils around their heads and bodies. Some might call the troll-like inhabitants monsters or shadow beings. Their skin is mottled with iridescent stains of color and appears composed from the underworld's miasma. They embrace, caress, and gently touch one another, pleased to welcome the visitor.

Will it change her—psychologically, emotionally, physically? Or will she bring some of the sunny world into the darkness? Can she pass back and forth or is she leaving the top-lit land for good? What would you do before the portal? Would you eagerly pass through? Maybe you have already decided. Do you consider the beings in the shadows threatening and repellant, majestic or beautiful? The artist has placed us in that alternate space where possibilities multiply. *We* are on the other side.

Gladys Nilsson's large watercolor *Checking Out the Other Side* (1987) expresses a desire to embrace the unknown, to leave the comfort zone, to move with curiosity and courage. It makes confronting the shadows an act of liberation, suggesting that if we make peace with new worlds, we might experience another consciousness and traverse multiple dimensions. Nilsson depicts a rent in the fabric of the everyday and the possibilities that might unfold from entering it. It is a clear assertion of realities adjacent to the one in which we live.

This embrace of a parallel reality characterizes much of that art that attracted Rob and Frances Kohler. The first time I visited their home, I recognized they were kindred spirits who knew the pleasures of the margins, the places off-map, the realm beyond the mysterious portal. We share a love for artists who explore and depict such places with clarity and precision, or assert that these places are *within* us. These artists often show us the vulnerable condition of being human, all the messy and multi-layered conditions of being in a body. Many makers in the Kohler collection acknowledge the existence of the unseen, the alien, the frightening, that which is below the surface, out of reach, just beyond the light. The collection often favors artists unafraid to enter darkness and the unknown in order to reveal a deeper truth.

Rob and Frances also chose work that shows artists pushing the limits of their craft. Didier William, for instance, radically reimagines figuration through the use of intertwined silhouettes and bodies carved into wood panels. Figures are elastic, slipping in and out of sight, and moving fluidly between dimensions. The eyes that coat the central body in *Dancing, Pouring, Crackling, Mourning* (2015; plate 86) are formed by cutting into the surface, excavating a pattern that is protective, enacting an apotropaic power. The eyes provide agency in other ways—a heightened awareness and ability to see the past, present, and future with supernatural clarity. These characteristics are necessary for bodies that are under surveillance, living in unfamiliar places, or protecting members of their communities.

Extremes in content and methods work hand in hand. In much of the imagery, artists reveal aspects of their selves usually reserved for intimates, written in private journals, or contemplated alone in a mirror. Anne Minich's *Feral Nun* (2012–13; fig. 2a–b) is a full-length self-portrait done in graphite and placed into a structure like a reliquary container with doors that close on the image. Minich presents herself, vulnerably and with tenderness, at age seventy-nine. She is also assertive and defiant, carrying

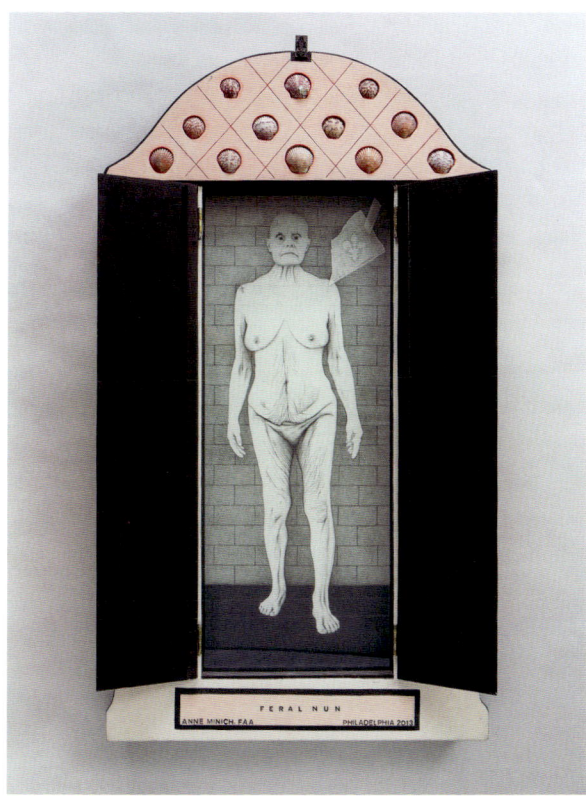 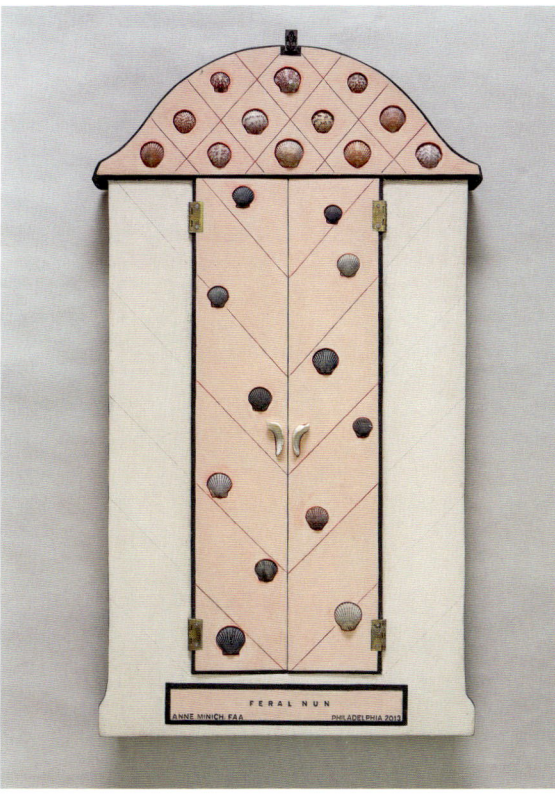

Fig. 2a–b Anne Minich, *Feral Nun*, 2012–13. Graphite on paper in mixed-media frame (wood, shells, and metal), 34 × 19 in. View with doors open and closed.

herself confidently and displaying the exquisite skill and attention that this personal altar requires. Minich made the drawing while recovering from cancer and chemotherapy. The subtly out of scale head was "an indication of feeling my body had taken over—I felt all body," she notes.[2] Her left foot steps forward into the future—she will survive this experience. Her right hand bears a bandaged finger—she has wounds—but she remains resilient and inspires others who might look to her for hope and strength. The Kohler collection shows how much artists have at stake in depicting lived experience.

Throughout the twentieth century and in the twenty-first, critics have periodically heralded a "return to figuration." Let us be clear once and for all: There has never been a "return to figuration" because the figure has always been relevant to humanity, perpetually top of mind for artists concerned with their communities and with understanding themselves, and aware of how bodies can powerfully convey our values. Luis Cruz Azaceta emphasized this when he asserted in an interview, "My concern is with humanity. I want to confront the viewer with life and with what we are doing to each other. I hope to awaken in the viewer a sense of compassion . . . Without compassion there is nothing."[3] Azaceta's remarks highlight a powerful undercurrent in the collection: empathy. The methods, subjects, and tone of much of the work convey an awareness of being in a body— the joy, sorrow, desire, hope, and disgust—a full range of what it means to be human.

As Rob Kohler describes in this volume, he and Frances began collecting with focus and intent in the early 1980s after visiting two large exhibitions of representational art. The first, *Contemporary American Realism Since 1960* (1981) was held at the Pennsylvania Academy of the Fine Arts (PAFA). The second was actually a series of eleven exhibitions coordinated simultaneously along 57th Street in Manhattan called *Bodies & Souls* (1983) organized by the Artists' Choice Museum. The PAFA exhibition, curated by Frank Goodyear Jr., was a large loan exhibition that situated contemporary realism within a long lineage in American art. The latter was led by artists working without a permanent venue, who responded "to the broader community's desire for greater access to contemporary representational art." They felt that over the previous decade, "an entire community of figurative artists were largely ignored by the institutions of the art world."[4]

Together the exhibitions presented a wide range of approaches to depicting the visible world, showing that "realism" is polyphonic, expressed in numerous registers, colors, tones, and speeds. Many exhibitions reexamined figuration at the time. In 1980 the Whitney Museum of American Art presented an eighty-year painting and sculpture survey of the figure from their collection. And in 1981 the Rutgers University Art Gallery presented *Realism and Realities: The Other Side of American Painting 1940–1960*, an exhibition that remains unmatched in its examination of the social, political, and psychological themes that concerned figurative artists during a period in which histories of abstraction dominate.[5] The Kohlers did not see these exhibitions, but those they did visit bore the impact of a field in transition, beginning to shrug off the formalist, teleological dogma that had plagued considerations of modern art in the United States. It was also the

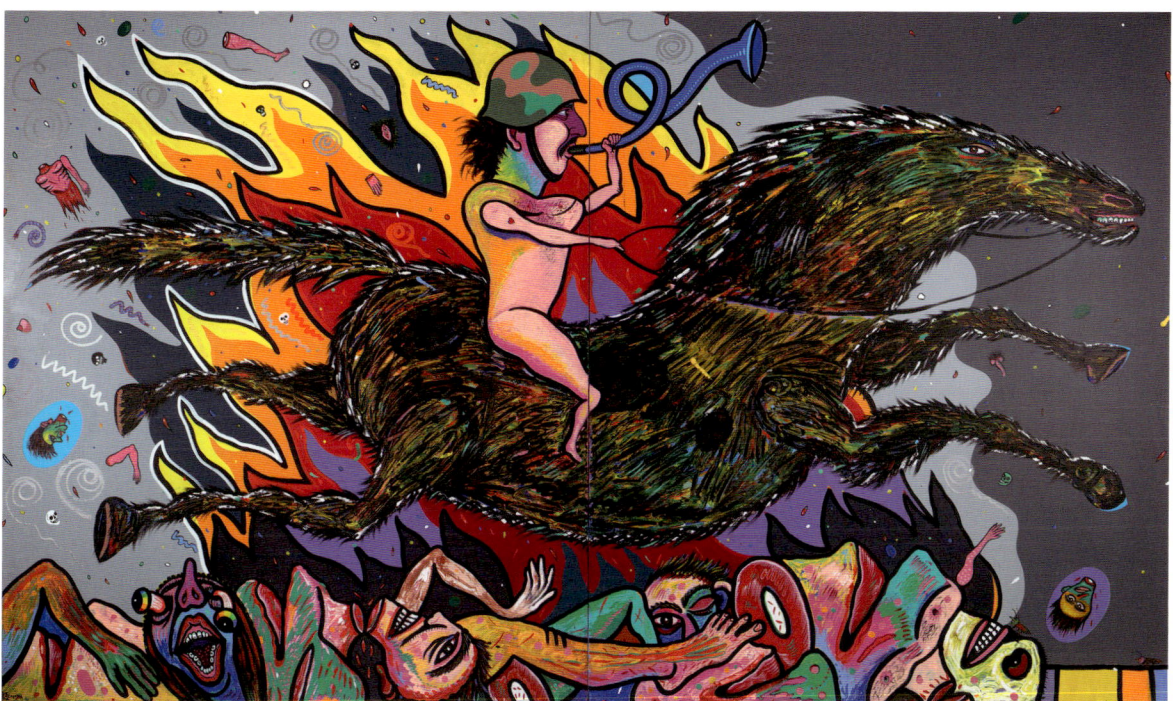

Fig. 3 Luis Cruz Azaceta, *Self-Portrait: Apocalypse Now—or Later?*, 1981. Acrylic on canvas, 72 × 120 in.

beginning of concentrated art world interest in how artists expressed identity and lived experience.

The exhibitions introduced the Kohlers to artists whose work they eventually collected, among them Azaceta, Robert Arneson, Robert Barnes, Jack Beal, William Beckman, Robert Colescott, Peter Dean, Martha Mayer Erlebacher, Rafael Ferrer, Gregory Gillespie, Red Grooms, Ed Paschke, and Philip Sherrod.[6] While each show was eye-opening, Rob reflected that *Bodies & Souls* was "more diverse and adventurous than *Contemporary American Realism*, including much that was expressionist, fantastic, raunchy, or all-out weird—a visual cornucopia. Here were artists established and unknown exploring all sorts of figuration, and energized by a sense of escaping or subverting mainstream orthodoxies."[7] For Rob, *Bodies & Souls* was a revelation. "I have a vivid memory of being there and feeling the excitement," he recalls. "It was . . . intimate and personal. The catalogue was our collecting and gallery guide on the edges of our expanding taste."[8]

John Yau, writing in his introduction for the Artists' Choice Museum catalogue, noted that the selections urged viewers to "be less concerned with styles and more intent on discovering the content of what we are seeing . . . An integral part of this exhibition is its quiet demonstration of connections and differences."[9] It was a narrative presentation, rather than one that emphasized "realism." He referred to it as a

troubling, provocative show. Many of the stories are not pleasant. Mortality, anger, frustration, loneliness, fear, intimacy, vulnerability, disillusionment—these are inescapable facts many have not tried to escape. The artists have continued to work without letting go of their doubts about the future of mankind. For them, the act of painting and making sculpture may provide a sanctuary but it is not an escape.[10]

Azaceta's monumental *Self-Portrait: Apocalypse Now—or Later?* (1981; fig. 3) was included in *Bodies & Souls* under the theme of "bizarre or fantasy works" at Marisa del Re Gallery. Azaceta, a Cuban exile who came to the US in the wake of Castro's revolution, has long been committed to confrontational antiwar imagery. Here, he references the four horsemen of the

Apocalypse from the New Testament book of Revelation—except Azaceta has made himself the single herald riding a creature that resembles a monstrous hybrid horse-rat. He sounds a twisted blue horn, springing over the grisly carnage of mutilated bodies, against a backdrop of further flying body parts and massive radiating flames. At the time, Azaceta was consumed with anxieties about nuclear war and the US government's abandonment of the working class and poor. Pablo Picasso's *Guernica* (1937, Museo Nacional Centro de Arte Reina Sofía) haunts the image, but Azaceta is more explicit in his indictment of power and its abuses.[11]

But Is It Real?

The PAFA exhibition was quiet and polite in comparison—nothing of the sort was included. Its curator, Frank Goodyear Jr., staked a claim for optical realism in his catalogue essay, including few works that bore deviations like gestural surface disruptions, stylization toward abstraction, or content that depicted extreme psychological situations. He contended that contemporary American realists approached painting from two main philosophies translated into methods: observation and transcription of only what one can see in their immediate visual field (represented by Alex Katz, for example) and using technology to collect information and objectively transfer that result to canvas (as in the work of Chuck Close). He wrote,

> The assertion of the visual perception of things based on two radically different aesthetics—one a commitment to the value of phenomenological information as the basis of art, the other an affirmation of the process and value of its translation into pictorial information—defines contemporary American realism. In either aesthetic, illusionistic images based on external evidence in the real world serve as the basis of pictorial structure; just as there were no "angels" in the oeuvre of Gustave Courbet, there are none in contemporary American realism.[12]

Despite Goodyear's claim, the Kohlers sought out artists whose representational work conveys perceptions beyond sight. All senses make it into art, including paintings made through a realist method. Reality is conditional, contextual, cultural, and situational. It is subjective, and the artists in the Kohler collection assure with veracity, tenacity even, that what you see is their reality. Gregory Gillespie, whose work was included in both the PAFA and Artists' Choice Museum exhibitions, expressed it in phenomenological and spiritual language, telling interviewers: "I know there are other structures of reality existing that we can't see."[13]

Gillespie's *Lydia and Her Demon* (1988; fig. 4), for example, is a double-portrait that shows a woman in a three-quarter view looking off into the distance. Her hair is neatly covered by a floral-patterned wrap that follows the curve of her skull. She wears a thin pale-green tank top and necklace. Next to her, just behind her right shoulder, is another being whose head and neck resemble an assemblage of flower petals and plant forms. Its head swells outward like a blossom and is much larger than hers. The eyes are narrow, set close, mouth and nose lie on a vertical axis along the face, with a third orifice at the forehead. Lines radiate out from each aperture and the flesh curves away and around its head. Its presence is unnerving, although it makes no gesture or expression of menace. The woman does not seem perturbed by its presence. Perhaps she is used to it— or perhaps she no longer sees it.

Lydia (1963–2015) was the daughter of Gregory and Frances Cohen Gillespie. An earlier portrait of her at age nine, *Leila* (1972–73; p. 33) by Frances Cohen Gillespie, is also in the Kohler collection. According to a family member, Lydia struggled with tenacious demons. She was diagnosed with bipolar disorder as an adult and battled addiction. Lydia worked through dependency issues and volunteered with a peer-led program helping those living with addiction in Greenfield, Massachusetts. It was an ongoing challenge for her to remain sober. She was in treatment at Austen Riggs Center in Stockbridge when her father died by suicide. A family member recalled, "She was certainly dealing with her demons for a long, long time, though a very sweet and loving person . . . Greg really was a caregiver to Lydia and hoped she would recover."[14]

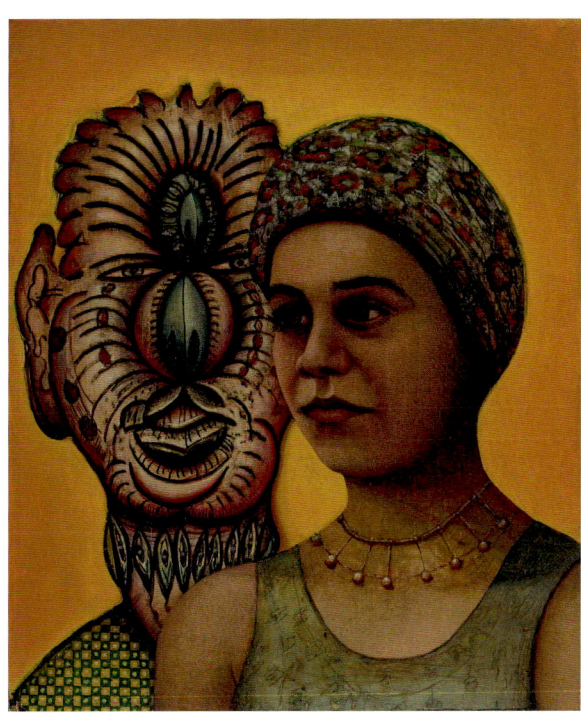

Fig. 4 Gregory Gillespie, *Lydia and Her Demon*, 1988. Oil and alkyd on panel, 17¼ × 14¼ in.

The demon, though Lydia's, appears in numerous instances in Gillespie's work of the period.[15] He knew it to morph, shapeshift, walk on all fours, and permeate the world in many other ways. We all have demons, Gillespie seems to say. They are tangible, sit next to us or ride our backs. They peer over our shoulders and listen to our thoughts; perhaps they even talk back. Why not visualize them? Maybe that is the best way to make peace with them and acknowledge they are companions. Find equilibrium together. Speaking about his own demons in relation to creativity, Gillespie claimed, "It's a continuous tension to stay in reality. Chaos and disorder are always threatening. It is a constant struggle not to let things get out of hand, to maintain some control . . . There is a lot of instability in the world and so I seek to make an art that is disturbing, provocative, self-challenging, and self-questioning. It is important to me that I use this anxiety for a worthy purpose."[16] For Gillespie, and others in the Kohler collection, these parts of one's personality were real, and essential ingredients of representation.

Jane Lund, a friend of the Gillespies, for a time made images that originated in her subconscious, presented in dreams that she translated in her waking life by restaging what she remembered by making reference photographs. As she worked, she allowed for free association to embellish the composition. She wrote, "In the way a dream bubbles up from that layer of the mind that knows all and reveals what it knows in such beautiful and tricky ways, my early paintings seemed to be symbolic disclosures of my inner being." Lund took these images to represent who she was, what shaped her personality and drives. "I have a deep love and wonder for the forms of life. This feeling has to come out somewhere, so I make pictures . . . Making images is a mysterious impulse that comes from some unknown place. An almost totally consuming need, not an end in itself, but rather a reflection of how I see and what I am."[17]

In the pastel *Party for Myself* (c. 1974–75; fig. 5) four women sit at a round table set with a white tablecloth and a single candle burning low at the center. A side table against a far wall holds another candle, plates, and bowls of food. The view beyond the windows at right shows that it is a

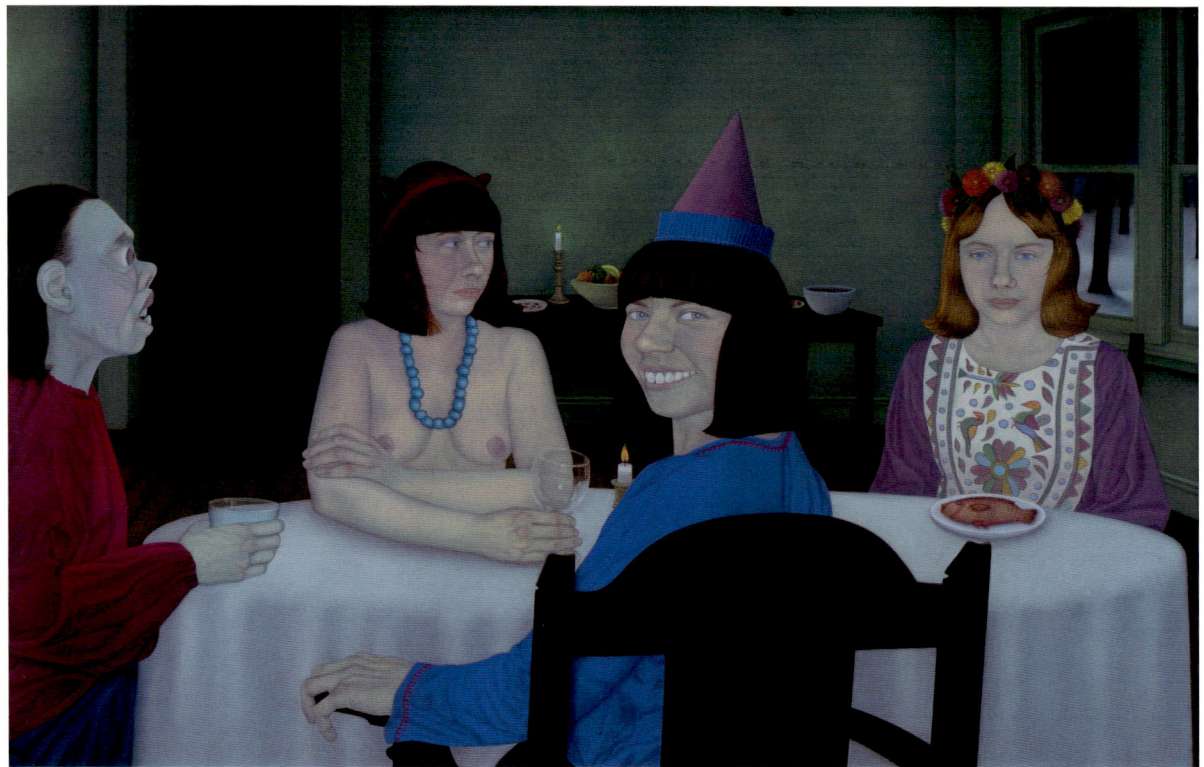

winter evening. The woman closest to us turns to smile, inviting us to join them. At right, another woman, in a lavender and white dress decorated with flowers and birds, wears a garland of flowers in her hair—perhaps marking the winter solstice and the gradual return of light. She is the only one with a plate before her, bearing a single fish. Her companion to the right is nude at least from the waist up, except for a large blue bauble necklace and a knit cap sprouting little horns. Finally at far left, the fourth guest looks off to the windows with large nearly lidless eyes, mouth agape. Her skin has a pale green pallor, a tone just lighter and bluer than that of the walls. Her features are slightly exaggerated, her nose upturned, her face creased with wrinkles, her hairline receded.

Lund describes this drawing as representing different aspects of herself. The woman in blue is her social, outgoing, and friendly personality; the woman at right is spiritual, aiming to be pure of heart and intentions; the woman to her right is Lund's sensual self, acting on her desires without shame; and the figure at left is the embodiment of self-loathing. They are all real and compose her full self. The greeting smile of the woman in blue may suggest that another aspect of self (rather than us) has joined the party. Lund says, "Even when I was younger, I had a strong sense of layers in ourselves . . . We all have these parts . . . and I was always making pictures of the divided self."[18]

In Deborah Kravitz's panel painting *Woman, Drawing, Door* (1975; fig. 6) a woman stands with her back to a large wooden door. It is secured in three places—near the top, with a two-by-four, and with bolts just above the handle. She grips pieces of charcoal tightly in her hands. Her eyes are glassy, as though she has not blinked for many minutes or is on the brink of tears. Tension is strung tight in her body, her shoulders slightly raised, arms taut, fists clenched, expression at the brink like a coiled spring. Her rigid, contained body contrasts with the wild excessive drawing of a creature on the door at her back. It lurches, reaching with clawlike hands, jagged mouth the full width of its head.

Kravitz described the image as a self-portrait in a long text sent to the Kohlers. The setting is a portion of water-stained, paint-peeling wall in her apartment's kitchen in Mission Hill, Boston. Because the neighborhood was rife with crime and break-ins at the time, Kravitz had the numerous locks installed at her door. The attempt to keep out unwanted presences, and the tension between what they were and the fear they triggered, coalesce in this compact, riveting image. It was a means to examine and come to terms with intergenerational trauma. She wrote,

> My fear of intruders resonated with the fear and anger inside of me, the result of childhood neglect and emotional abuse. The monster-woman drawing pictured on the door behind the two-by-four bolt did not really exist. The pieces of charcoal I hold imply that I drew the monster, that I am the source of the monster-woman. The rage I felt toward my mother at that time made me feel both monstrous and empowered. The rage was caused by and at the same time was an antidote to the worthlessness my mother, an abused child herself, projected onto me. She boiled with black clouds of depression and rage, and wrapped me in her darkness, which I absorbed along with her love. The self-portrait along with many other paintings was part of an attempt to understand my real self and to come to terms with both the anger and the love I felt for my mother.[19]

Throughout modernist criticism, arguments against representation turn on misunderstandings and misreadings of realist art. Just because what is represented can be apprehended and named does not mean it cannot also carry multiple meanings, as in Kravitz's self-portrait. When painted imagery looks "real" it does not necessarily mean the artist's concern is solely with illusion. Some who use a realist method embrace materiality and process, and give equal weight to the design underpinning the narrative or feeling conveyed. The modernist prejudice against realism or representational painting in general has a long and complex history. Clement Greenberg and subsequent generations of formalist critics instilled a distrust and even disgust of representational painting that became institutionally ingrained in theory, museum practice, and academia, and among collectors.[20]

As early as 1940, Greenberg asserted that realist painters were uncritically imitating a dominant art form (literature) with an incongruous medium. To him, painters had destroyed purity in their art by aspiring to encompass the properties of another art (narrative, description). In doing so they had betrayed what was unique to their practice to leave it "perverted and distorted." For Greenberg this mishandling occurred when painters "reached such a degree of technical facility as to enable them to pretend to conceal their *mediums*. In other words, the artist must have gained such power over his materials to annihilate it seemingly in favor of *illusion*."[21]

Many American realists of multiple generations identified with the layers of meaning to be found in Italian, German, and Flemish painting of the fourteenth through sixteenth centuries.[22] These panel paintings present worlds that look familiar, uncanny in their similarity to ours (or their contemporaries'), but their conditions of reality are charged from the outset. Because of their apparent fidelity to the real—as in the work of the

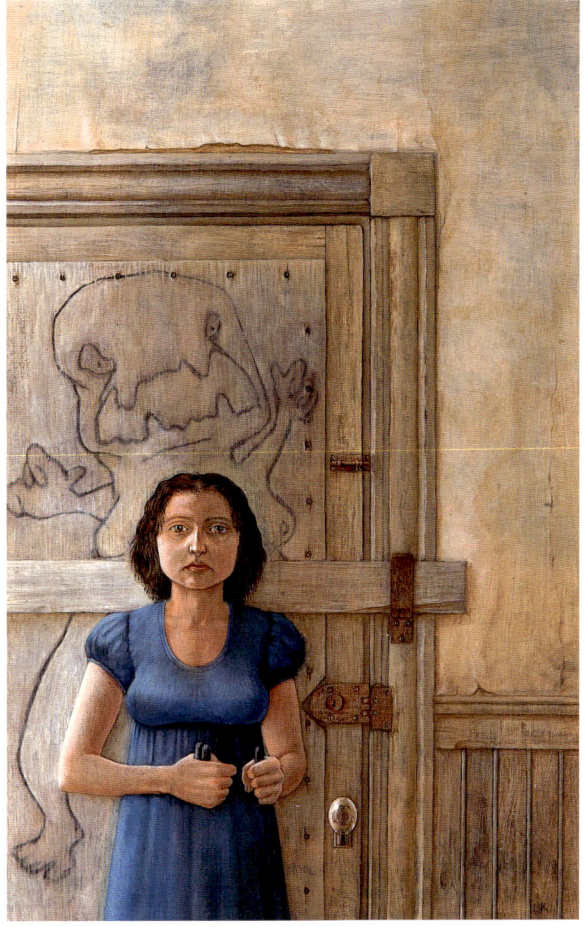

Fig. 6 Deborah Kravitz, *Woman, Drawing, Door*, 1975. Oil on panel, 13½ × 8¼ in.

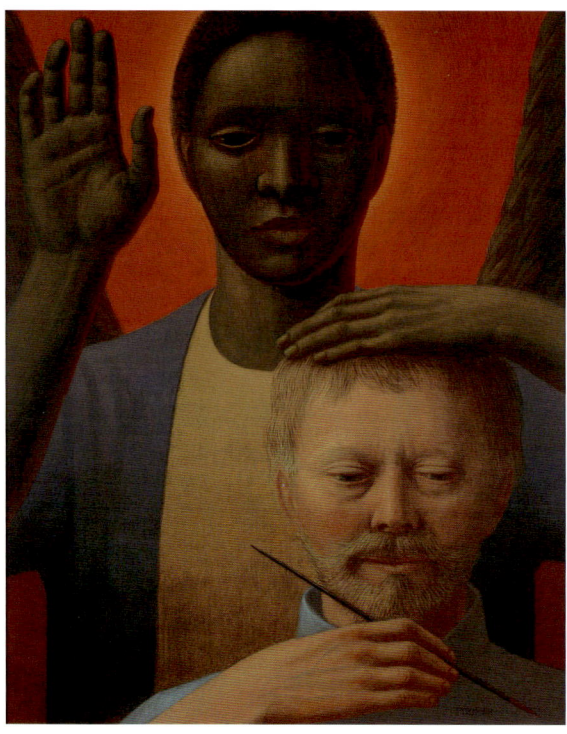

Fig. 7 George Tooker, *Dark Angel*, 1995–96. Egg tempera on gesso panel, 24 × 19 in. The Pennsylvania Academy of the Fine Arts, Philadelphia, Henry C. Gibson Fund, 2007.7

American realists who adored them—we can forget that what we see is of the imagination, reality heightened, intensified, in order to embody religious symbolism or other coded references layered in objects and gestures with multiple meanings. What is presented *is real* but it is also ideas, feelings, a belief system. George Tooker (fig. 7), who persisted in making small realist panel paintings during the height of institutionalized modernism, told an interviewer in 1957, "Uccello and the early Sienese masters were doing what I'm trying to do." But emphasizing the modern condition of his disorienting scenes of subways, offices, and waiting rooms, he added, "I am after painting reality impressed on the mind so hard that it recurs as a dream."[23]

Looking at the body or objects before him in his studio, Gillespie challenged himself to look closer and longer, trying to apprehend and depict detail that shows veils and processes happening beneath the skin. It was as though he was trying to be inside what he was painting in order to feel it, not just see it. He aimed for patient, mindful viewers to recognize that elision with what he was painting. Gillespie believed there was a reality beyond our senses and asserted,

> I know that, and I want to be able to suggest that in the painting too . . . There are always contradictory notions . . . conflict in the painting. There's wanting to make it as real as possible in a sensuous way—yet wanting it to be very transitory and ephemeral at the same time. I know that my flesh is made of chemicals and molecules. I know that what I'm seeing is like a dream. I know consciousness is something totally different but yet in some powerful way connected to this physical/chemical organization.[24]

By 1980, Goodyear, like other critics and curators, was operating with a concept of realism connected to objectivity and clinical depiction. For many, it was then still seen as conservative in terms of how it mirrored the world. What Gillespie was describing was his awareness that what we call "reality" is mutable, fluid, and based on bodily and unconscious perceptions. The limits of perception or rather its extent are governed by what we are in our physical and cognitive being. Artists deploying the tools of realism are constantly negotiating this recognition of an internal reality and external stimuli, processing them together to craft microworlds.

Whose Realism?

In the years leading to a reassessment of figurative art in the early 1980s, many writers were so entrenched in formalist criticism that they incessantly indexed representational paintings to modernist practices. Critics tried to understand them in that trajectory, where they were doomed to be seen as an aberration, though there are ways to discuss some realist impulses as having kinship with abstraction, and they are part of that thread in modern art. These revisionist approaches came decades later. Even those sympathetic to realism felt compelled to discuss it in relation to modernist aesthetics for the art world to pay attention.

In 1969 painter and critic Sidney Tillim tried to make sense of the representational "impulse" he felt was prevalent in the art world, prompted by two exhibitions of so-called new realism, *Realism Now* (curated by Linda Nochlin at Vassar College Art Gallery, May 8–June 12, 1968) and *Aspects of a New Realism* (presented at the Milwaukee Art Center, June 21–August 10, 1969).[25] He found the works on view "anything but homogenous," and rationalized that this resulted from "where an artist stood in relation to modernist art when he made his commitment to figuration."[26] This conversation occurred when many artists in the Kohler collection were in their early careers. Although some, like Gregory Gillespie, recalled having their integrity questioned by being representational painters at art schools where faculty were still obsessed with Abstract Expressionism, others studied in places where that pressure was not at play. Teachers at the School of the Art Institute of Chicago, San Francisco School of Fine Arts, and PAFA, for instance, encouraged figuration across styles.[27]

Tillim could find no unifying method, style, or philosophy of contemporary representation. Among the painters he found an "almost anarchic disagreement. They all have completely individual, if not perverse, takes on the history of modernism in art."[28] As if on cue, Chuck Close, in an interview with Cindy Nemser published months later, derided figurative art's "outworn humanist notions" and suggested that new critical interest in realist painting derived from curators and critics hostile to the "avant-garde." Close stated, "I have very little sympathy or interest in the figurative art being shown today. I object to the lumping together of everybody who works from life or from photographs under the title of realism or superrealism. The term is too vague and I see very few common denominators."[29] Close's perception rings true to the ongoing reception of representational art from that period and today.[30] Practitioners of realist methods for image-making are often surveyed together, regardless of cultural impulses, politics, or the philosophies behind their methods. In many cases these artists share motivation with artists who do not work like them. Integrating them helps us better understand their relative positions in a broader context.[31]

Tillim, an artist who shifted from abstraction to figuration around 1960, had his own struggles with reception (Donald Judd called the realist paintings a "serious mistake") and perhaps sought to understand the impulses that drove his contemporaries. While he tried to untangle contemporary realist practices from modernism, Tillim located its relevance outside of aesthetics and related to the immediate and urgent context of the ongoing civil rights movement and American war in Vietnam. Realist art had the capacity to transmit "individual pride to humanity . . . Racial issues and issues of identity are synonymous, but the identity of the human race is also at stake." For Tillim, "the issues involved in the question of realism, or representation . . . are ultimately moral ones." Realism was a method that might realize the "deeper social and psychological function of form."[32]

This was absolutely on the minds of activists and image-makers of all genres. The head of the Student Nonviolent Coordinating Committee's (SNCC) Photo Agency, Julius Lester, put it like this in 1967: "Power is not only political, power is also self-confidence. And so you can't have self-confidence if the images you see reflect somebody else's world . . . how somebody else looks. How can you have confidence in yourself?" He continued, emphasizing the role of self-representation. "[Black Americans] should be allowed the opportunity to know their own images . . . We are going to look at ourselves with our own eyes and define ourselves (if we must) after we've taken a good look around and found that we're a beautiful people."[33] Robert Neal's *Street People* (1986; fig. 8) embodies that determination to depict a confident, aware, beautiful Black man on a city street just as snow begins to fall. Neal had by this time had a full life and career, and this later expression of grace conveys the fullness of his own experience as a Black man who had experienced the terrible and hopeful arc of the twentieth century. Here he sees this man's humanity clearly, and perhaps infuses the figure with his own self-reflection about where he is now, confident and painting with the full range of his talent.

Critic Benjamin Buchloh has been as confrontational toward representational painting as Clement Greenberg. In an essay published around the time of *Contemporary American Realism* and *Bodies & Souls* he reaffirmed a dogmatic view of modernism according to a prescribed teleological and formalist model that does not correlate to why artists make work or their social and community practices. Buchloh, reacting to art world attention to a specific group of figurative artists (mostly Europeans and all male, among them Georg Baselitz, Sandro Chia, and Francesco Clemente, and Americans such as David Salle and Julian Schnabel) gave inordinate weight to their presence as representatives of contemporary figure painting, a condition created, as he notes, by money, social taste, and a fear of missing out. As he put it, "The mock avant-garde of contemporary European painters now benefiting from the ignorance and arrogance of a racket of cultural parvenus who perceive it as their mission to reaffirm the politics of a rigid conservatism through cultural legitimation."[34]

They (and by extension, other figurative artists) yearned for "a past culture that serves as a fictitious realm of successful solutions and achievements that have become unattainable in the present," and sought to end modernism and "deny the dynamic flux of social life and history through an extreme form of authoritarian alienation from these processes."[35] Buchloh asserts that various modes of twentieth-century realism (Neue Sachlichkeit) "cleared the way for a final takeover by such outright authoritarian styles of representation as fascist painting [in Europe]."[36]

This reactionary assessment of realist modes disregards their powerful role in criticizing authoritarian regimes and the oppressive power structures they maintain to dehumanize people. Buchloh's response, understandably, was single-mindedly focused on the European political and social context and a fascist strategy of historical amnesia that he suspected underlay the promotion and reception of so-called Neo-Expressionist

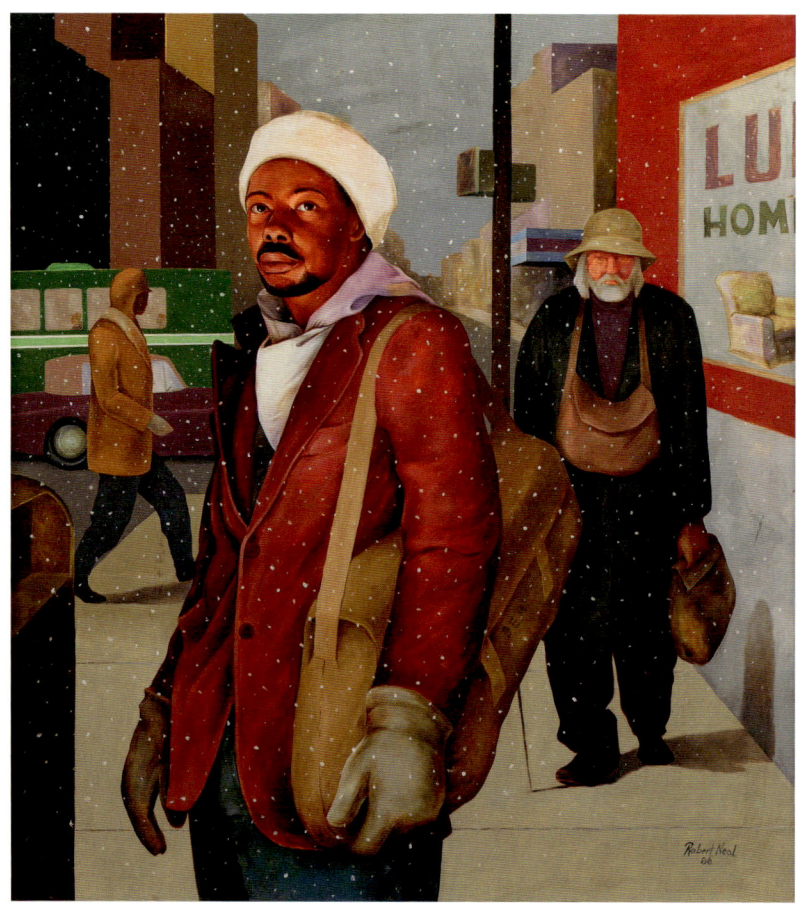

Fig. 8 Robert Neal, *Street People*, 1986. Oil on canvas, 35 × 31 in.

painters. This may be so, but an additional and equally nefarious force was the relentless focus on a Wall Street–style art-as-speculation climate in 1980s New York. Buchloh's writing, like that of most of his colleagues connected with the journal *October*, disregarded the conditions of art making, education, and discourse outside New York, whether in Minneapolis or Birmingham. For many of the critics consumed with defining the art world at the time, and who viewed the supposed return of figurative painting as a moral crisis, these places did not exist, and therefore the artists working there were invisible. Artists in these communities, such as Nilsson (Chicago), Gillespie (Northampton), Joan Brown (San Francisco), Barbara Bullock (Philadelphia), and others at the core of the Kohler collection, operated apart from the debates in New York by choice; their self-worth, conceptions of success, and community did not revolve around that city.[37]

Buchloh also argued that unless pictures incorporate actual things, materials, modernist facture, showing clear evidence of the hand, that it scarcely matters what is represented because of *how* it is represented. His example is modernist collage, and he credits its "experience of increased *presence* and autonomy of the self" to detritus from daily life incorporated as experience and "revealed as fissures, voids, unresolvable contradictions, irreconcilable particularizations, pure heterogeneity." To Buchloh, what he considers illusory images—realist painting—deliver "false consciousness" because the artist conceals their presence through their method and therefore enacts treachery on the viewer by eliminating "perceptual clues to all its material, procedural, formal, and ideological qualities." In this way realist painters conduct "aesthetic self-negation" due to "particularization, and restriction to detail."[38]

Attacks on realism as conservative or as a method coopted by fascism during the 1930s did not hold in the political climate of the 1980s and beyond, in part because of its use by various communities as a means for clear visibility—making present those who had been rendered absent or their identities erased from the broader narrative of American art. Intimating that figuration, and specifically a crisp approach to realism, aligns with fascist ideology fails to account for the decades of antifascist representational painting made in Black, queer, and pluralistic communities that cut an additional path through the history of modern art, one that was not mutually exclusive of supposed avant-garde strategies.

Buchloh's denigration of representational painting makes no space for queer artists and their allies opposing the disastrous Reagan administration. Azaceta, Arneson, Ida Applebroog, Roger Brown, Sue Coe, Leon Golub, Frank C. Moore, and David Wojnarowicz, for example, took on the bigotry that led to needless deaths during the AIDS crisis, the madness of nuclear proliferation, and the funding of regimes in Central and South America. These artists are self-aware, concerned with the present moment, not trying to replicate the past but using its methods to gather the living world around them, to assert presence and counter violence. These modes are meaningful because they communicate clearly. But they can also hold secrets or speak in code to specific communities.

Craig Calderwood incorporates multiple materials, including fabric, thread, paint, and graphite, into figural work that opens up new possibilities for representing the body. They want viewers to have sensorial

Fig. 9 Craig Calderwood, *Notes on ♀ and ♂ from My Eight-Year-Old Self*, 2018. Paint and thread on upholstery fabric, 51 × 46 in

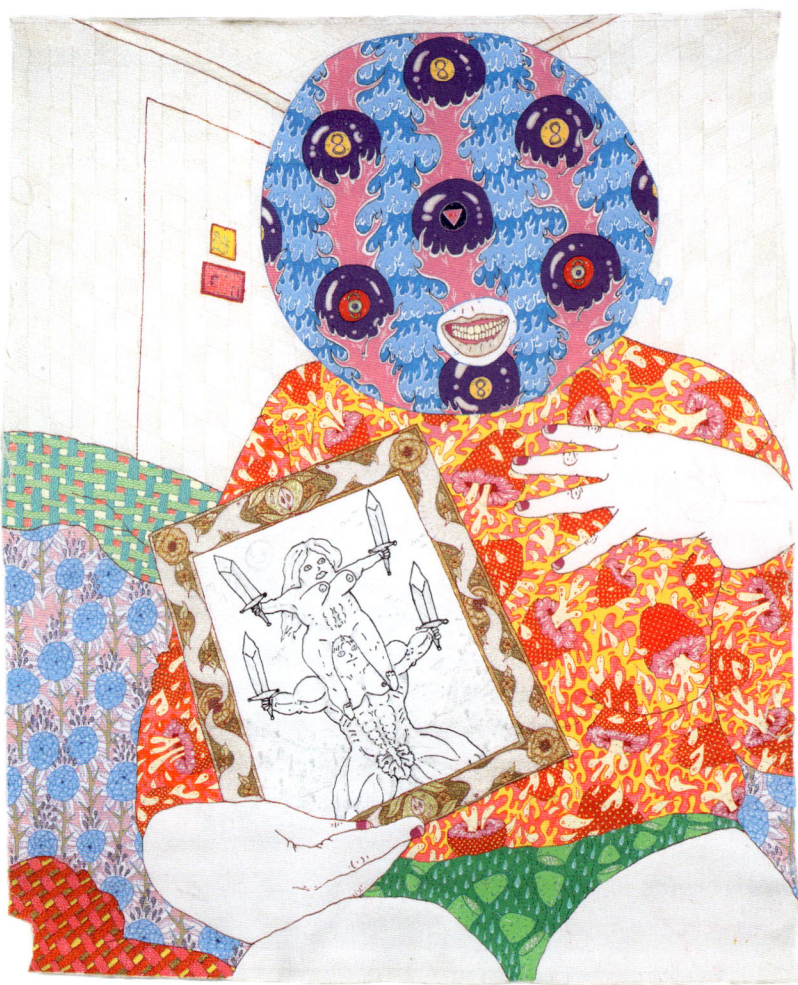

experiences before the work, to connect and know intimacy through how these intricate images are composed. They noted in a 2018 interview,

> I come at making a piece in a *constellative* way. Like when you experience something intensely, like a death, a friendship, love, bigotry, etcetera—those moments that define those feelings and events are dense with information. When you experience something like that, everything from that moment gets imprinted on you. The textures of the space, the smells, faces, feelings, patterns, the taste in your mouth, all arrange themselves within that memory . . . I sort of come at an idea or theme for a piece with that mindset, and then try and code everything in symbols and patterns. By developing a piece with this cache of imagery I can tell stories that can remain sacred and private. This way of communicating is a part of queer and trans hirstory; it's a tool for survival that over the years has become my primary mode of conceptualizing work. It feels akin to flagging with a hanky, or making that specific *cruising* eye. It's insider information. It's the Queens' Vernacular.[39]

Calderwood's *Notes on ♀ and ♂ from My Eight-Year-Old Self* (2018; fig. 9) embodies all of the aspects of meaning making they value. The person seated on a sofa gestures with their left hand over their heart and holds up a drawing for us to see in their right: two figures rendered in thin black lines, each holding two swords in outstretched hands. One figure sits on the shoulders of the other so that together they make a stack. The person at the base is extremely muscular, thick strong legs, solid, tight brick wall of an abdomen, swelling biceps. A leaf covers their genitals. The figure on top has long, thick hair and emphatic, protruding torpedo-like breasts and a sculpted torso. While we might be tempted to gender them, based on the scant information provided, and the references to, as Calderwood told me, "Venus and Mars" in the gender symbols of the title, they present as one interconnected, interlocked figure. They exude strength together and are aspects of one body. It is a drawing Calderwood made many times when they were young.[40]

The figure holding the drawing also resists binaries. Despite the emphatic patterning, which contrasts with the clean and clear rendering of the hands and legs, this is a solid figure whose presence in this room is tangible, convincing. They are present, and appeal to us to connect the offered drawing with the tender gesture toward their body—their heart and soul. Their green briefs are decorated with a pattern of cucumbers sliced at the tip and their raucous, joyful shirt is a dazzling array of juicy berries spilling forth sweetness. A large, inflated mask surrounds the figure's head, with a small opening for the mouth, which manifests with barred teeth. Is this a smile? A grimace? A nervous response? It could be all simultaneously— though the Magic 8 Ball pattern on the mask gives the message "HI" in its pink triangle.

While the figure could be communicating with us, this could also be a self-portrait in which Calderwood engages across time with their eight-year-old self, holding the image that was inside them, a clue to their identity to reassure them about it as an older person. Everything in this densely packed image comes together to center on the relationship between drawing, gesture, and the centered 8 Ball answer, meeting at viewer's gaze. It is a comforting image, one that asserts that everything is OK. The elaboration of detail serves the content. Calderwood says, "One of my goals is to destabilize a person's ability to approach my work with an idea of a binary gender. By flooding my pieces with pattern, and by sometimes taking away secondary sex characteristics, it sort of guides the viewer into reading the work differently. I want to disrupt the scrutinizing heteronormative gaze that seeks to fetishize or be abhorred by the trans body."[41]

Realism as a Liberatory Practice

Calderwood's remarks emphasize how representational and realist methods are liberatory practices that can be used to assert presence for those omitted from dominant narratives or harmfully depicted by those outside their communities. Realism and representation are a means to show embodied human experience. They can help us imagine the world we want to live in. Representational art has been transformational and critical for artists who want to make themselves and their communities visible on their own terms. It provides the agency to see and be seen, to show relationships, pleasure, and autonomy. Representing ourselves is a powerful means of celebrating our full humanity.[42]

These possibilities in realist painting have a long history. Virtuoso draftsman and painter Charles White asserted in 1940, "Paint is the only weapon I have with which to fight what I resent. If I could write, I would write about it. If I could talk, I would talk about it. Since I paint, I must paint about it."[43]

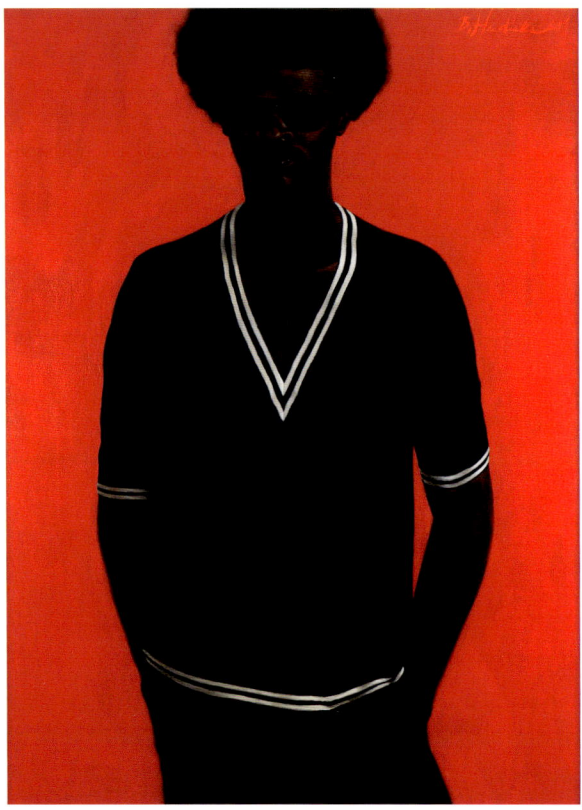

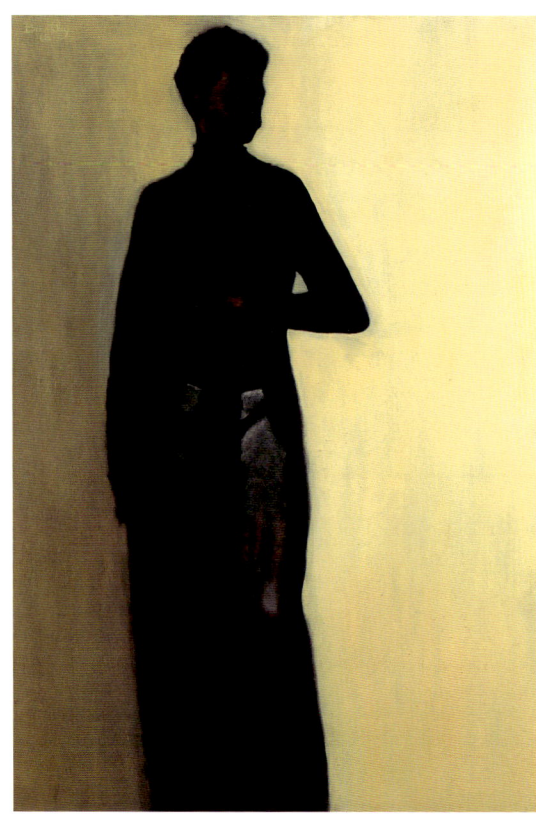

Fig. 10 Barkley Hendricks, *J. S. B. III*, 1968. Oil on canvas, 48 × 34⅜ in. The Pennsylvania Academy of the Fine Arts, Philadelphia, gift of Mr. and Mrs. Richardson Dilworth, 1969.17

Fig. 11 James Sherman Brantley, *Brother James*, 1968. Oil on canvas, 60⁷⁄₁₆ × 40¼ in. The Pennsylvania Academy of the Fine Arts, Philadelphia, John Lambert Fund, 1970.1

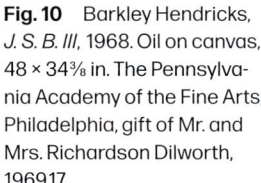

Speaking about photography, Dawoud Bey has asserted, "There were precious few places where one would have encountered Black folks in all of their gloriously celebrated human complexity. While these [negative] images filled the public arena, Blacks always knew that those images were not theirs. And the photographic image became important to the visual construction of Black community."[44] Painting has, of course, also been a critical facet of communities taking back representation and creating the images they know of themselves. Artists such as Barkley Hendricks and James Sherman Brantley, studying at PAFA in the 1960s, understood the power of redirecting agency to Black artists in communion with Black subjects (figs. 10–11), depicting one another and their peers, as they learned the nuances of their craft.

Leslie Barlow, an artist based in Minneapolis, has cultivated a painting practice that is inherently about community. Relational representation is a core value of her work. She writes that stepping into this tradition allows her to "challenge the norms and hierarchy of who is painted, what stories are amplified, and by whom . . . Visual culture is one of the sites in which narratives of belonging are produced and propelled." Barlow surveyed the visual field and found a "lack of representation of Black, Indigenous, people of color, mixed race and transnational/transracial adoptee experiences." Part of her aim is to reshape the way Americans "perceive identity, race, and family."[45]

This consciousness formed the foundation of her series *Within, Between, and Beyond* (2019–21), a collaborative project that includes filmed interviews and paintings of families made up of plural races.[46] Barlow had the inspiration to begin related work on the fiftieth anniversary of the 1967 Supreme Court case *Loving v. Virginia*, which ruled that laws banning interracial marriage violated the Equal Protection and Due Process Clauses of the Fourteenth Amendment of the US Constitution. Her painted portrait of writer Nicole Asong Nfonoyim-Hara and her family—*Nicole and Seth and Their Daughter (and Daughter to Be), in the Kitchen* (2020; fig. 12)—can be viewed on its own or with a film in which Nicole and her husband, Seth, share their experiences with family and race. The painting radiates

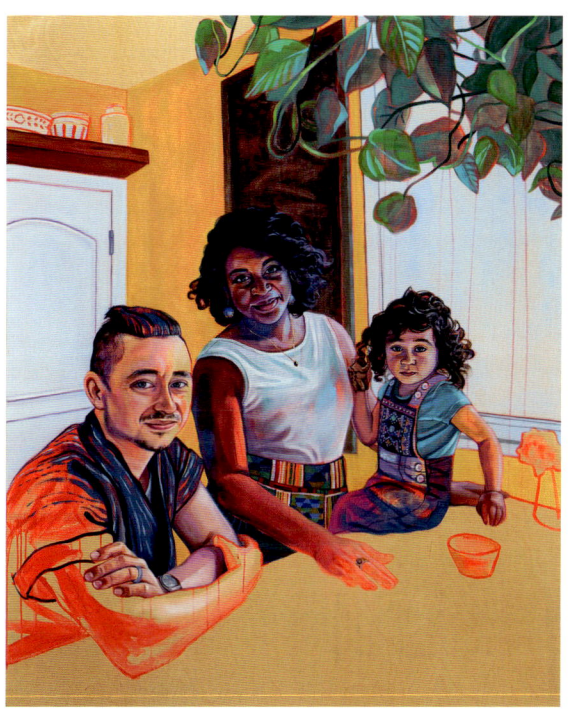

warmth: Nicole is surrounded by her daughter, partner, and a thriving houseplant. Barlow's title indicates that their family will soon grow as well, and suggests that future generations will carry on a commitment to love and compassion.

Barlow's practice flows from the ethos "nothing about us without us," a phrase that originated in the diverse disability community. Riva Lehrer, an uncommonly sensitive and skillful portrait painter, lives that premise in her attention to people in her orbit living with disabilities. Her series *Circle Stories* was collaborative, made through mutual trust and conversation that led to all aspects of the resulting portraits. Lehrer chose the circle because it is "the wheel of a wheelchair . . . the universal symbol of impairment"; and for "the Collective, my circle of safety." None of the paintings were commissions; all are of people Lehrer admires in her community.

Lehrer's portrait of writer Mike Ervin and designer Anna Stonum (1998; fig. 13) began—like others in the series—with "listening. A portrait began with days, even months of conversation. We spoke honestly about the relationship between our bodies and our work, after which I'd go home and make thumbnail sketches based on what my subject had said. We adjusted the sketches again and again until we agreed on an image." The process "actively demanded a collaborative ethics of representation."[47] Ervin and Stonum, who are married, sit side-by-side in wheelchairs, looking out at us, meeting our gaze. He reaches over affectionately to hold her right leg and she meets his hand with her own. Behind them an electrical storm sizzles in the sky, perhaps hinting at their passion, or the dynamics of their relationship. Lehrer wanted to convey their "language of communion . . . The kind of automatic intimacy that exists between any couple. Nothing special, just two people in a marriage. Which was the point."[48]

The transformational possibilities of representational painting are especially evident in Philadelphia, a place where realist methods have been taught at multiple art schools, most notably, of course, at PAFA. For Charles Searles, understanding form and how to reproduce it served a personal and spiritual need. As a young man, he spent time studying and drawing from African sculpture at the University of Pennsylvania Museum of Archeology and Anthropology. Searles felt a deep connection to the sculpture and those who had made it and, inspired by the objects, eventually started carving. He recalled, "It was sort of frightening because I had never seen anything like this before. They were strange looking . . . They had this power. They almost felt like they were alive . . . I began to feel more myself in the sculpture because some of the figures, the faces just resembled me, you know."[49]

Searles enrolled at PAFA and during the course of his studies was awarded prestigious traveling scholarships that enabled him to visit Morocco, Nigeria, and Ghana in the summer of 1972. On returning to Philadelphia he became involved with his friend, artist Barbara Bullock, in the Ile-Ife Black Humanitarian Center, led by dancer and choreographer Arthur Hall. Ile-Ife quickly became a major center of the Black Arts Movement across genres and an essential intergenerational cultural center in the region. Karen Steptoe Warrington, a founding member of Hall's Afro-American Dance Ensemble, explained, "To see this whole village of Africans who weren't born in Africa here [at Ile–Ife] . . . was satisfying

Fig. 12 Leslie Barlow, *Nicole and Seth and Their Daughter (and Daughter to Be), in the Kitchen*, 2020. Oil and acrylic on panel, 60 × 48 in. Courtesy of the artist.

Fig. 13 Riva Lehrer, *Mike Ervin and Anna Stonum*, 1998. Mixed media on paper, 22 × 21 in. Courtesy of the artist.

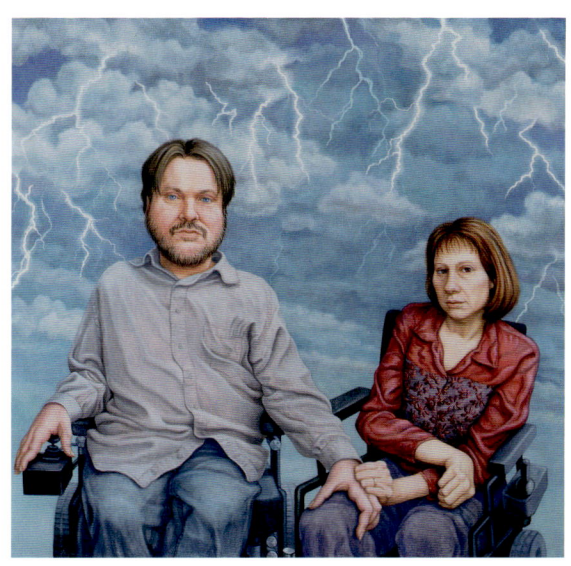

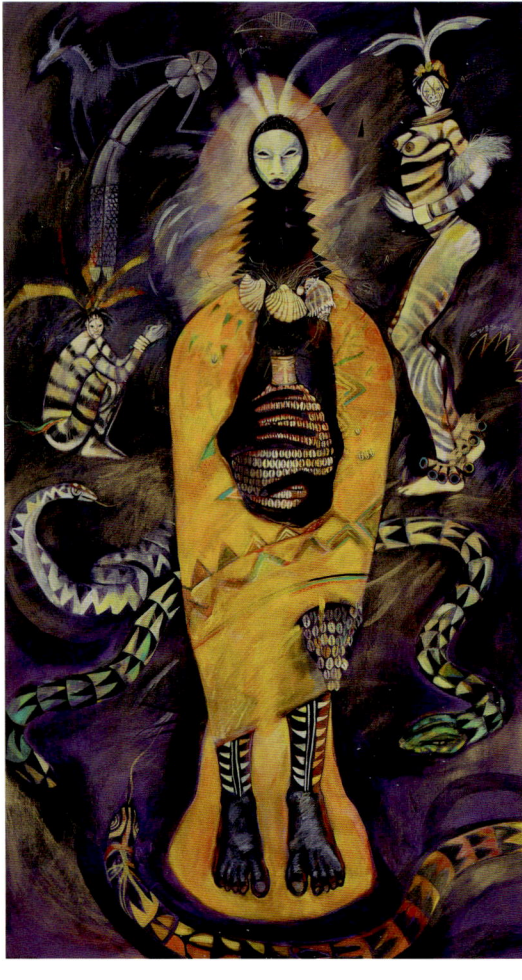

Fig. 14 Barbara Bullock, *Remembrance*, 1985. Acrylic on canvas, 74 × 40 in.

something inside all of us, because we never really just fit in that little box that [white society] put us in. So then people started figuring out [that Ile-Ife provided] the affirmation of knowing who you are and being celebrated for who you are."[50]

Both Searles and Bullock taught at Ile-Ife and their work began to integrate their personal understanding of African culture. It was critical to both of them that they work with students of all ages and openly discuss what it meant to be Black in their generation—who they wanted to be and how they wanted to honor ancestors and prepare a new generation. Searles's experience in Nigeria had a profound effect on the way he incorporated pattern in his work. He reflected on how in Africa he had seen people using pattern upon pattern in dress, in everyday aesthetic choices. "In Africa, these people would mix the patterns together. For example, they would have a print pattern for a skirt and a different print pattern for the top. The men would wear print patterned pants and a different one for the top. So I became very aware of these combinations of patterns . . . that became a strong influence in the paintings."[51]

Searles's *Dancer #1* (1974; plate 87), a gift from the artist to Susan and Barkley Hendricks, was the first in his *Dancers* series. A dazzling performance equal to the reputation of the dancers active with Hall, the painting highlights the artist's skillful control over more than a dozen separate patterns unified in a dynamic figure. Arms curved in serpentine lines, hand outstretched, and feet rising up with rhythm, the woman actively conjures music from the color and shapes that sway with her body.

Bullock also made images of dancers, but as often also depicted bodies active in spiritual ceremonies, initiation rites, and sacred performances. *Remembrance* (1985; fig. 14) shows a central figure clothed in a deep yellow garment, hands clutching a cowrie shell–covered vessel, rising up tall on bare feet. The figure is in a state of transformation, spirits, snakes, and dancers swirling around them. Flashes of bright yellow and orange contrast with a deep purple background. Bullock's artistic practice is inseparable from her spiritual practice: she has made altars for ancestors and spirits, and her paintings can be understood to attract and honor spirit. She reflects, "Journeying through my African American life, I have found an intuitive need to create forms which are protective spirits . . . They are important in my life as I intend to travel both physically and spiritually through many open areas to become stronger in my creative manifestations and closer to my ancestral heritage."[52]

Searles and Bullock were enriched by meeting the artist Twins Seven-Seven, who came to the art department at Ile-Ife while they were teaching there. Bullock explains the impact he had:

[He] explained to Charles and me that he was an artist, and a musician, and a dancer. He went on and on, and we were like, how do you have time to do work? My God. But when we saw his work, it was like another world, just extraordinary. The forms and the meanings—you could look at it for forever and you'd still never see everything in it. He was Yoruba. So there were a lot of spirits in his work . . . Well, it was the whole thing, that you can paint spirits. You can draw spirits, you know? And it's that whole thing of the freedom of your belief, you know? He would talk about the forest in his work, and about the magicians. I was just so inspired, deeply inspired, and just really loving what he did. And I just knew it was going to change me.[53]

His monumental work *The Spirits of My Reincarnation Brothers and Sisters* (2006–7; plate 126), a later version of an earlier work at the Philadelphia Museum of Art, shows a group of musicians gathering amid a grove of trees, playing instruments and singing. Some beat drums, another strums a stringed instrument, while others sound wind instruments. This is no ordinary band of players. The artist stands in the center surrounded by "his brothers and sisters on this earth," not biologically related siblings, but people he considered his community. Each of their bodies and the trunks and leaves of the trees are covered in faces. They represent beings in the spirit world, surrounding and protecting Twins and his loved ones.

The title refers to Twins's status as an *abiku* child. When an *abiku* child is born, the spirit world tries to reclaim him, which results in an earthly death in childhood or shortly thereafter. Twins believed he experienced this death several times. He recalled that he had been born as a twin six different times to his mother, who lost all twelve of these children within their first few years of life. Only when he was born a seventh time, again as a twin, did he survive, though his twin sister would not. This painting thus not only celebrates his life and community, but also honors all of those who precede us in the spirit world.

Paying attention to the hum that connects us to our ancestors, learning together with generations older and younger than us, these are the ways we persist and thrive as a culture. For artists who came to the United States from the Caribbean, often escaping dangerous political regimes, or leaving, as so many immigrants have done, difficult conditions for the hope of better circumstances, representing their stories and their journey has been affirming. Azaceta and Didier William, mentioned earlier, came to the US from Cuba and Haiti, respectively. Their state as exiles, and as people spiritually connected to another place, comes through in their work, sometimes explicitly, often in veiled ways understood among intimates.

Rafael Ferrer came to the US from Puerto Rico in 1966. He initially established himself in Philadelphia and made a reputation in the late 1960s and 1970s for installation and conceptual work, frequently with performance components. In those pieces he often included natural elements, grease, ice, leaves, items from nature, and set things up to be affected by the passing of time during an exhibition. Things decayed, melted, started to rot. Ferrer reflected on the tone behind some of this work: "Dada was my turn-on because it is opinionated, disrespectful, and embraces humor, the blacker the better. It is filled with wit, irony, cynicism, and pessimism."[54]

After seeing Alex Katz paint outdoors, Ferrer had an epiphany and turned to painting. He was close to many painters, including Benny Andrews, Roger Brown, and Alice Neel, but also had strong friendships with Mel Edwards, Marisol Escobar, Ree Morton, Yvonne Rainer, and

Paul Thek. He remarked, "We were all brothers [sic] sharing a particular reality, aware of what was *really* going on, but when you're in it, you're traveling through the world like a knife through butter. You know your strength and we know that we are not against each other; we are allies in a situation that is ongoing. But we're not making alliances in order to get ahead, we're part of the scene, and each one has to deal with it on their own."[55] This eclectic mix of friends, whose practices varied greatly, stimulated Ferrer as he dedicated himself to painting in the late 1970s.

Ferrer started to apply the tools of representational painting to suggest the complexity of his immigrant experience. He made numerous self-portraits and portraits of the people in his community and on visits to the Caribbean. *El Bolero* (1983–84; plate 84) commemorates a reunion of friends playing music together and singing. Music was central in Ferrer's life. He was a drummer and played professionally as a young man. Here a small gathering of close friends shares the joy of making music, guitarists and percussionists interlocking rhythms as a singer takes the melody while strumming along. His companions all look toward him in admiration, feeling the shifts and nuances of the tune together. The saturated colors in the composition suggest a nighttime scene lit by torches, perhaps at a beachside restaurant or the patio of a friend's home.

Juan González, who was born in Cuba and came to the United States in 1961, made a sacred altar to his family and identity in *Nacimiento (The Birth* (1979; fig. 15a–b). Modeled on fifteenth- and sixteenth-century altarpieces that he saw on a trip to Florence, Italy, it is a watercolor executed in a miniaturist technique, painted with the use of a magnifying glass and jeweler's lamp. González fit the watercolor into a wooden cabinet to give an impression of a religious object. It shows a stagelike setting, a marble terrace overlooking a memory landscape of Cuba. González's mother sits at lower right as though enthroned and his father is at the center holding a shepherd's crook. The artist told a writer that he spent over a month

Fig. 15a–b Juan González, *Nacimiento (The Birth)*, 1979. Watercolor on paper on wood, 6⅛ × 6¾, tabernacle frame 15 × 15 × 10⅝ in. Overall tabernacle and detail of watercolor painting.

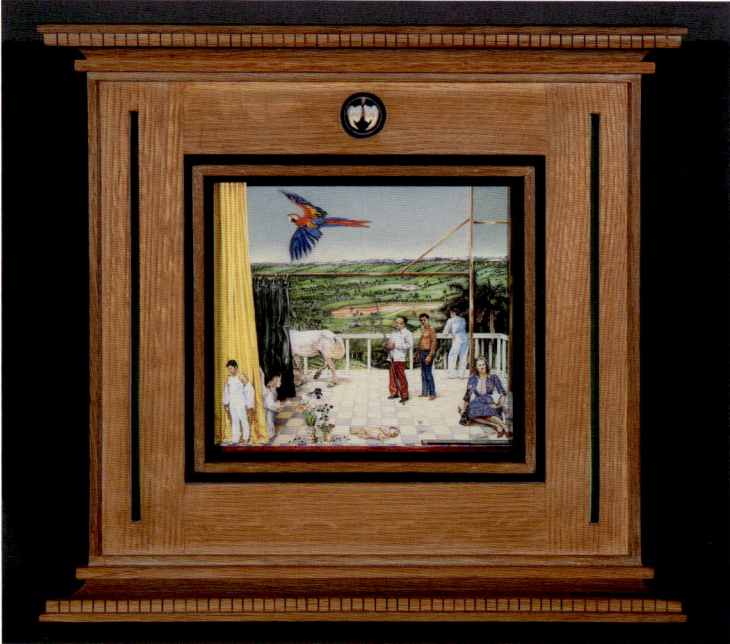

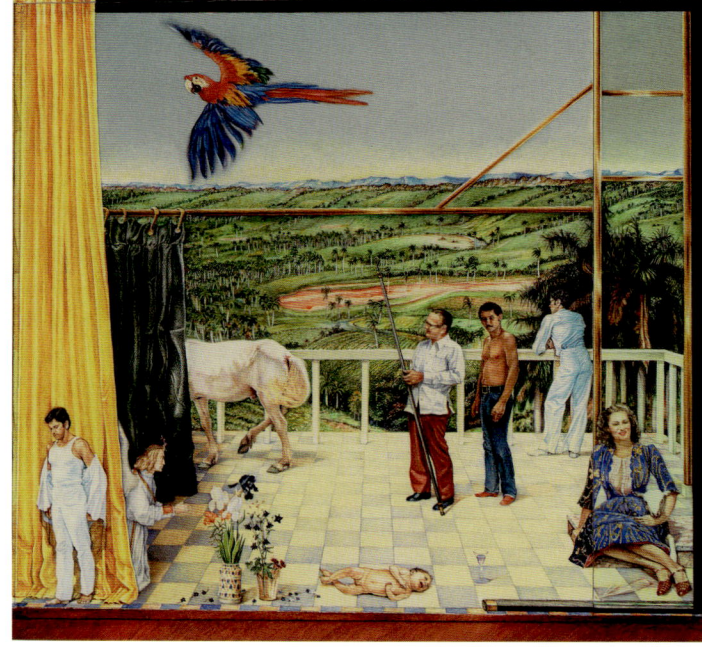

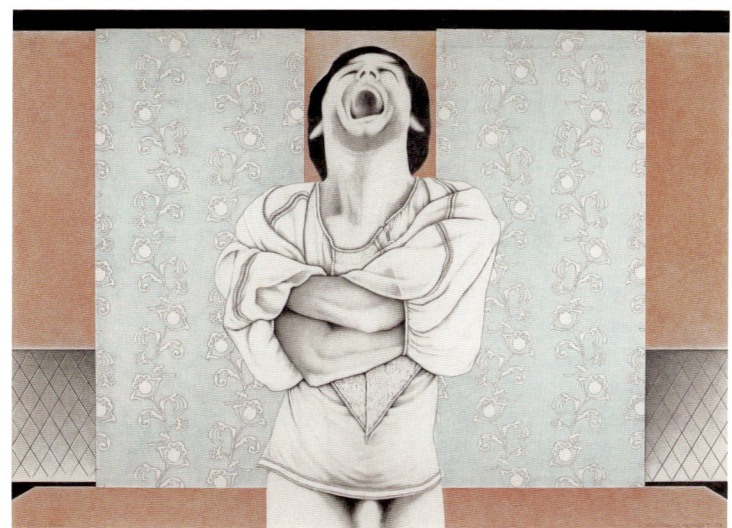

painting his mother's portrait in the retable, "trying to get at some psychological truth about my relationship with her. I just couldn't let go until I felt I had that."[56]

González's lover at the time, Ronald McKenna, stands behind his father, just off center.[57] The artist appears twice, once from behind, looking back toward Cuba, and again in the lower left, discarding a white garment. Fiery wings appear in a small roundel above the scene, embedded in the wooden box. The whole composition honors where González came from and the life he was living in 1979. It places it in an invented space, partly inside and out, a tangible place though constructed from caprice and memory. Anne Minich, who was very close to González, remembers him as wickedly funny and that "he had a killer ability for extreme patience and detail." Just a year before he painted *Nacimiento* Minich drew him in *Hungry Jesus* (1978; fig. 16) and a related drawing showing him in sequential moments of dancing. Minich's vision of her friend is that of a saint or martyr, calling out in pain or ecstasy, experiencing an altered state. He holds himself, arms wrapped around in a garment that seems like it could also constrain. Minich's González is a figure of extremes, passionate and mercurial, sexy yet disturbing.

Sexuality is a thread throughout the Kohler collection, with artists of all identities making imagery that is forthright about desire. In *The Priestess* (1974–75; plate 48), Jane Lund depicts herself seated and nude, except for sheer tights, shoes, and an animal mask, powerfully present and

Fig. 16 Anne Minich, *Hungry Jesus*, 1978. Graphite and colored pencil on ragboard, 27½ × 37¹⁵⁄₁₆ in. Minneapolis Institute of Art, gift of funds from Robert and Frances Coulborn Kohler, 2018.87

Fig. 17 Roland Ayers, *Orgasm*, 1969. Ink on paper, 11¼ × 11½ in.

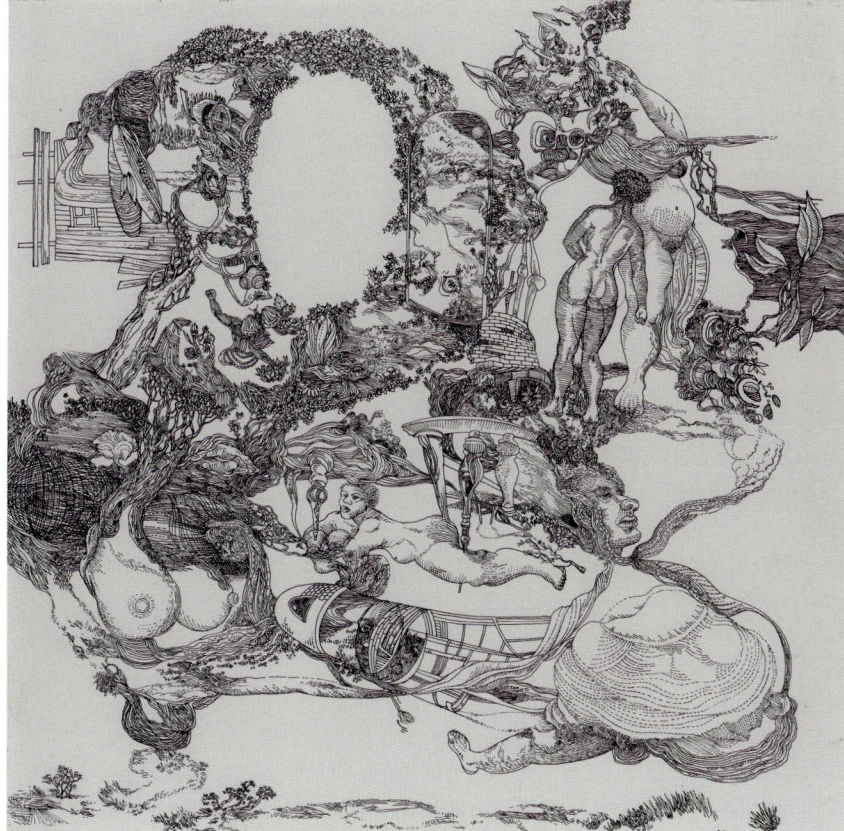

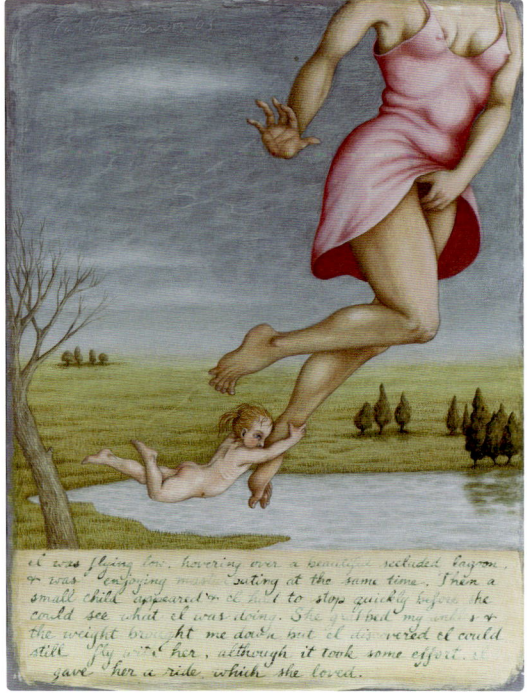

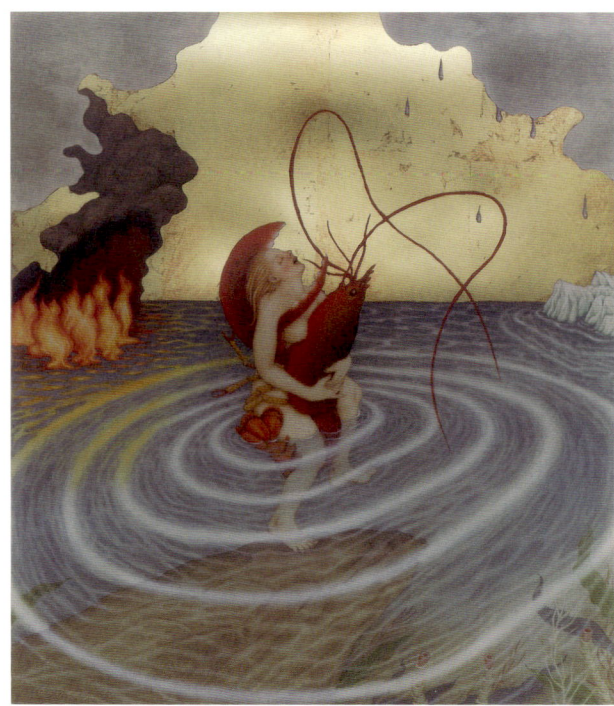

Fig. 18 Tabitha Vevers, *Flying Dream (Anonymous),* 2003. Oil on galvanized steel, 12 × 9 in.

Fig. 19 Tabitha Vevers, *Shiva (Fire and Ice),* 2011. Oil and gold leaf on ivorine, 16 × 14 in.

Fig. 20 Tabitha Vevers, *Eden (Eveandadam VI.07a),* 2007. Oil and gold leaf on ivorine, 9⅜ × 9⅞ in.

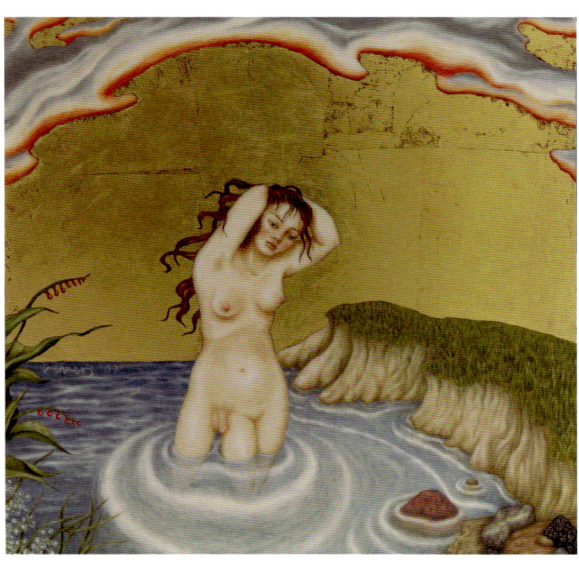

in control. Her left hand holds a phallus, which according to the artist was a ceramic vase she acquired in Portugal. She remarked on seeing the pastel recently, "Holding the phallus and depicting myself this way was a means to counter the oppression women have experienced. I am going to show you my strength, confidence, and power."[58] Roland Ayers's ink drawing *Orgasm* (1969; fig. 17) is a slow unfurling of imagery that entangles itself in a circular composition made up of bodies, flowers, butterflies, leaves, fruit and vegetables, clouds, and myriad other forms. They grow and curl back as though blooming out into the sky and then dissipate like clouds in the high atmosphere blown by winds. Ayers manages to convey the simultaneous merging with the universe and feeling outside oneself in ecstasy.

Tabitha Vevers regularly incorporates sexual pleasure in her work, as in a relaying of a dream (fig. 18) or a painting of a woman making love with a crustacean (fig. 19). She also reimagines Eden with bodies that evade binaries, open and fluid, existing without shame in a new world (fig. 20). This theme underscores a dual imperative in her practice, "to take the female figure back from art history and on a personal level, to own my own body, my sexuality. I came of age in the 1970s, amid the sexual revolution and the rise of feminism, but none of this was reflected in the official canon of art history . . . I set out to correct that . . . Painting narrative, figurative paintings . . . went against the tide of what male artists were doing." Vevers made a point to work small, encouraging close looking, fostering intimacy with the viewer. "I enjoyed luring viewers in with the quiet beauty of the detail and luminosity of the paintings and then giving them a good wake-up slap when they realized what they were actually looking at."[59]

Some of these artists imagine a better world, or a place in which joy and community are foregrounded, and we are free to be ourselves. Gina Litherland's women exist in harmony with the landscape, communing with all species of creatures and part of the whole ecosystem (plate 73). She says, "I think of them as utopian and in some way counteracting the disrespect for nature that has got us where we are today. I like the view of eco-feminism, that the suppression of nature and the suppression of women (and I would include Indigenous people and people of color) are linked together . . . In my paintings the women are forming alliances with animals and plants."[60]

Visualizing a better world, and dealing directly with forces inside oneself or in our environment in order to make it real, is always critical, but doing so is a matter of urgency now. The artists represented in the Kohler collection come from communities that are under existential threat by authoritarian leaders and political decisions that aim at undoing protections for the earth as well as human rights. Sue Coe, a passionate activist and antifascist artist, has been making prints about threats to democracy and to peace for many decades. Her whole body of work, including recent prints that explicitly target Donald Trump's totalitarian aspirations and the impact of his cruel policies, models courage and truth-telling. In other works, she shows what might come of a world at peace, unburdened by war, pollution, and bigotry. Coe shows how artists can use their voices to demand justice for all people, a necessary and brave counter to the terrifying state of the world. If we can imagine an alternative to a world full of pain, perhaps together we can make it real. When things seem their darkest, artists give us a sense that this is possible.

Conclusion: These Things Take Time

The art historian Suzanne Hudson has argued that by 1990, a time in which the Kohlers were especially active in collecting, "painting was, to many critics and practitioners, a thing of the past." Its irrelevance was revealed over slow decades, supplanted by conceptual and technological practices. "It was only with the emergence of a group of expressionistic painters . . . who were active internationally in the early 1980s," Hudson says, "that painting assumed widespread visibility again."[61] As we have seen, claims like this privilege a specific market-driven ecosystem of the art world—critics and theorists, collectors and curators who pursued and promoted the next big thing as though imitating a confused dog chasing its own tail. Painting— representational, realist—never lost visibility and critical relevance. The emergence of prominent attention to a specific group of gestural painters was a function of a hungry market devising ways to promote large, gestural figurative paintings adjacent to Abstract Expressionism, a reliable blue-chip commodity.

In the meantime, artists continued to make slow, meditative, careful painting—crafting intensely personal, clear, and detailed images. It has been a vital thread in twentieth and twenty-first century art. They shifted with changes in culture, in critical engagements with politics, identity, methods. A fickle, distracted, and exploitative part of the art world has largely ignored it and its antecedents, likely owing to the challenge of marketing artwork that defies labels, requires slow looking, deals with difficult though deeply human content, and is modest in scale. The honesty and willingness to probe emotionally volatile subjects may have kept some curators, critics, collectors, and dealers away. Frances Cohen Gillespie (plate 2) drew on these methods to "escape my emotional problems through a developing love of the allegorical via the purified world of image-making. I could rectify the confusion of reality through the concentration of my selections . . . I would like my paintings to breathe . . . I don't imitate the things I stare at, but their presence lends me courage to invent and is a reminder that life is more complex than anything I can set down with clarity."[62]

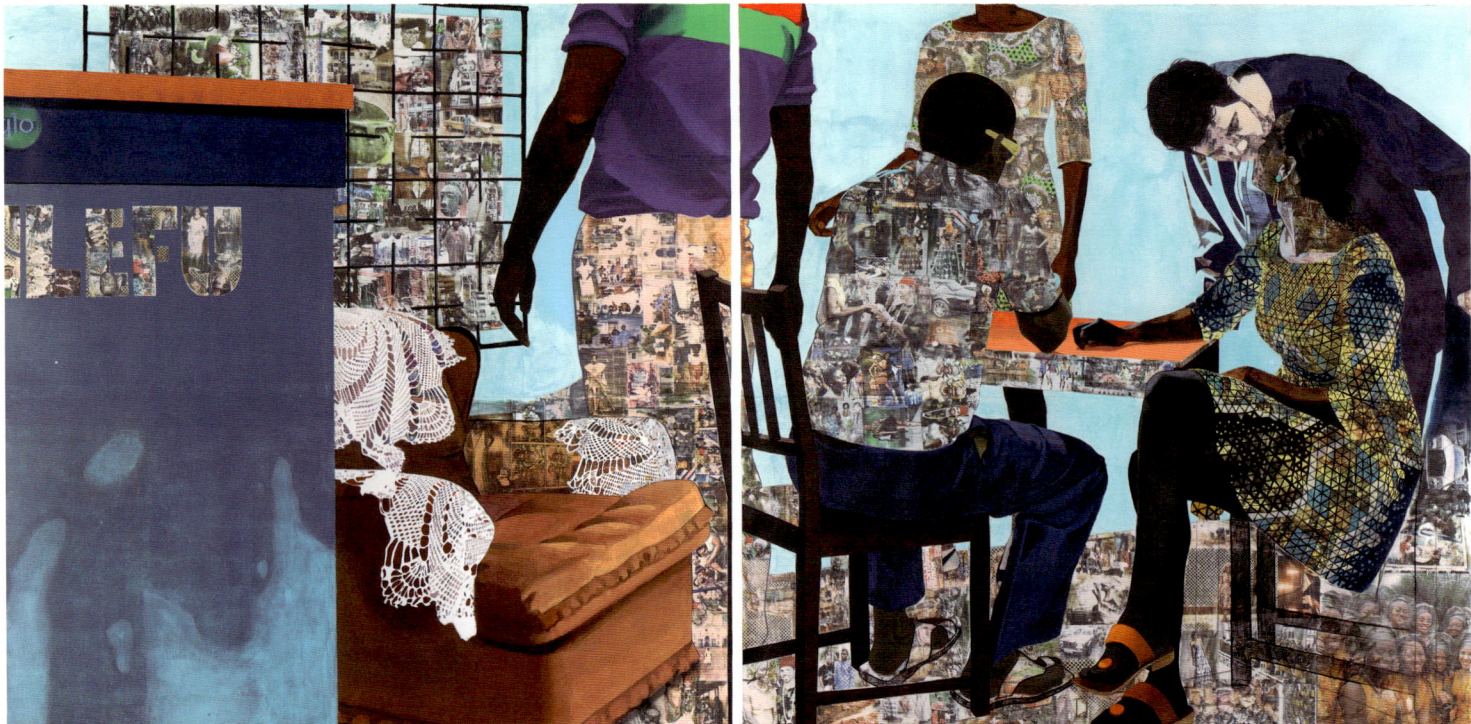

Fig. 21 Njideka Akunyili Crosby, *I Always Face You, Even When It Seems Otherwise*, 2012. Acrylic, pastel, charcoal, colored pencil, collage, and Xerox transfers on paper, two panels, each 78 × 78 in. The Pennsylvania Academy of the Fine Arts, Philadelphia, museum purchase, 2012.29a&b

Her husband's ethos was also rare in an art world that privileged immediacy and serial production, and refuted the hand:

The most important thing I've learned all these years is the value of patience with each painting. In this culture, it's like we're all on speed and we're trained to go after things in a very compulsive way . . . I've learned to take my time with my paintings. They just take as long as they need to take, sometimes years, and when I'm into a piece I keep reminding myself to slow down even more so things can happen without there being too much force of will, or at the very least a balance is set up between will and playfulness.[63]

A new generation of figurative artists has pushed back at market pressures to produce, to be a brand, to make things for clients. PAFA graduate Njideka Akunyili Crosby (fig. 21), for instance, has established boundaries that allow her to stay true to who she is and prevent exploitation by the market. She noted in a 2023 *New York Times* profile, "Something I've been very clear about with everybody I work with is, my pace is slow and you cannot push me or force me to work faster." She continued, "I'm not a machine, I like taking my time . . . Normally I would have said, it takes me about three months to do a work, but it's slowly been extending into longer. I've slowed down to get what I need."[64] What she needs may be what connects us—the time to be present and understand who we are in a constantly shifting world. The need to be grounded for ourselves and our loved ones.

The artists in the Kohler collection played a long game, of investing in deeply personal subjects communicated clearly to their viewers, not knowing whether they would find an audience, but putting everything into these self-contained worlds. They should know, we are here, and we are ready to go with them to the other side.

Notes

1. Kerri ní Dochartaigh, *Thin Places: A Natural History of Healing and Home* (Minneapolis: Milkweed Editions, 2021), 249.

2. Anne Minich, e-mail correspondence with the author, June 23, 2025.

3. Luis Cruz Azaceta, from an interview with Friedhelm Mennekes, *S.O.S.* (Atlanta: Georgia State University Art Gallery, 1990), 3; quoted in *Luis Cruz Azaceta: The AIDS Epidemic Series* (New York: Queens Museum of Art, 1990), 22.

4. "Who & What Is the Artists' Choice Museum," in *The Artists' Choice Museum Presents Bodies & Souls, Paintings and Sculpture* (New York: Artists' Choice Museum, 1983), 4. The participating galleries were Tatistcheff & Co., Kornblee, Marisa Del Re, Midtown, Alex Rosenberg, Tibor de Nagy, David Findlay Jr., Inc., Marlborough, Sherry French, A. M. Sachs, and Sutton.

5. Patricia Hills and Roberta K. Tarbell, *The Figurative Tradition and the Whitney Museum of American Art* (Newark [DE]: University of Delaware Press, 1980) and Greta Berman and Jeffrey Wechsler, *Realism and Realities: The Other Side of American Painting, 1940–1960* (New Brunswick: Rutgers University, 1981).

6. Those on view at the time that caught their eye, but that they never committed to for one reason or another, included Roger Brown, Paul Cadmus, Leon Golub, Mark Greenwold, Lester Johnson, Catherine Murphy, Jim Nutt, Peter Saul, and James Valerio. Rob and Frances did not acquire work unless they both agreed; one might convince the other, but if not, they respected these parameters. They also bought art on a relatively modest income for most of their collecting life.

7. Rob Kohler, "Passionate Figuration," in this volume.

8. Rob Kohler, e-mail to the author, June 21, 2025.

9. John Yau, "Introduction," in *Bodies & Souls*, 5.

10. Yau, "Introduction," 6.

11. Luis Cruz Azaceta, e-mail correspondence with the author, June 19, 2025.

12. Frank Goodyear Jr., *Contemporary American Realism Since 1960* (Boston: New York Graphic Society, 1981), 32.

13. Gregory Gillespie, "The Artist on His Work," *Massachusetts Review* 19, no. 1 (1978), 130. These statements were adapted from his interview responses in Abram Lerner and Howard Fox, "An Interview with Gregory Gillespie," in Abram Lerner, *Gregory Gillespie* (Washington, DC: Smithsonian Institution Press, 1977), 28–29.

14. Peggy Gillespie, e-mail correspondence with the author, June 18, 2025.

15. Demons take on several appearances and forms in Gillespie's work. In *Pear and Demons* (1987–88) they appear as winged bird-hybrids draped with snakes. For this and other variations see *Gregory Gillespie*, foreword by John Yau (New York: Forum Gallery, 1996).

16. Gregory Gillespie, "Notes from the Artist," in *Gregory Gillespie: New Works* (New York: Forum Gallery, 1999), 6, 9.

17. Jane Lund, "A Note by the Artist," *Massachusetts Review* 18, no. 1 (1977), 90–91.

18. Jane Lund, telephone conversation with the author, June 24, 2025.

19. Deborah Kravitz, "My Life in Pictures," 2015, unpublished manuscript. Courtesy of Rob Kohler.

20. For more on this see Robert Cozzolino, "Bernard Perlin and the State of Modern Painting at Mid-Century," *Record of the Princeton University Art Museum* (2012–13), 58–73.

21. Clement Greenberg, "Towards a Newer Laocoon," in John O'Brien, ed., *Clement Greenberg: Collected Essays and Criticism Volume I: Perceptions and Judgments, 1939–1944* (Chicago: University of Chicago Press, 1986), 24.

22. For more on this see Robert Cozzolino, "Medieval/Modern: Gothic Impulses in American Modernism," in Joyce Robinson, ed., *A Gift from the Heart: The James and Barbara Palmer Collection* (State College, PA: Palmer Museum of Art, 2013).

23. Selden Rodman, *Conversations with Artists* (New York: Devin-Adair, 1957), 210.

24. Gillespie, "The Artist on His Work," 130.

25. For more on Tillim see Katy Siegel, "Critical Realist: Sidney Tillim," *Artforum* 42, no. 1 (September 2003), https://www.artforum.com/features/critical-realist-sidney-tillim-167353/.

26. Sidney Tillim, "A Variety of Realisms," *Artforum* 7, no. 10 (1969), 42.

27. Donald D. Keyes, "Interview with Gregory Gillespie," in Donald D. Keyes, *A Unique American Vision: Paintings by Gregory Gillespie* (Athens, GA: Georgia Museum of Art, University of Georgia, 1999), 50. See also Robert Cozzolino, "Raw Nerves: 1947–1973," in Maggie Taft and Robert Cozzolino, eds., *Art in Chicago: A History from the Fire to Now* (University of Chicago Press, 2018), 143–52, and Robert Cozzolino, *Elizabeth Osborne: The Color of Light* (Philadelphia: Pennsylvania Academy of the Fine Arts, 2009), 10–13.

28. Tillim, "Variety of Realisms," 42.

29. Interview with Chuck Close, *Artforum* 8, no. 5 (1970), 55.

30. Sarah Lehrer-Graiwer, "Ordinary People: Photorealism and the Work of Art Since 1968," *Artforum* 63, no. 7 (March 2025), https://www.artforum.com/events/ordinary-people-photorealism-moca-la-1234727418/.

31. A good example of this is Melissa Ho, ed., *Artists Respond: American Art and the Vietnam War, 1965–1975* (Princeton, NJ: Princeton University Press, 2019).

32. Tillim, "Variety of Realisms," 43. See also Sidney Tillim, "The Reception of Figurative Art: Notes on a General Misunderstanding," *Artforum* 7, no. 6 (1969), 30–33.

33. Quoted in Kellie Jones, "Civil/Rights/Act," in Teresa A. Carbone and Kellie Jones et al., *Witness: Art and Civil Rights in the Sixties* (Brooklyn, NY: Brooklyn Museum, 2014), 19.

34. Benjamin D. Buchloh, "Figures of Authority, Ciphers of Regression," in Brian Wallis, ed. *Art After Modernism: Rethinking Representation* (New York: New Museum of Contemporary Art, 1984), 132. Reprinted from *October* no. 16 (Spring 1981), 39–68.

35. See for instance Buchloh, "Figures of Authority," 115.

36. Buchloh, "Figures of Authority," 108.

37. For more on this see Cozzolino, "Raw Nerves," esp. 146–152.

38. Buchloh, "Figures of Authority," 118–19.

39. Craig Calderwood, quoted in Toshio Meronek, "See You in Hell: This Queer Artist's Work Resists the Gender Binary," *Them*, September 7, 2018, https://www.them.us/story/craig-calderwood.

40. Craig Calderwood, telephone conversation with the author, June 26, 2025.

41. Craig Calderwood, quoted in Meronek, "See You in Hell."

42. Recent projects that assert this premise for the figure include Ekow Eshun, *The Time Is Always Now: Artists Reframe the Black Figure* (London: National Portrait Gallery, 2024) and Koyo Kouoh, ed., *When We See Us: A Century of Black Figuration in Painting* (London: Thames & Hudson, 2022).

43. Willard Motley, "Negro Art in Chicago," *Opportunity* (January 1940), 22.

44. Dawoud Bey, "Swagger," in Rebecca Walker, *Black Cool: One Thousand Streams of Blackness* (Berkeley, CA: Soft Skull Press, 2012), 154.

45. Leslie Barlow, "Precious & Infinite," in *Kith & Kin: A Collection of Works by Leslie Barlow* (Minneapolis: Wise Ink Creative Publishing, 2022), 77.

46. The interviews are led by Lola Osunkoya and the filming was done by Ryan Stopera. They can be accessed on Barlow's website: https://www.lesliebarlowartist.com/projects/within-between-and-beyond-videos.

47. Riva Lehrer, *Golem Girl: A Memoir* (New York: One World, 2020), 253.

48. Lehrer, *Golem Girl*, 258.

49. Susanna W. Gold, "These 'African Feelings,'" in *Africa in the Arts of Philadelphia: Bullock, Searles, and Twins Seven-Seven* (Philadelphia: Woodmere Art Museum, 2020), 33.

50. Gold, "African Feelings," 17.

51. Gold, "African Feelings," 35–36.

52. Nannette Acker Clark, *Barbara Bullock: Spirit Rain* (Philadelphia: Afro-American Cultural and Historical Museum [now the African American Museum in Philadelphia], 1988). Reprinted in Klare Scarbrough, *Barbara Bullock: Chasing After Spirits* (Philadelphia: La Salle University Art Museum, 2016), 77. See also her comments in Andrea Packard, "Power and Inquiry in the Art of Barbara Bullock," in *Ubiquitous Presence: Selected Works by Barbara Bullock* (Swarthmore, PA: List Gallery, Swarthmore College, 2022), 16.

53. "A Conversation with Barbara Bullock, Lowery Stokes Sims, Leslie King Hammond, William R. Valerio, and Barbara Bullock," in *Barbara Bullock: Fearless Vision* (Philadelphia: Woodmere Art Museum, 2023), 26–27.

54. Rafael Ferrer, "Rapping with Rafi: An Exchange with Rafael Ferrer," interview by Vincent Katz, in Deborah Cullen, ed., *Retro/Active: The Work of Rafael Ferrer* (New York: El Museo del Barrio, 2010), 36.

55. Deborah Cullen, *Rafael Ferrer* (Los Angeles: UCLA Chicano Studies Research Center Press, 2012), 53.

56. Irene McManus, *Dreamscapes: The Art of Juan González* (New York: Hudson Hills Press, 1994), 78.

57. Anne Minich, e-mail correspondence with the author, June 30, 2025.

58. Jane Lund, telephone conversation with the author, June 25, 2025.

59. Tabitha Vevers, e-mail correspondence with the author, June 25, 2025.

60. Gina Litherland, e-mail correspondence with the author, June 23, 2025.

61. Suzanne Hudson, "After Endgame: American Painting in the 1990s," in Alexandra Schwartz et al., *Come as You Are: Art of the 1990s* (Montclair, NJ: Montclair Art Museum, and Berkeley and Los Angeles: University of California Press, 2015), 46.

62. Frances Cohen Gillespie, "The Artist on Her Life and Work," *Massachusetts Review* 17, no. 2 (1976), 358.

63. Gillespie, "Notes from the Artist," 5.

64. Robin Pogrebin, "Njideka Akunyili Crosby Wants to Take It Slow, Despite Her Rapid Rise," *New York Times*, May 21, 2023, https://www.nytimes.com/2023/05/21/arts/design/njideka-akunyili-crosby-zwirner.html.

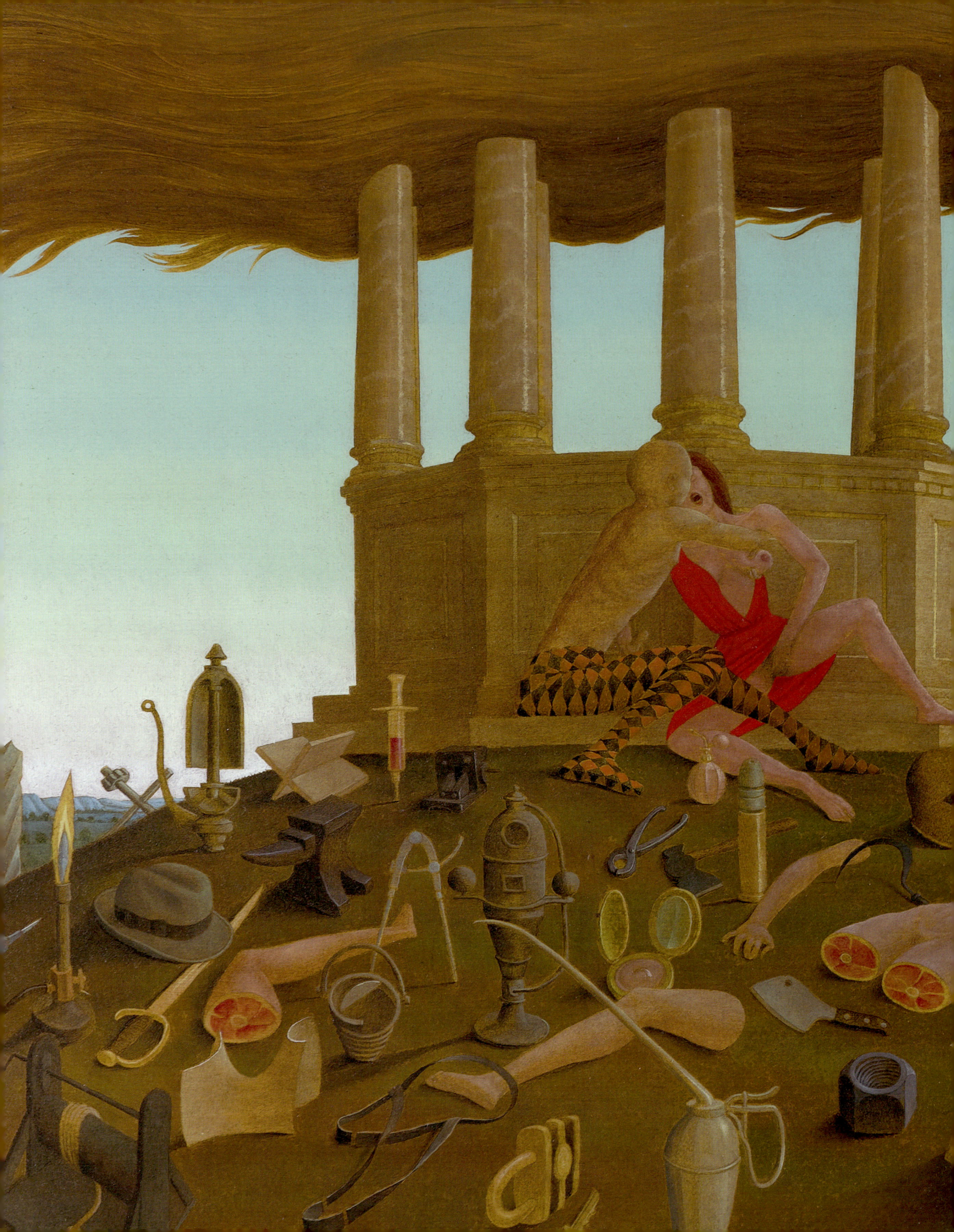

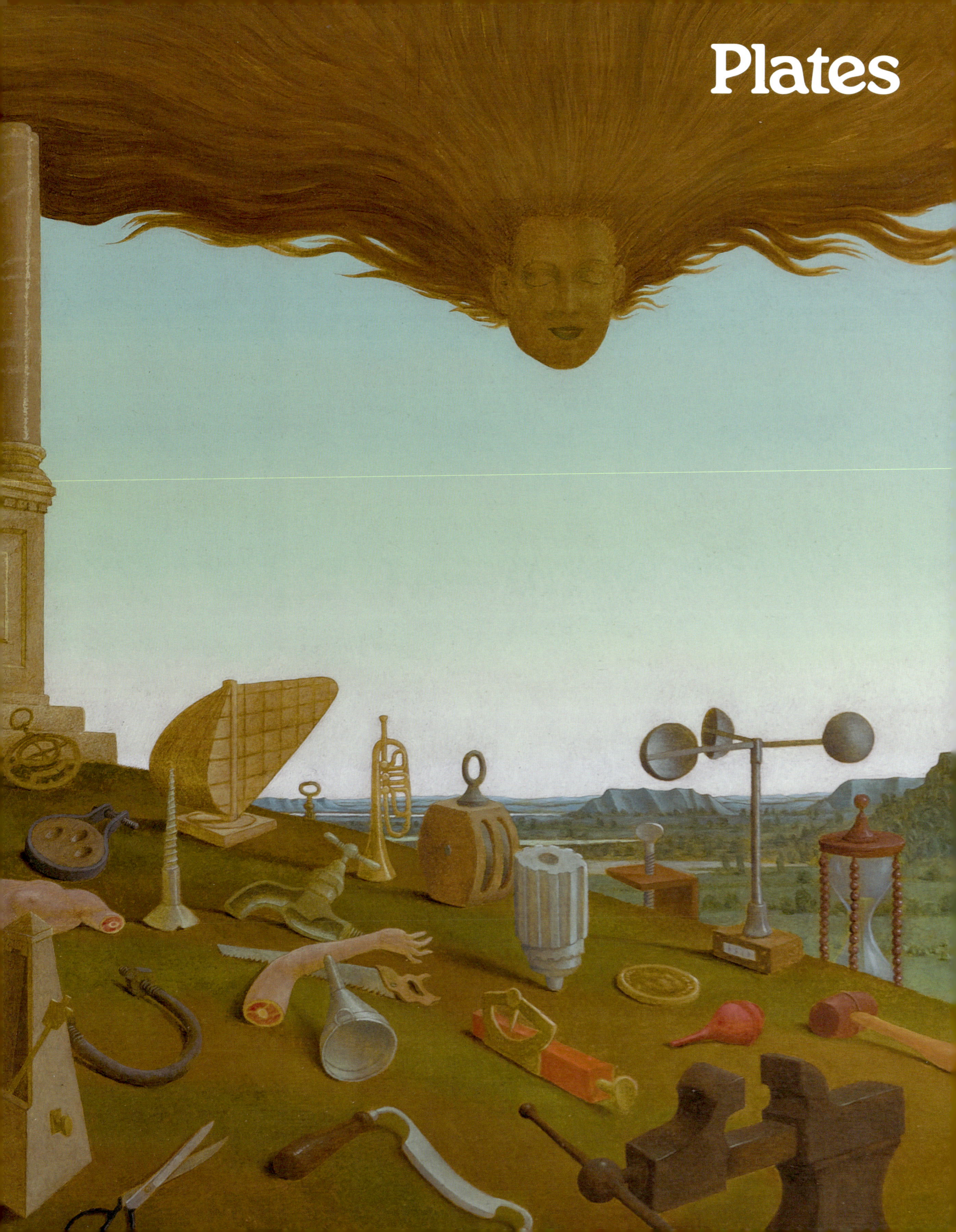

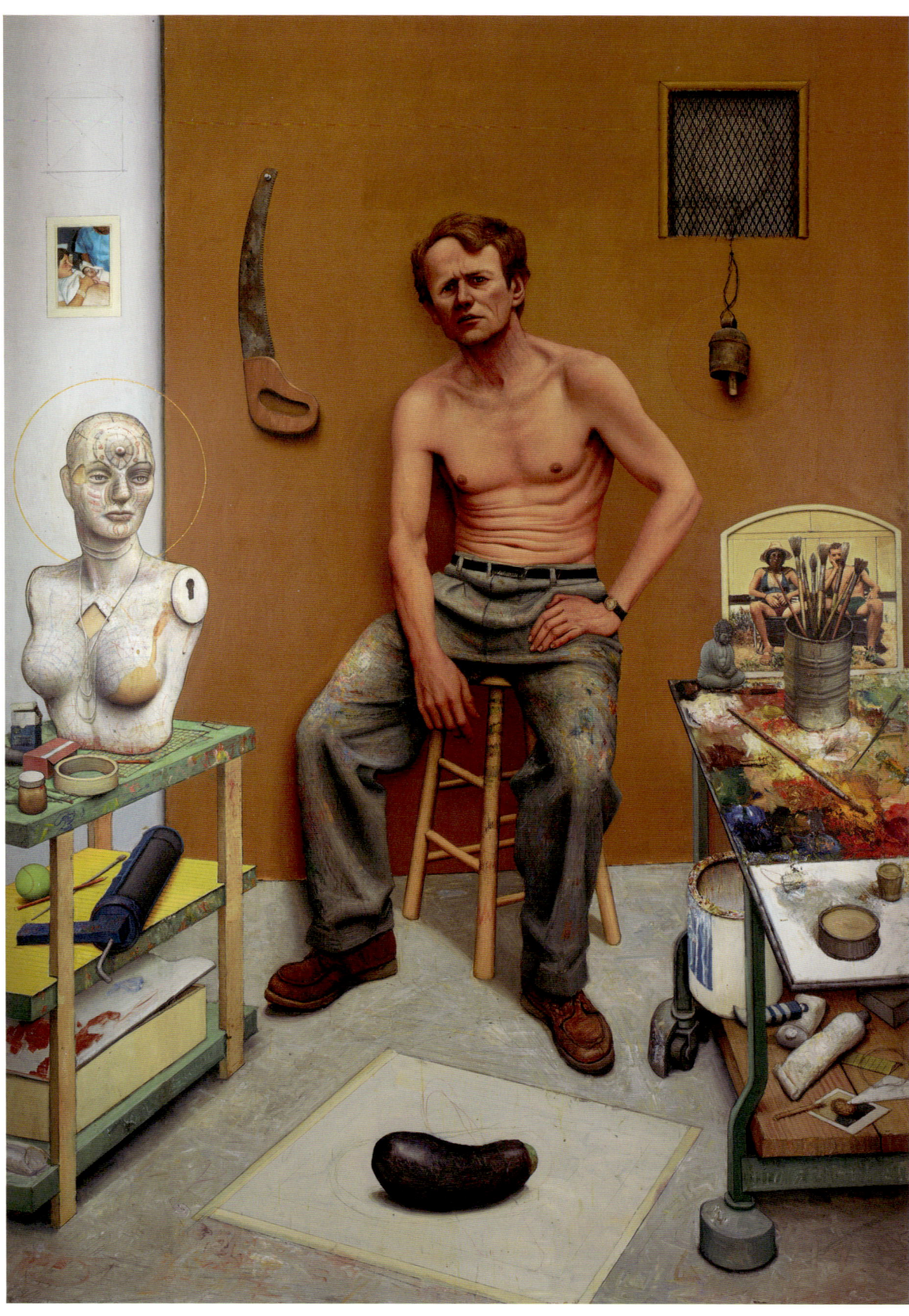

Gregory Gillespie
(1936–2000)

William Beckman
1993. Oil and alkyd on panel, 98 × 86 in.

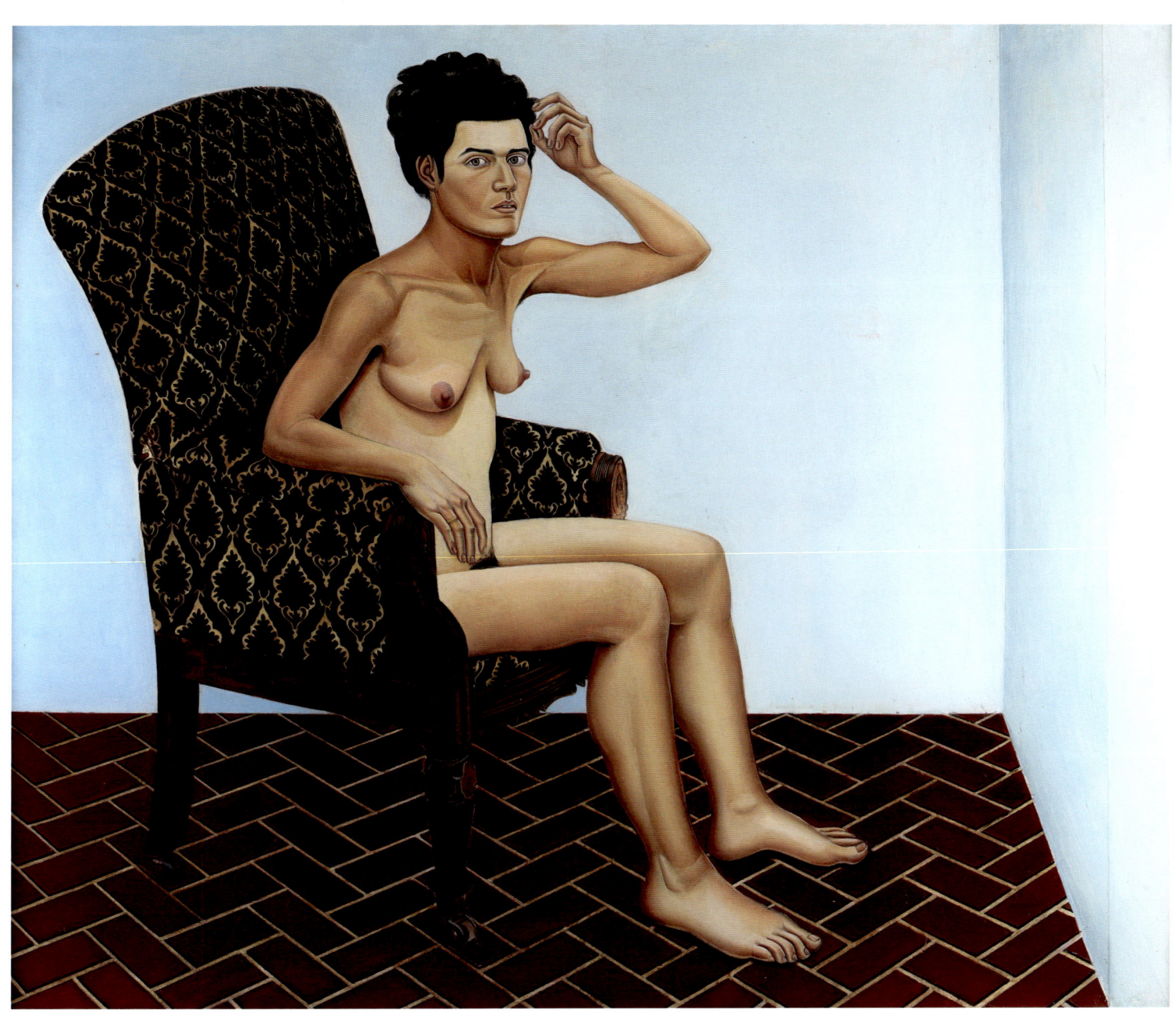

2

**Frances Cohen
Gillespie**

(1939–1998)

Nude Self-Portrait in Chair

c. 1972. Oil on panel, 48 × 57 in.

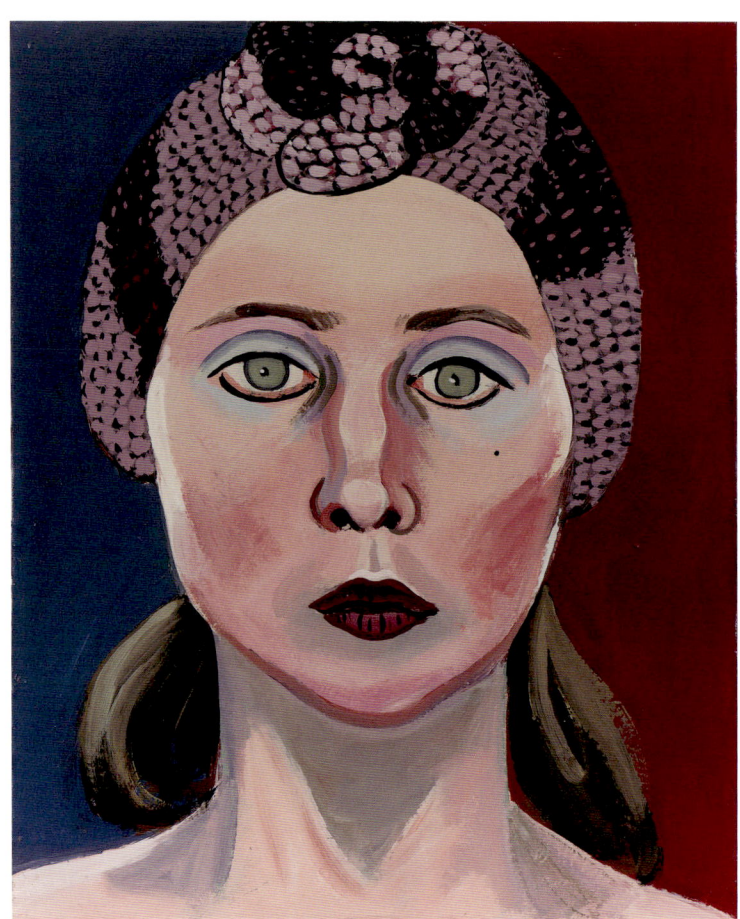

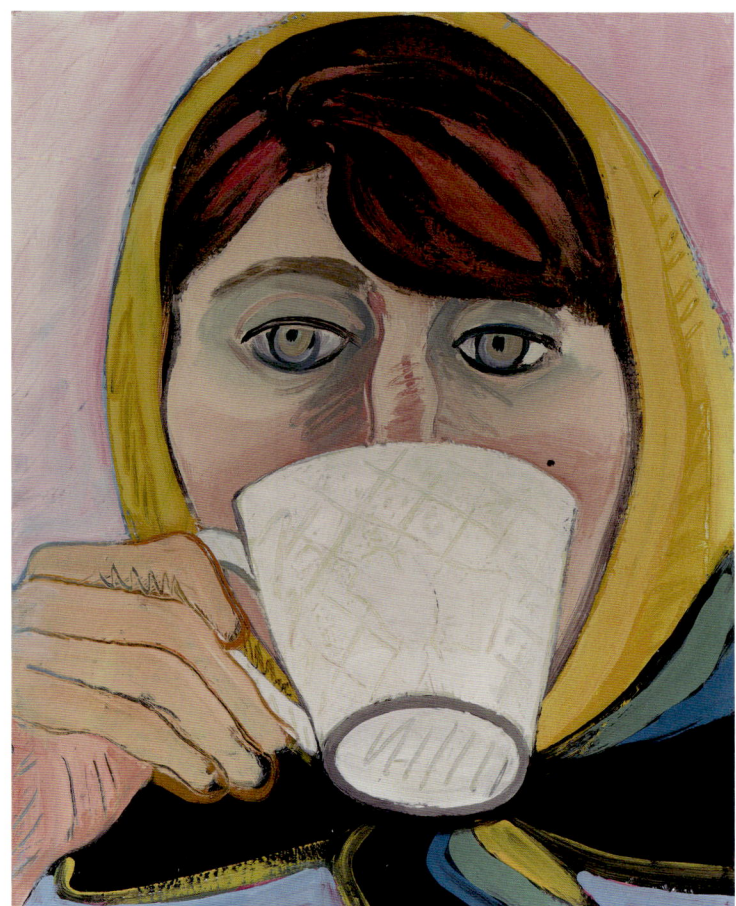

3
Joan Brown
(1938–1990)

Self-Portrait in Knit Hat
1972. Enamel on canvas, 20 × 16 in.

4
Joan Brown

Self-Portrait in Scarf Drinking Tea
1972. Enamel on canvas, 20 × 15¾ in.

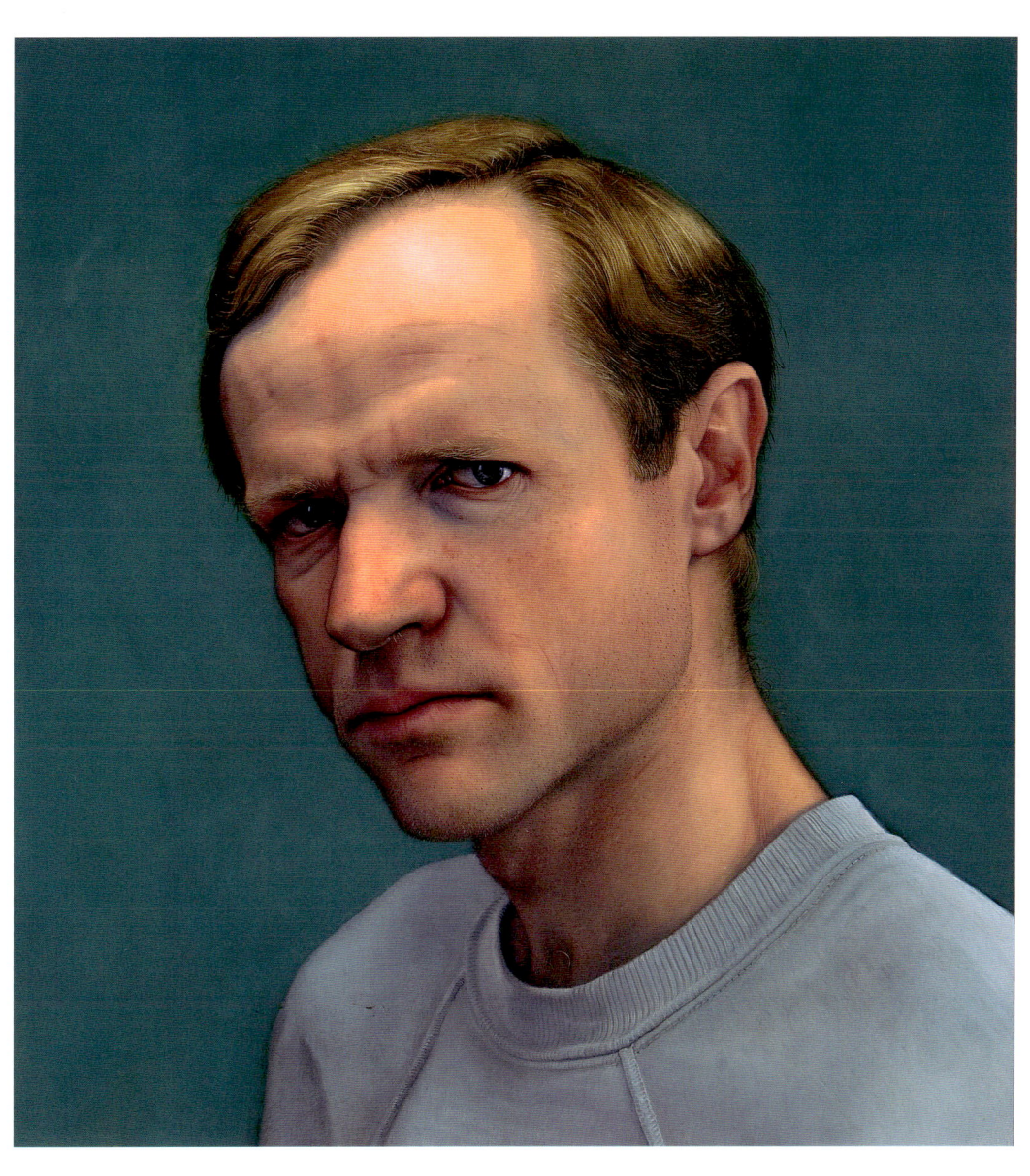

5
William
Beckman (b. 1942)

Self-Portrait
1980. Oil on panel, 15¼ × 13¼ in.

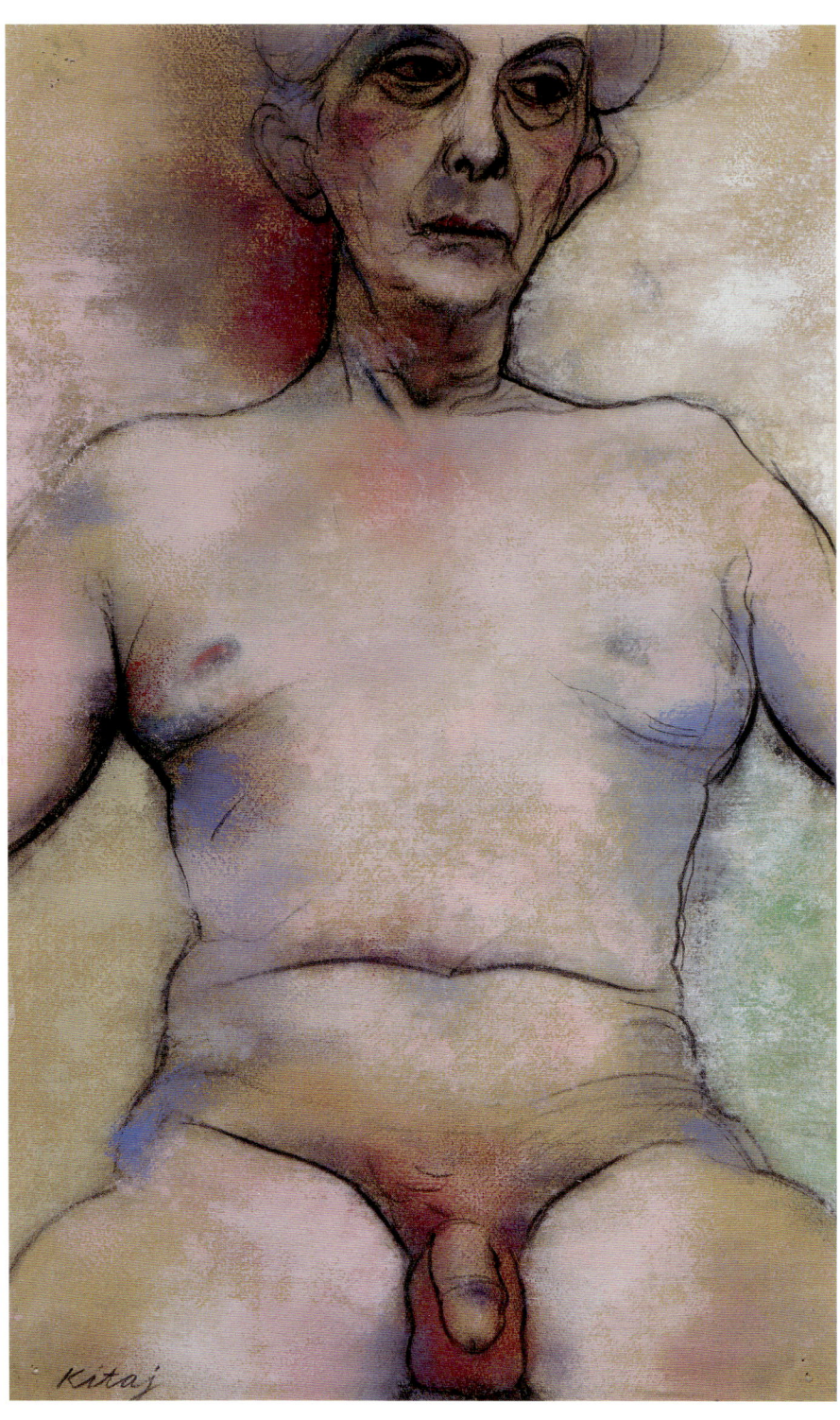

6
R. B. Kitaj
(1932–2007)

Quentin
1979. Charcoal and pastel on paper,
25¾ × 15¾ in.

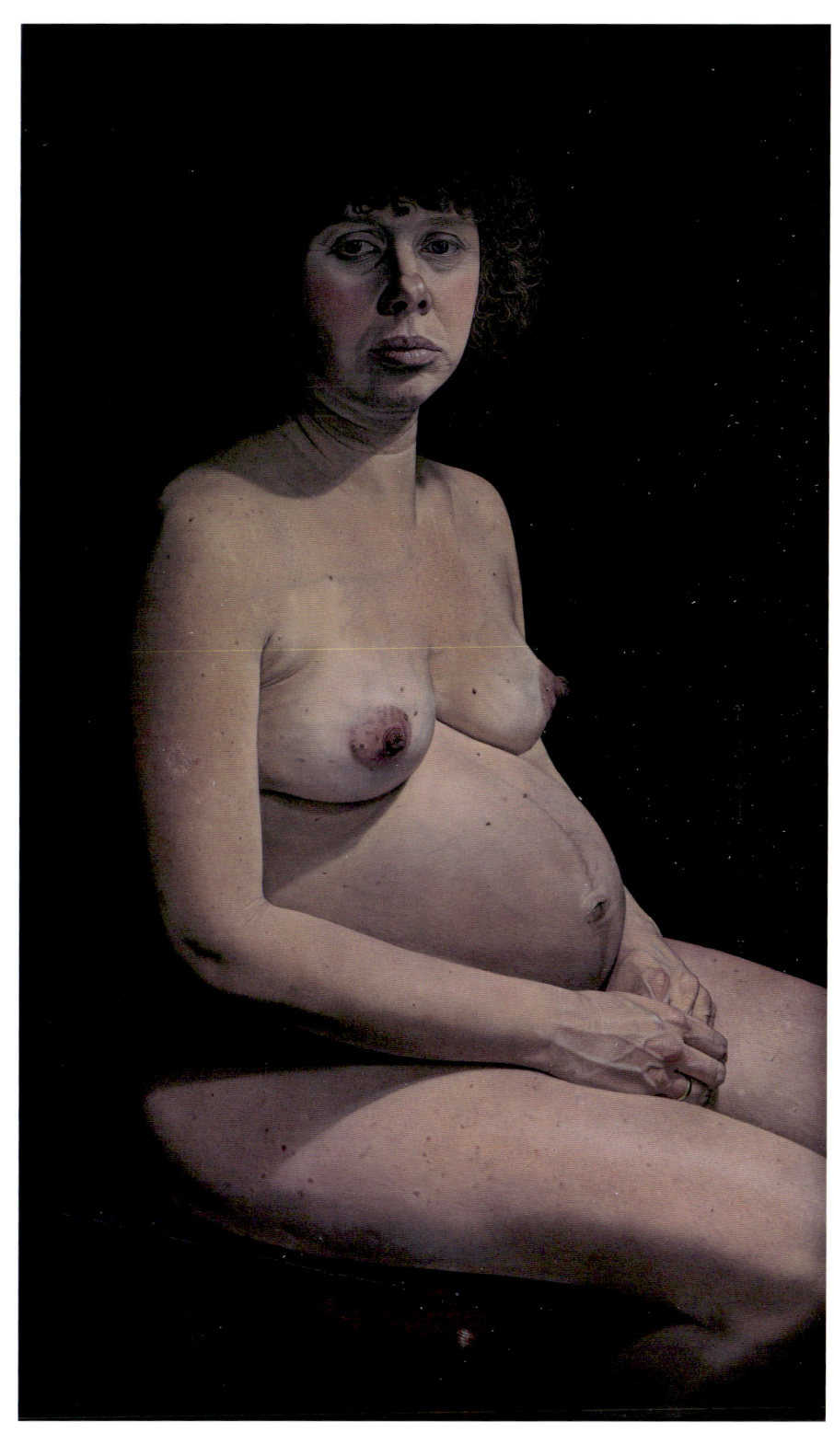

7
Jane Lund
(b. 1939)

Pregnant Woman
1978. Pastel on paper, 28 × 22 in.

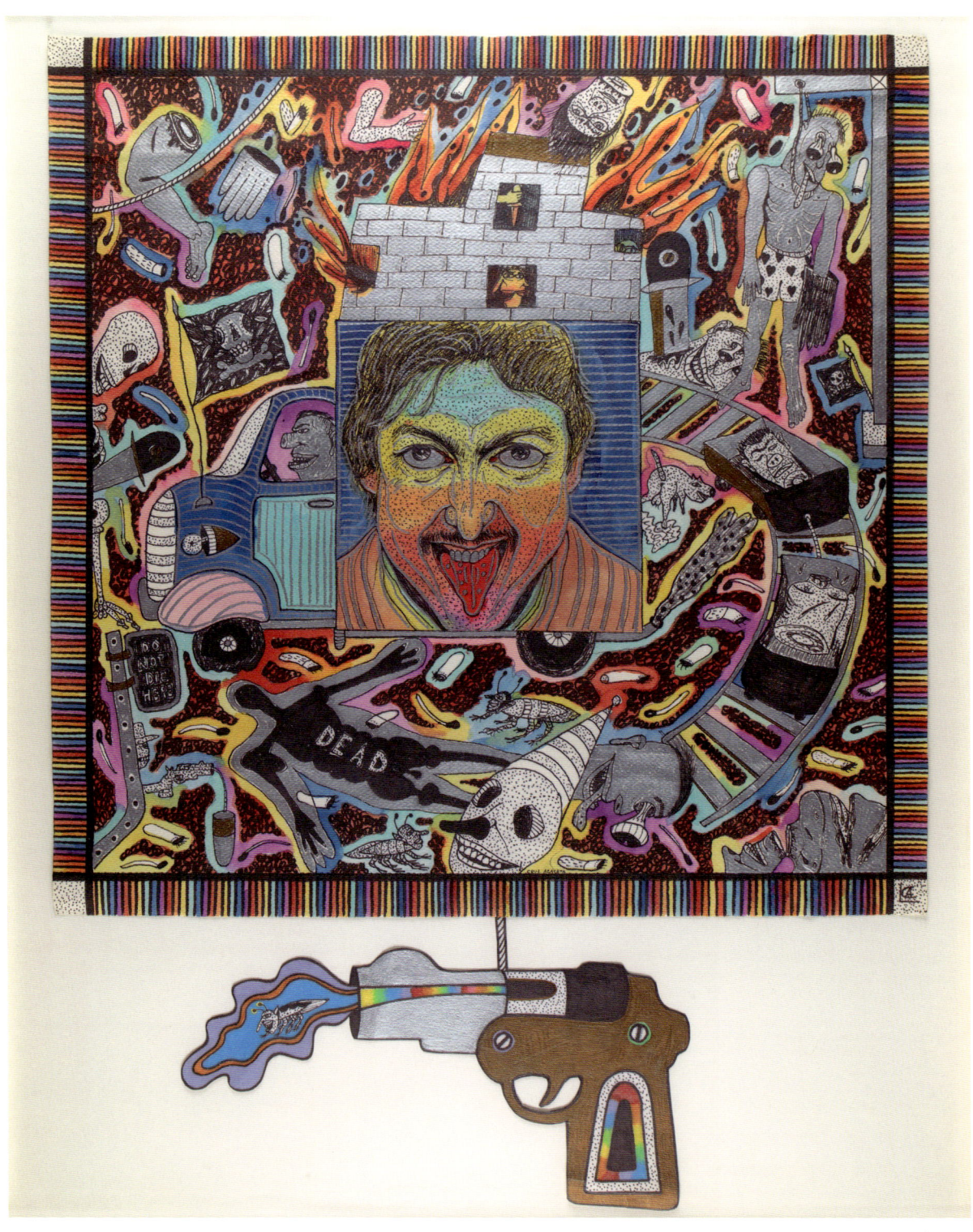

8
Luis Cruz
Azaceta (b. 1943)

Self-Portrait: Pistol and Other Small Things
1981. Watercolor and colored pencils on paper,
32 × 25 in.

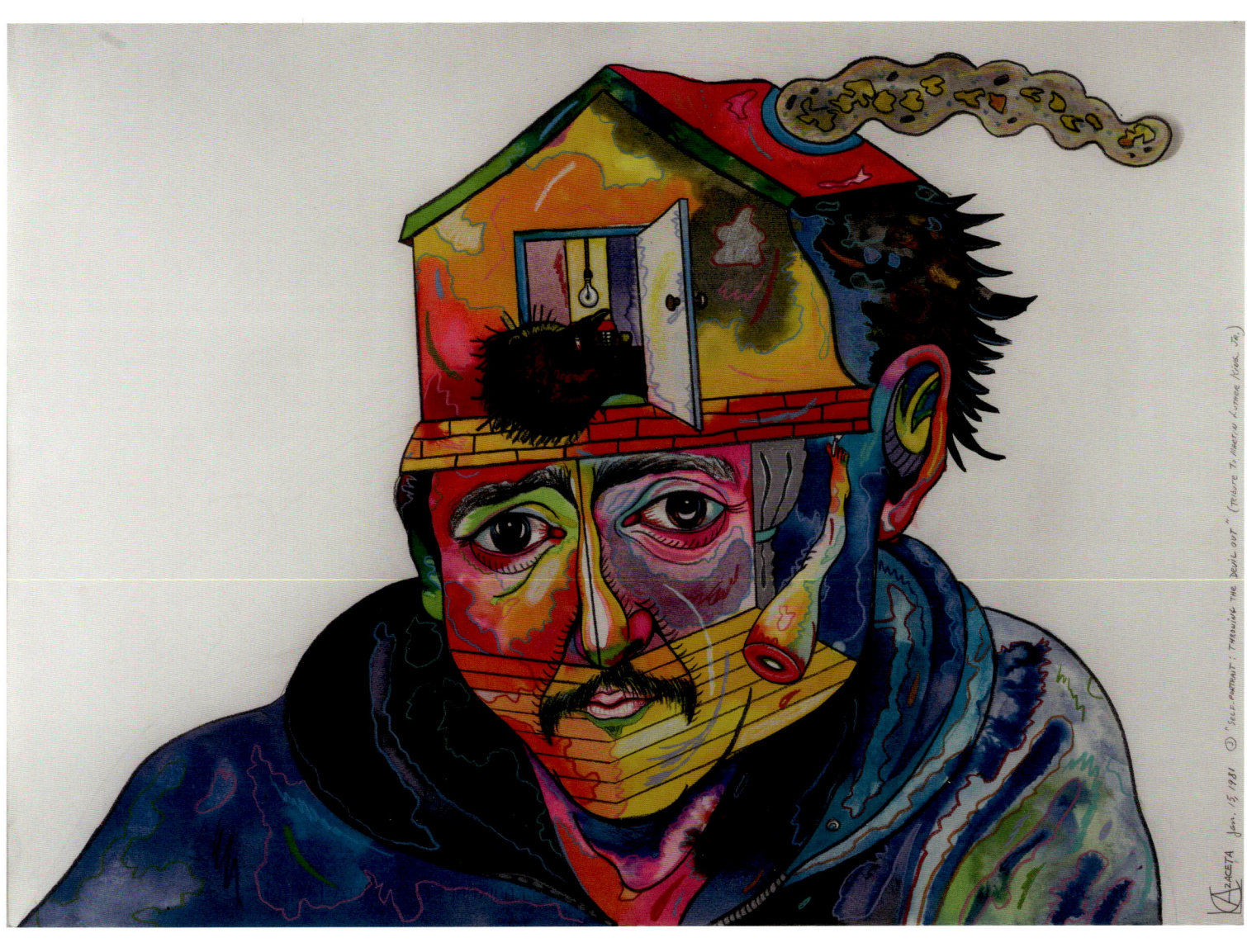

9

Luis Cruz Azaceta

Self-Portrait Throwing the Devil Out
1981. Ink and colored pencil on paper,
22 × 30 in.

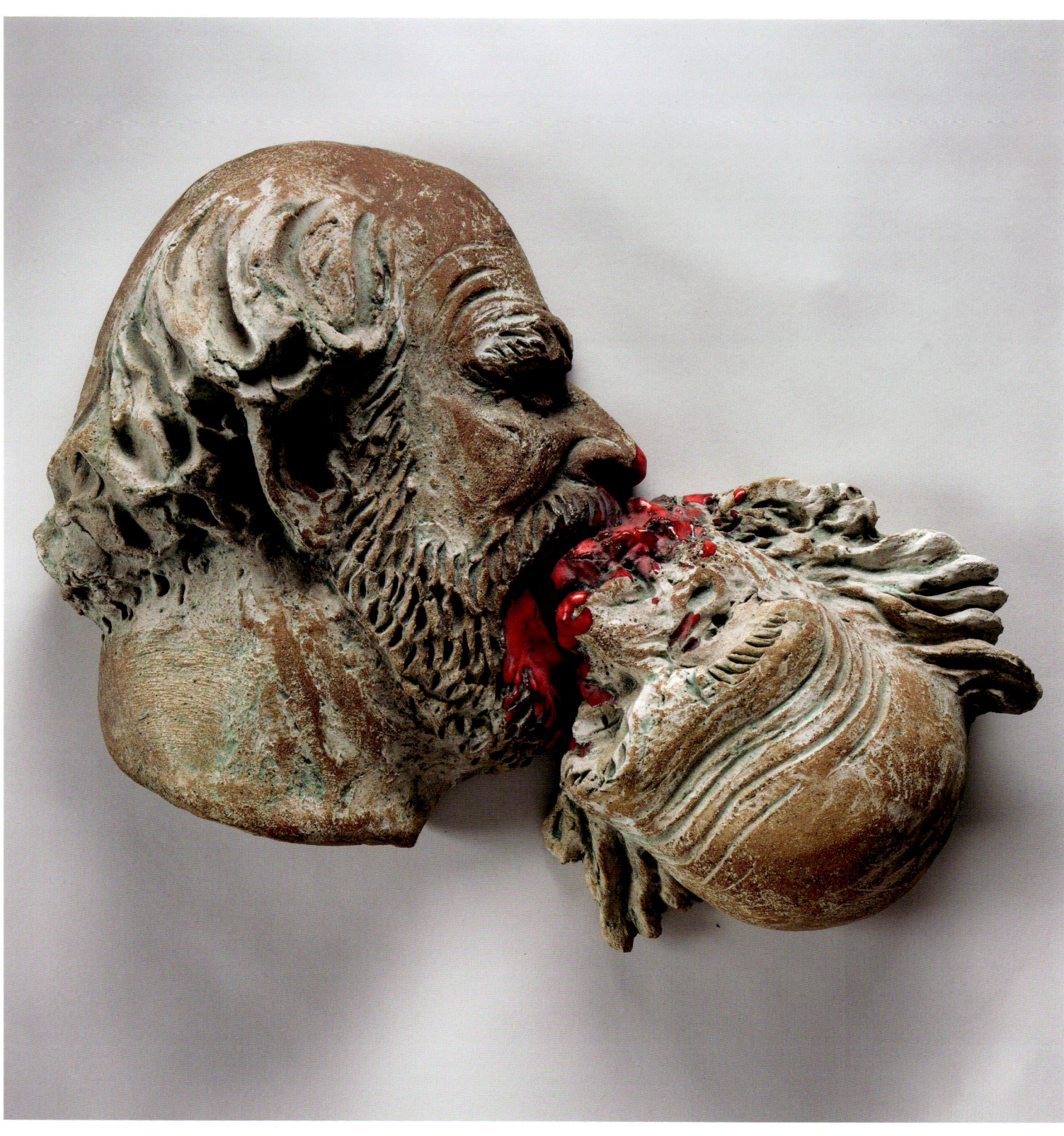

10

Robert Arneson   *Head Eater*

(1930–1992)   1991. Glazed ceramic, 15½ × 21½ in.

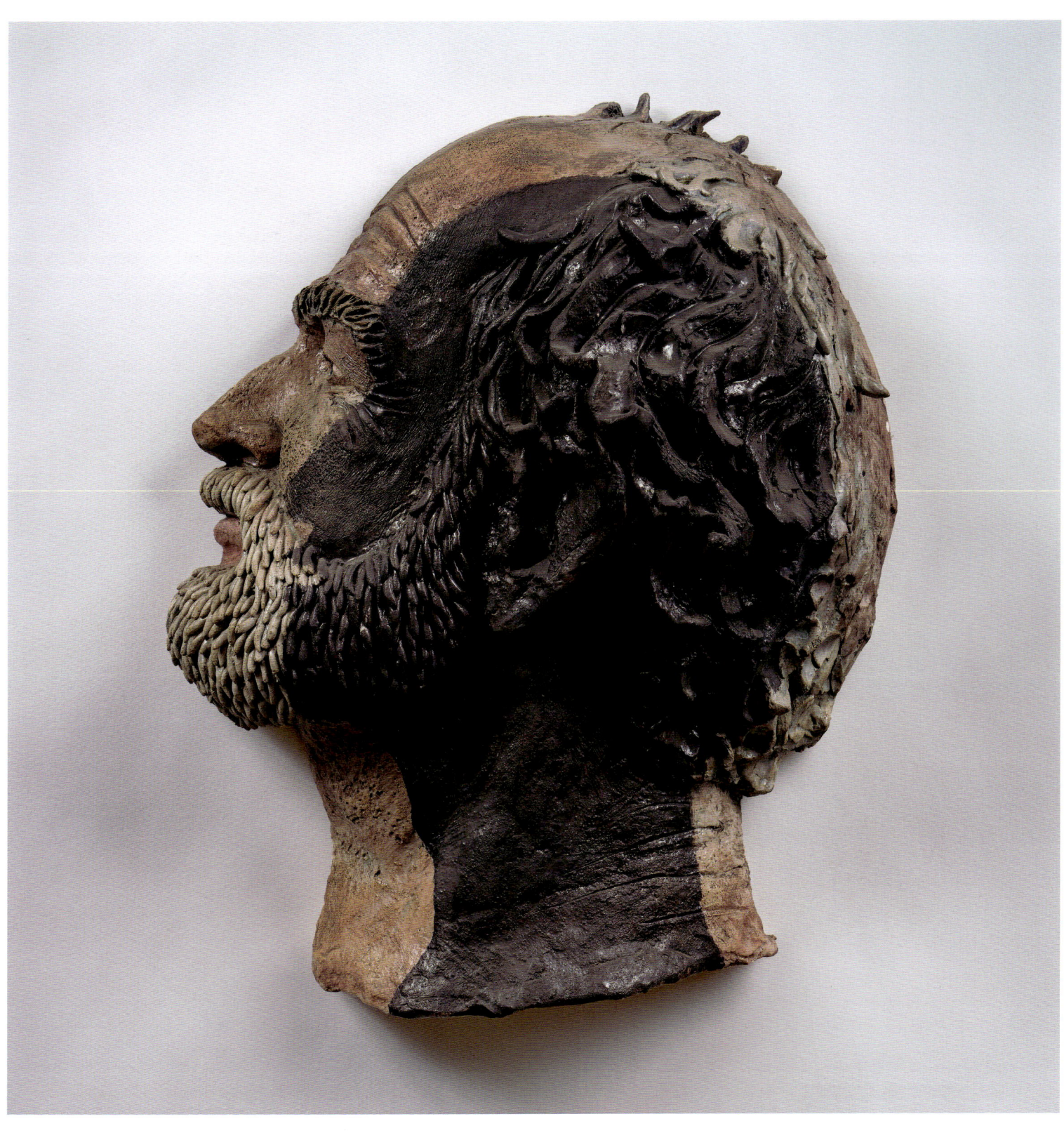

11
Robert Arneson

Untitled (Double profile)
1978. Glazed ceramic, 16 × 14 × 4 in.

83

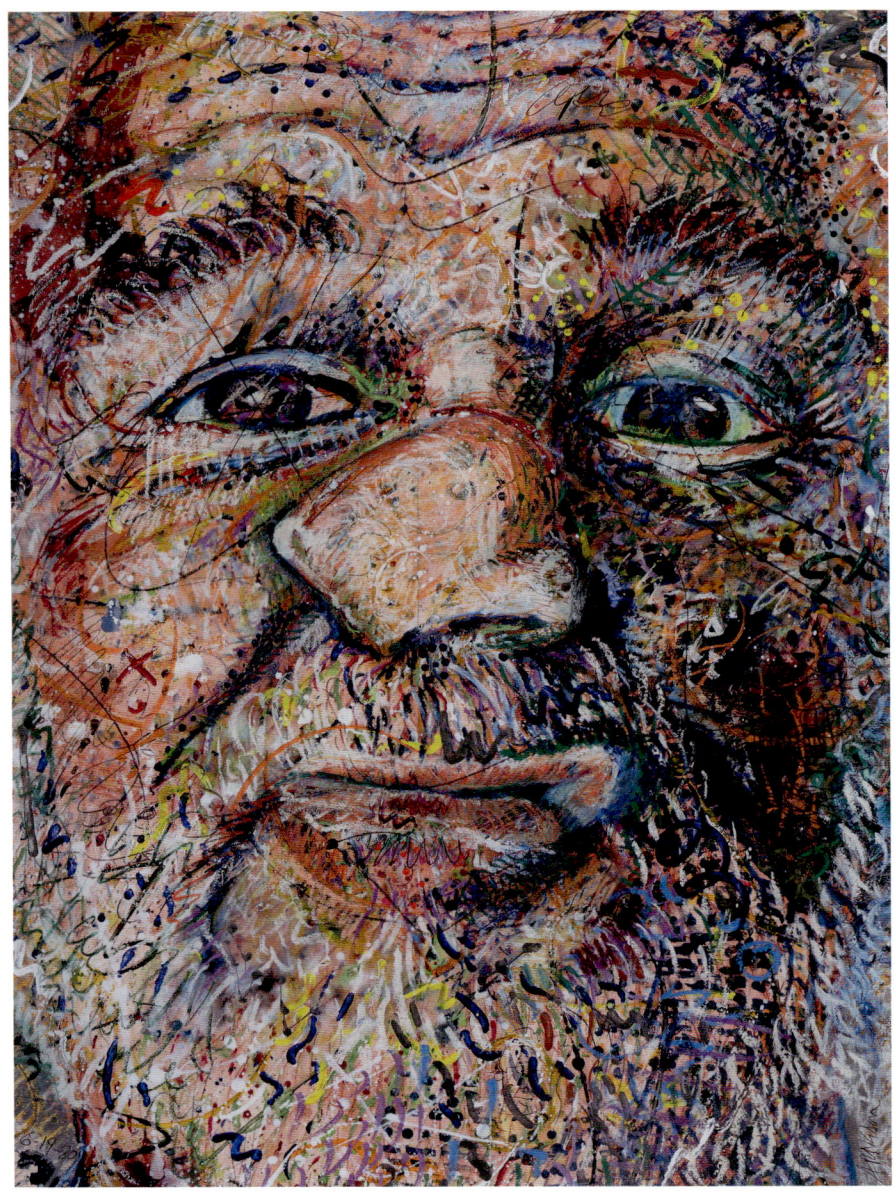

Study for *Nasal Flat*
1980. Pastel and acrylic on paper,
31½ × 27¾ in.

12
Robert Arneson

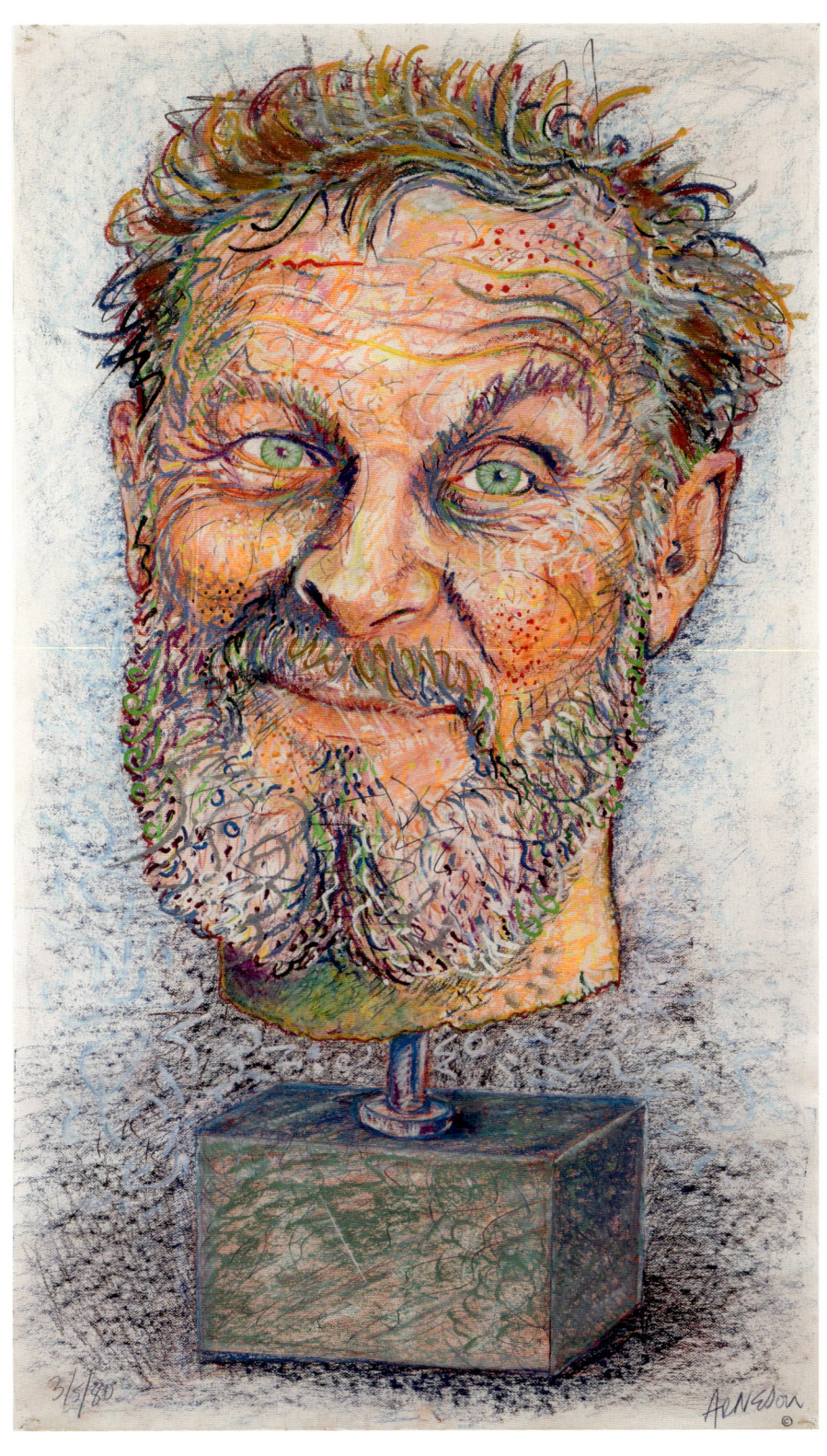

Robert Arneson

Roy De Forest-Witness
1980. Oil pastel, acrylic, and conté crayon
on paper, 51$\frac{1}{12}$ × 30 in.

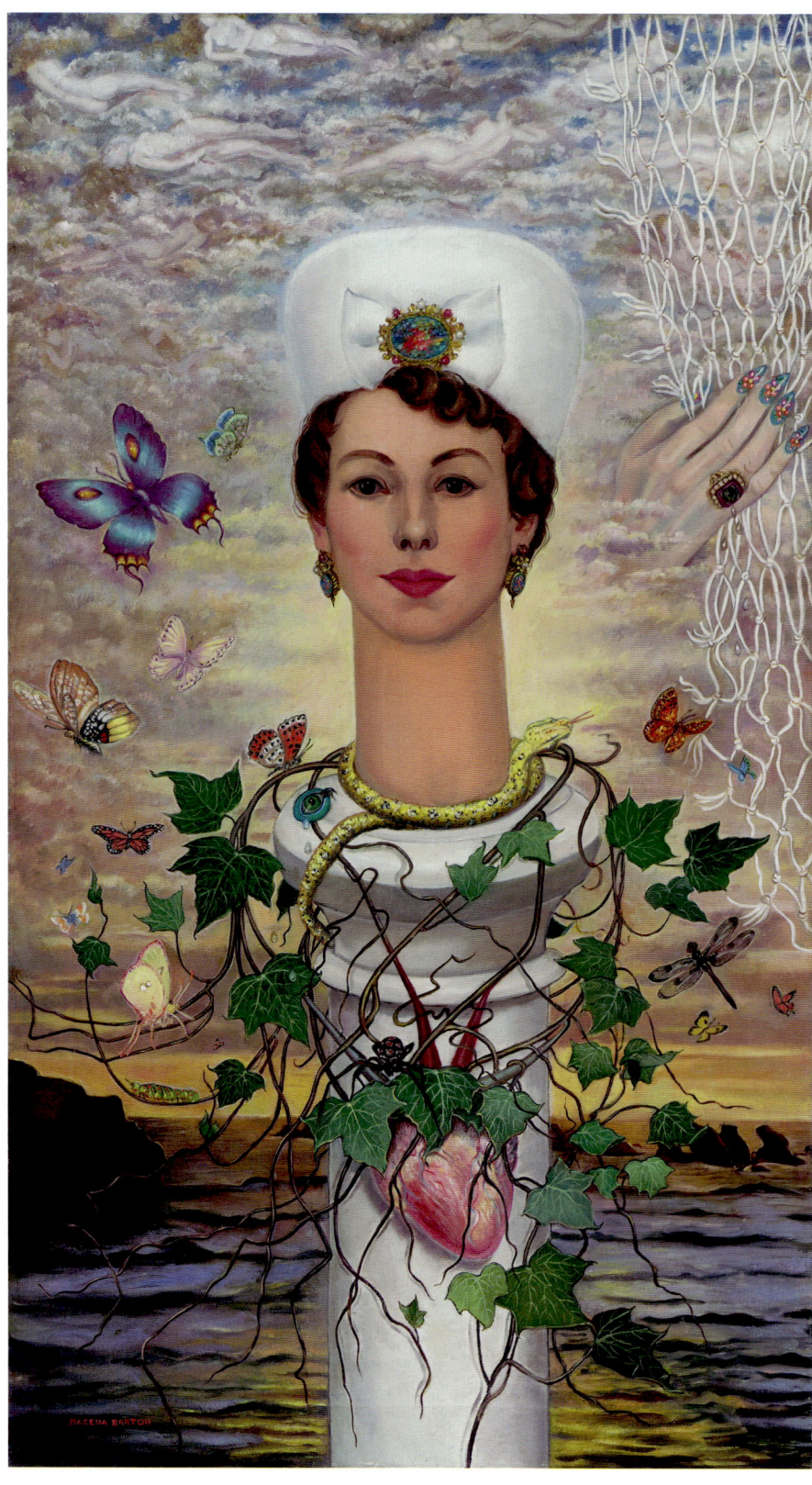

14

Macena Barton
(1901–1986)

Self-Portrait

1940s. Oil on canvas, 36 × 20 in.

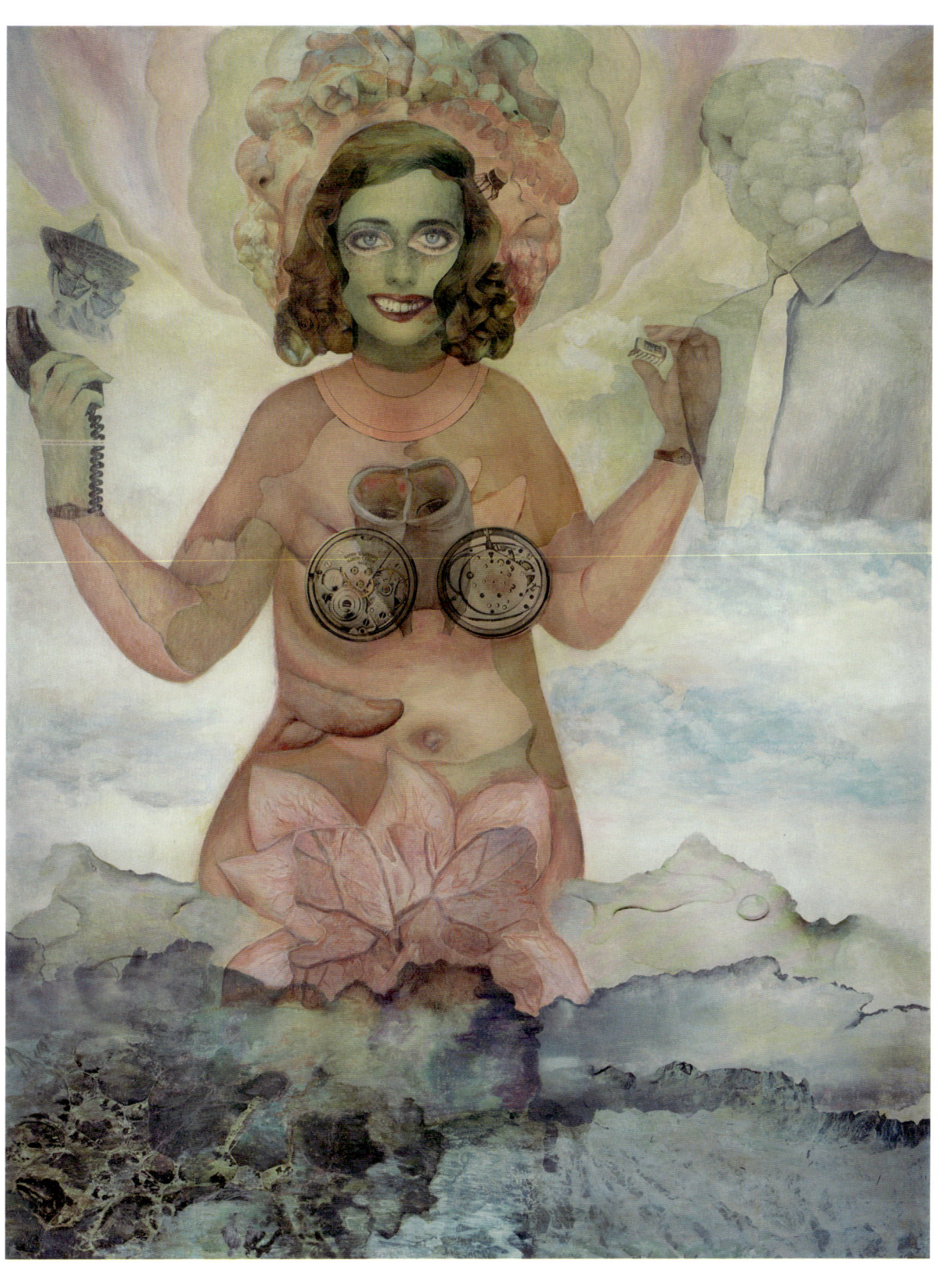

15
Vera Berdich
(1915–2003)

Olympia (A Mechanical Doll)
c. 1960s. Oil on canvas with collage transfer,
48 × 36 in.

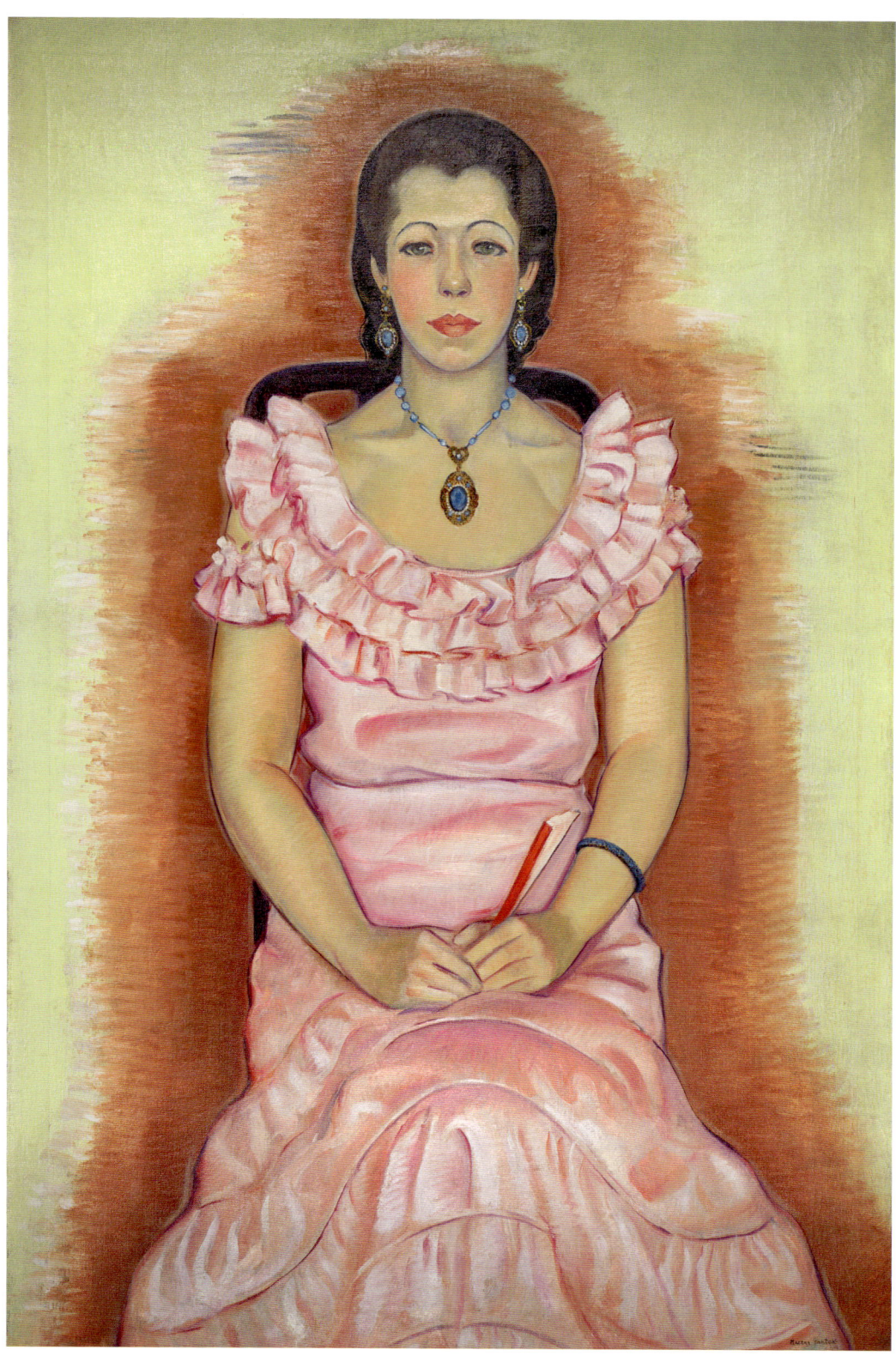

16
Macena Barton

Untitled (Rosanna in pink)
c. 1935. Oil on canvas, 48 × 38 in.

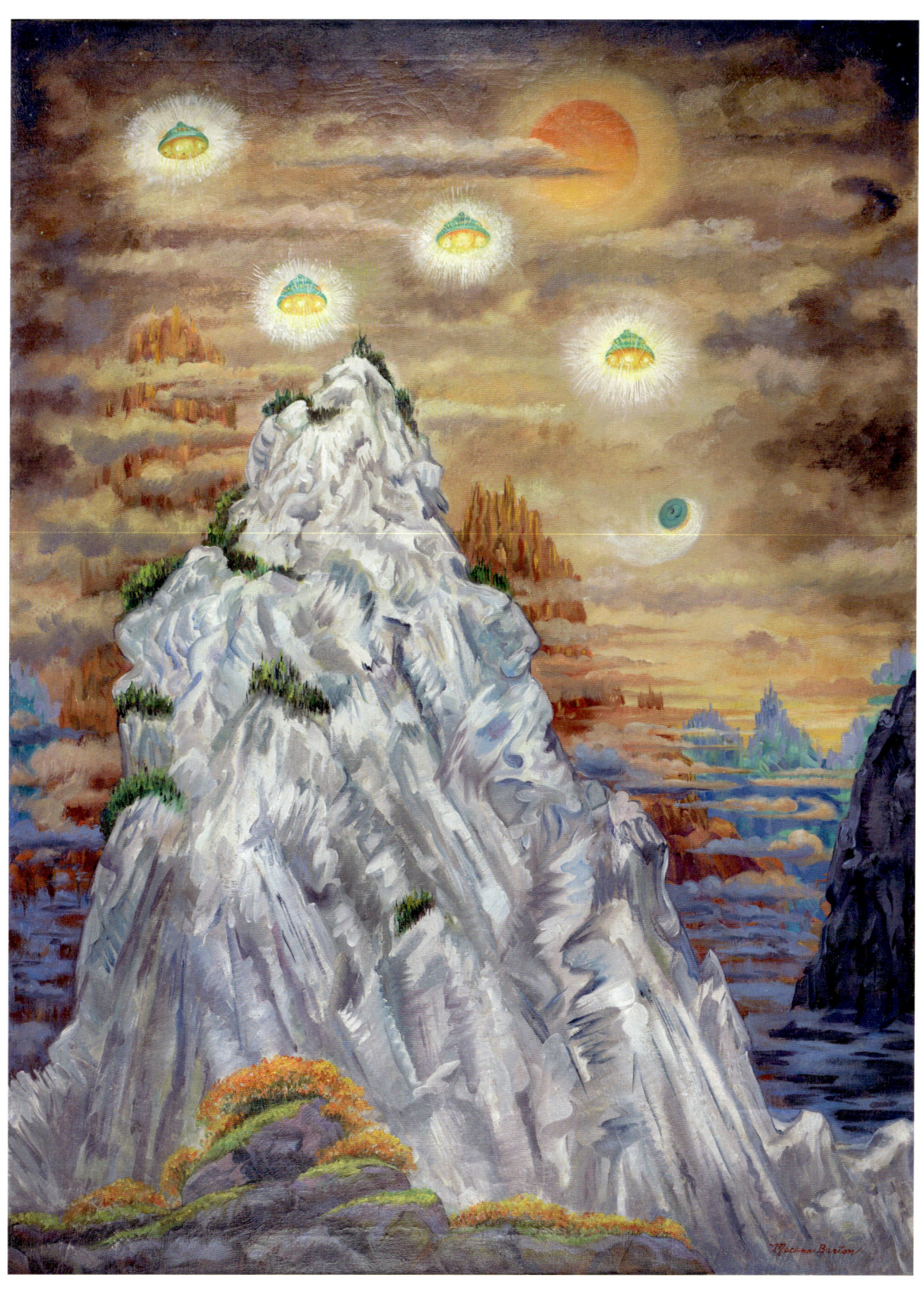

17
Macena Barton

Untitled (Outer space)
1962. Oil on canvas, 50 × 62 in.

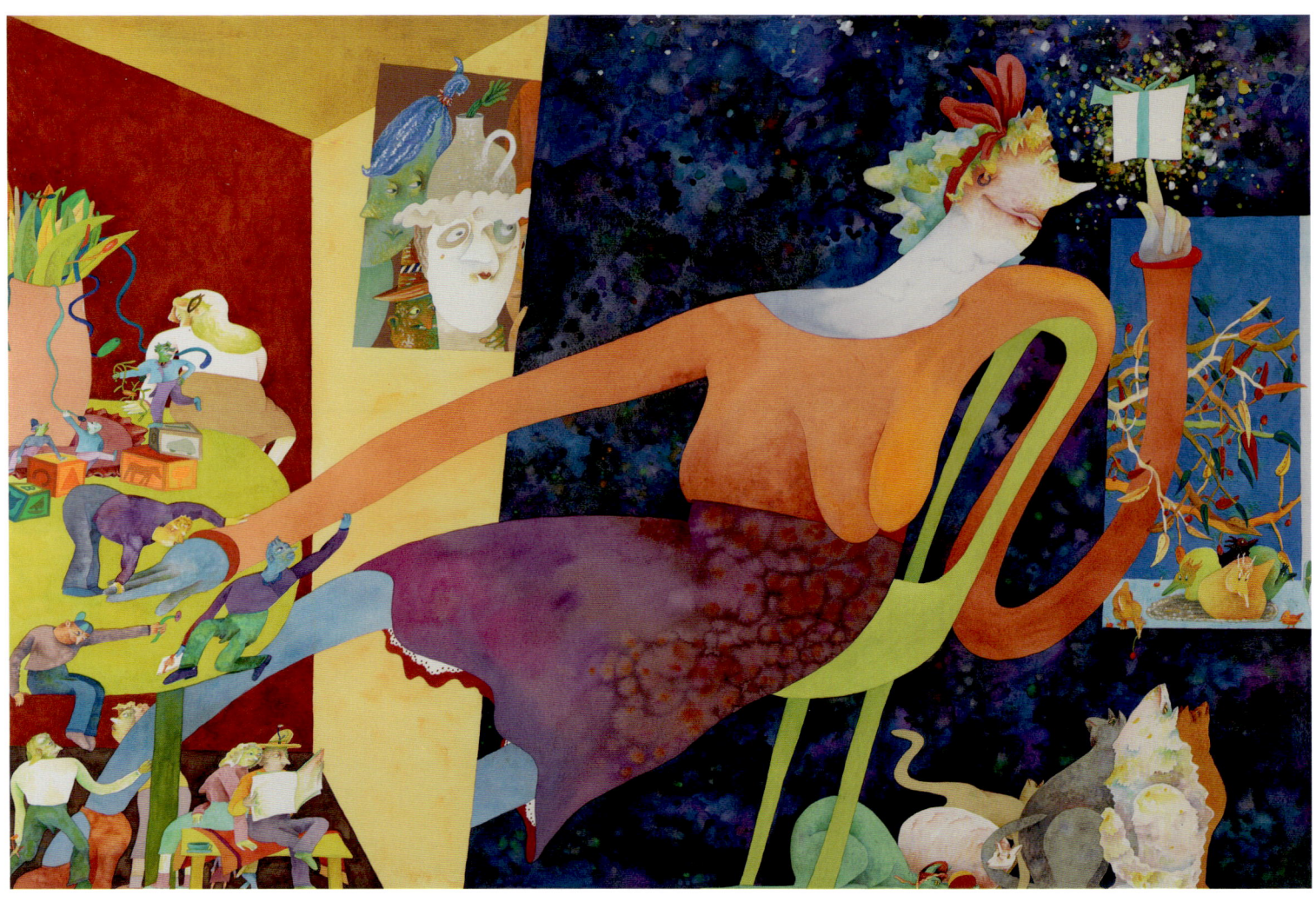

18
Gladys Nilsson
(b. 1940)

Gift Box
1999. Watercolor and gouache on paper,
40¾ × 60 in.

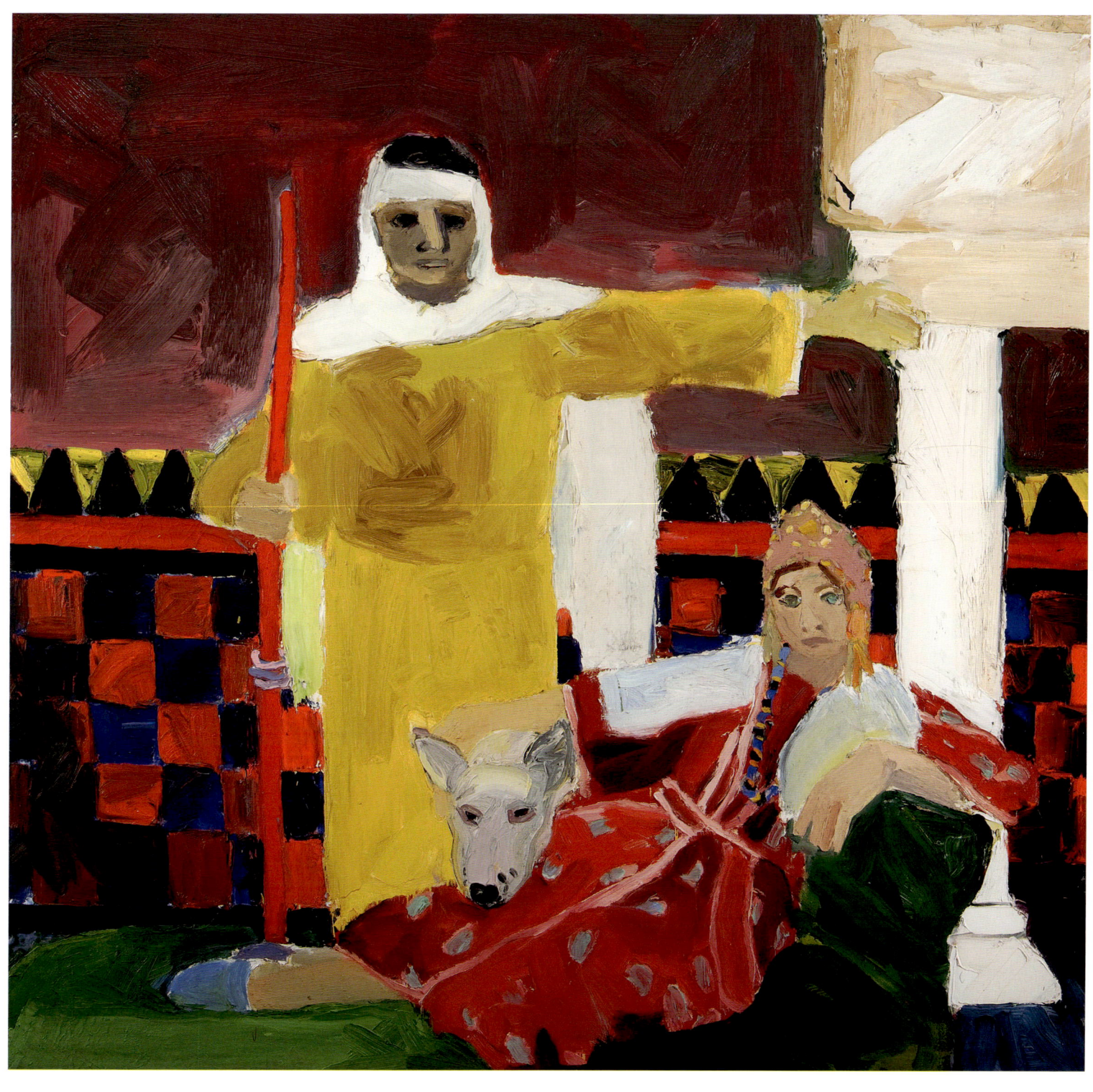

19
Joan Brown

Bob, Sultana, and Guard
1961. Enamel on canvas, 72 × 72 in.

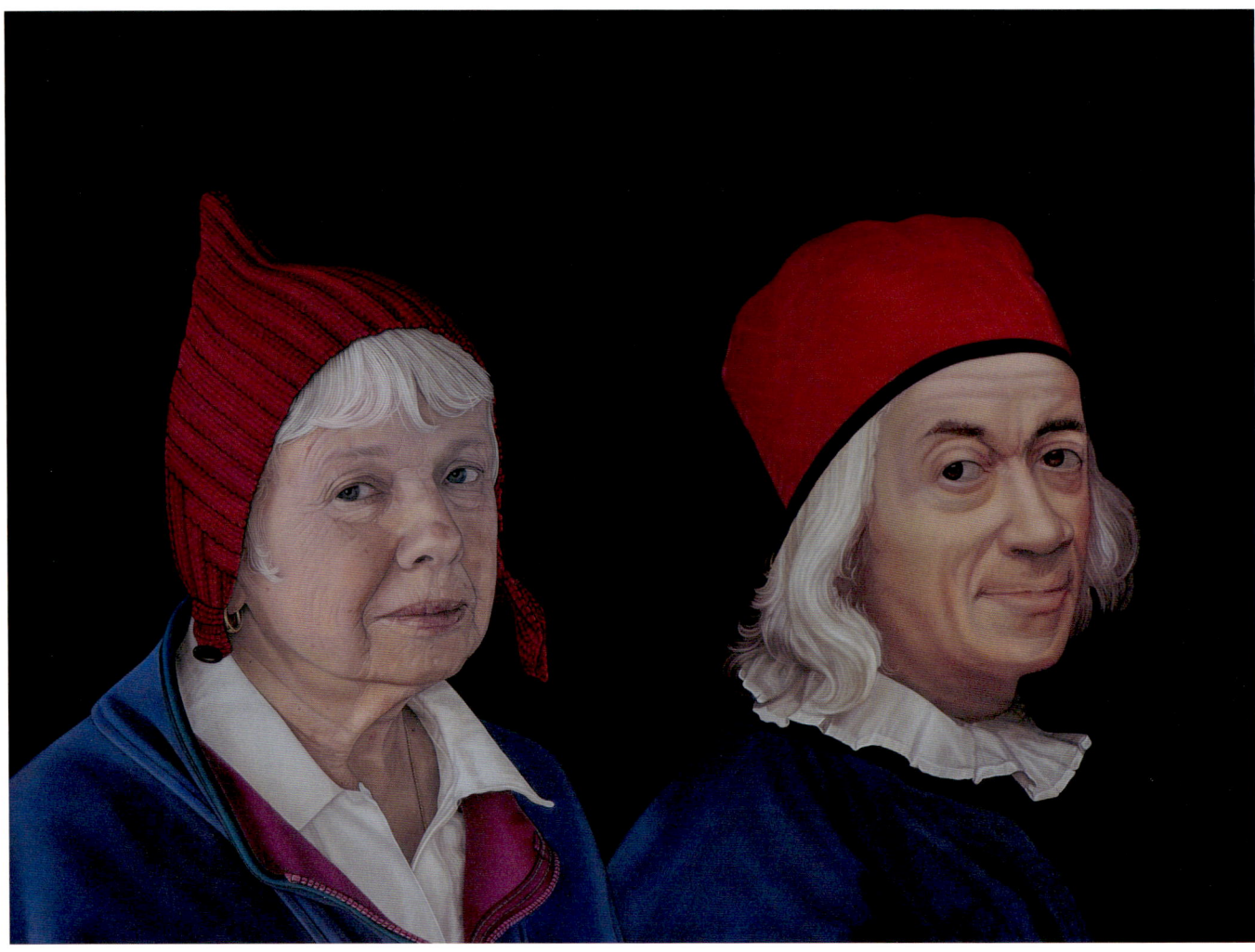

Jane Lund

*Artists of a Certain Age: Self-Portrait
with Jean-Étienne Liotard, 1702-1789*
2016. Pastel on paper, 20 × 27 in.

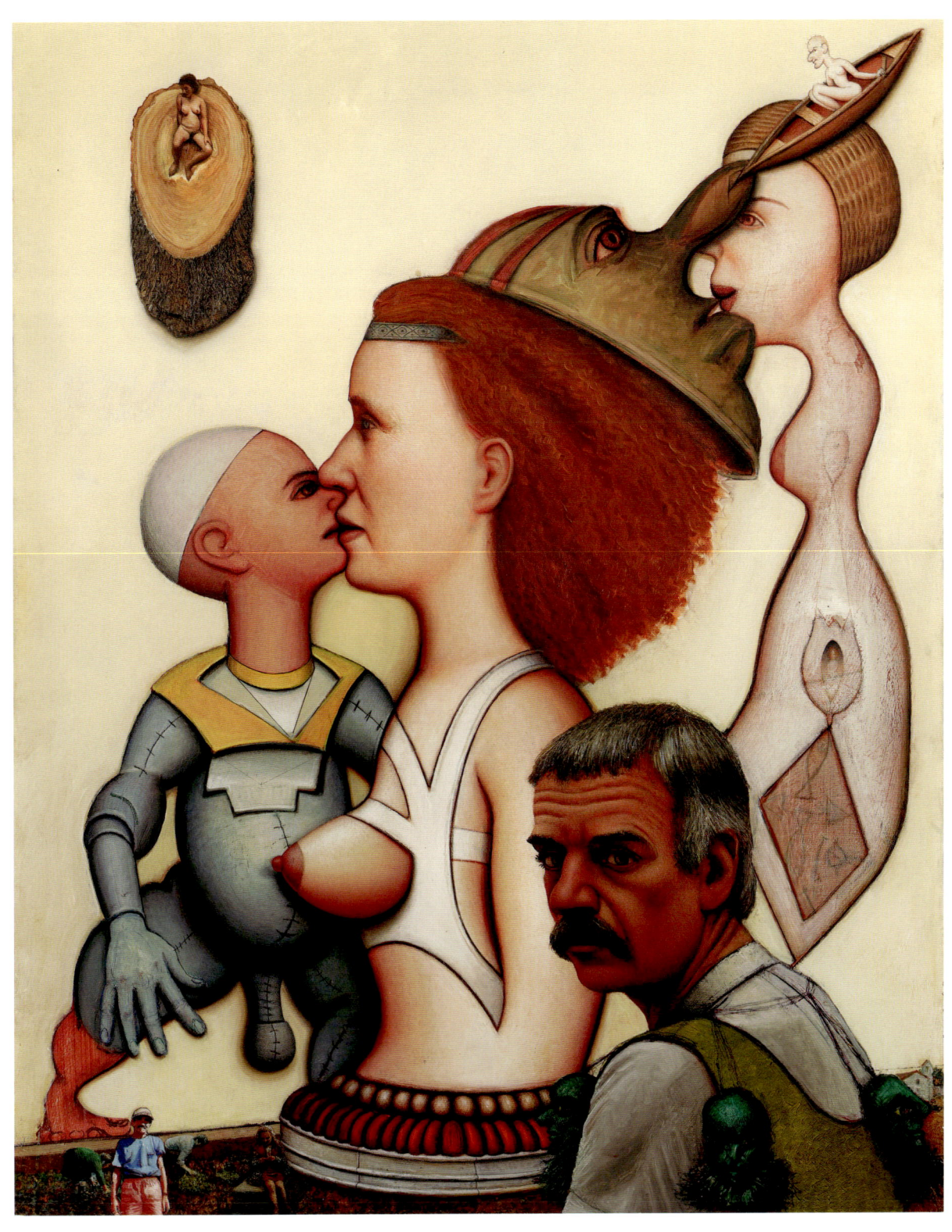

21

Gregory Gillespie

Self-Portrait with Mother and Son
1991–92. Oil on panel, 48 × 37¼ in.

93

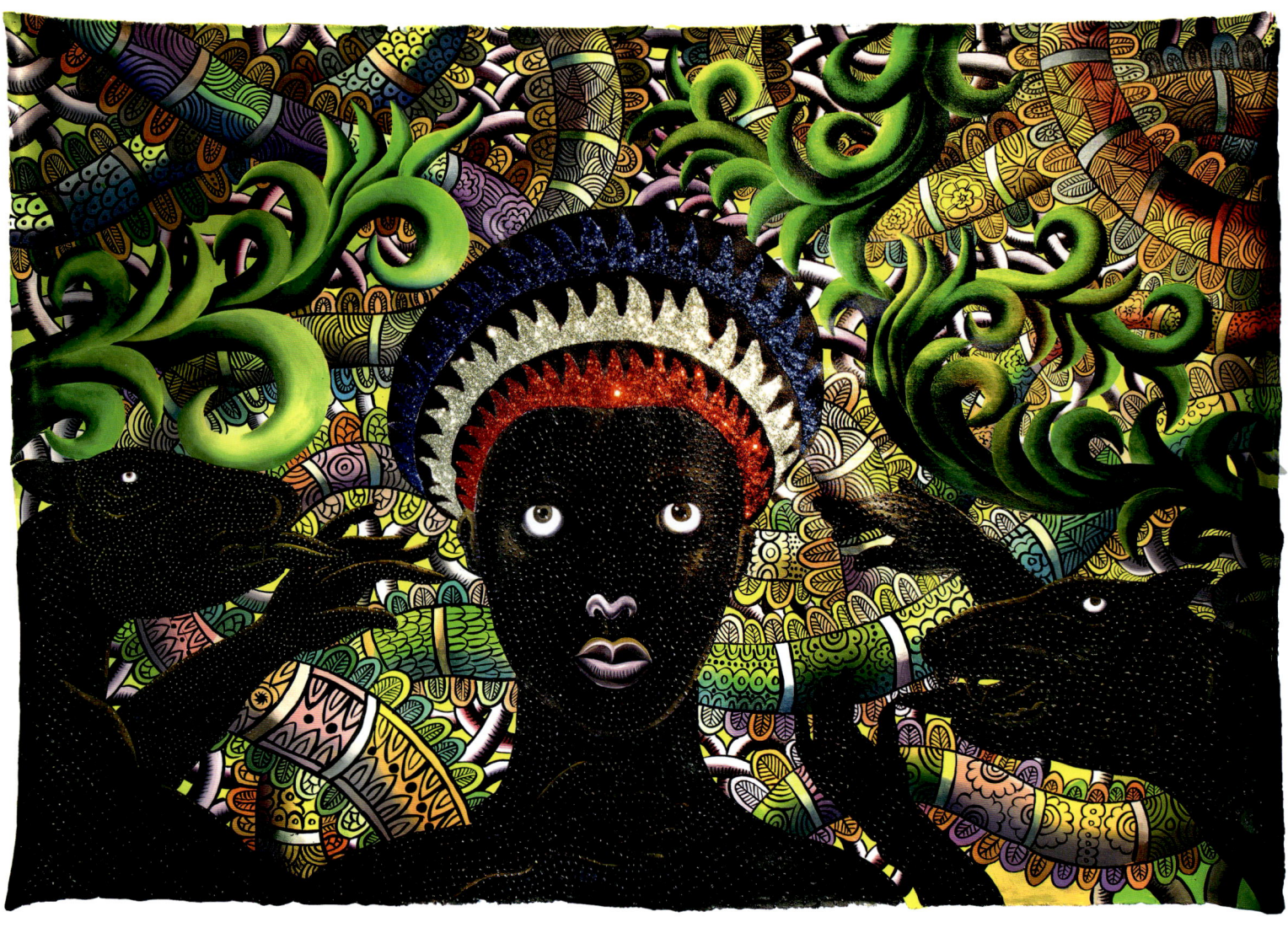

22

Henry Bermudez   *Miss America*

(b. 1951)   2019. Acrylic and glitter on canvas, 50 × 72 in.

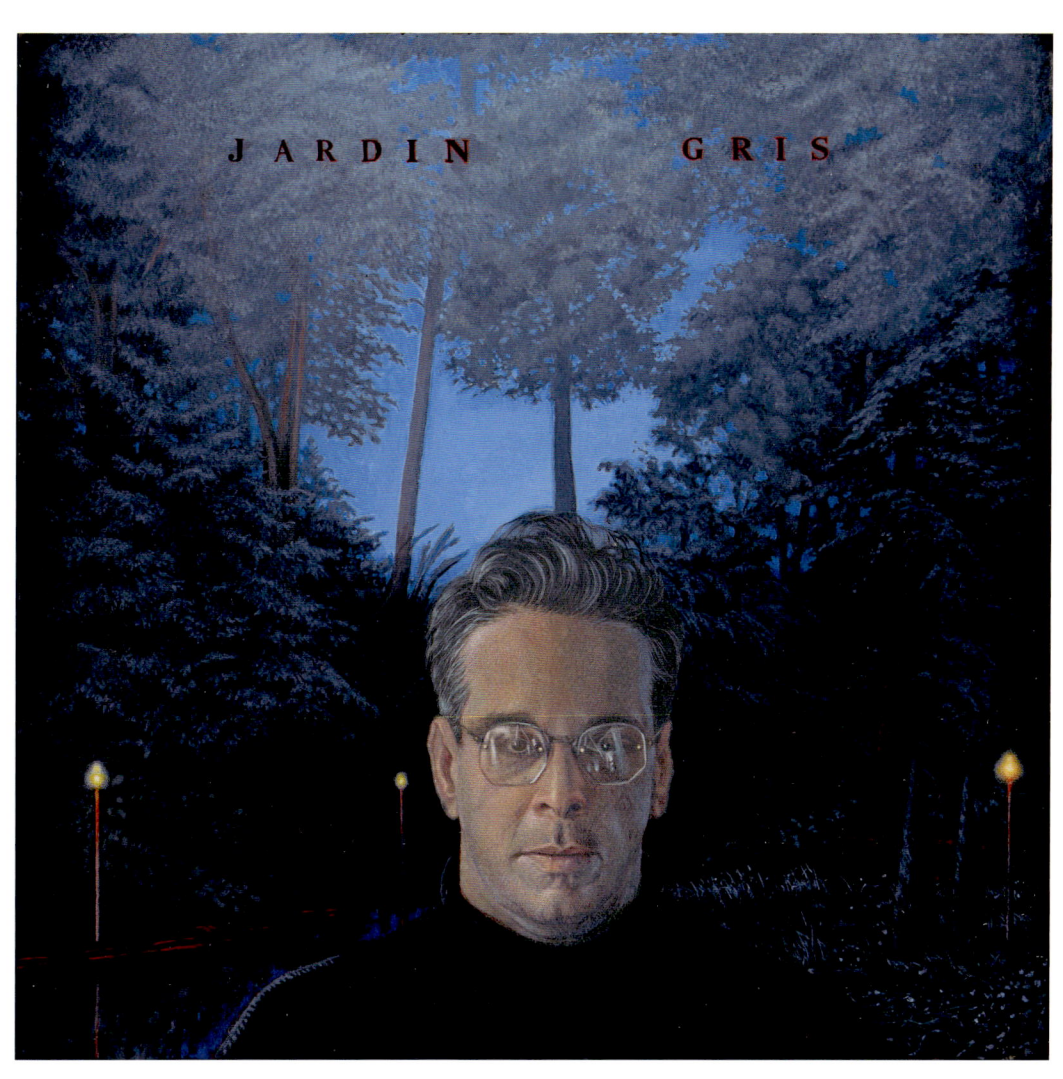

23
Juan González
(1945–1993)

Jardin Gris
1989. Acrylic and tempera on canvas,
15¾ × 15¾ in.

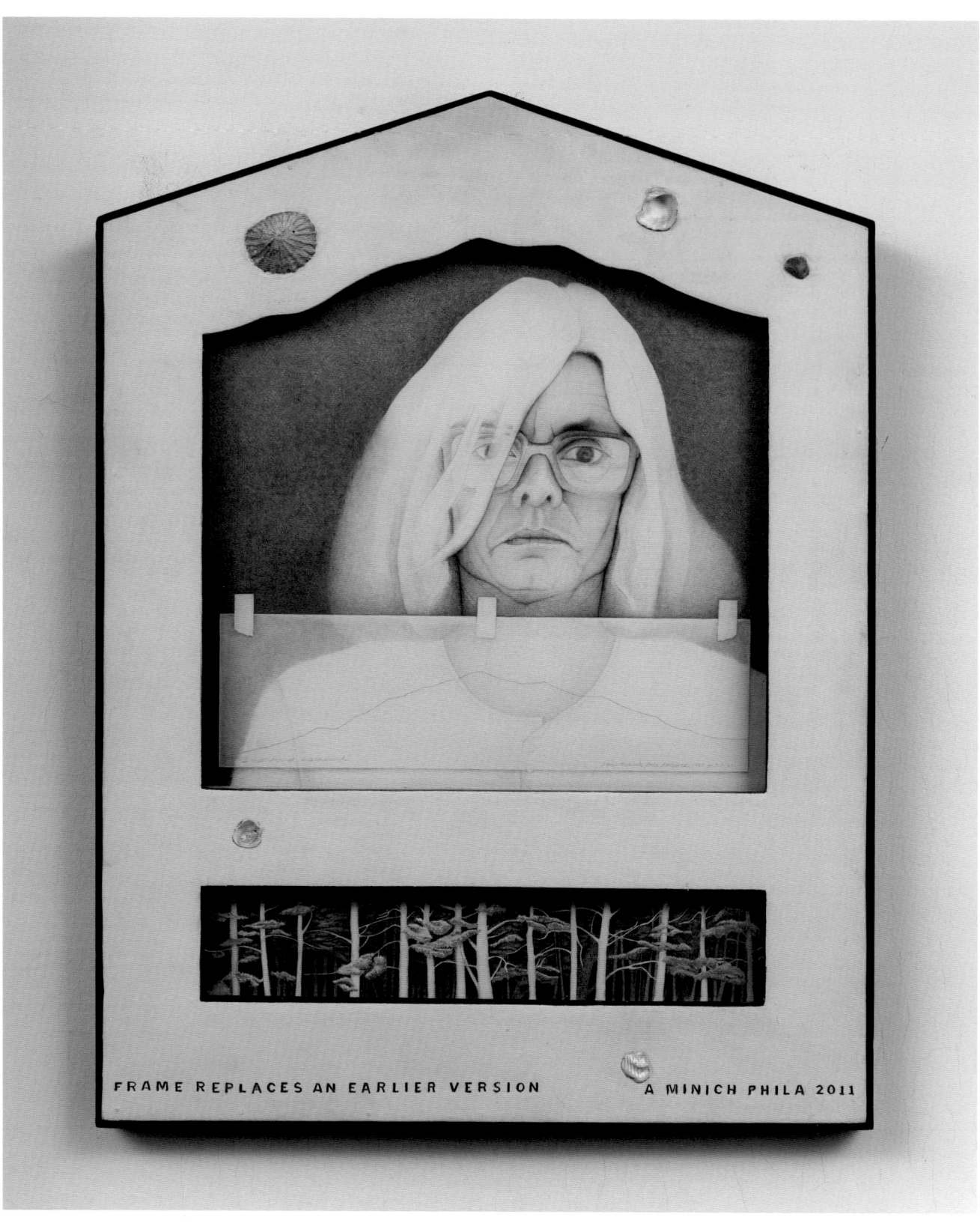

FRAME REPLACES AN EARLIER VERSION   A MINICH PHILA 2011

24
Anne Minich
(b. 1934)

Imposition at Monadnock
1988 and 2011. Graphite and colored pencil on
paper, wood frame with shells, 26¾ × 20 in.

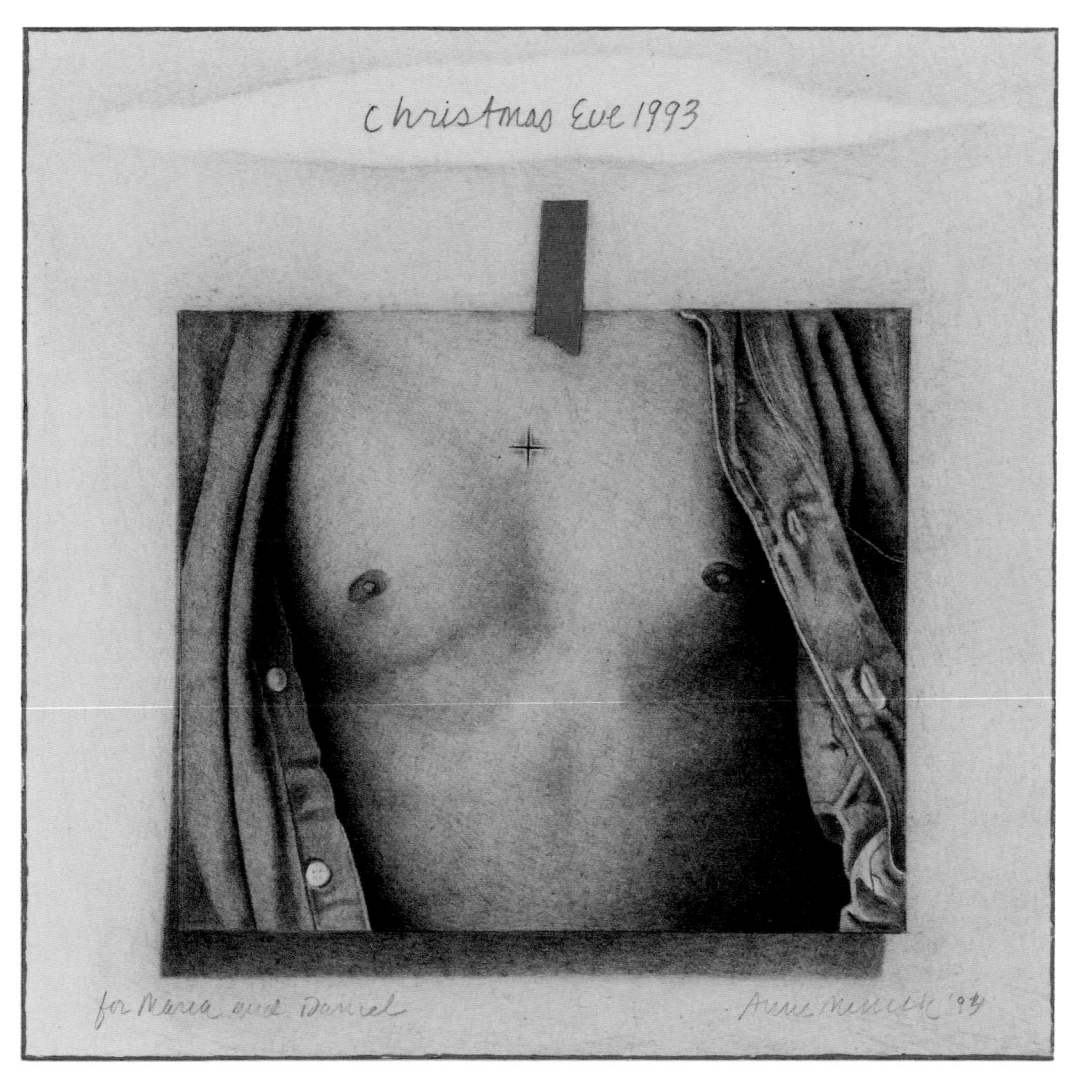

Christmas Eve 1993, for Maria and Daniel
1993. Graphite and gold paint on artist's
board, 8 × 8 in.

Anne Minich

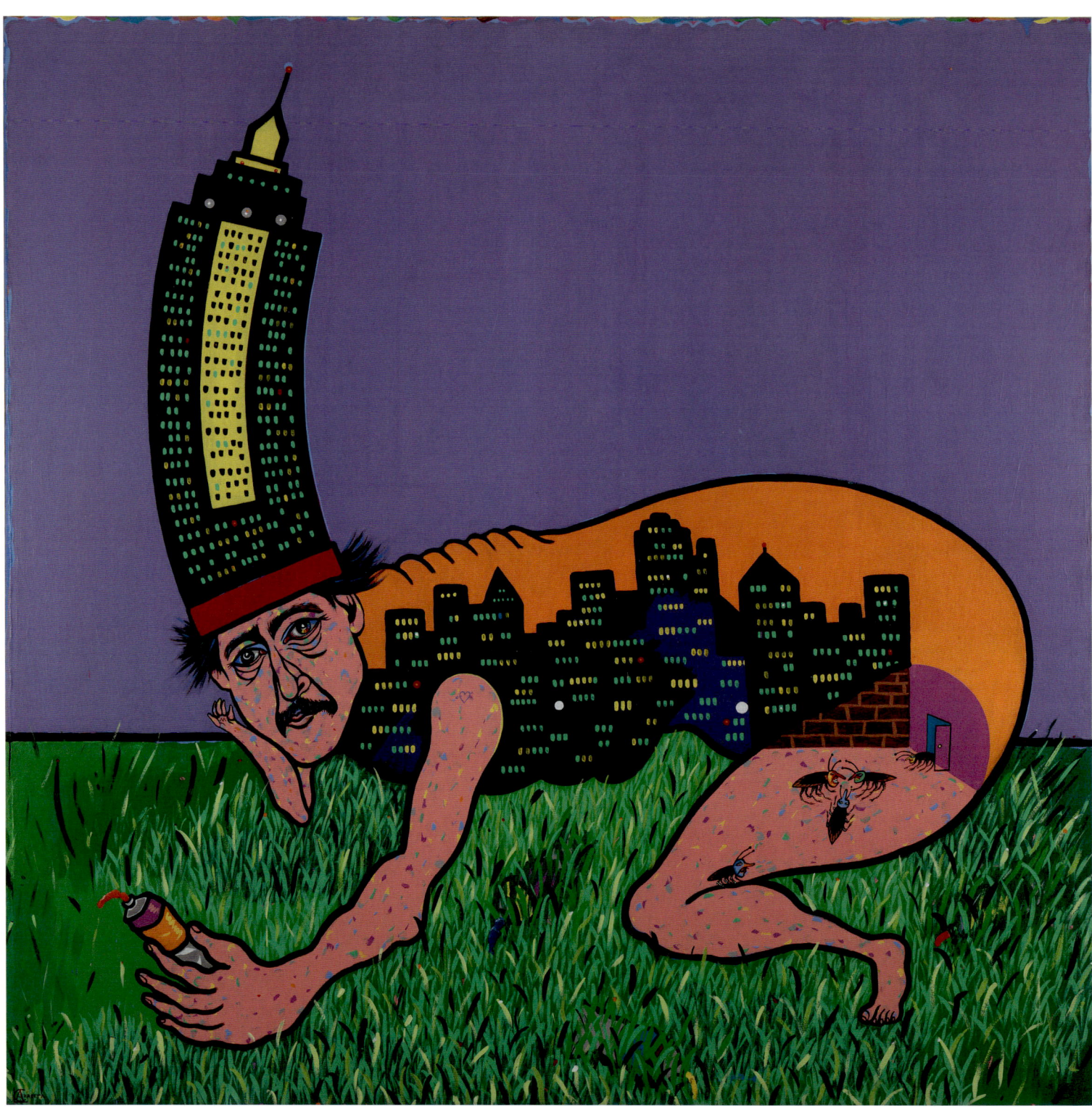

26

**Luis Cruz
Azaceta**

Self-Portrait as Cockroach
1981. Acrylic on canvas, 66 × 66 in.

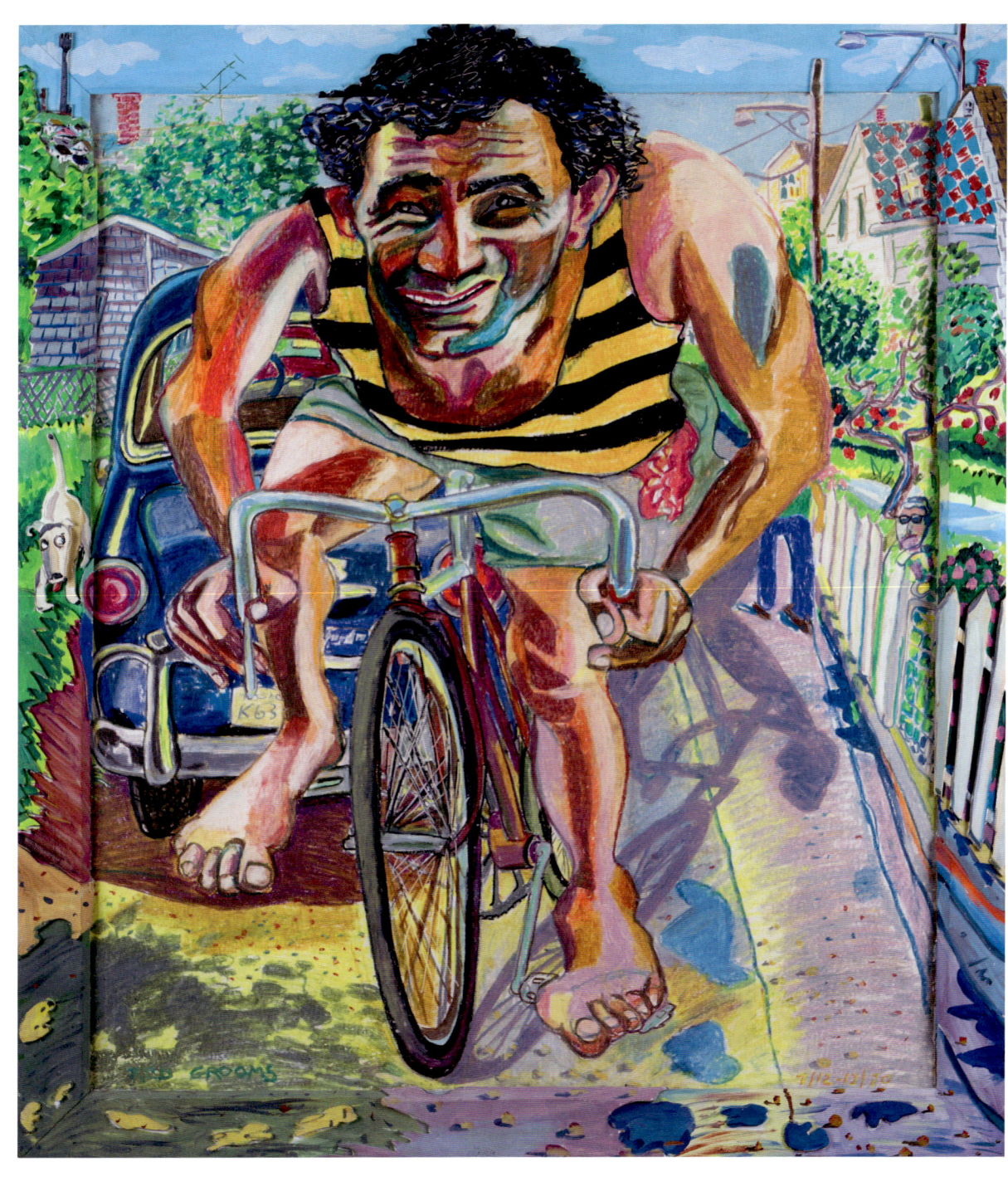

27

Red Grooms

(b. 1937)

P'town Bicycle (Arthur Cohen)
1971–74. Crayon on paper and acrylic on
wood, 56½ × 49 in.

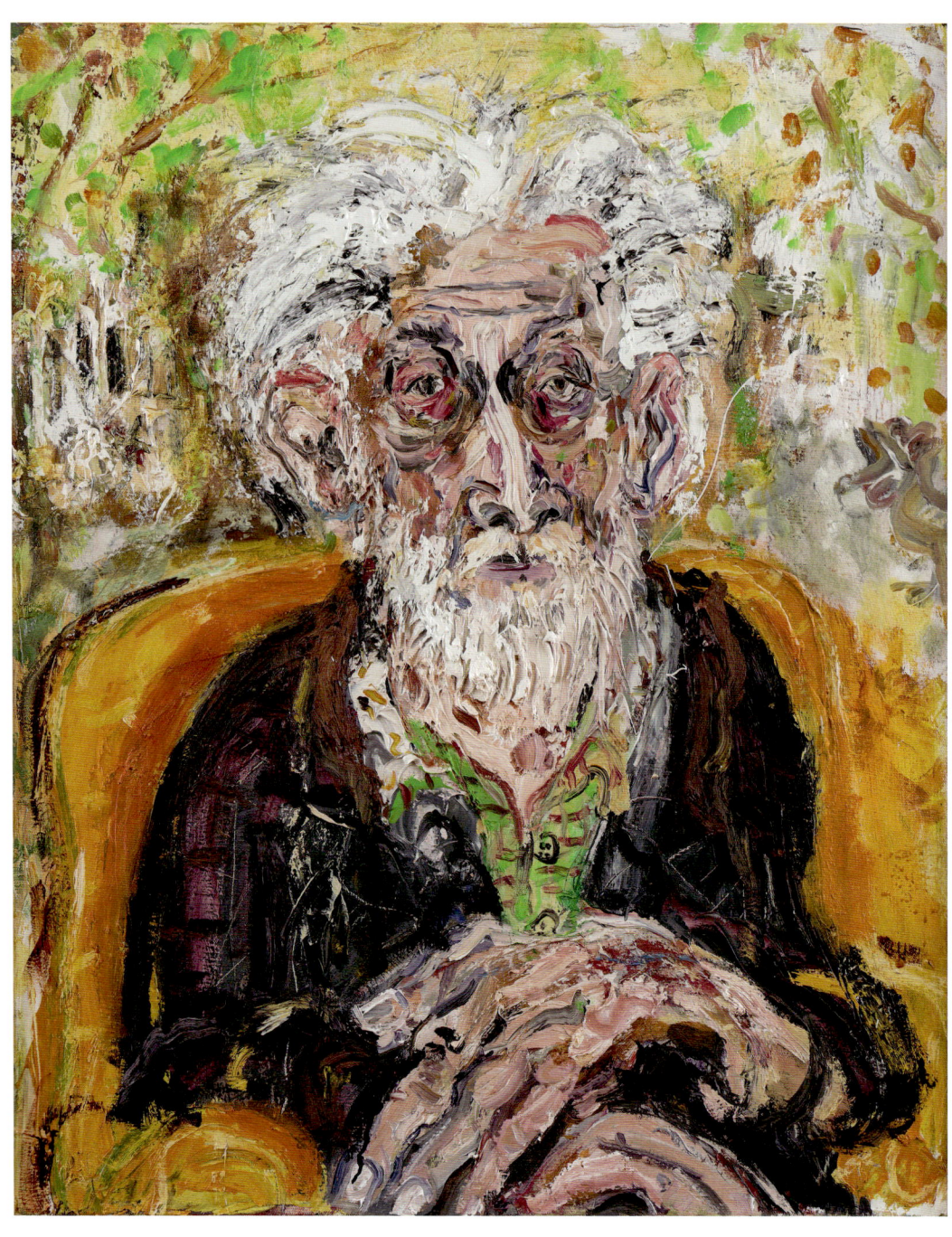

28
Sam Messer
(b. 1955)

Jon in Yellow Chair
1992. Oil on canvas, 28 × 22 in.

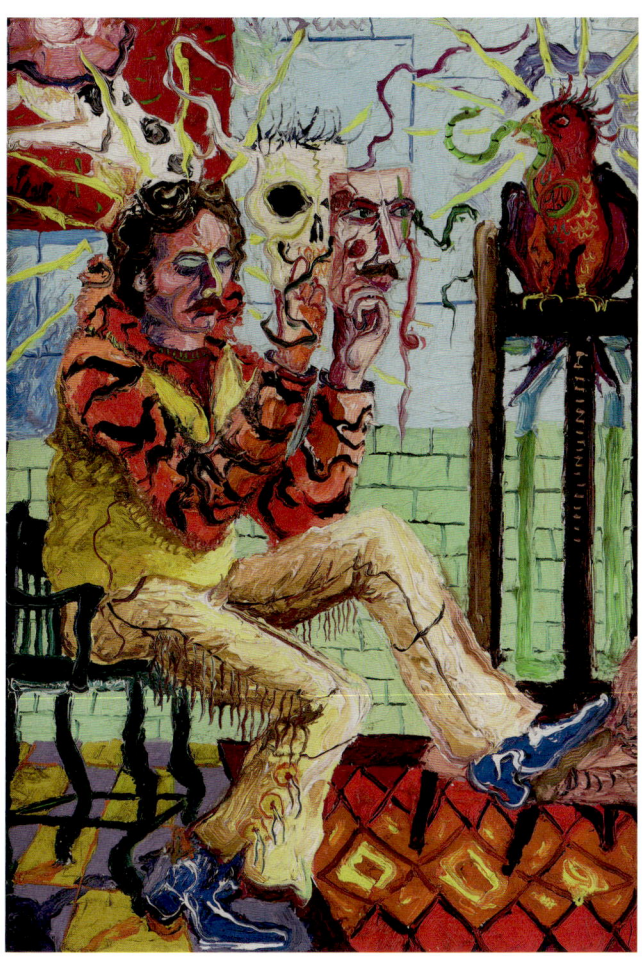

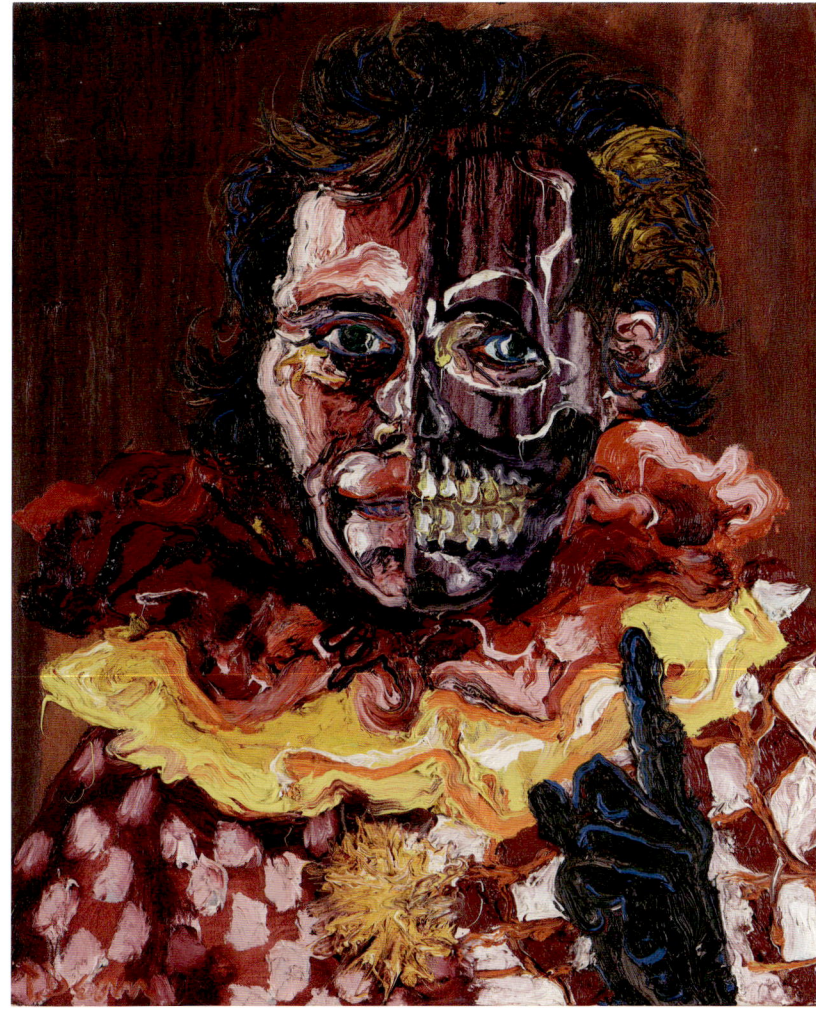

29
Peter Dean
(1934–1993)

Untitled (Self-portrait with
two masks)
n.d. (mid-1970s). Oil on Masonite,
15¾ × 10½ in.

30
Peter Dean

Portrait of the Artist
1981. Oil on canvas, 27 × 22 in.

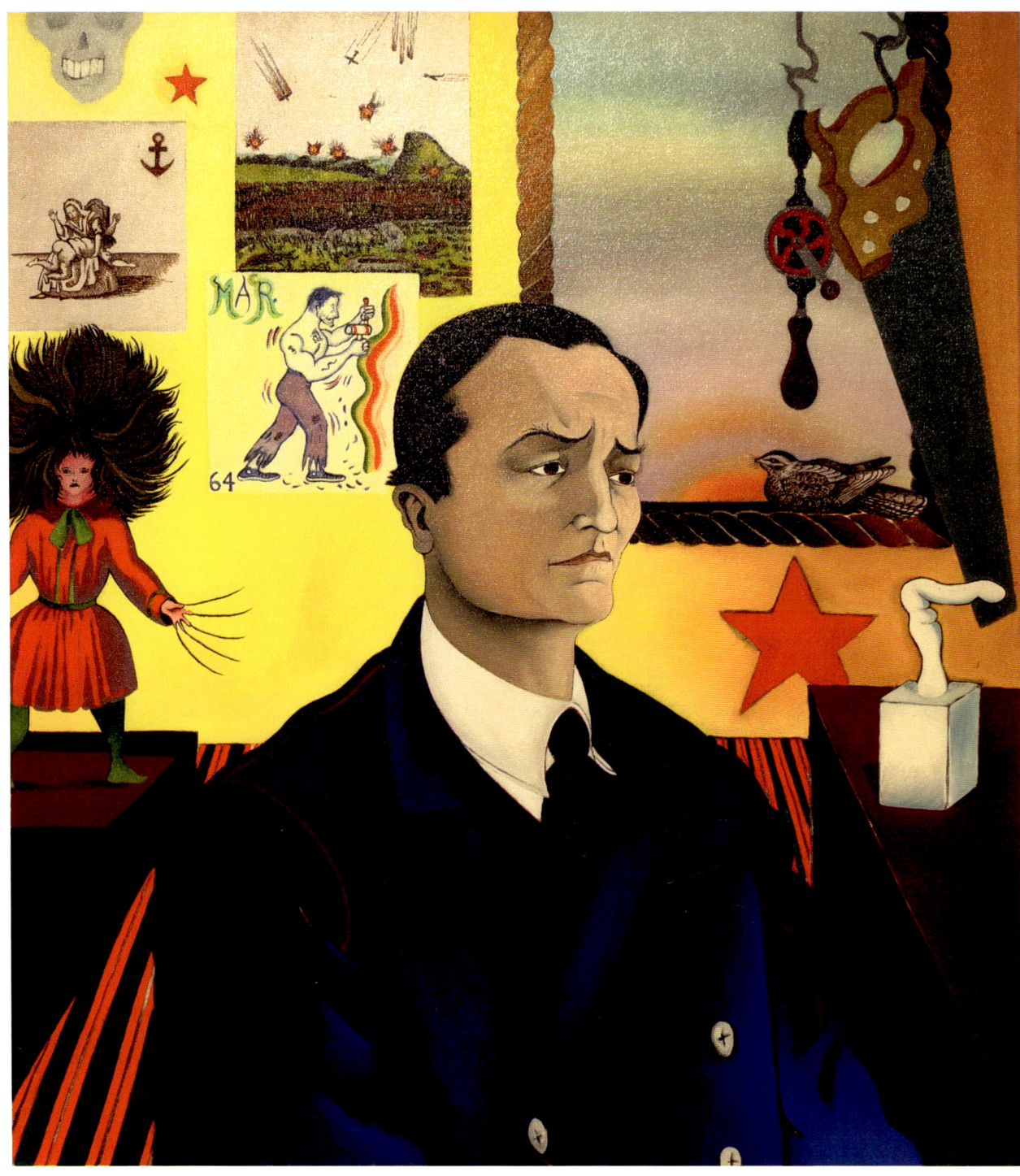

31
Joanna Beall
(1935–1997)

Portrait of HCW(esterman)
1963. Oil on canvas, 46 × 40 in.

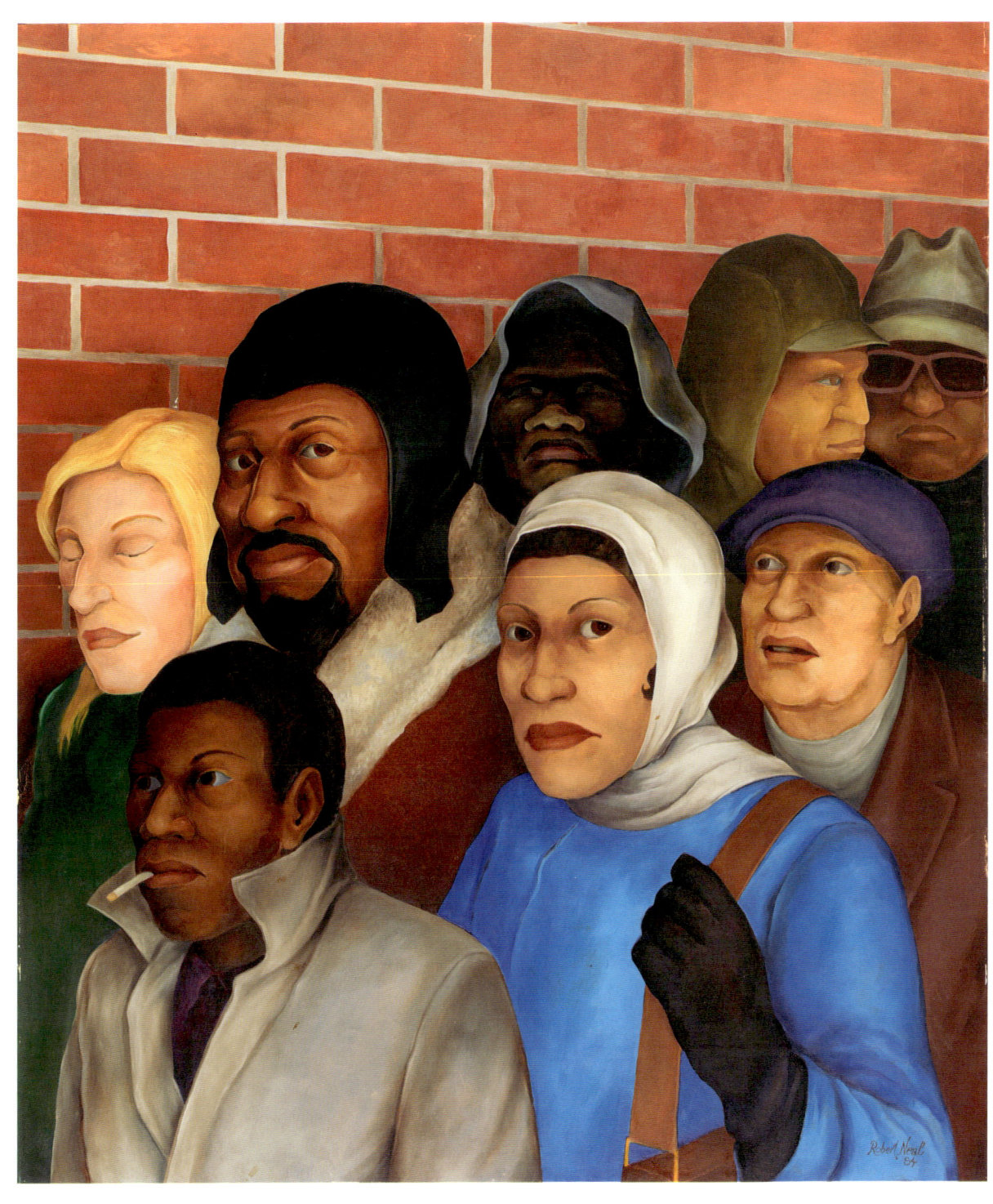

32

Robert Neal

(1916–1987)

Cheese and Butter Line

1984. Oil on canvas, 36 × 30 in.

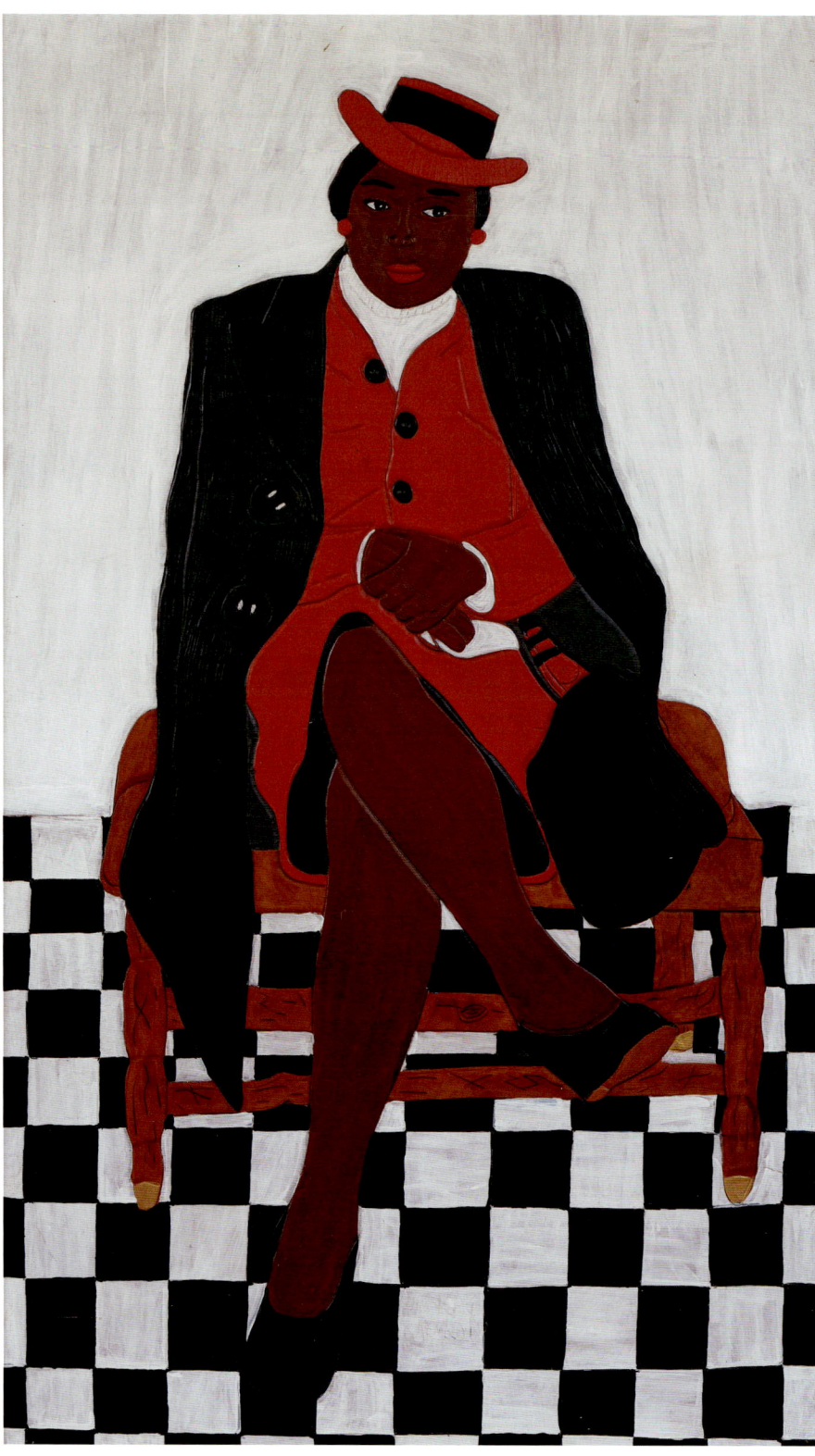

33

Winfred Rembert   *Sugar Cane*

(1945–2021)   2009. Dye on tooled leather, 52 × 29½ in.

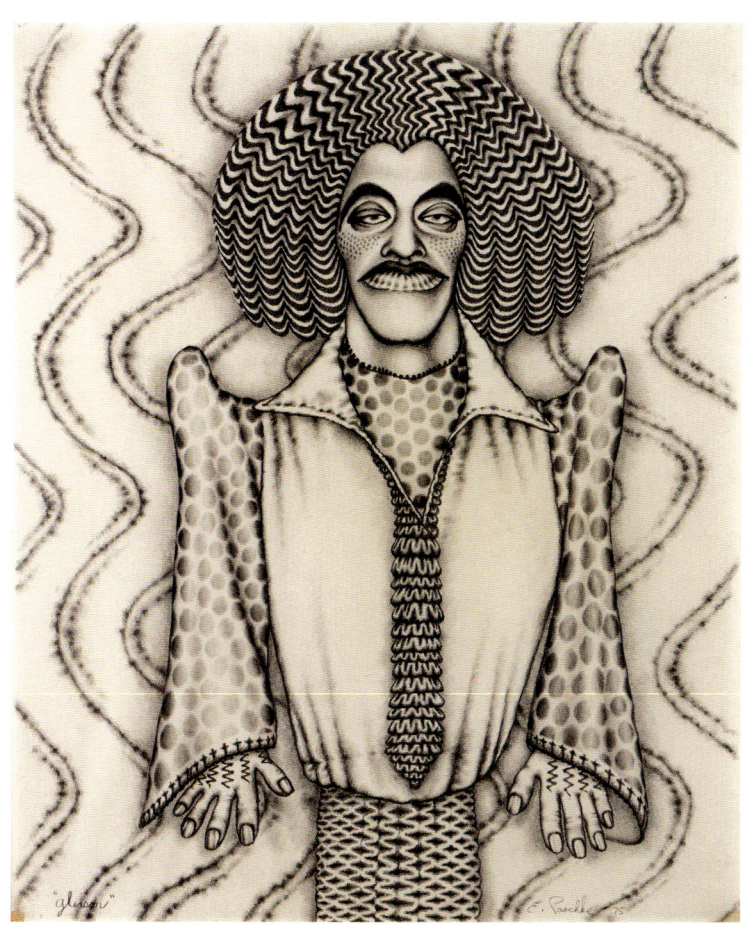

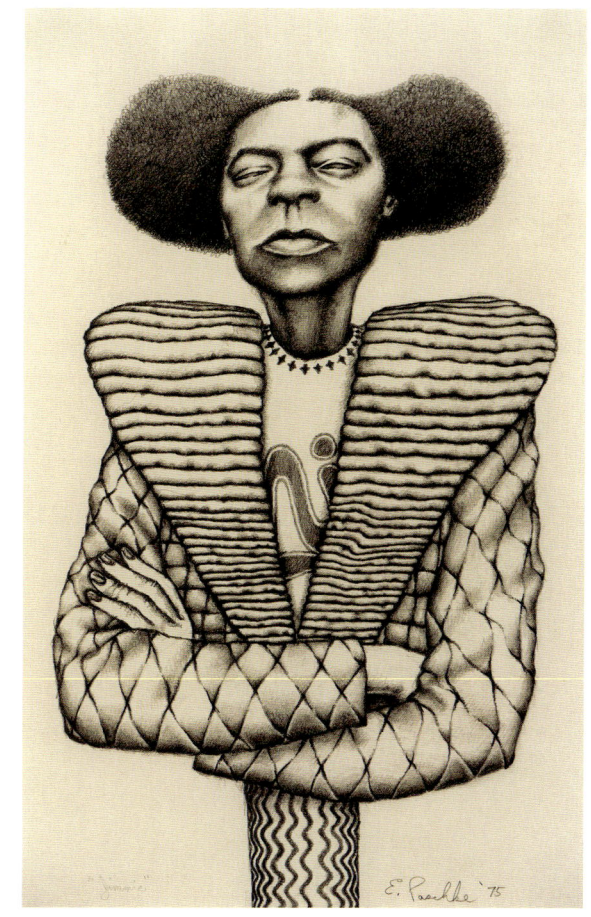

34

Ed Paschke

(1939–2004)

Gleason

1975. Graphite on paper, 29 × 23 in.

35

Ed Paschke

Jimmie

1975. Graphite on paper,
22 × 13½ in.

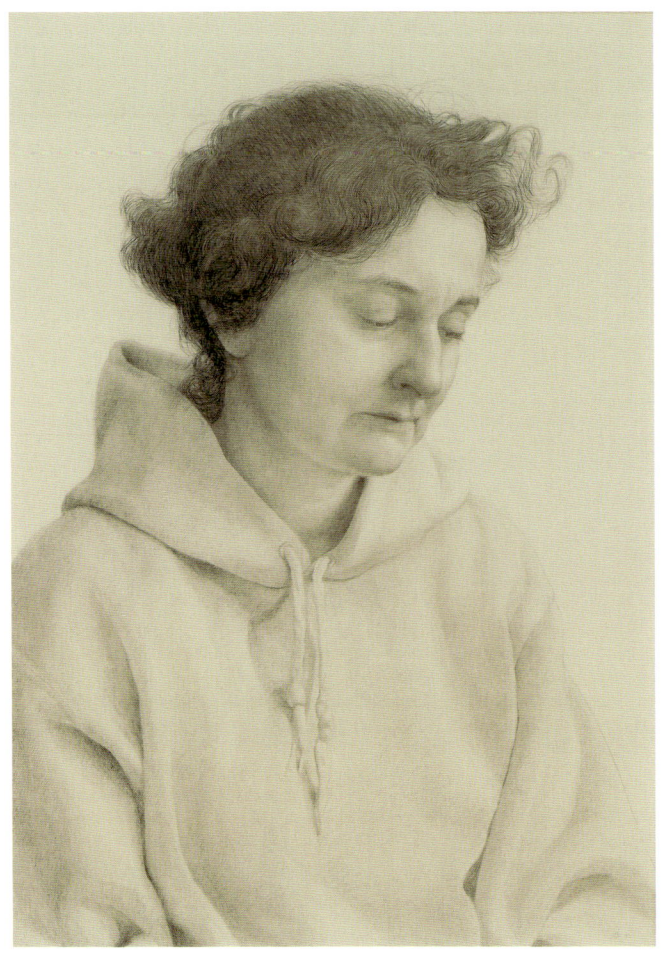

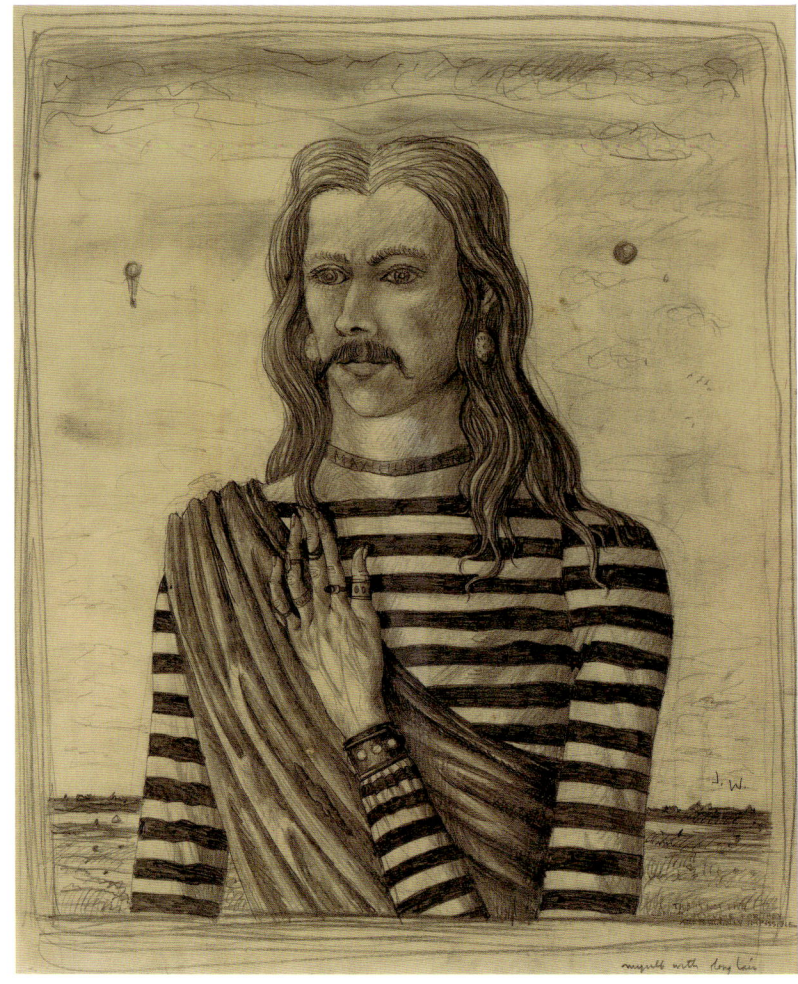

36
Deborah Kravitz   *Self-Portrait*
(b. 1951)   1996. Pencil on panel, 14½ × 10¼ in.

37
John Wilde   *Myself with Long Hair*
(1919–2006)   1940. Graphite on paper, 20¾ × 18 in.

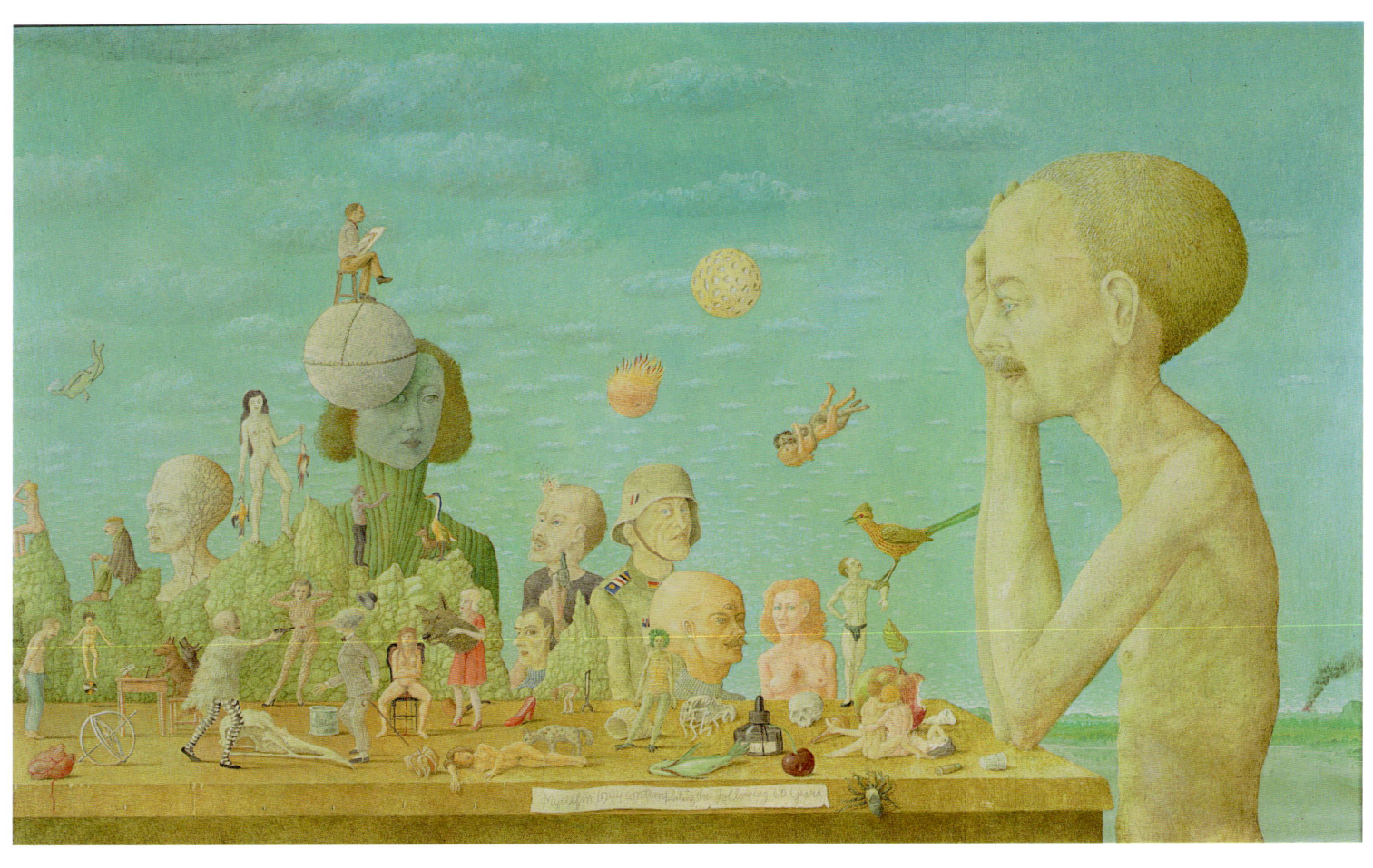

John Wilde

*Myself in 1944 Contemplating
the Following 60 Years*
2004. Oil on panel, 24 × 40 in.

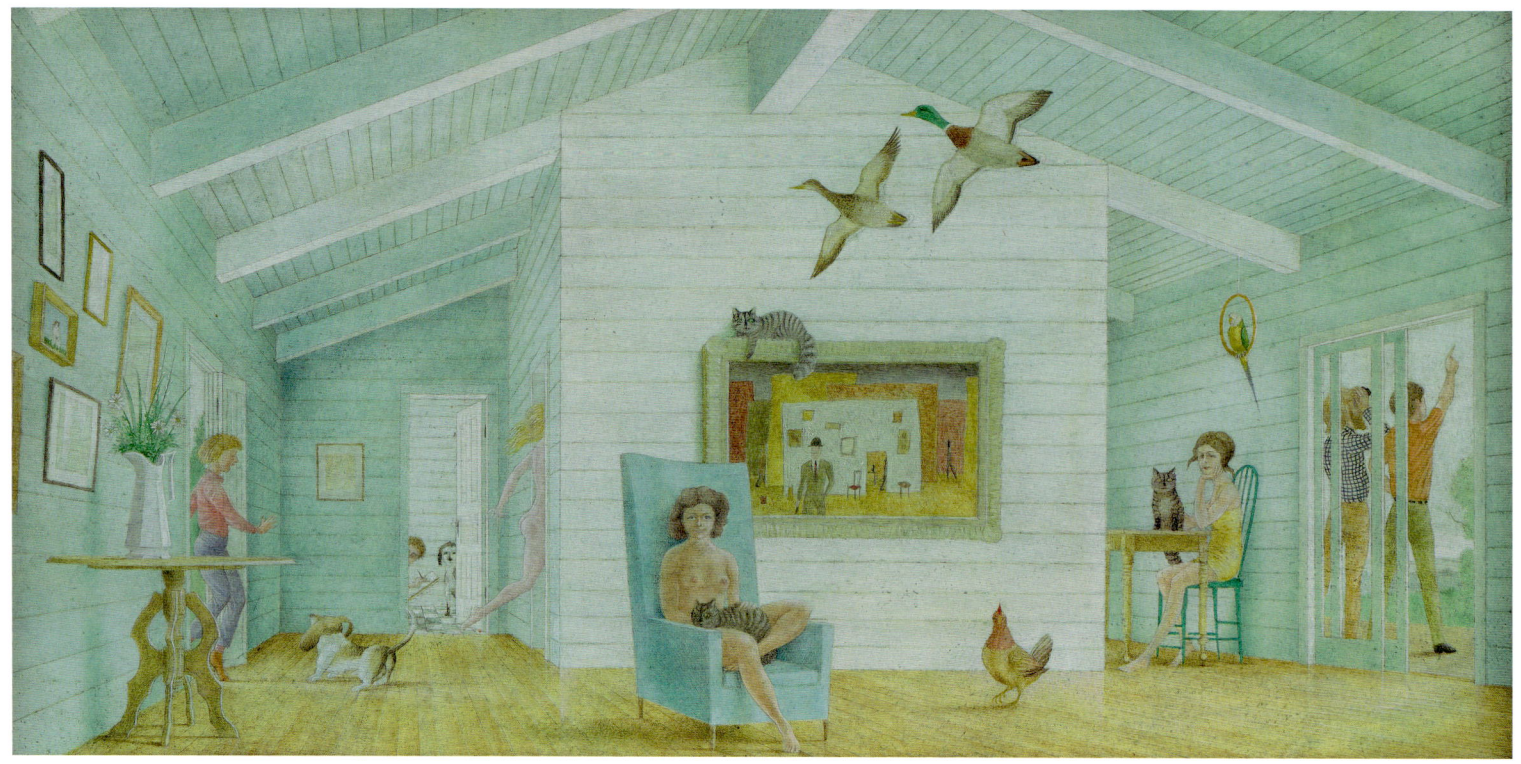

39
John Wilde

Family Portrait I, Inside
1971. Oil on panel, 9¼ × 19¼ in.

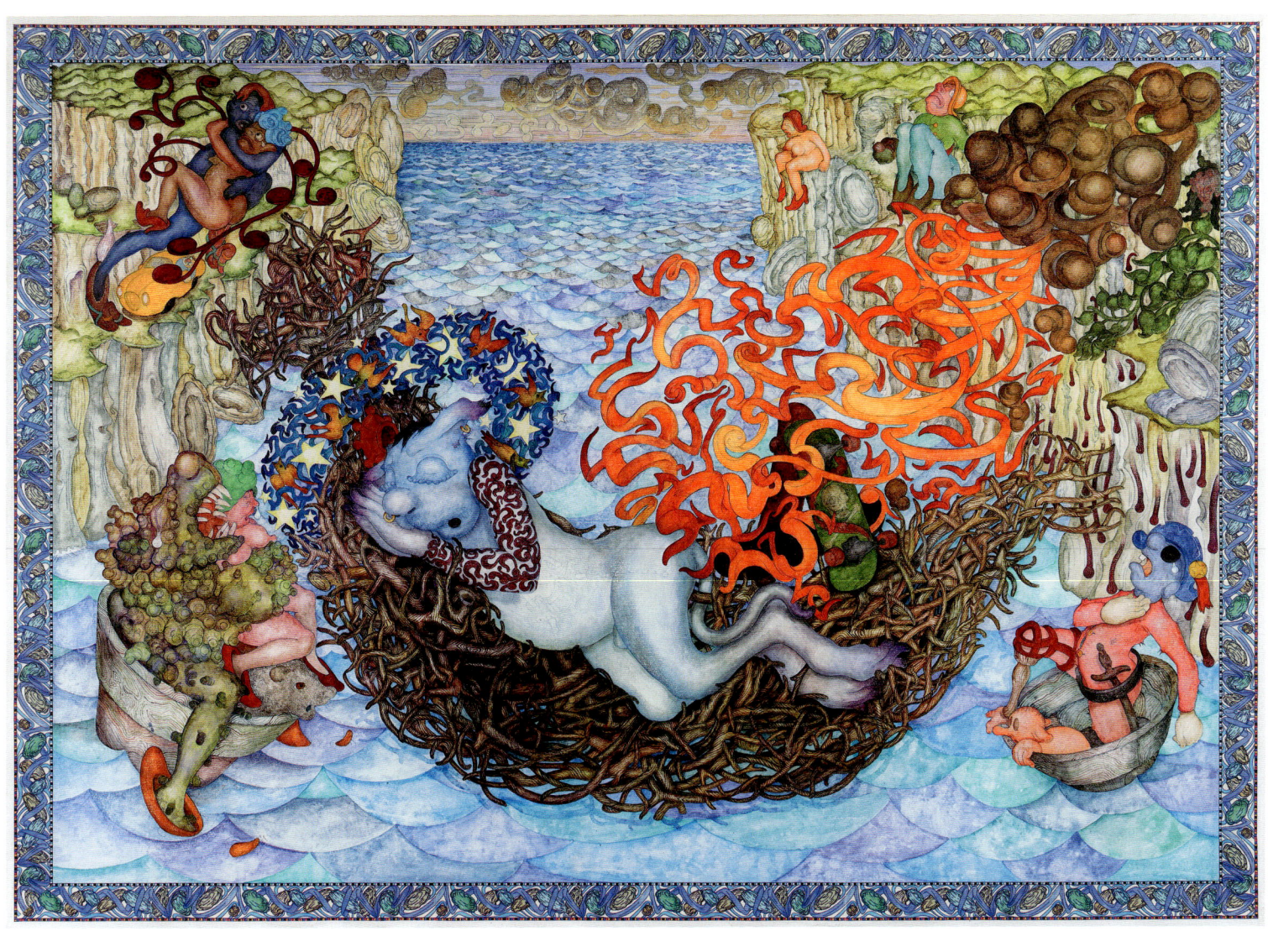

40
James Barsness
(b. 1954)

Bifrost Bridge
2005–6. Acrylic, ink, and paper on canvas,
51½ × 69½ in.

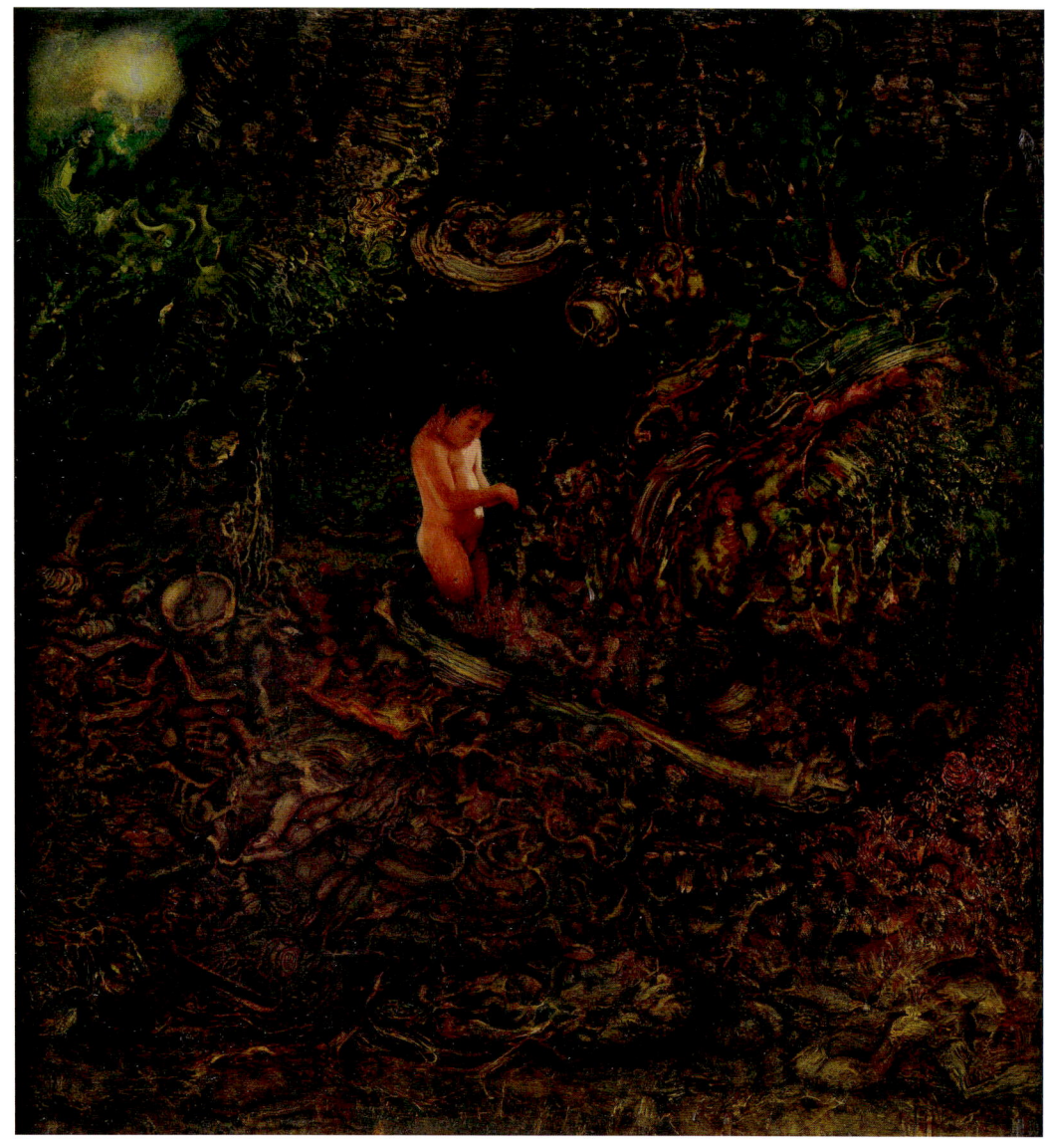

41
Gregory Gillespie   *Julianna*
1991. Oil on panel, 16½ × 15 in.

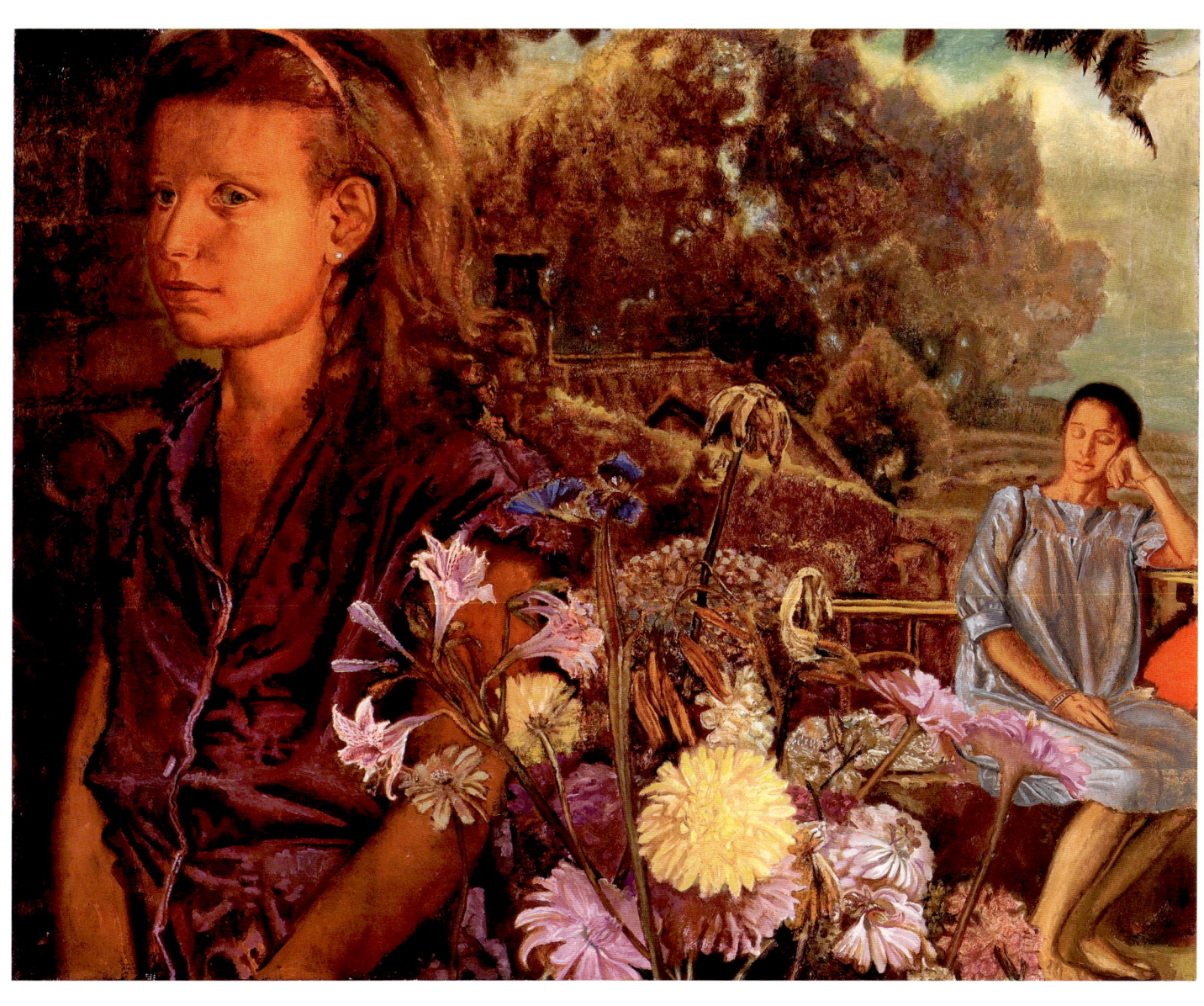

42
Frank Galuszka
(b. 1947)

Greta with Flowers
c. 1985. Oil on canvas, 26 × 32¼ in.

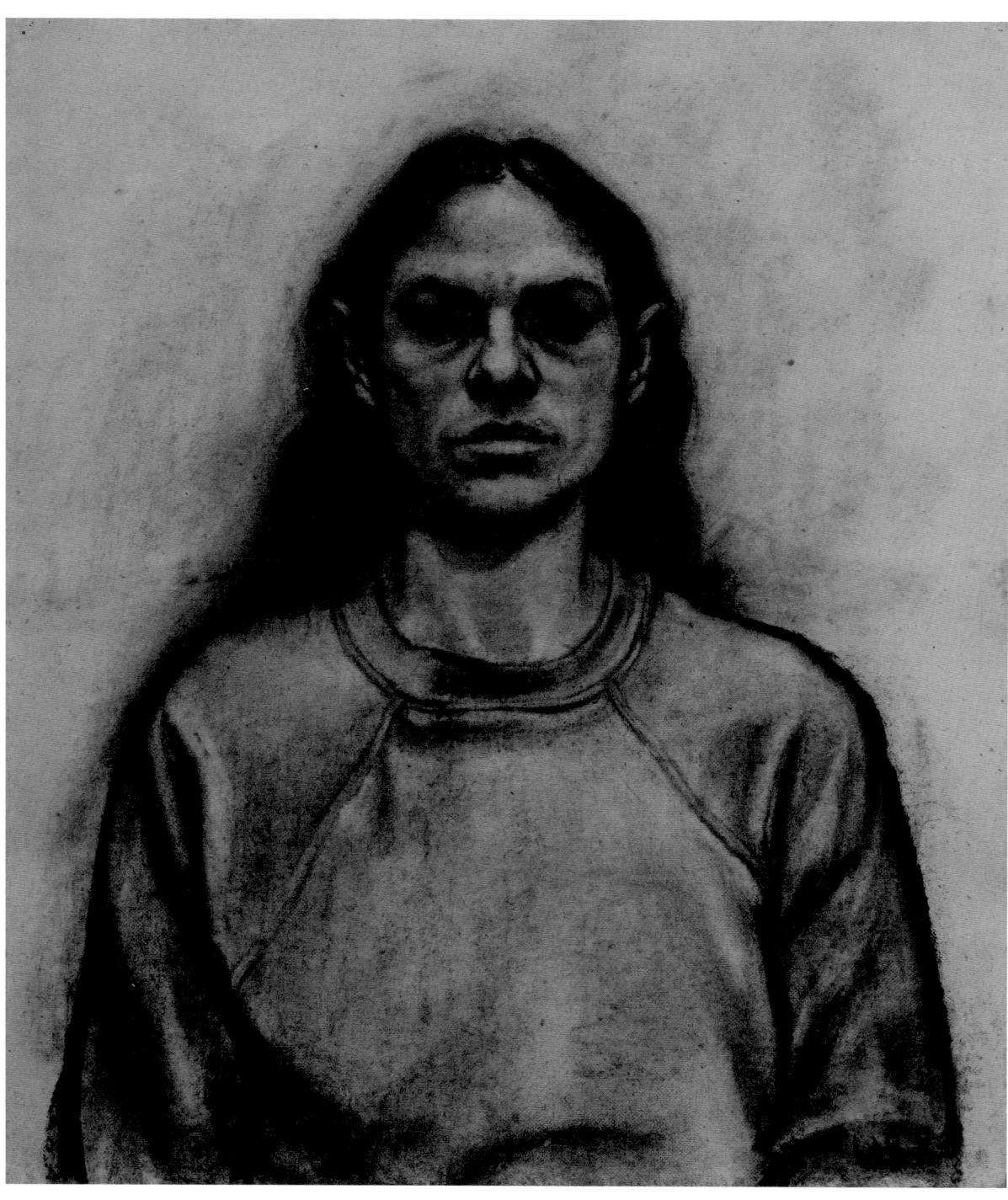

43

**William
Beckman**

Diana in Sweatshirt
1983. Charcoal on paper, 29½ × 24½ in.

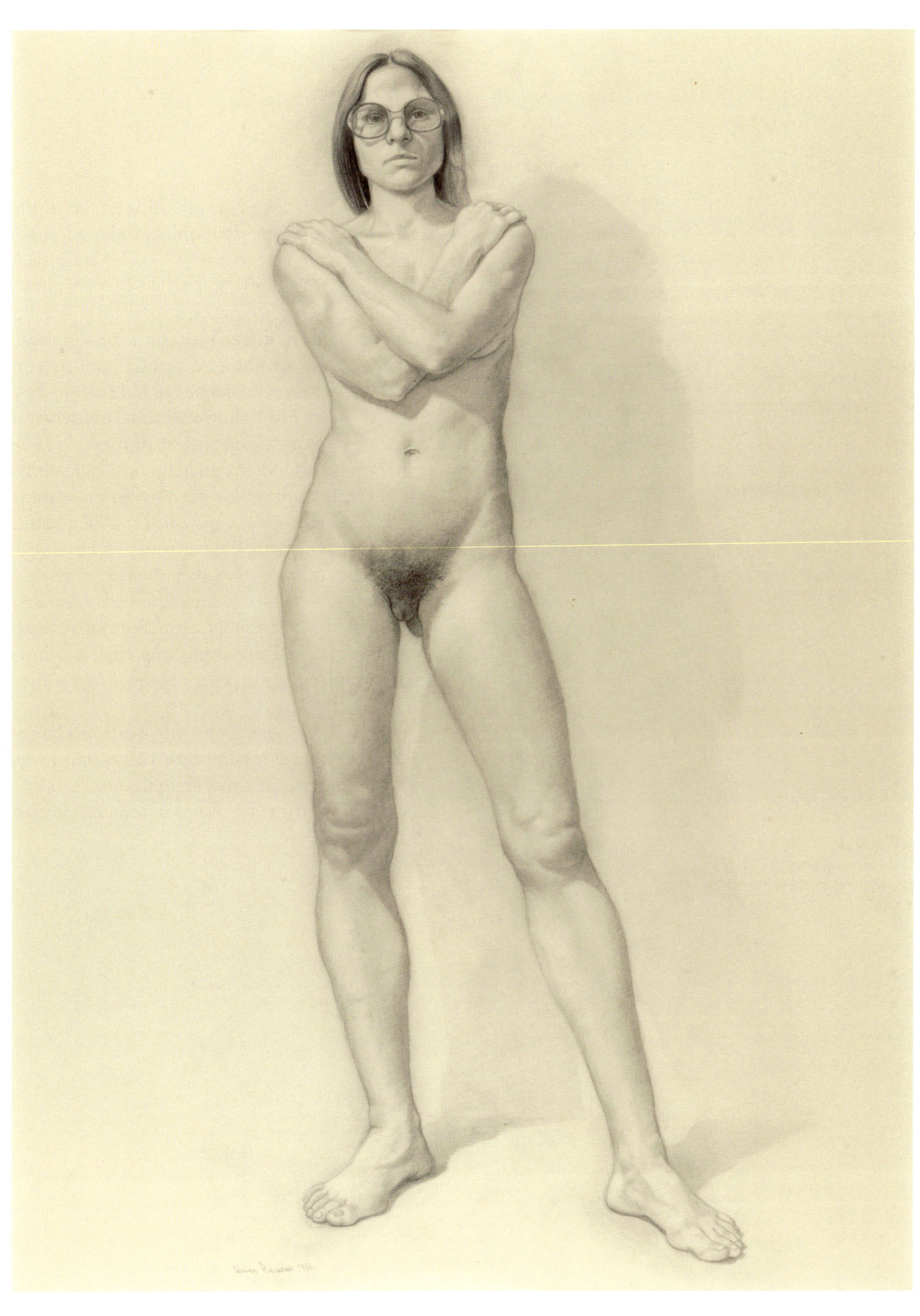

44
William Beckman

Study for *Diana IV*
1980. Pencil on paper, 30 × 28 in.

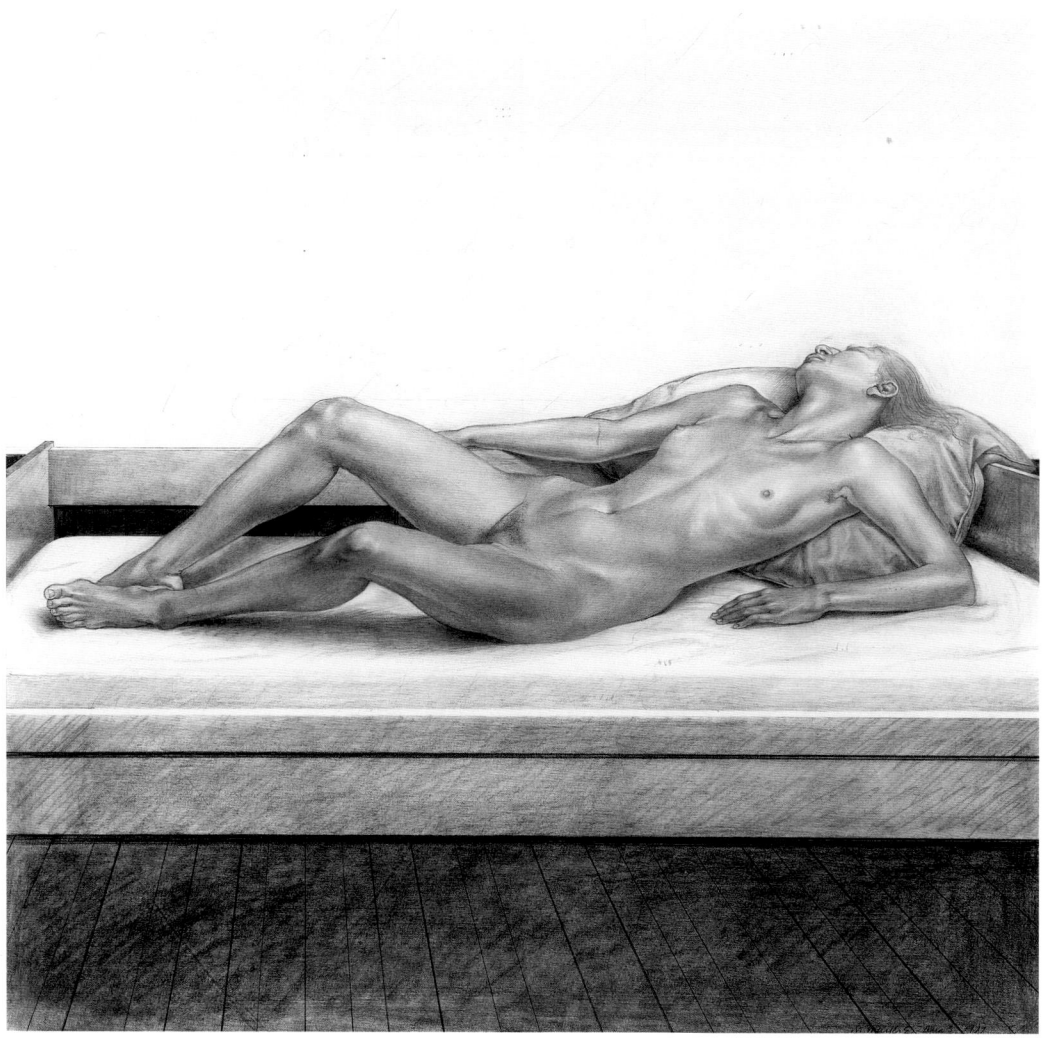

45
Martha Mayer
Erlebacher
(1937–2013)

Study for *Reclining Nude*

1977. Graphite and watercolor on paper, 16 × 16 in.

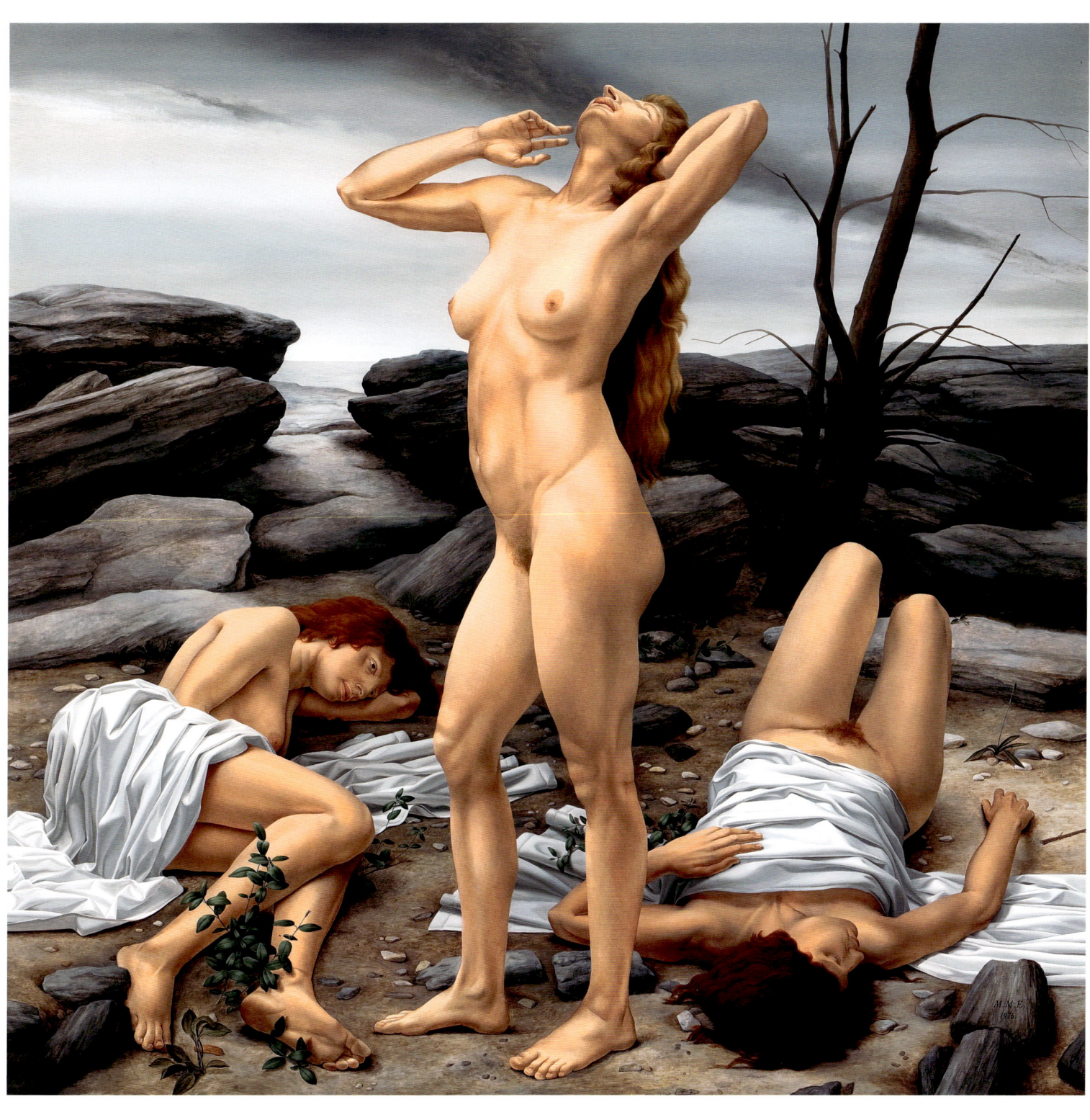

46
Martha Mayer
Erlebacher

In a Garden
1976. Oil on canvas, 64 × 64 in.

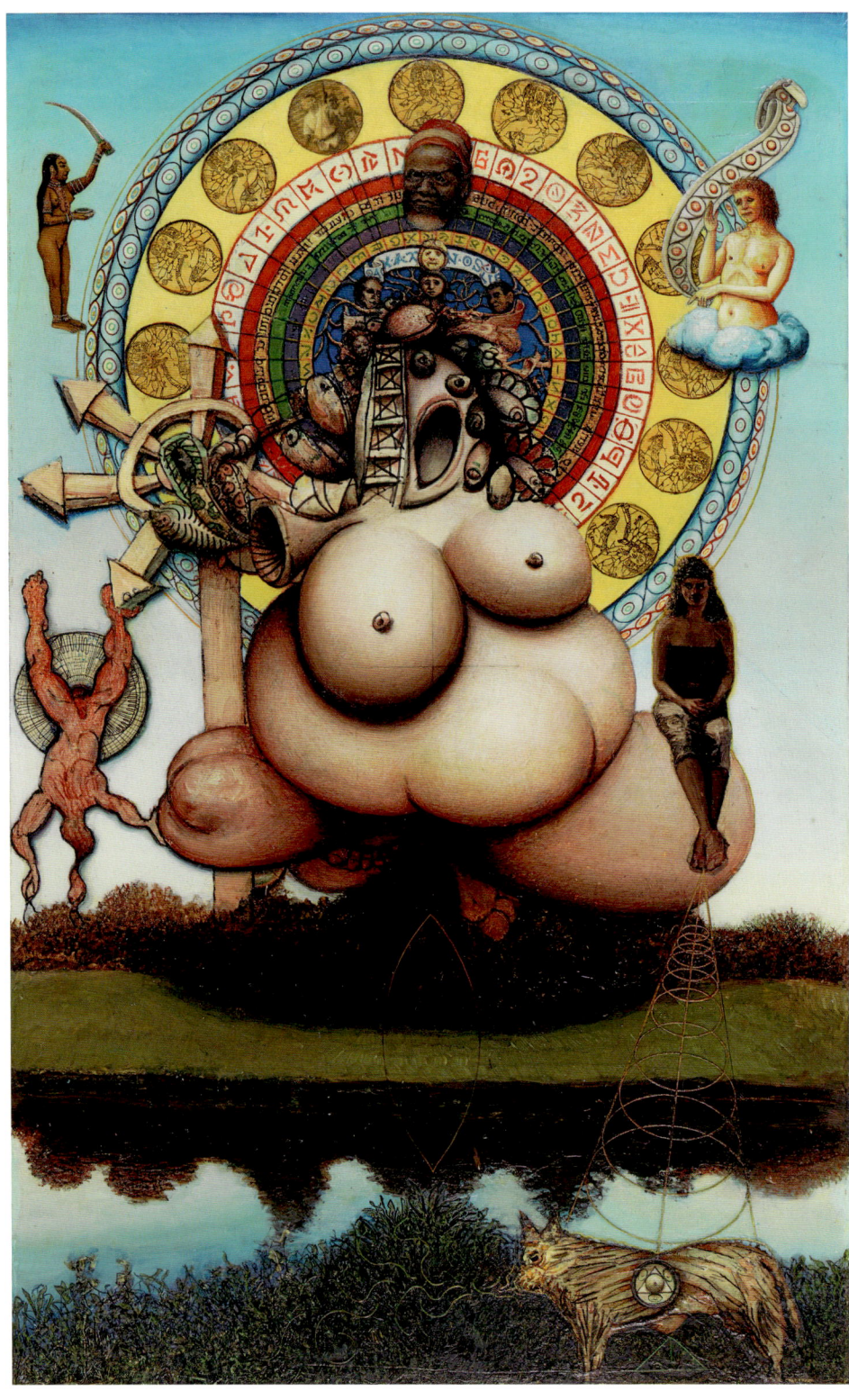

47
Gregory Gillespie

Wheel of Birth
1983–90. Oil and alkyd on panel, 29½ × 18 in.

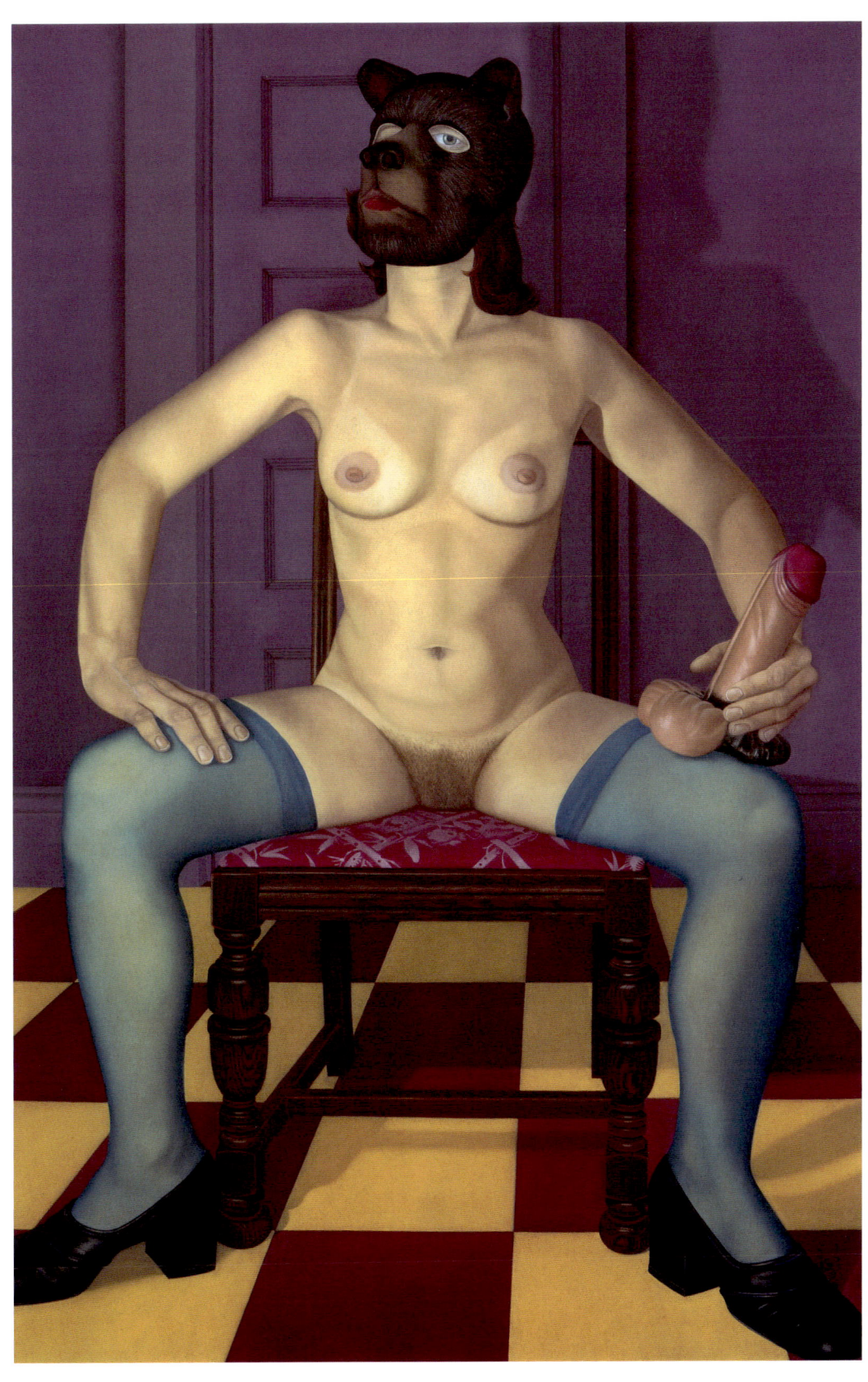

48
Jane Lund

The Priestess
1975. Pastel on paper, 36¾ × 24¼ in.

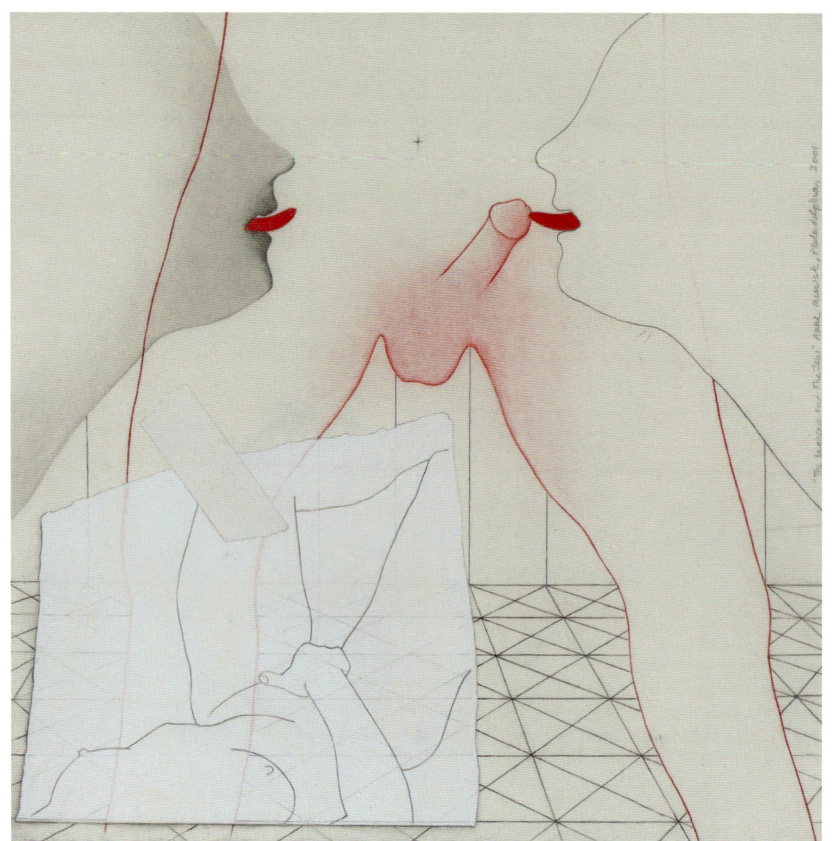

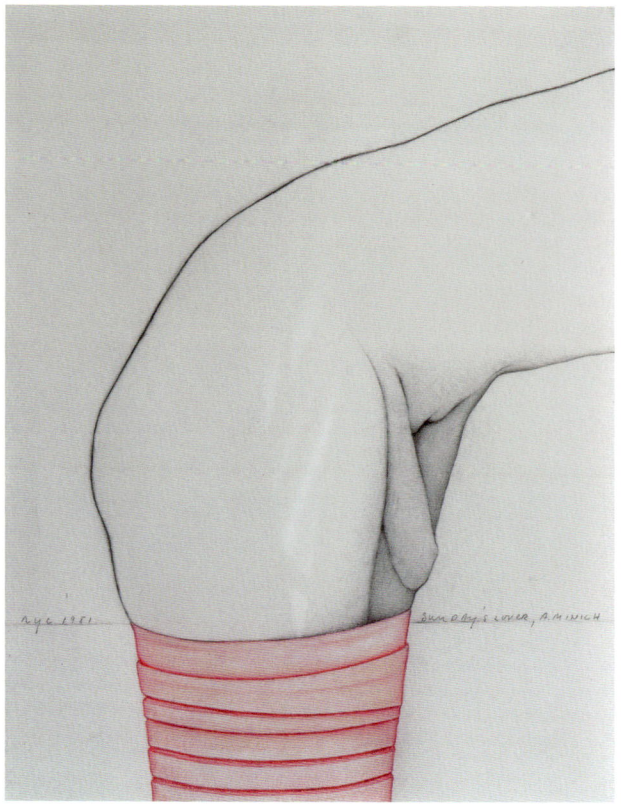

49
Anne Minich

The Anglican and the Jew
2001. Graphite, colored pencil, and
watercolor on paper, 10 × 10⅝ in.

50
Anne Minich

Sunday's Lover
1981. Graphite and colored pencil on
paper, 10⅜ × 7¾ in.

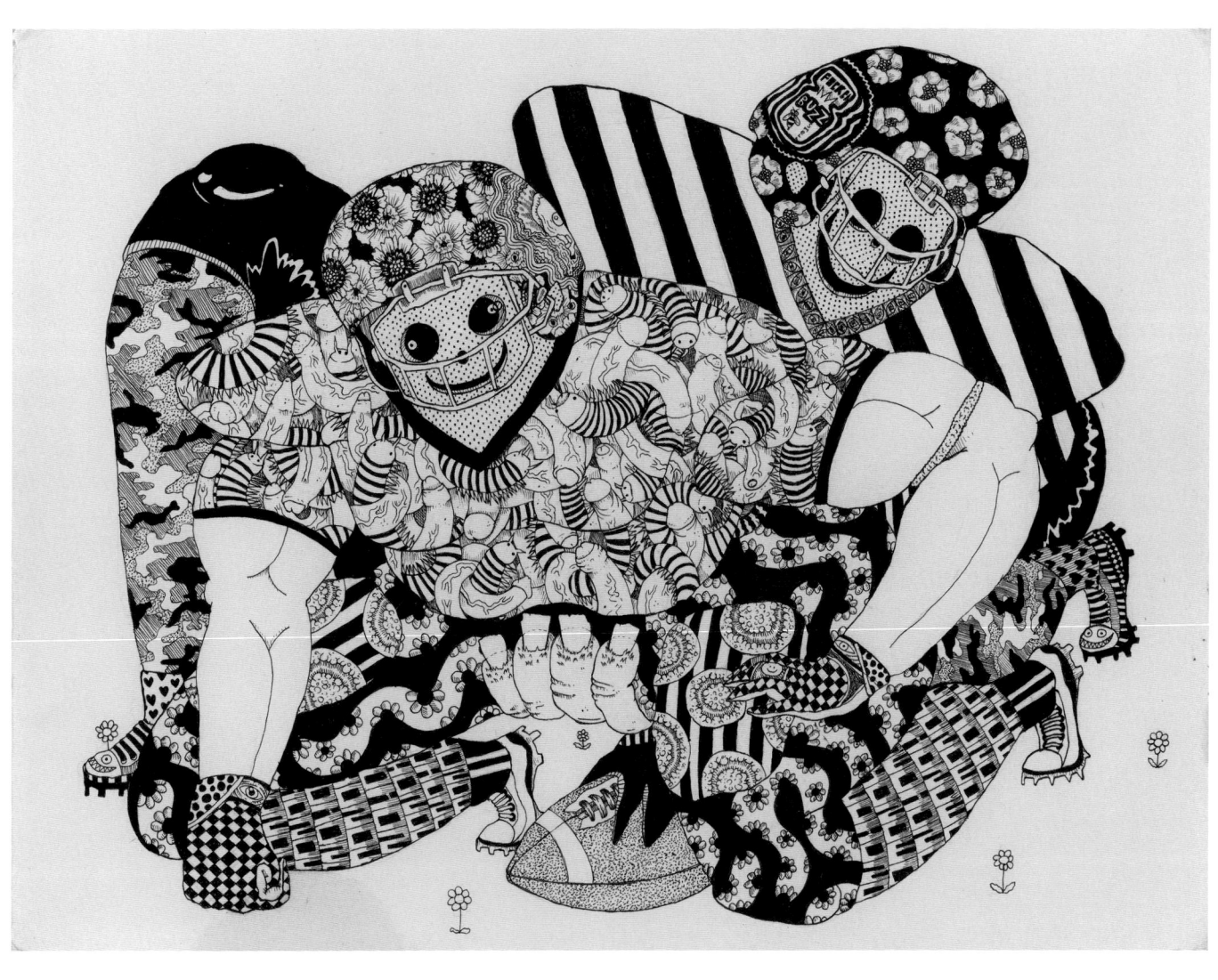

51

**Craig
Calderwood**

(b. 1987)

Ringworm Inspection

2019. Pen on paper, 11 × 14 in.

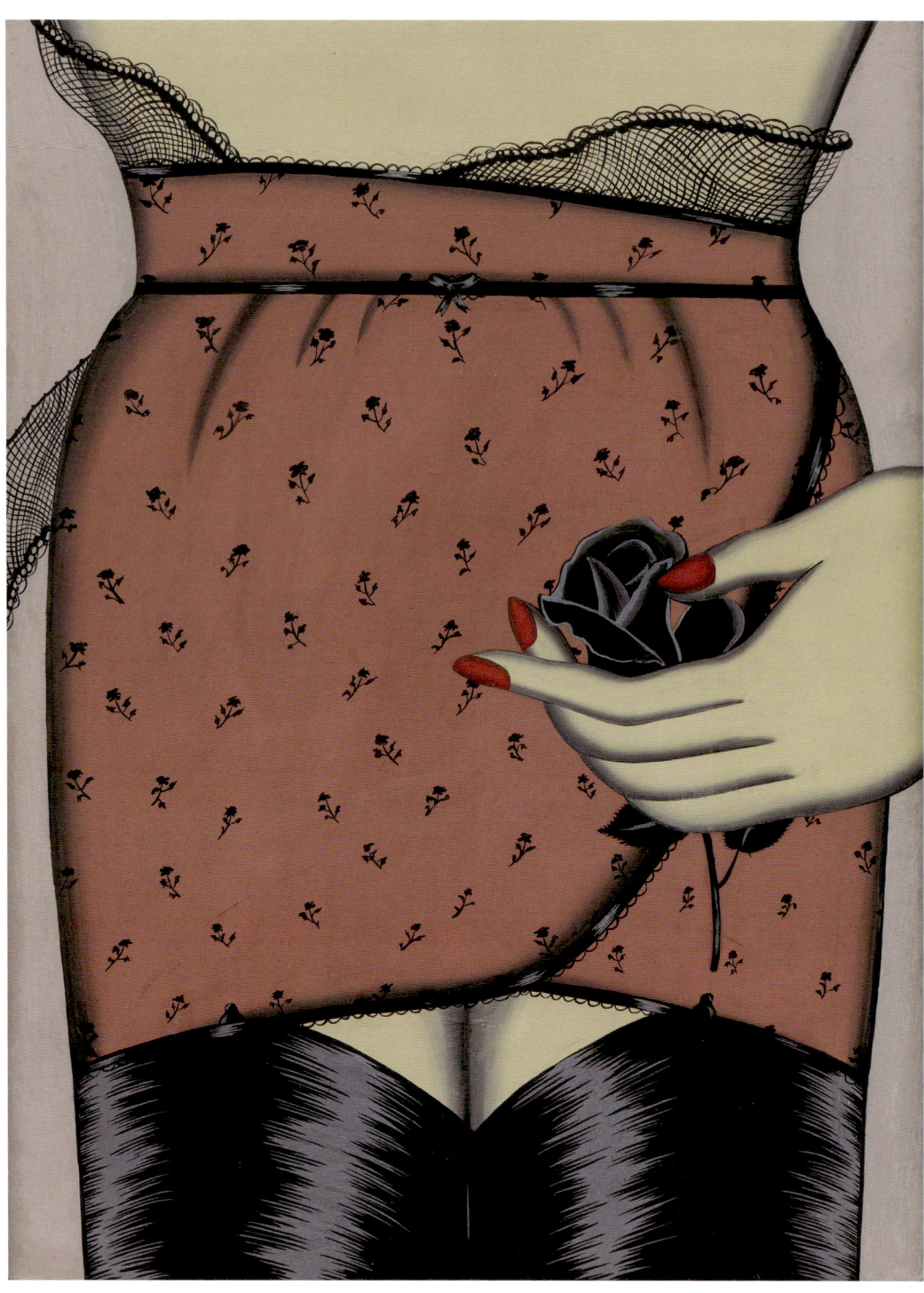

52
Christina
Ramberg
(1946–1995)

False Bloom
1971. Acrylic on Masonite, 17 × 12¾ in.

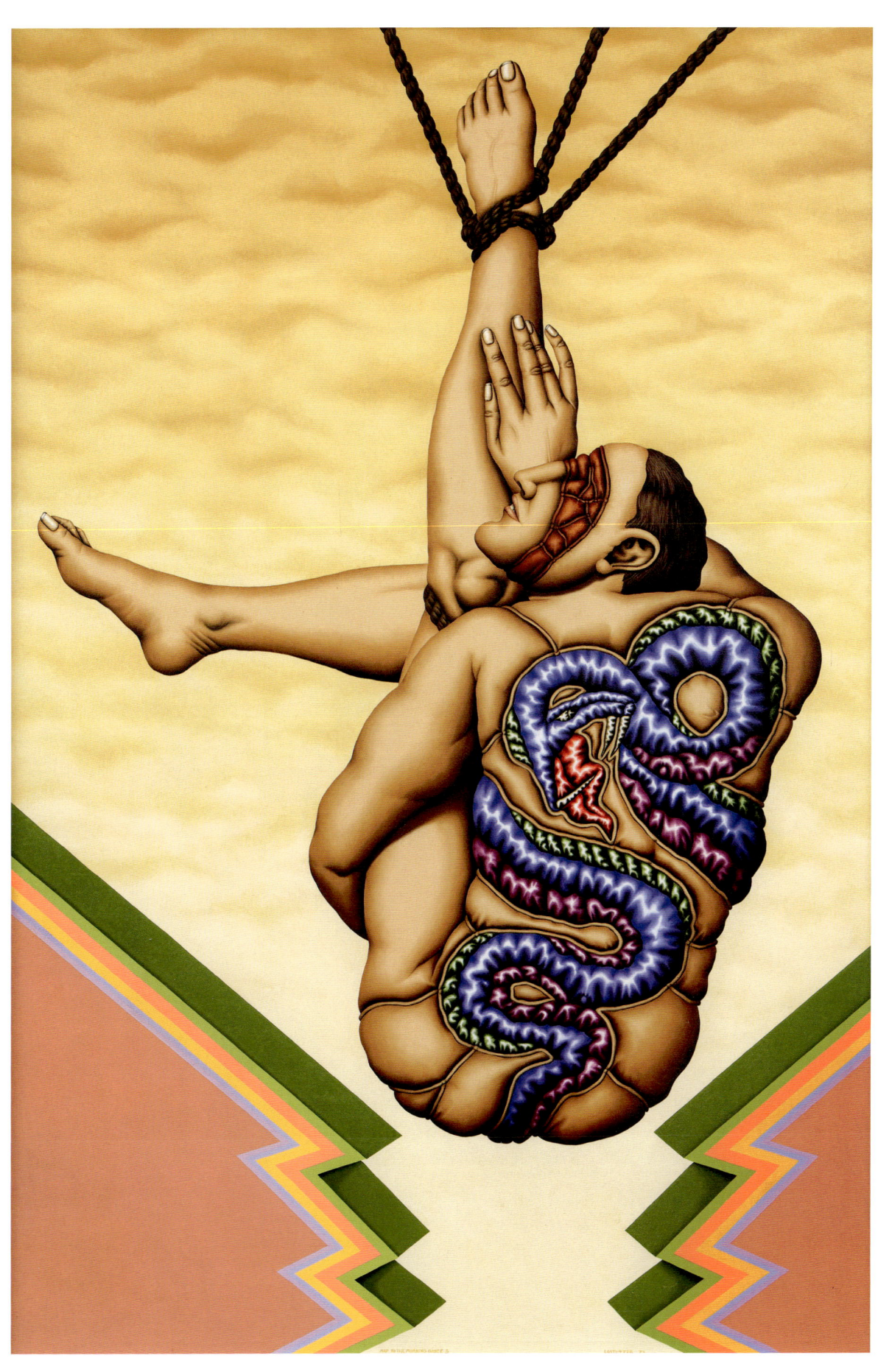

53

Robert Lostutter *Map to the Morning Dance 3*

(b. 1939) 1973. Oil on canvas, 66 × 43½ in.

121

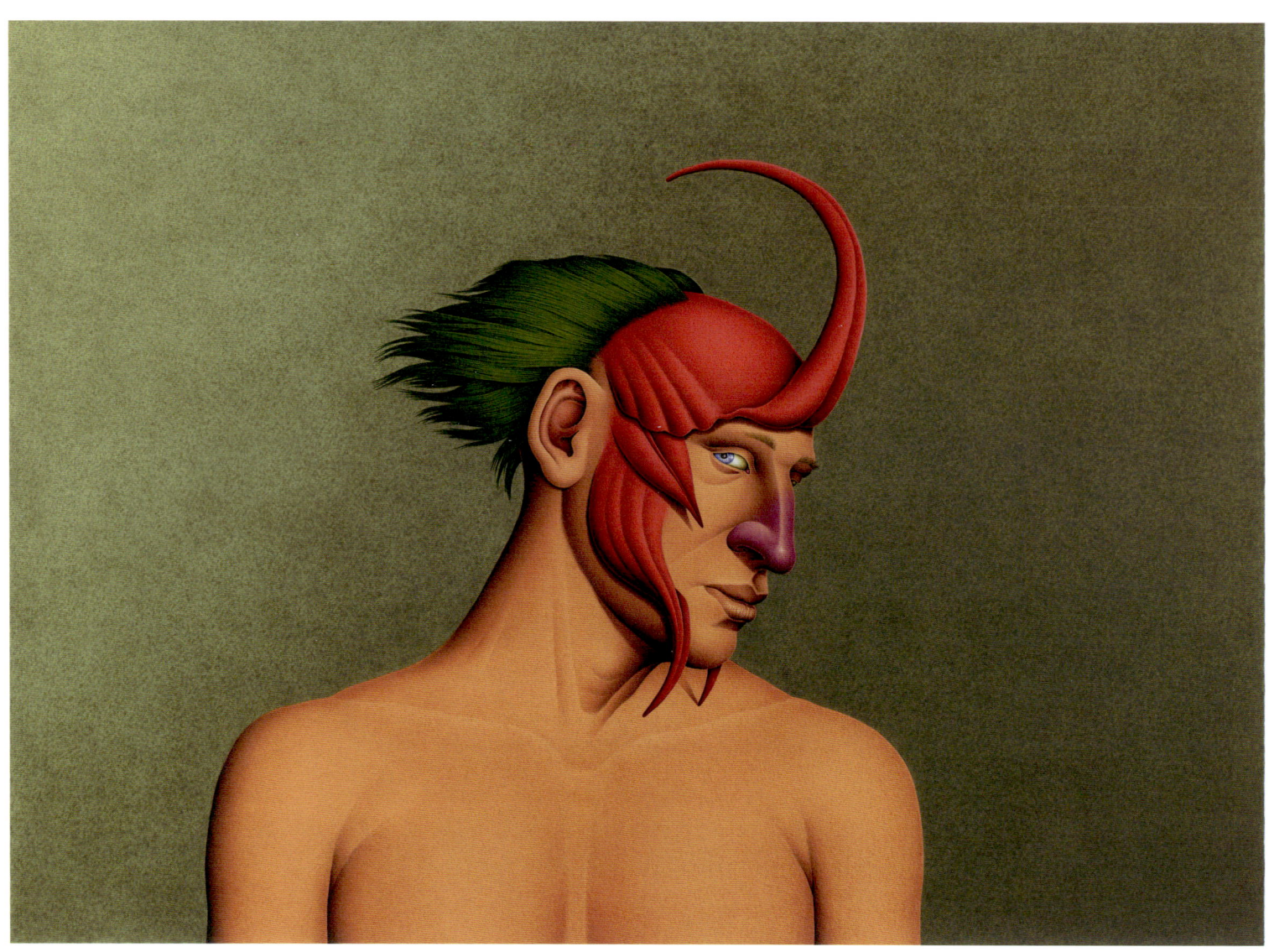

54
Robert Lostutter

Red Masdevallia
2004. Watercolor on paper, 35 × 43 in.

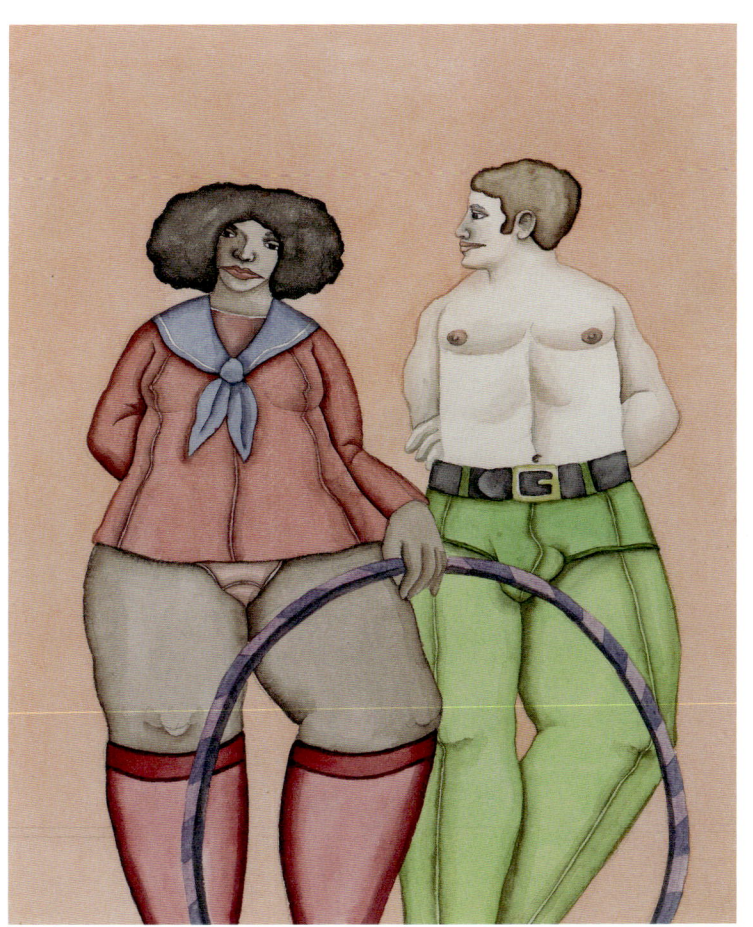

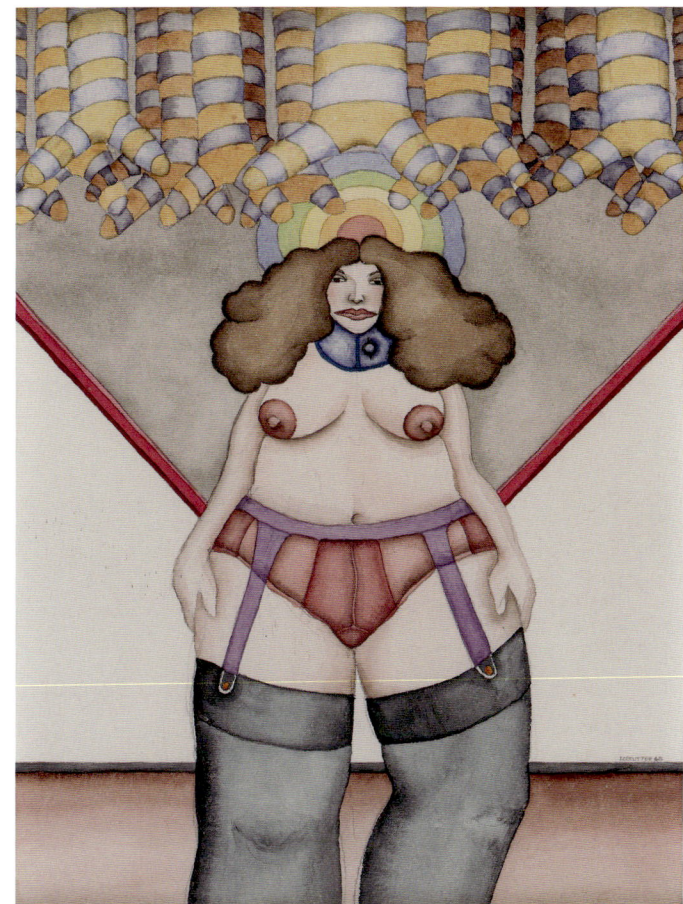

Untitled (Two standing figures
with hoop)
c. 1968. Watercolor on paper,
10¼ × 13 in.

55
Robert Lostutter

Untitled (Woman in stockings)
1968. Watercolor on paper,
10½ × 13 in.

56
Robert Lostutter

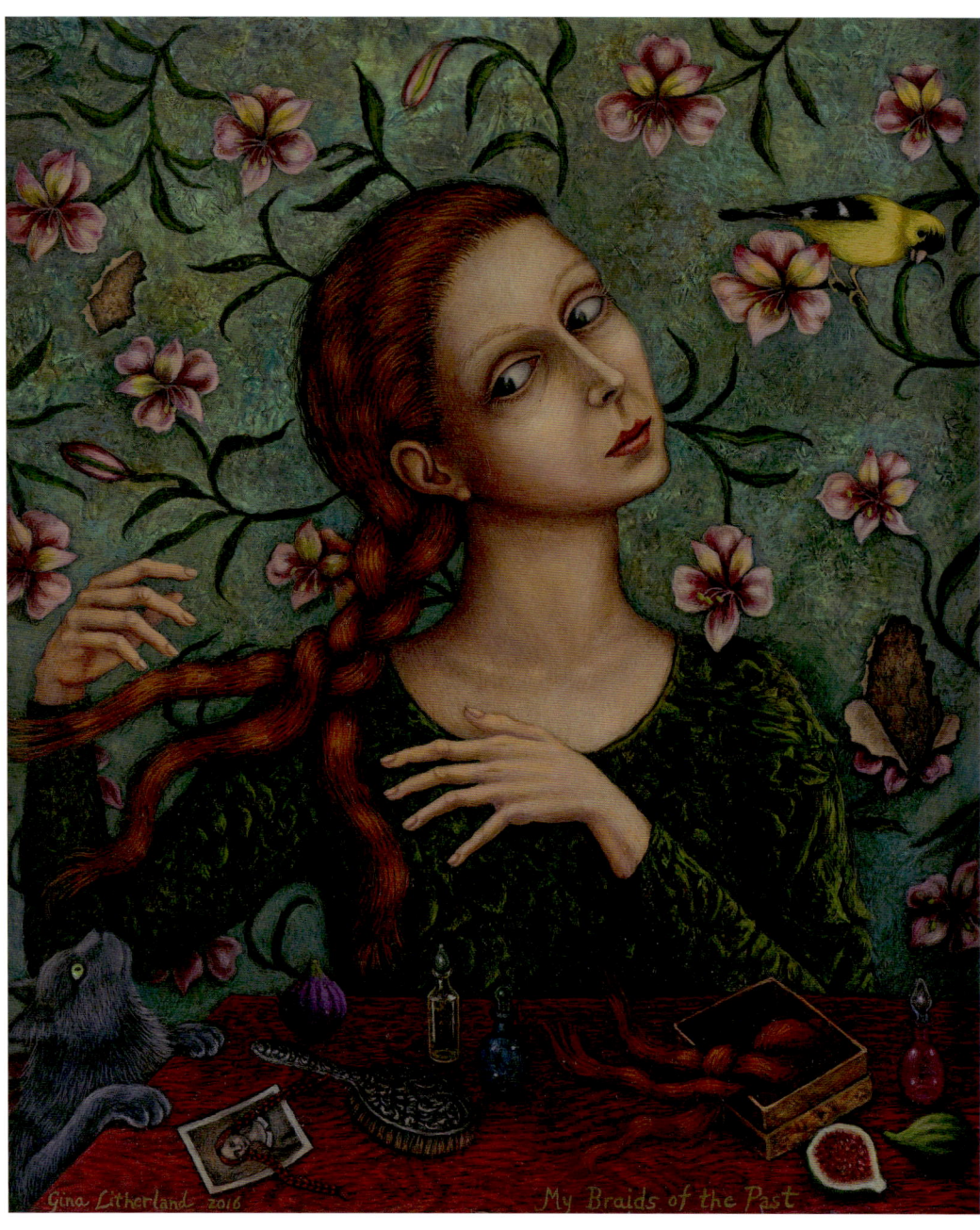

57

Gina Litherland

(b. 1955)

My Braids of the Past
(for Marosa di Giogio)

2016. Oil on panel, 14 × 12 in.

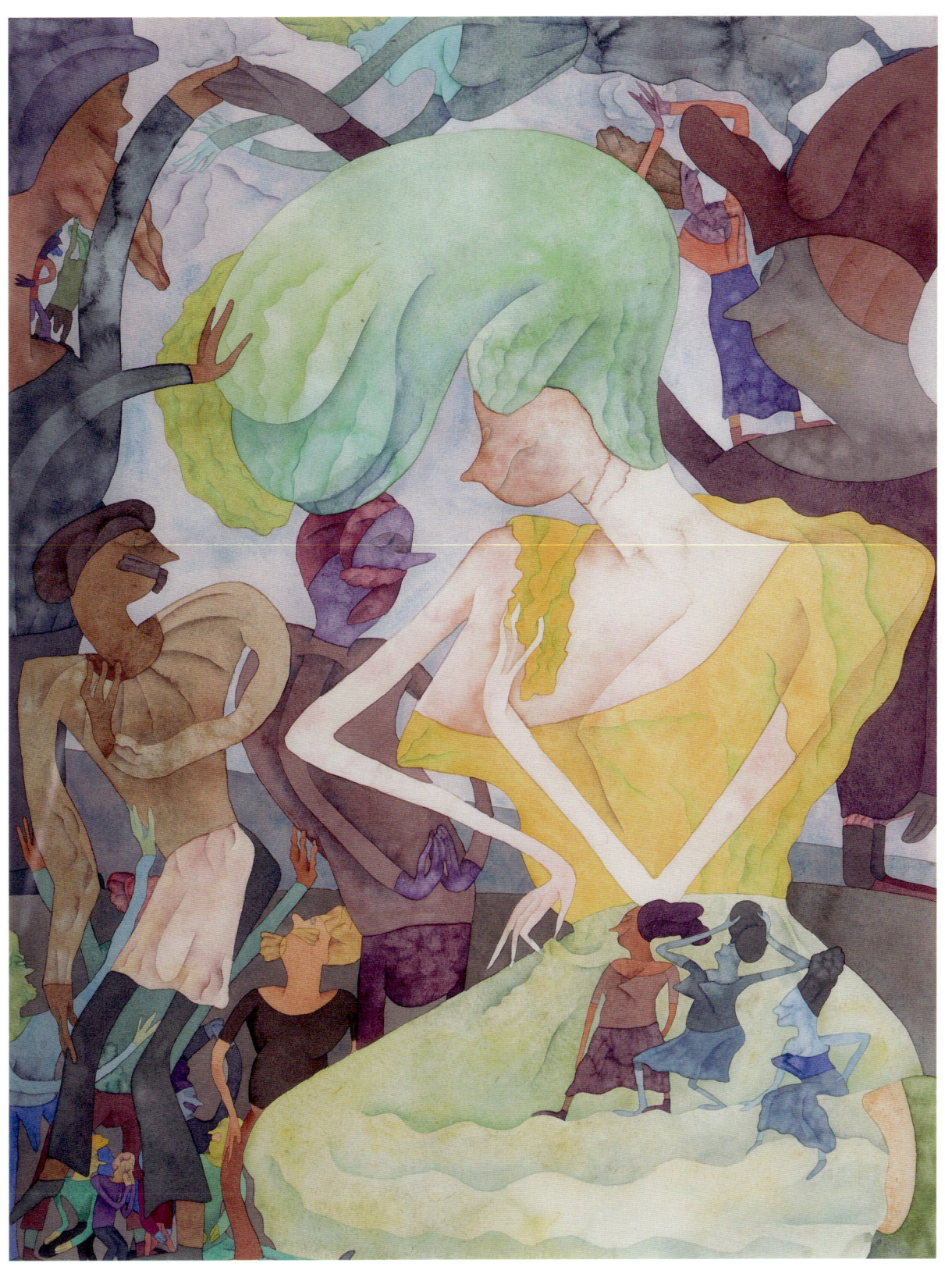

58
Gladys Nilsson

Hairdresser's Surprise
1977. Watercolor on paper, 33 × 25½ in.

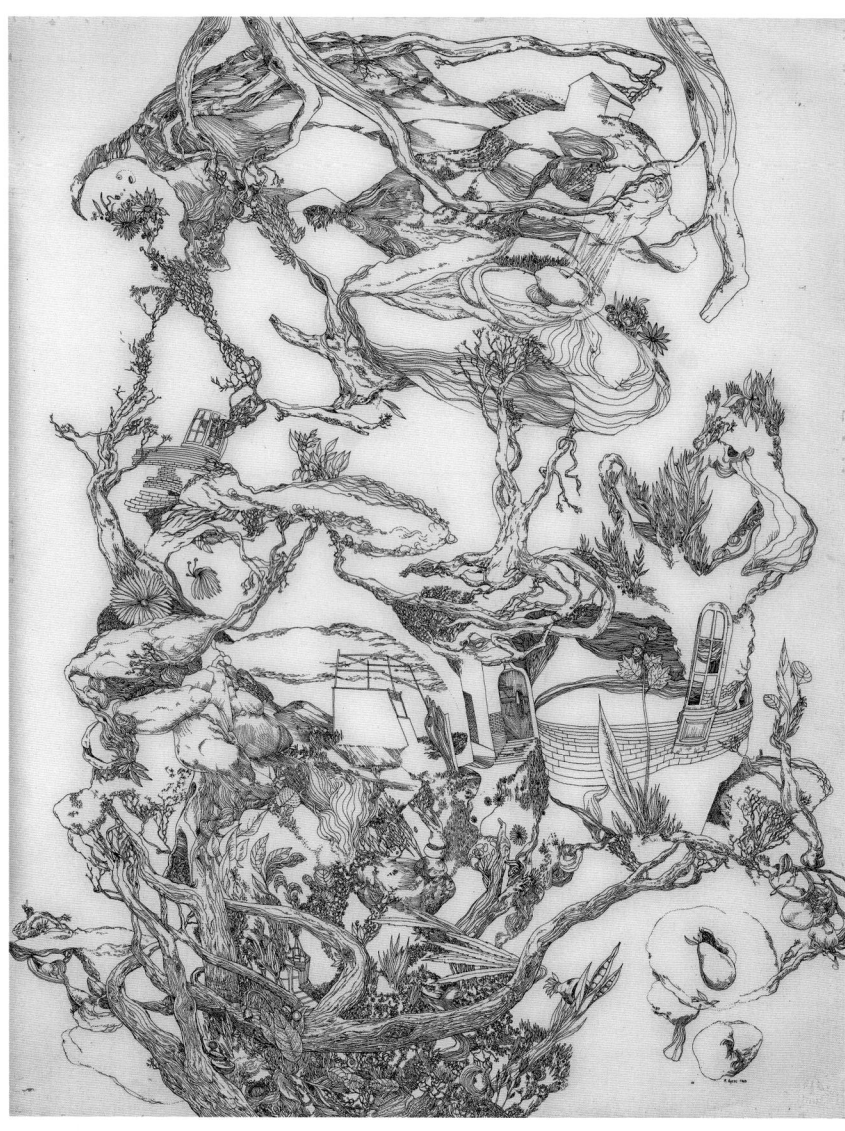

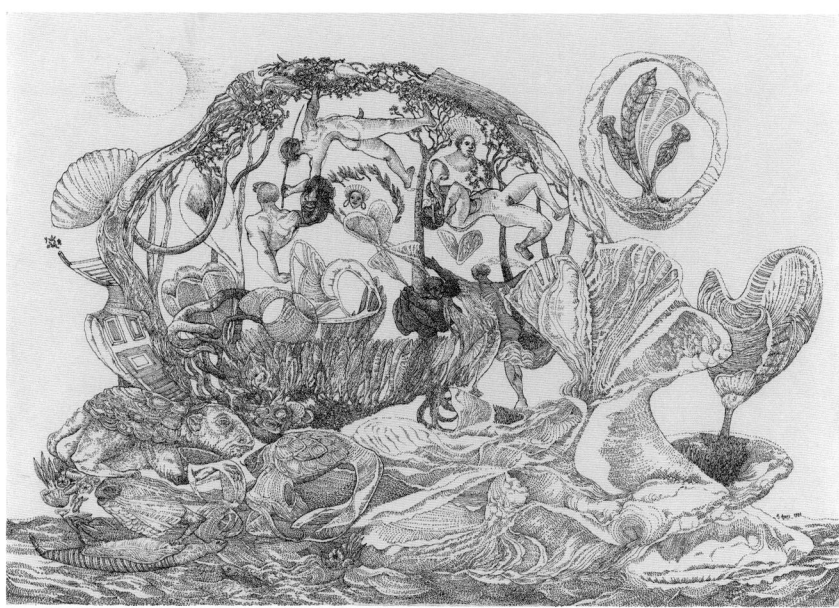

59
Roland Ayers
(1932–2014)

Trees
1969. Ink on paper, 23 × 17½ in.

60
Roland Ayers

Swing
1972. Ink on paper, 5 × 7 in.

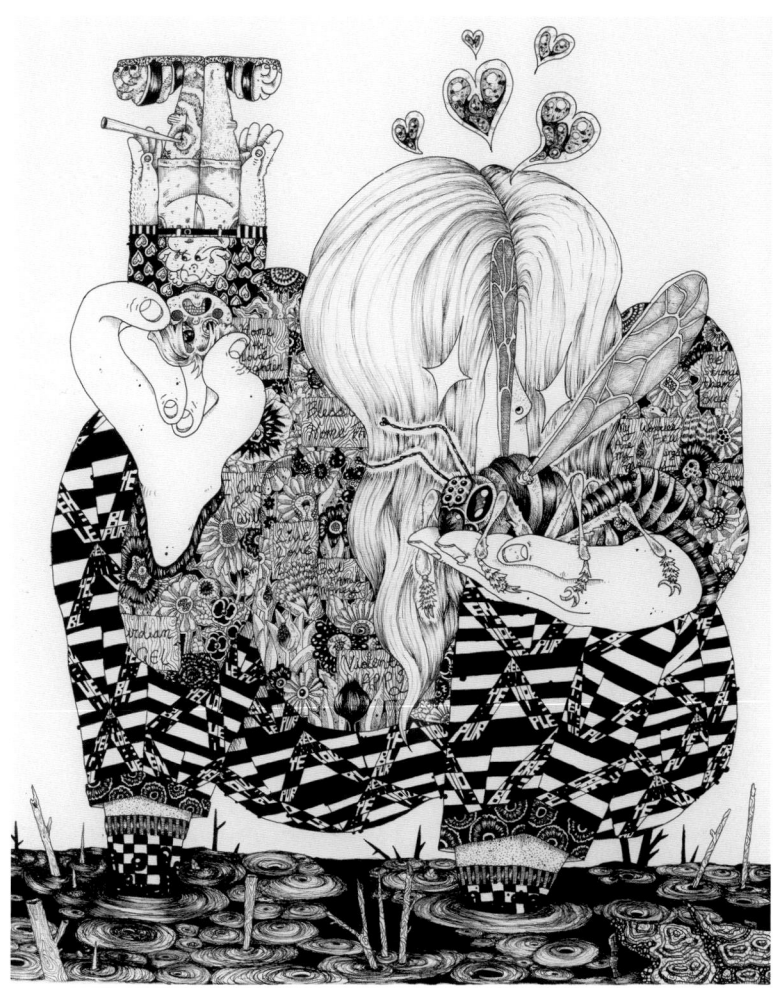

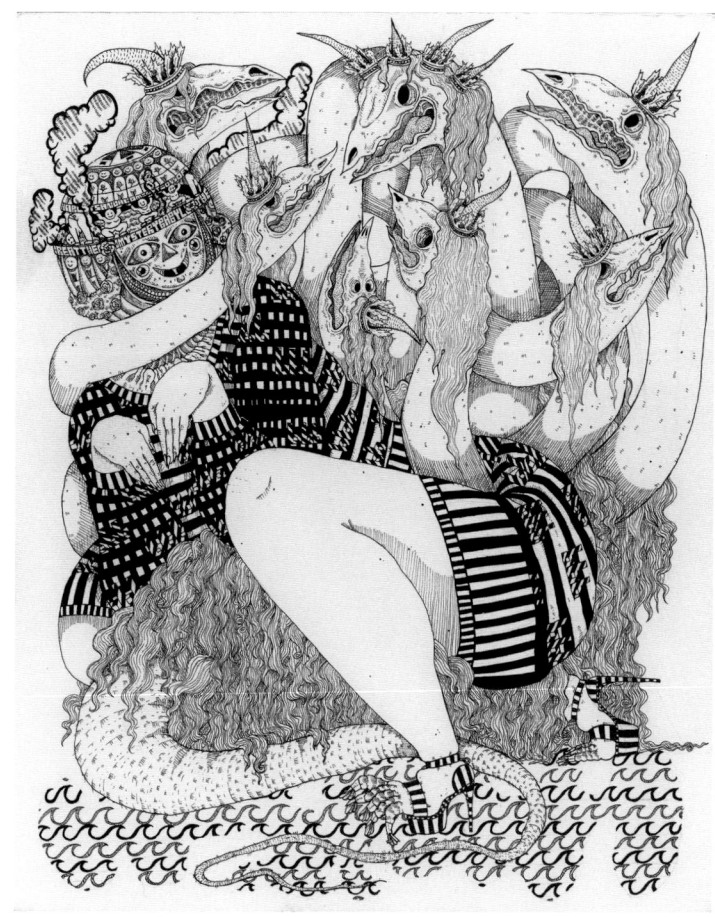

61

Craig Calderwood

Meat Bees

2023. Ink on paper, 18 × 14¼ in.

62

Craig Calderwood

You Can Tell by the Beast Between Her Legs

2019. Pen on paper, 14 × 11 in.

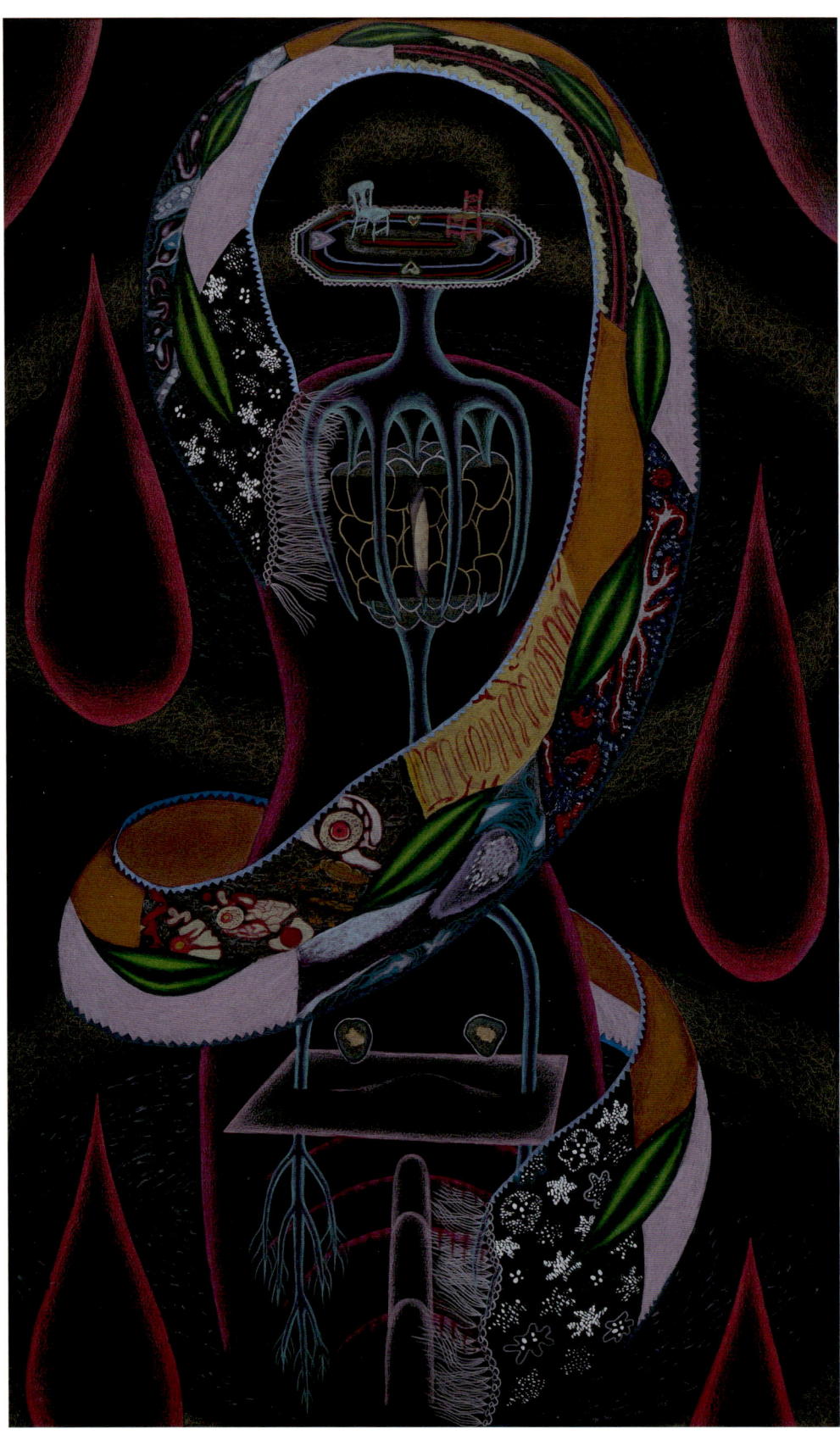

63

Marcy Hermansader

(b. 1951)

Alterations in the Blood

1985. Colored pencil, acrylic, and fabric on paper, 30 × 18 in.

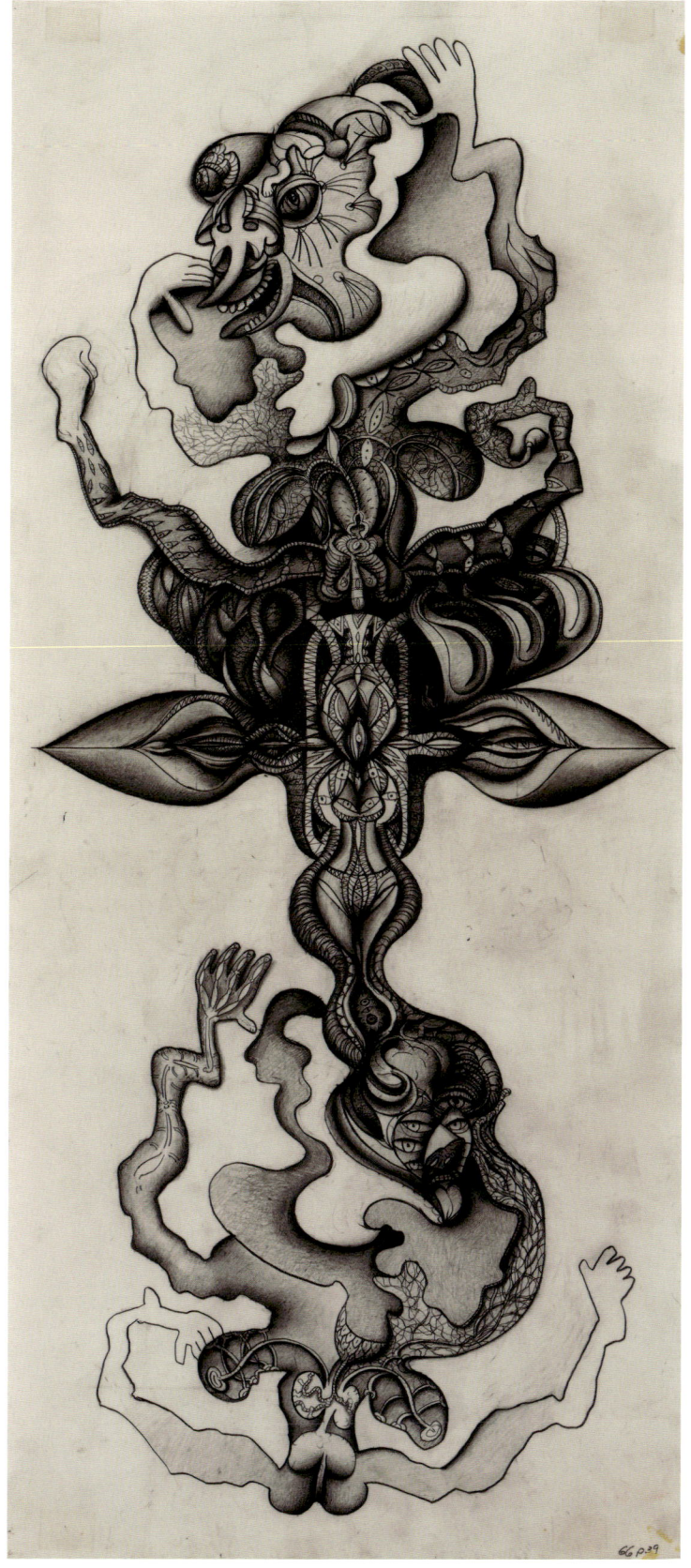

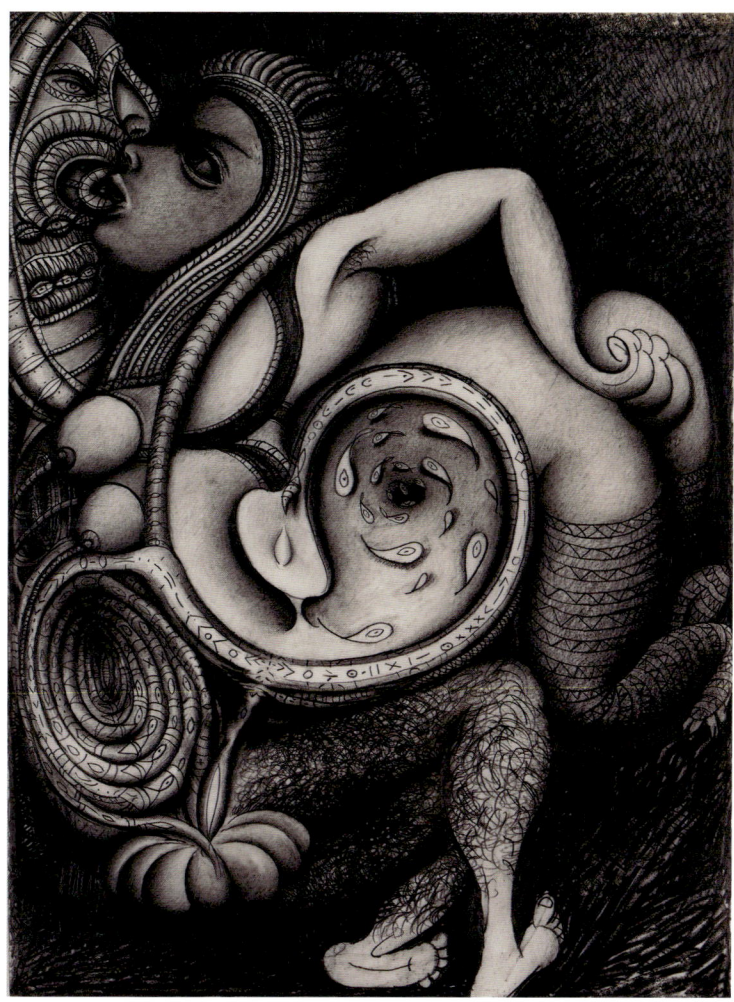

Manic Depression

64

Gregory Gillespie

c. 1987. Graphite on Mylar,
29¼ × 12¾ in.

The Kiss

1987 and 1996. Oil and
pencil on lithograph on panel,

65

Gregory Gillespie

21 × 17½ in., artist's frame

129

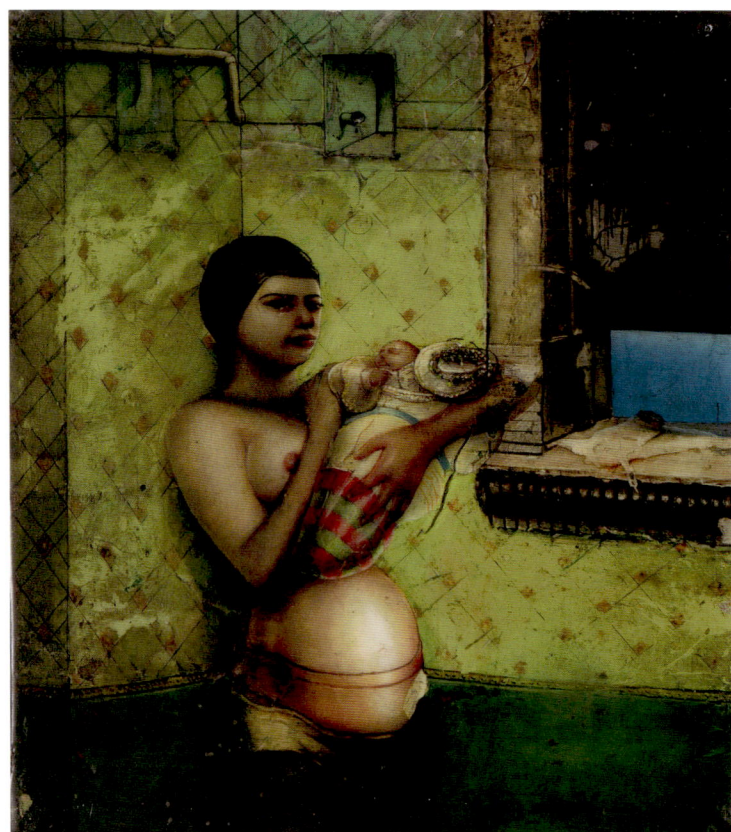

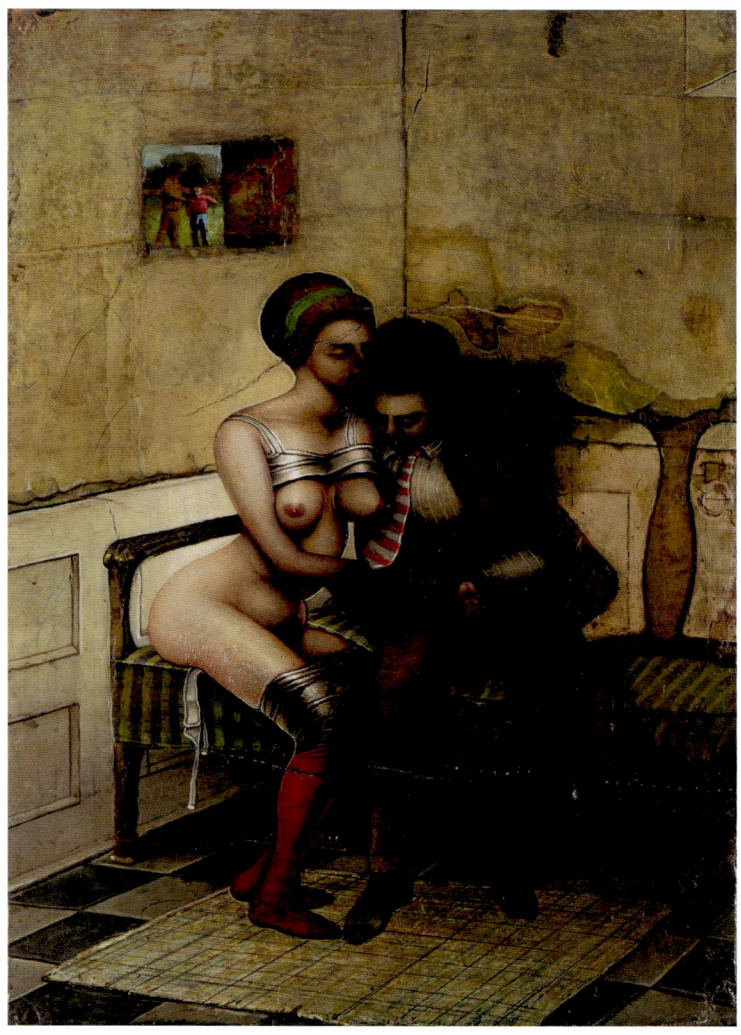

66
Gregory Gillespie

Woman with Baby
1968. Mixed media, 7½ × 6½ in.

67
Gregory Gillespie

Seated Couple
1967. Oil on panel, 9 × 7 in.

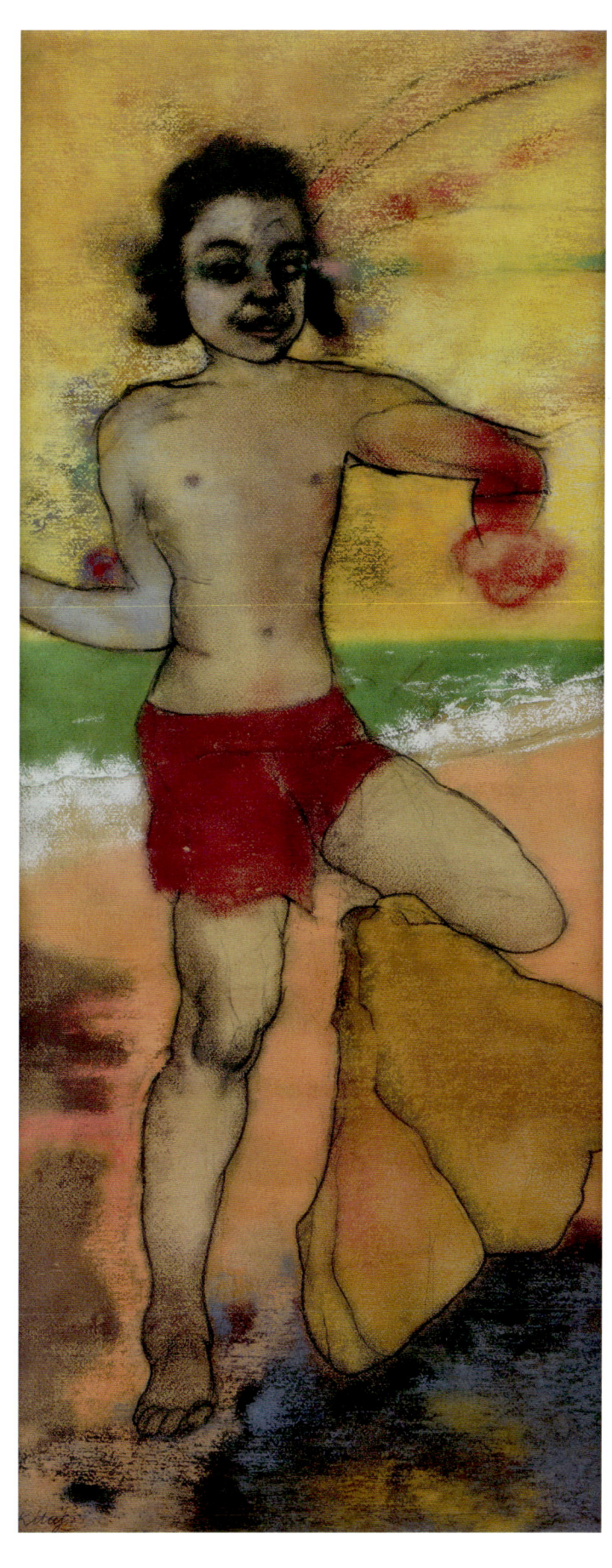

Bather (Psychotic Boy)
1980. Pastel and charcoal on paper,
52¾ × 22½ in.

R. B. Kitaj

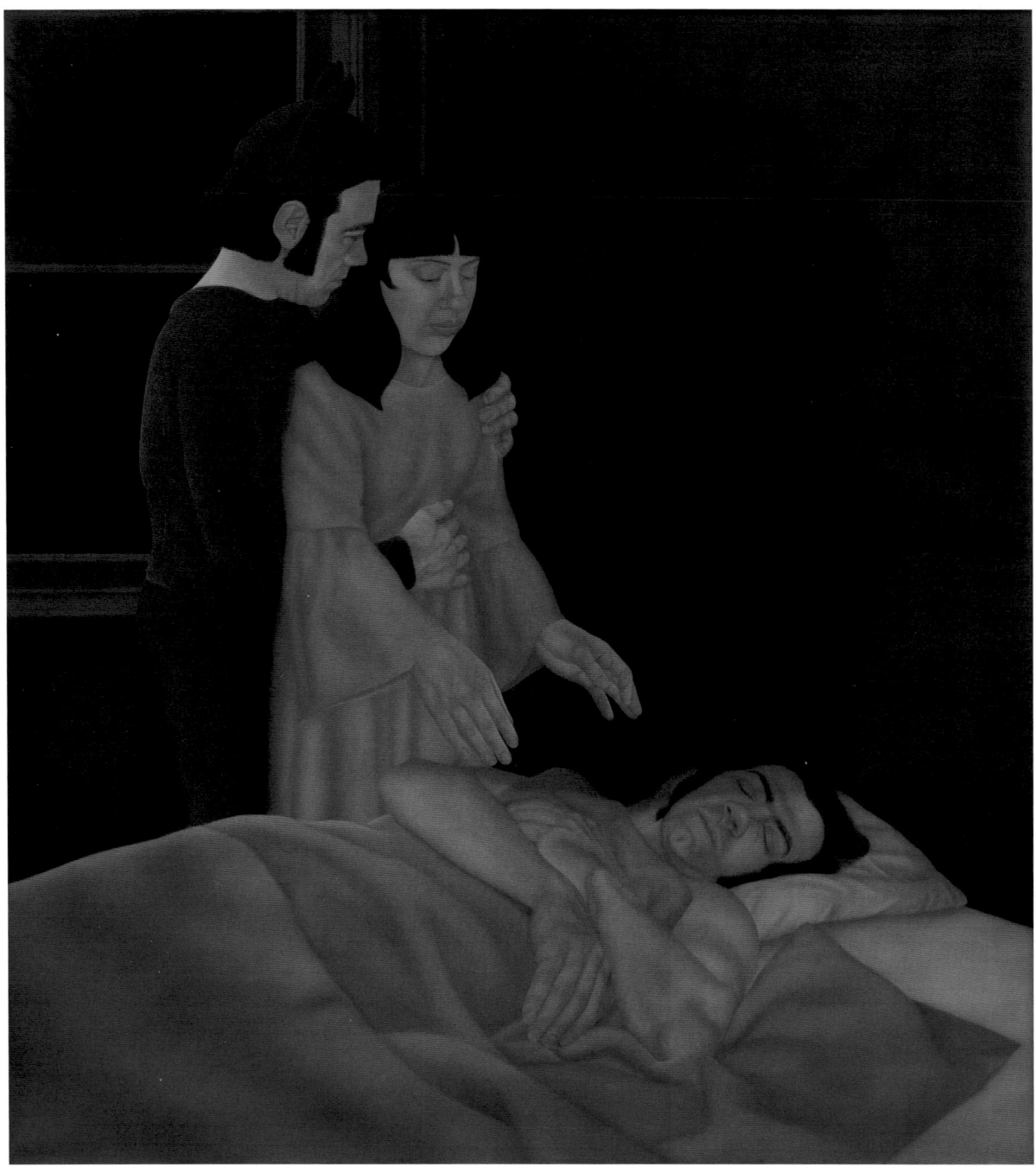

69
Jane Lund

The Choice
c. mid- to late 1970s. Pastel on paper, 33 × 30 in.

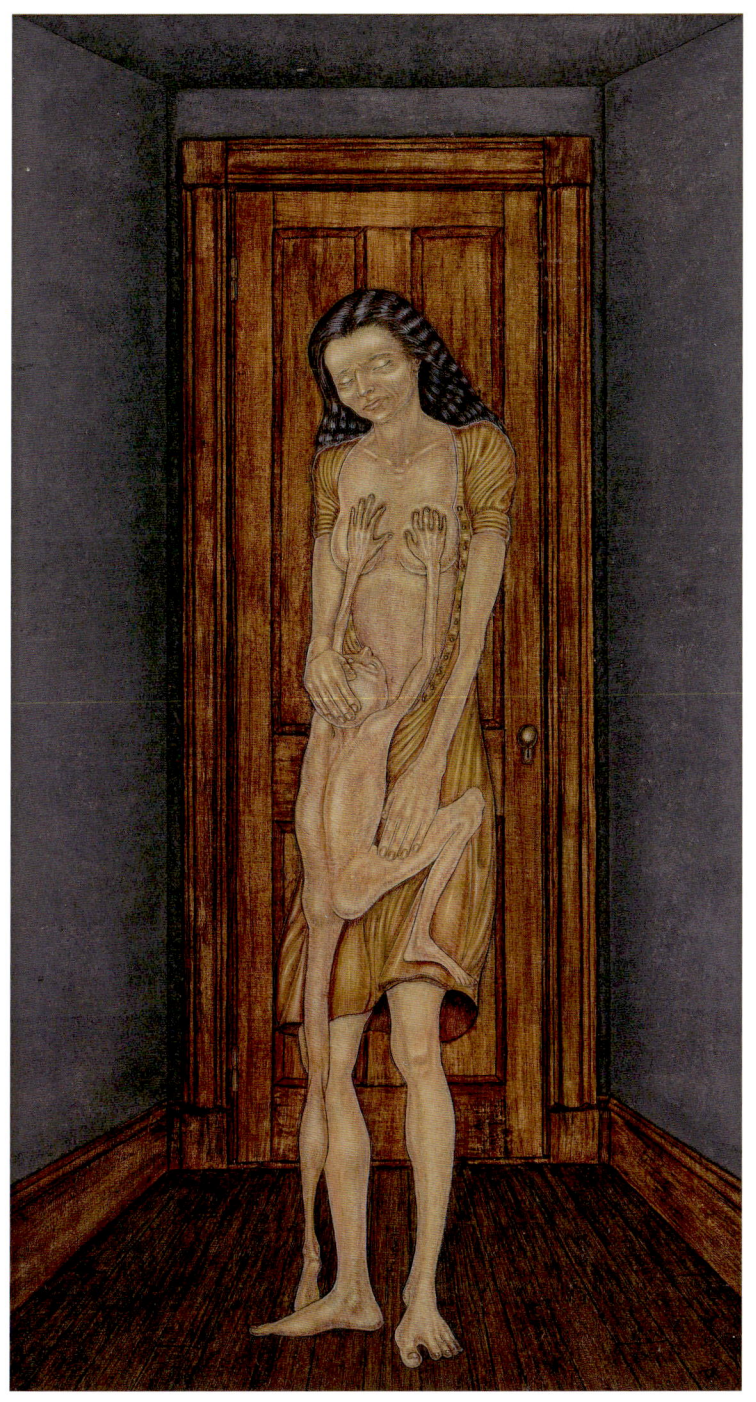

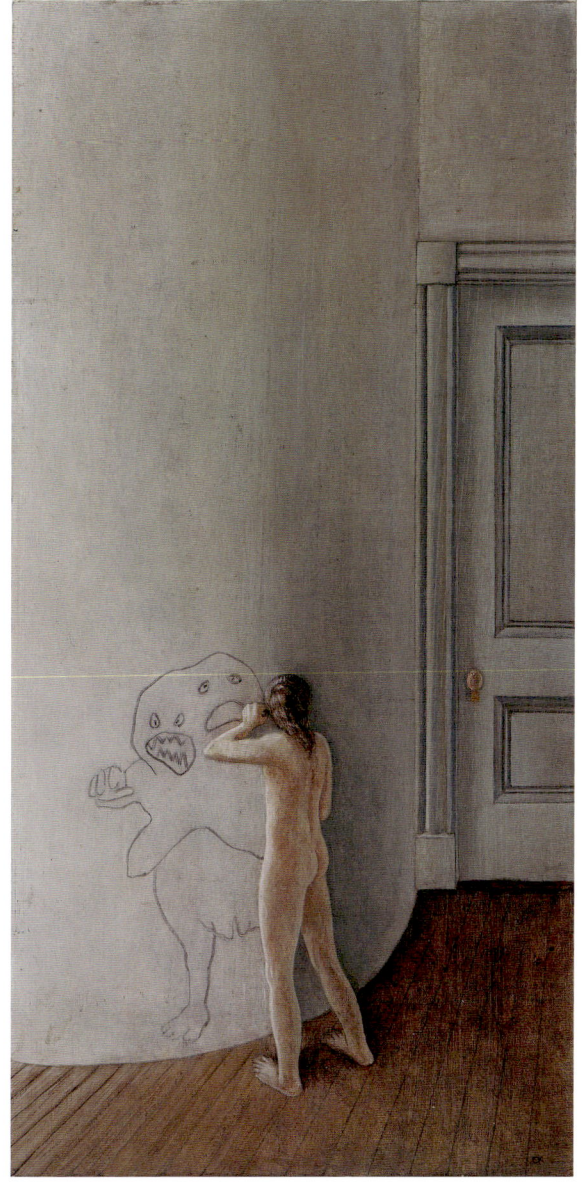

70
Deborah Kravitz

Mother and Child in Front of Door
c. 1972. Acrylic on panel, 23 × 6¼ in.

Girl Drawing II
(Girl Drawing Door)
1978. Acrylic on panel,
14½ × 7 in.

71
Deborah Kravitz

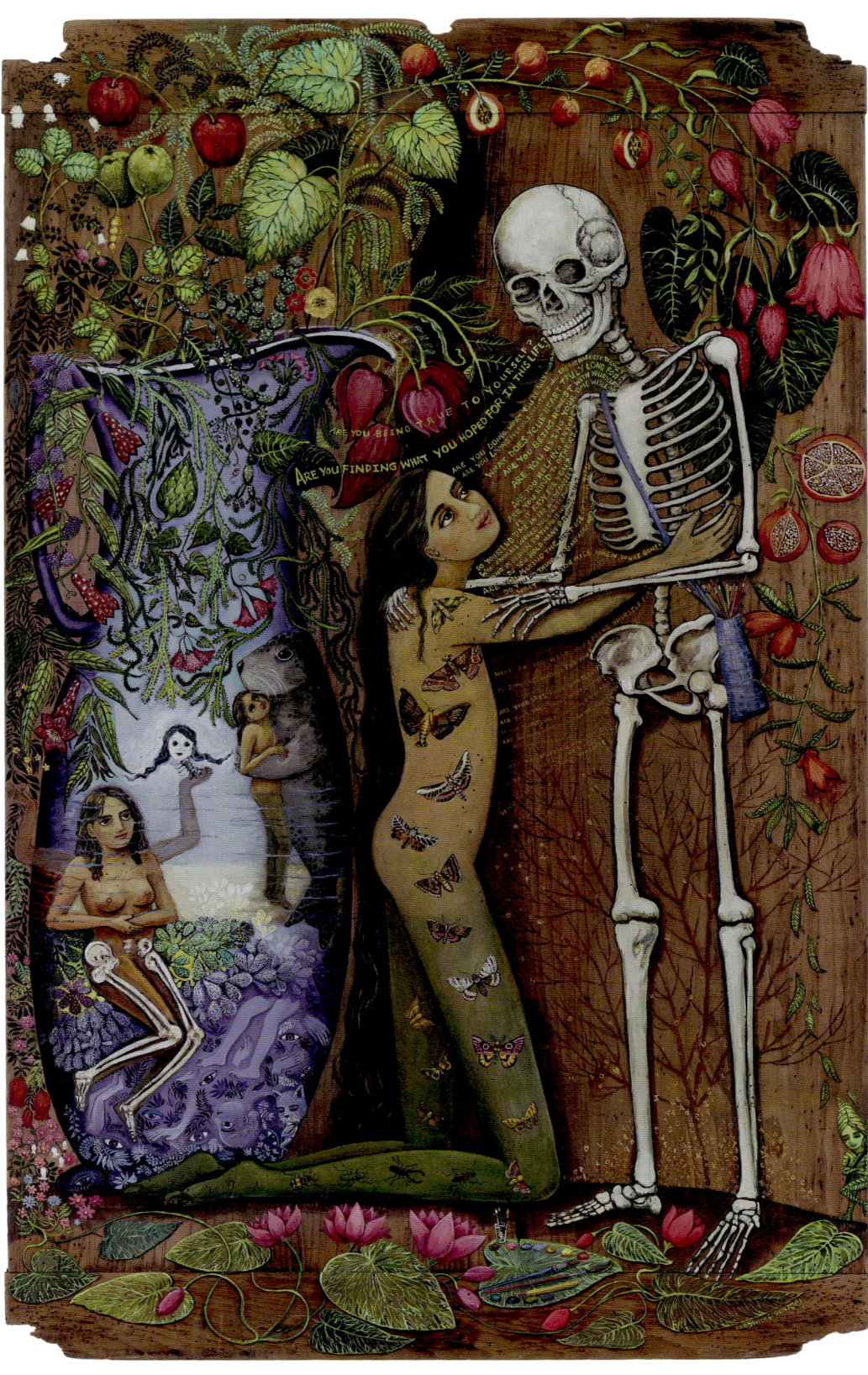

72

Irene Hardwicke
Olivieri (b. 1959)

The Painter and Her Skeleton
2019. Oil on wood, 31½ × 20 in.

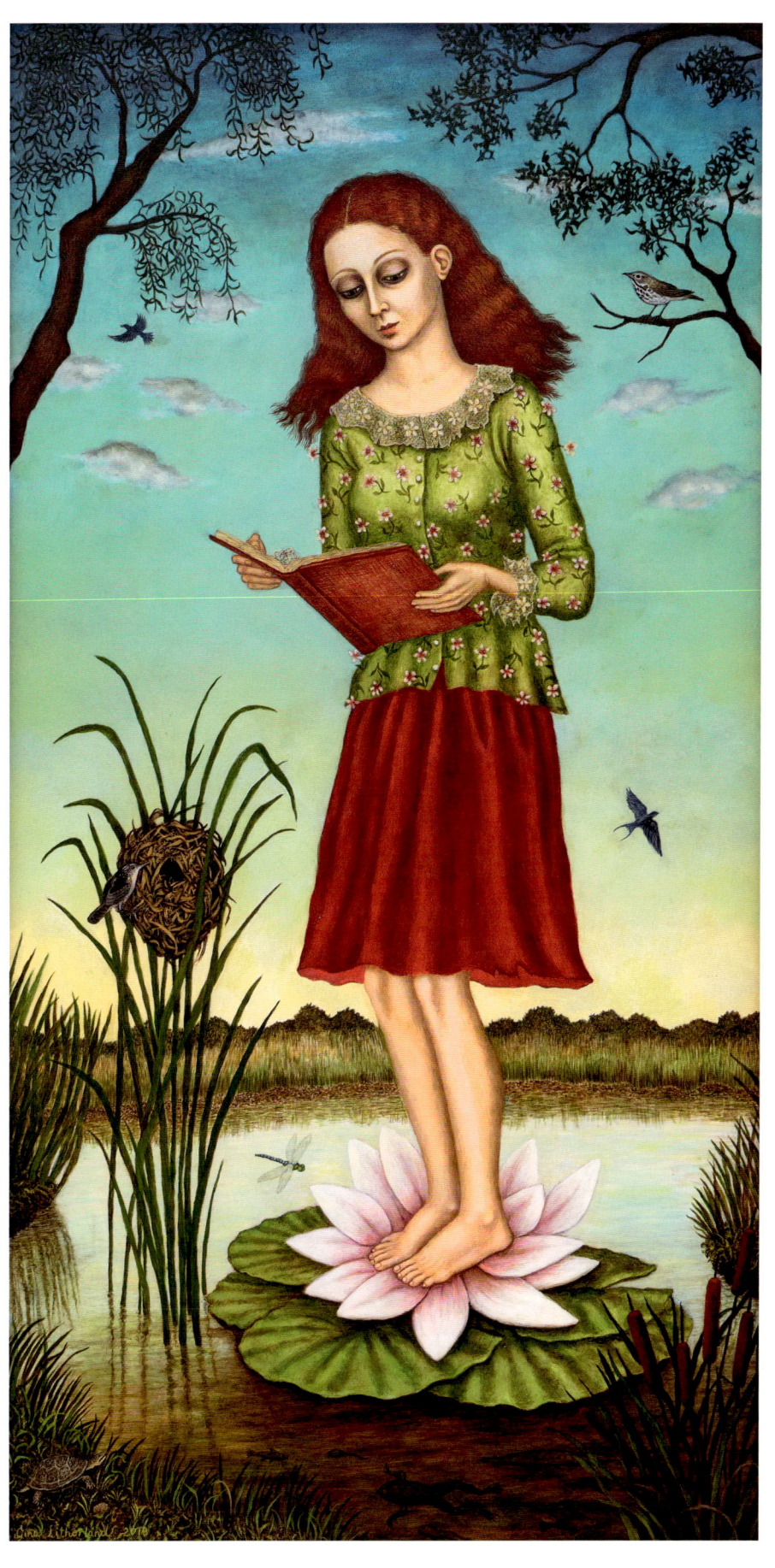

73

Gina Litherland

Pistis Sophia

2018. Oil on panel, 36 × 18 in.

135

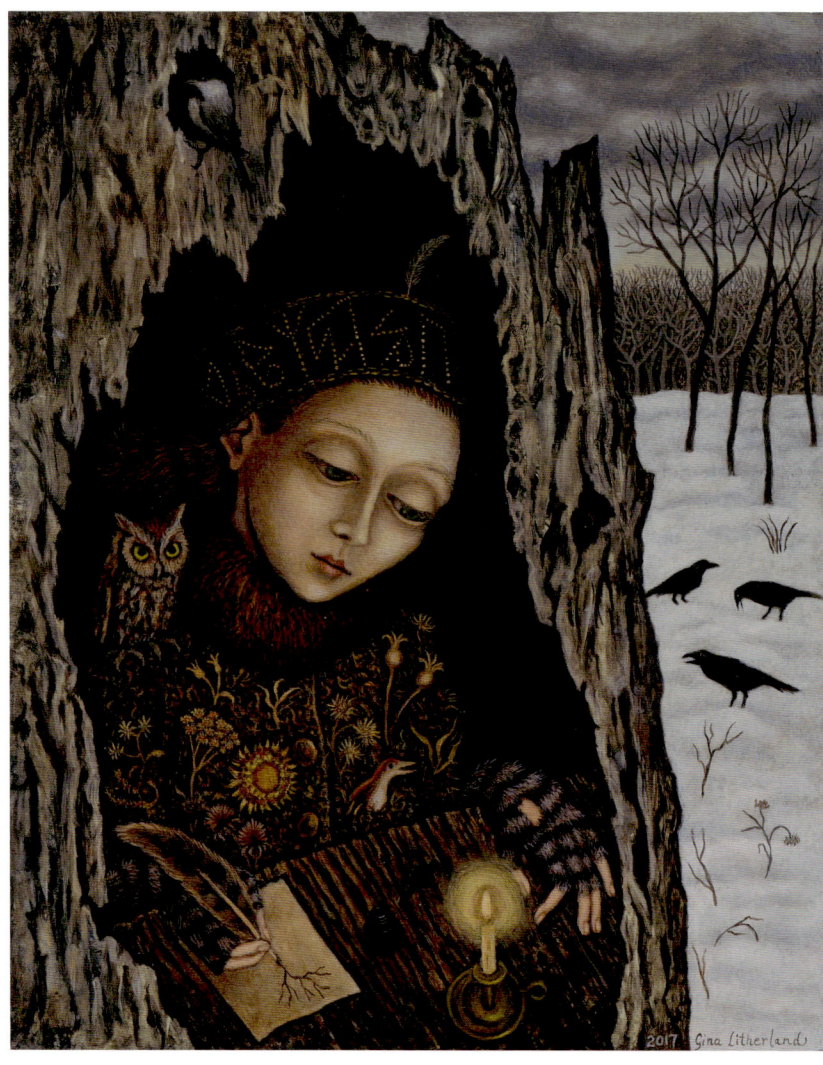

74
Gina Litherland

Winter Solstice
2017. Oil on panel, 9¼ × 7½ in.

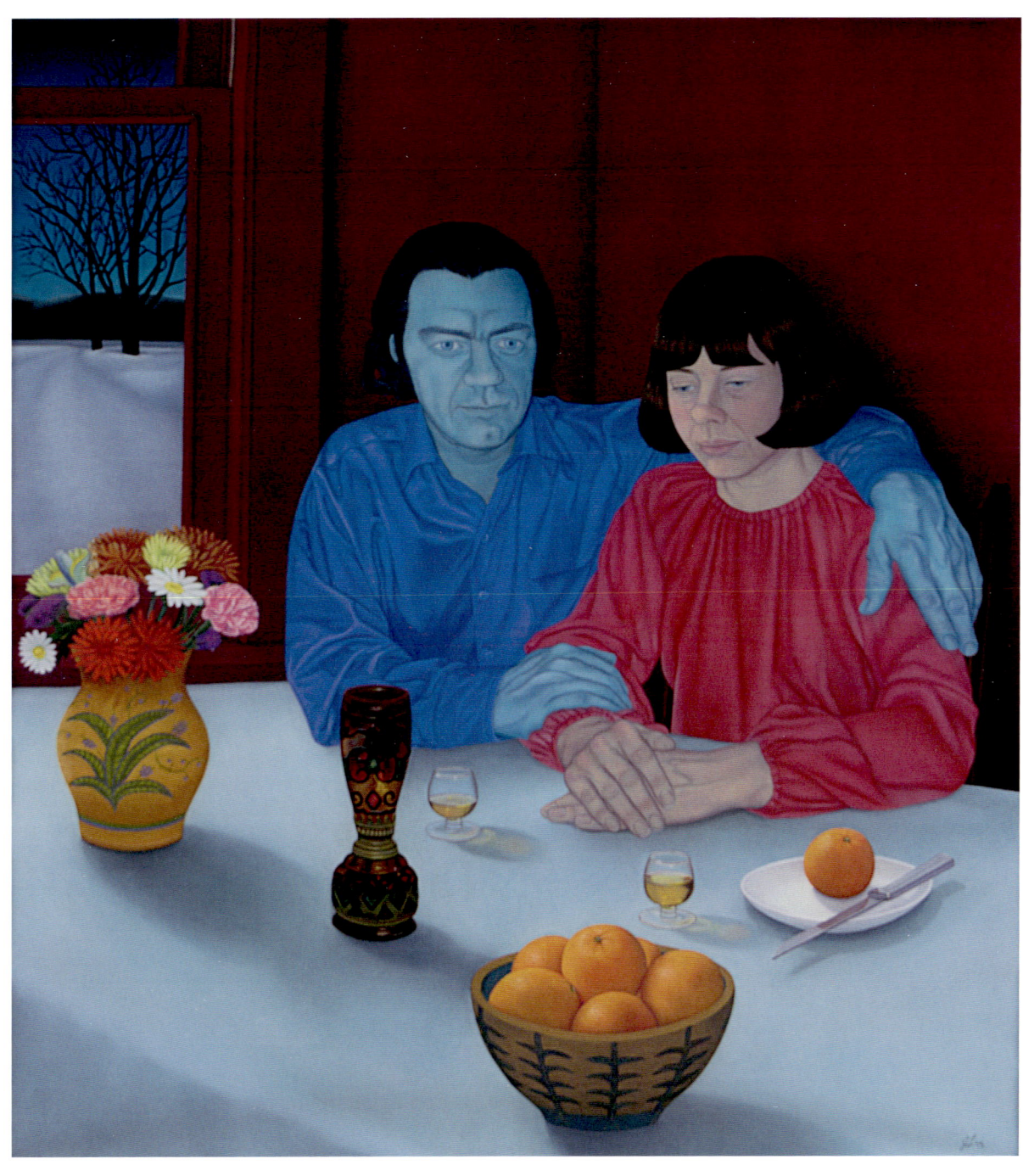

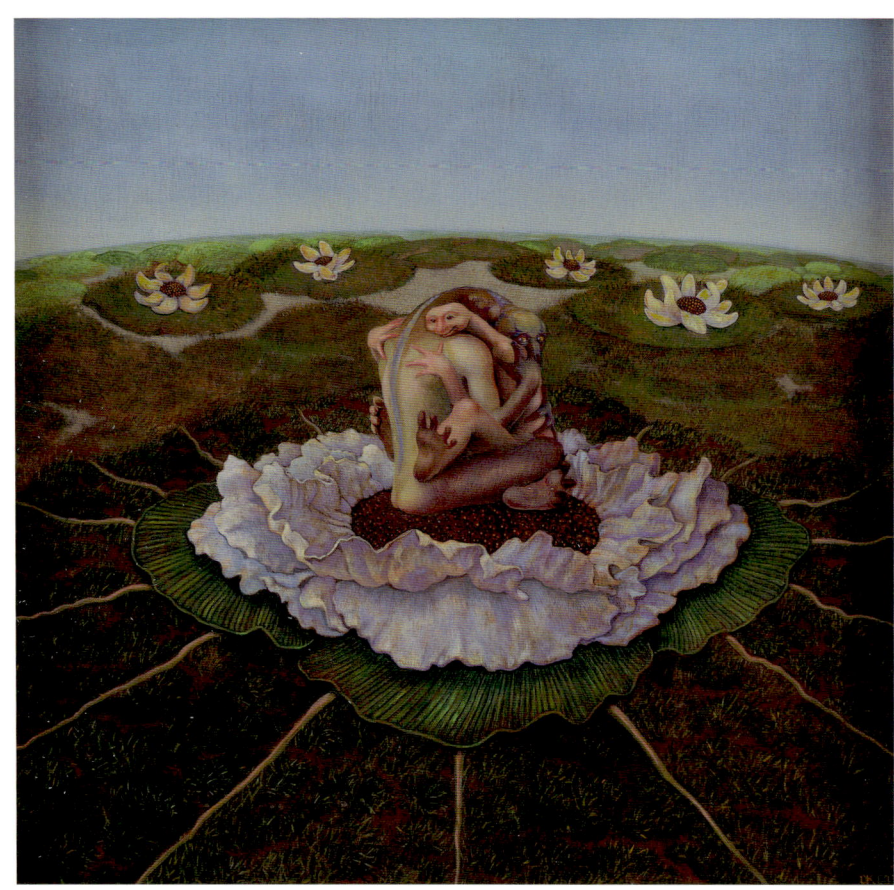

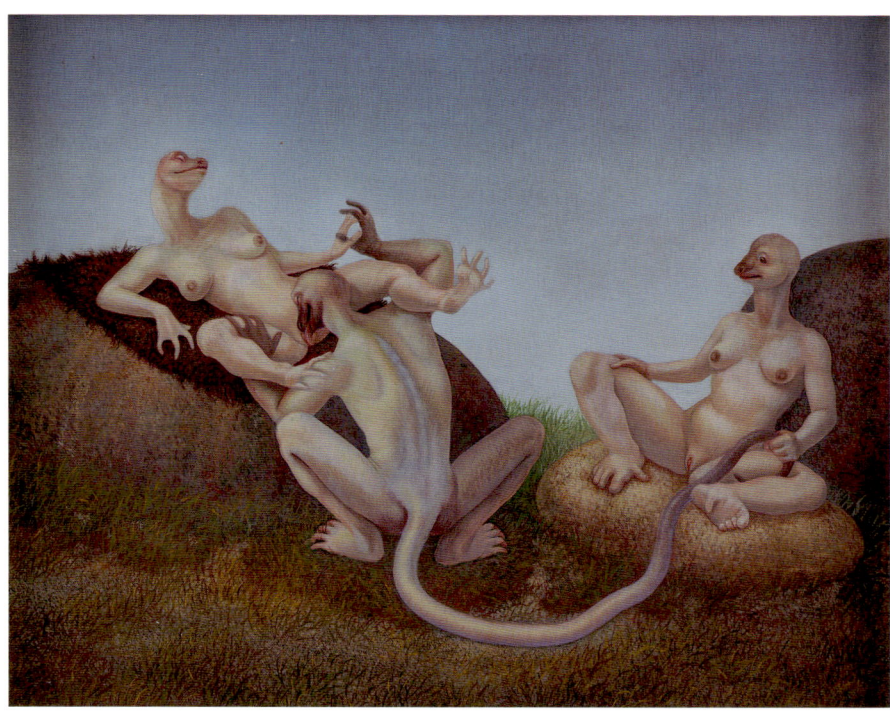

76
Deborah Kravitz
Within the Lotus
1983. Acrylic on panel, 8¼ × 8¼ in.

77
Deborah Kravitz
Ceremony
1982. Acrylic on panel, 6⅛ × 7⅝ in.

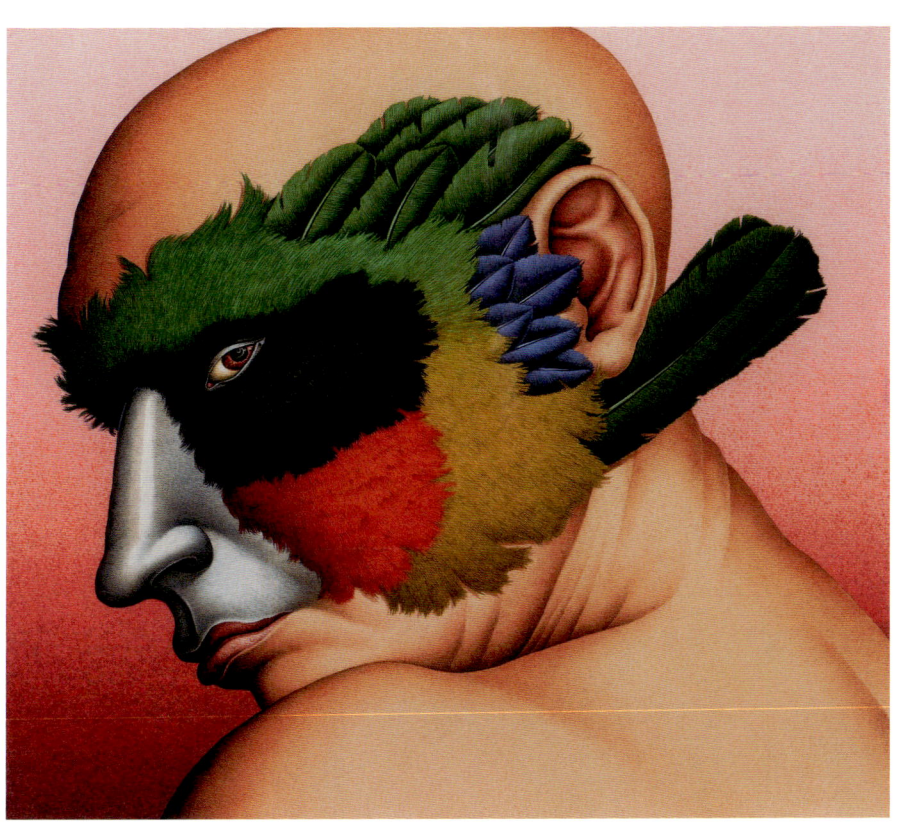

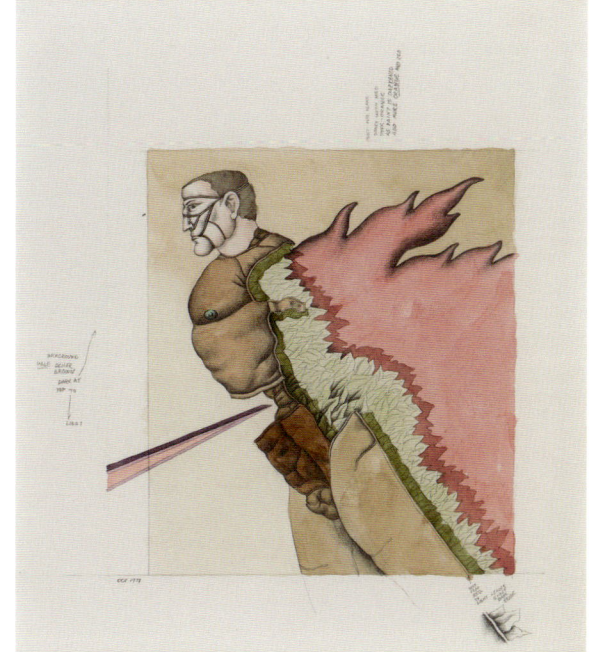

Red-Throated Bee-Eater

78

Robert Lostutter

1978. Watercolor on paper, 12½ × 14 in.

Untitled (Burning man)

79

Robert Lostutter

1971. Watercolor and graphite on cardstock, 7¾ × 6¾ in.

139

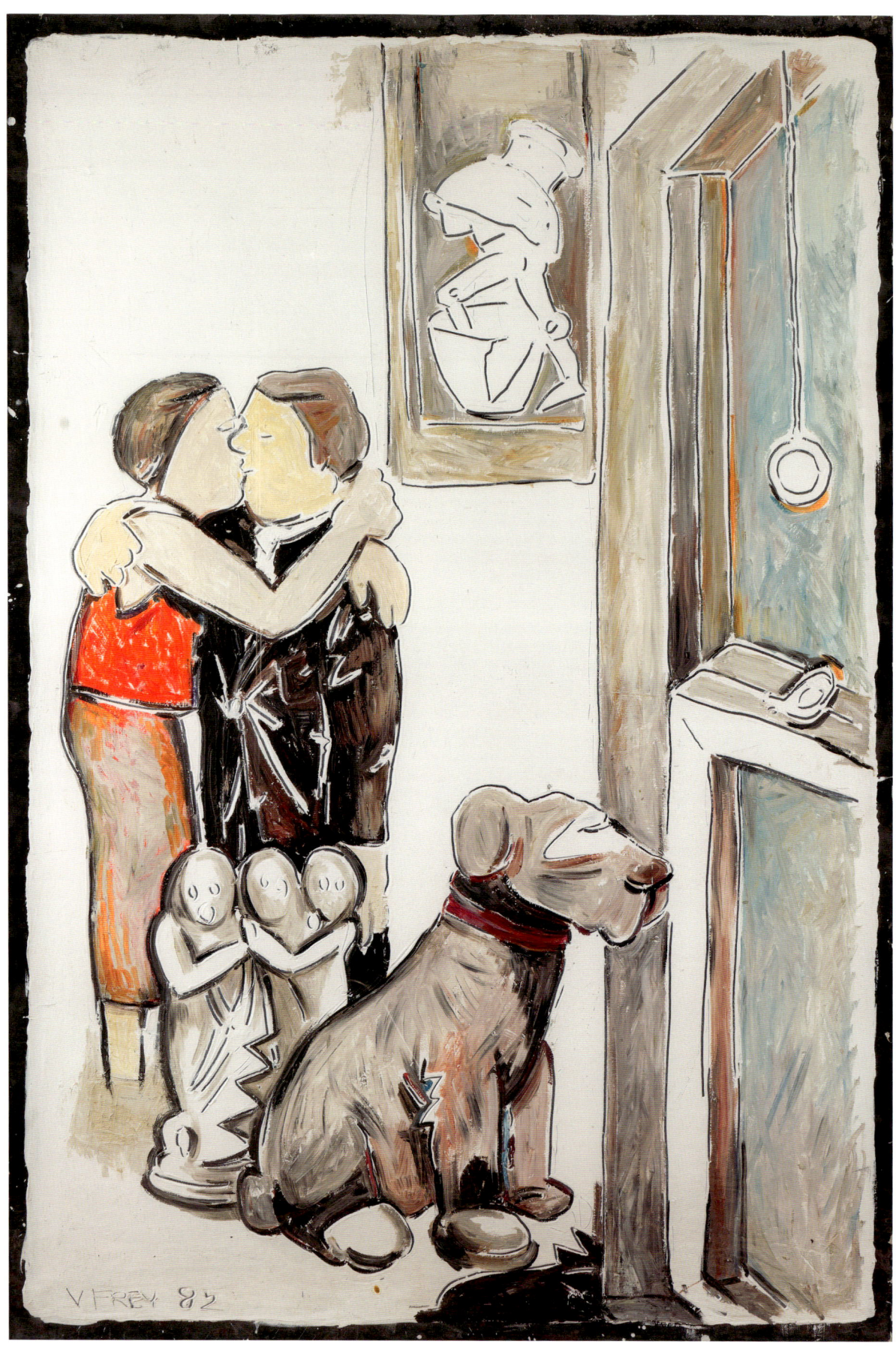

80
Viola Frey
(1933–2004)

Untitled (Kissing couple and dog in window)
1982. Oil on paper, 60 × 40 in.

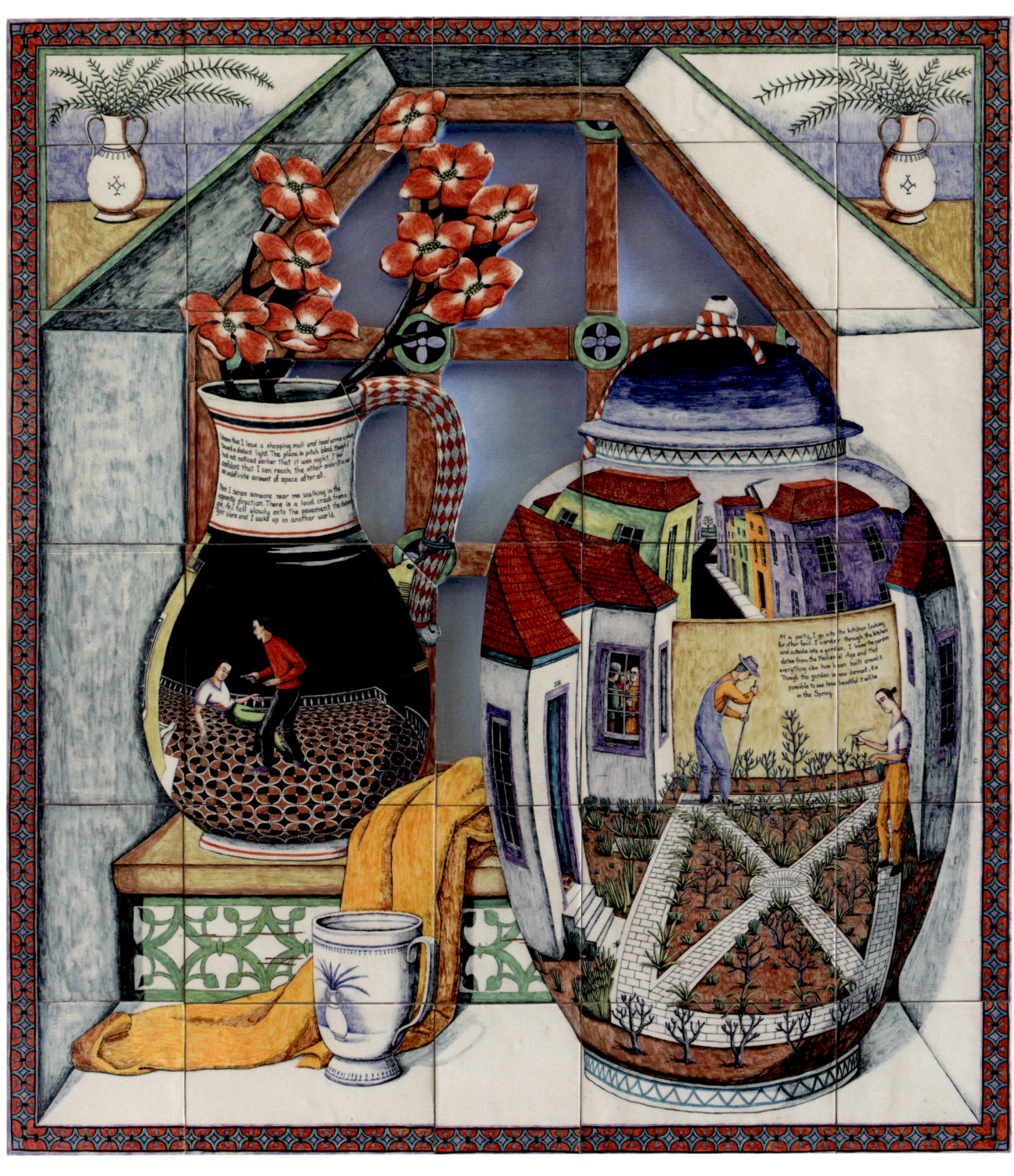

81
Anne Kraus
(1956–2003)

The Dormant Garden
2001. Glazed whiteware, 36 × 32 in.

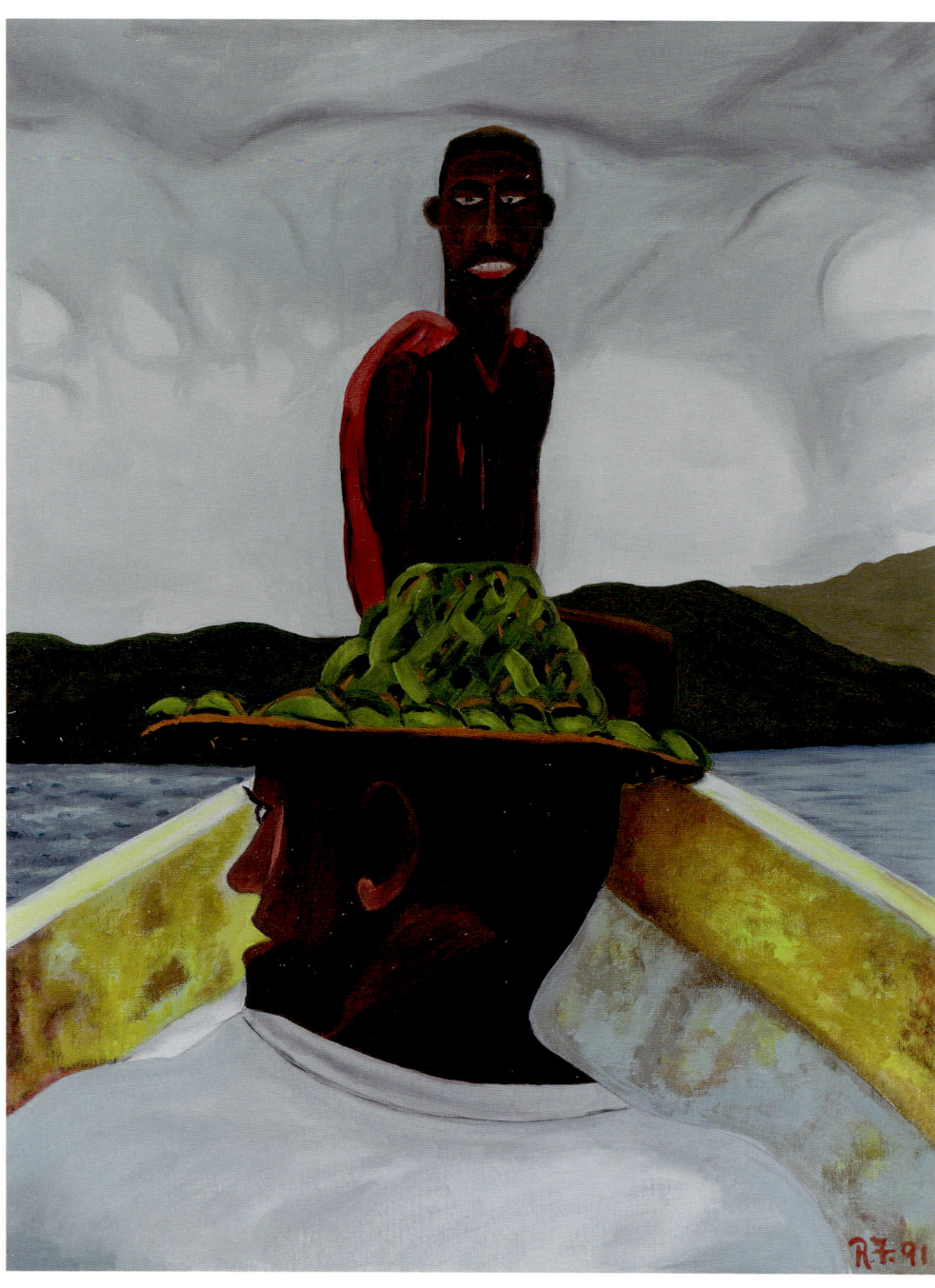

82
Rafael Ferrer
(b. 1933)

Sombrero de Palma
1991. Oil on canvas, 24 × 18 in.

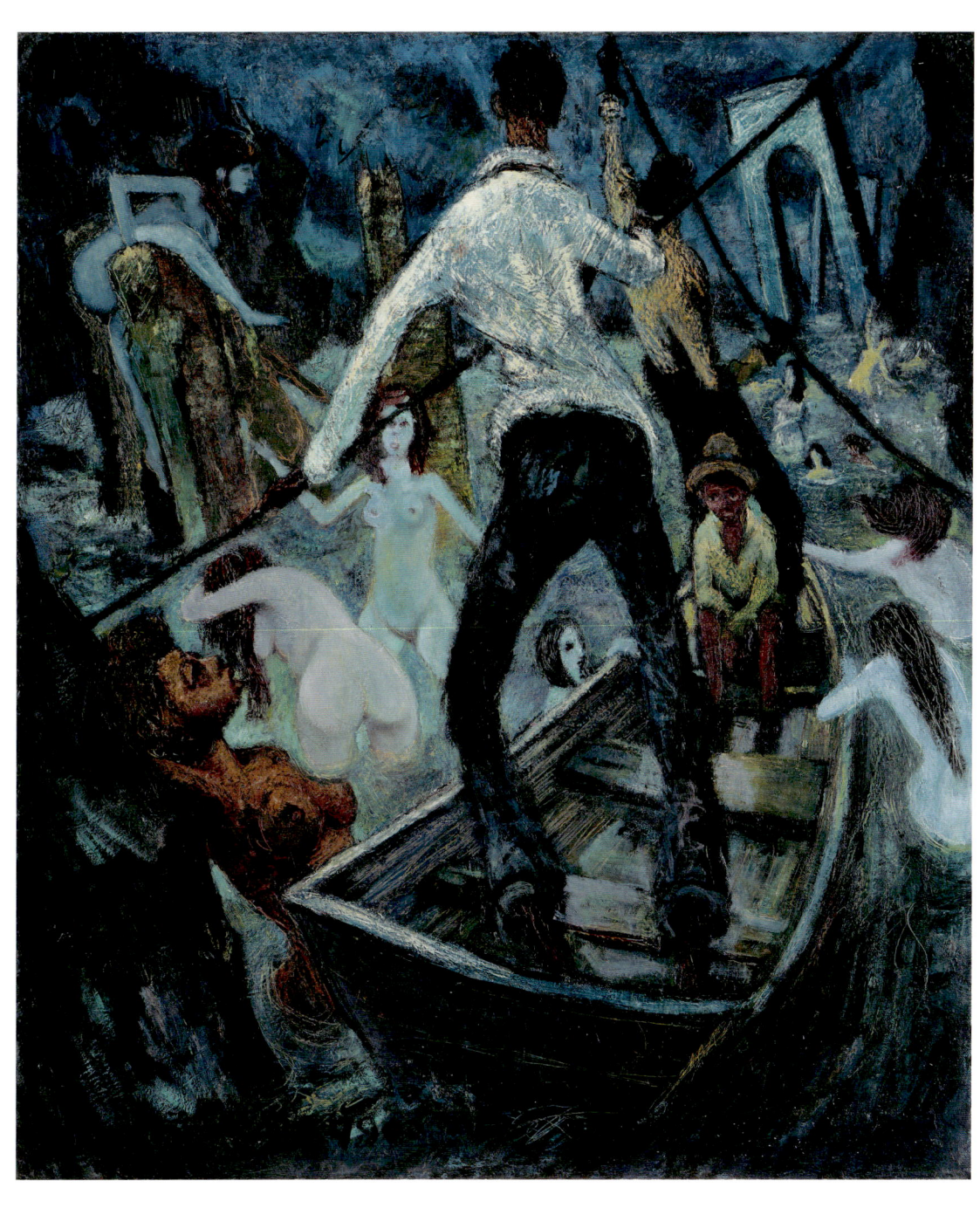

83
Paul F. Keene Jr.   *Odysseus*
(1920–2009)   1949. Oil on linen canvas, 24 × 20 in.   143

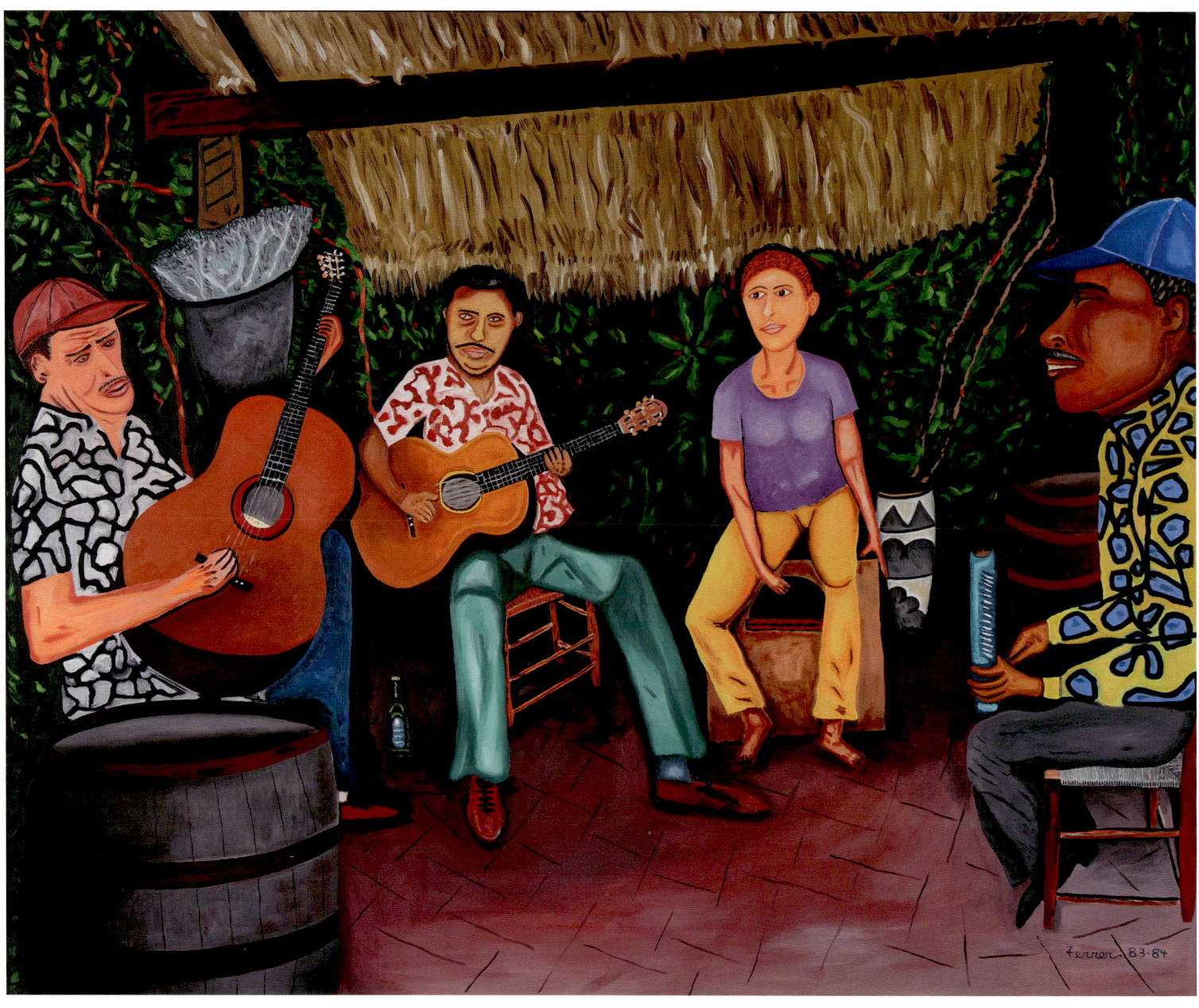

84
Rafael Ferrer

El Bolero
1983–84. Oil on canvas, 60 × 72 in.

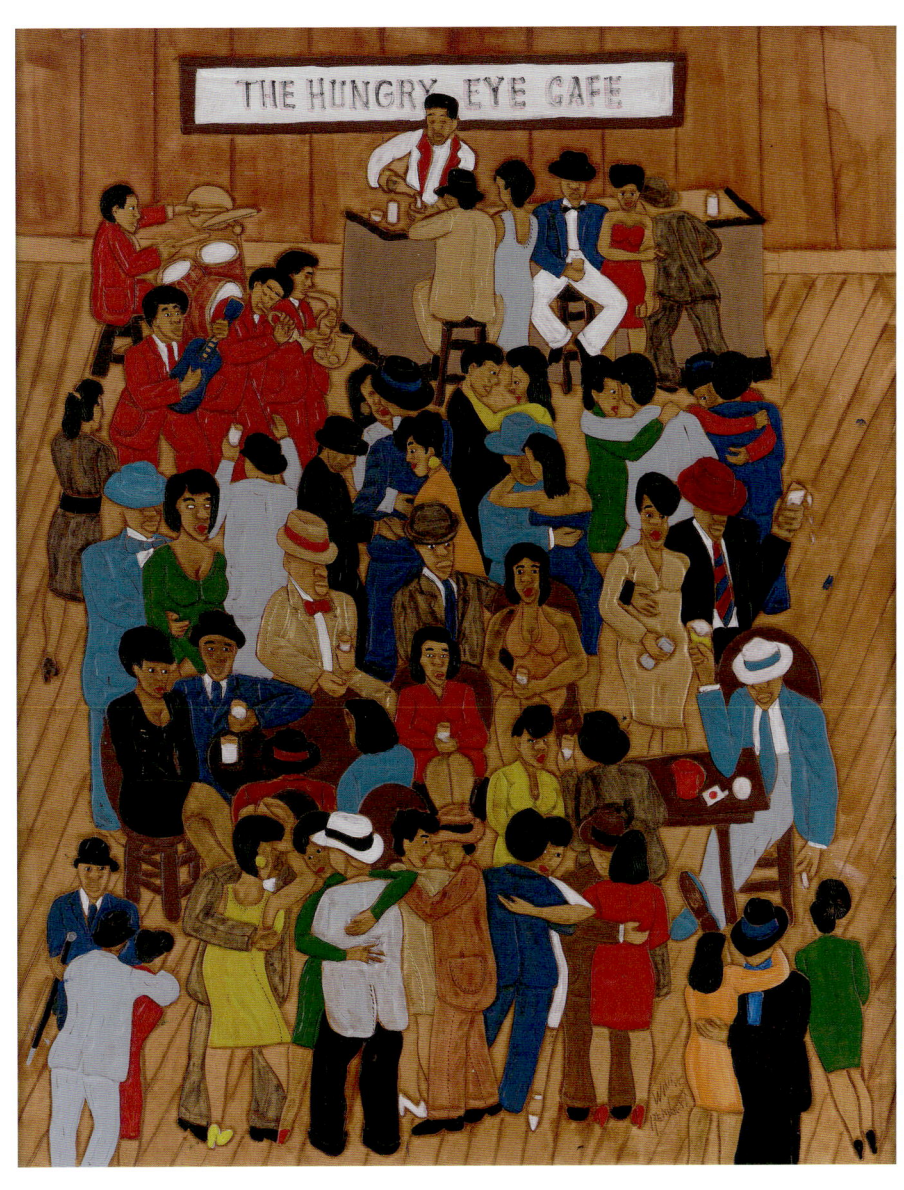

85
Winfred Rembert

The Hungry Eye Cafe #2
2006. Dye on tooled leather, 31½ × 24¼ in. 145

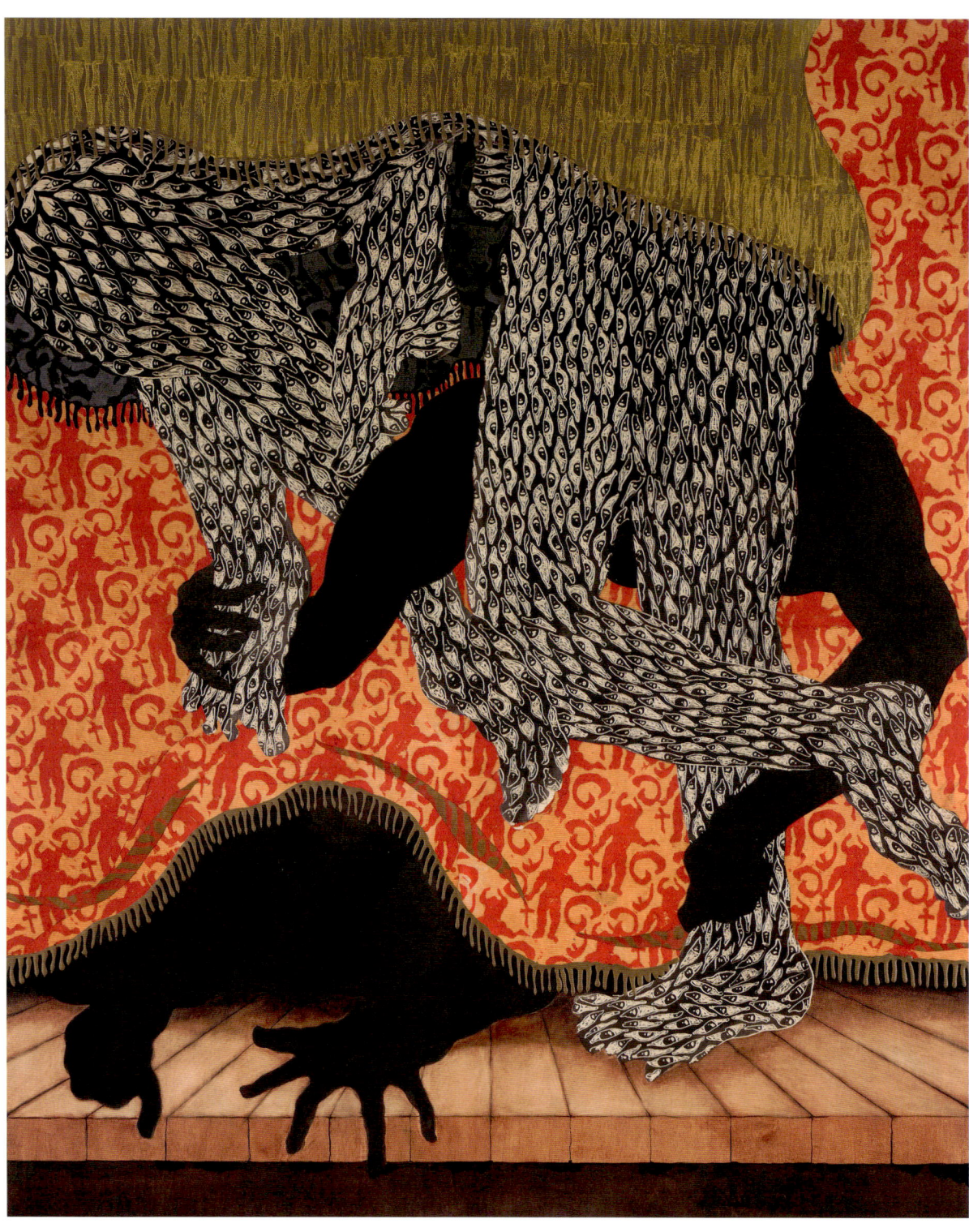

86

Didier William

(b. 1983)

Dancing, Pouring, Crackling, Mourning

2015. Collage, acrylic, and stain on panel
with carving, 60 × 48 in.

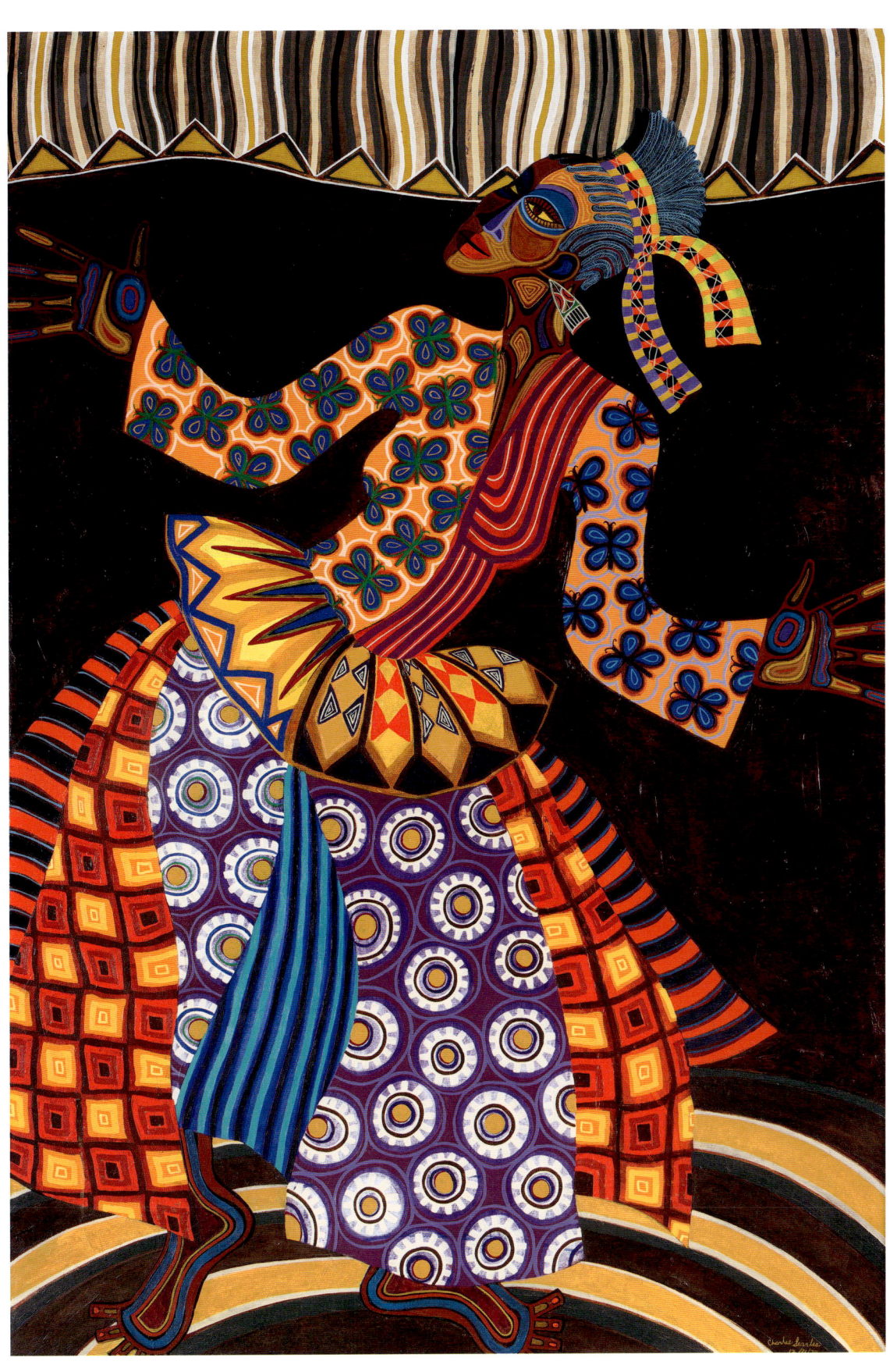

87
Charles Searles
(1937–2004)

Dancer #1
1974. Oil on canvas, 70½ × 46½ in.

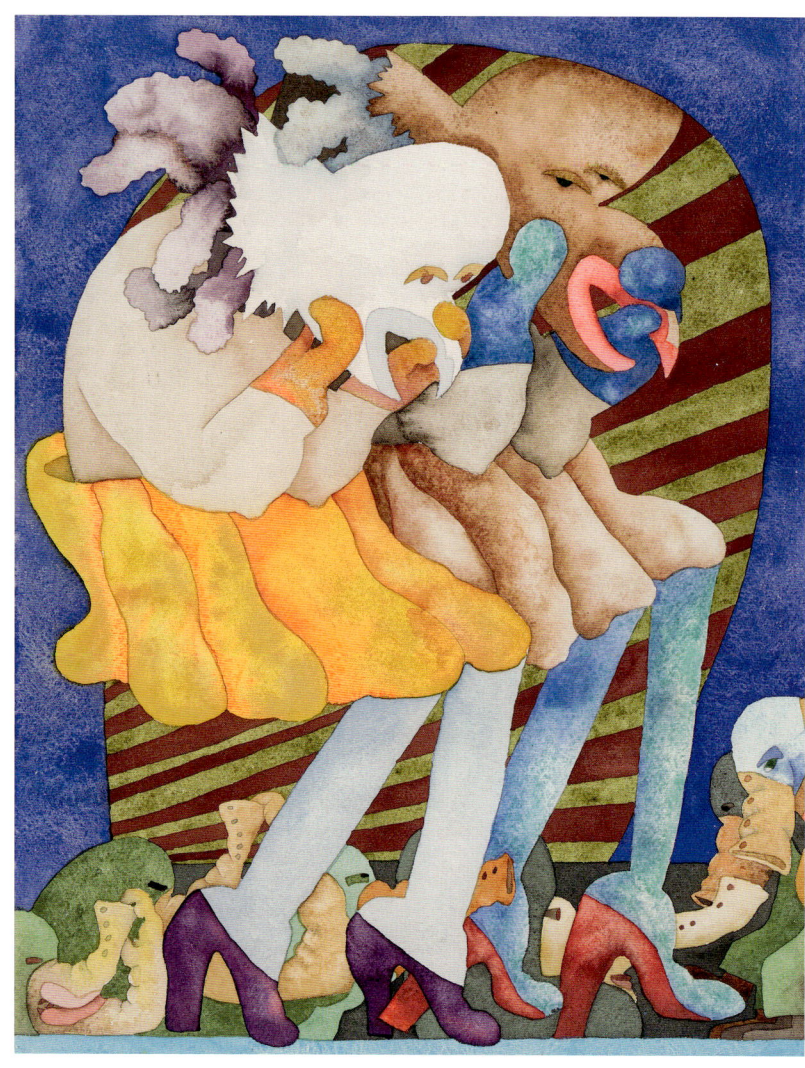

Archway Peckercysters

88
Gladys Nilsson

c. 1968. Watercolor on paper,
14¾ × 11¼ in.

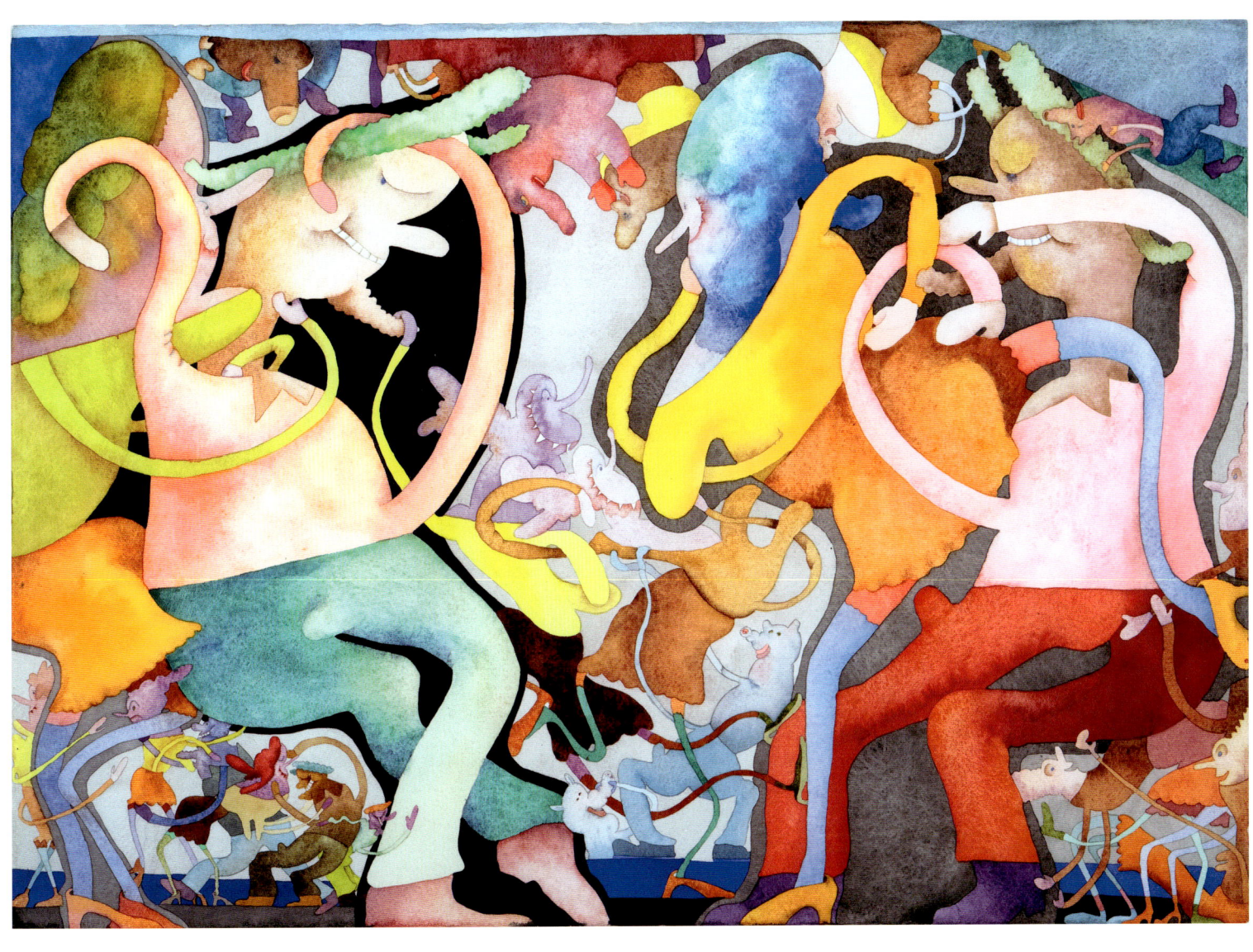

89
Gladys Nilsson

To Couples: DeKaled
1969. Watercolor on paper, 22¼ × 30½ in.

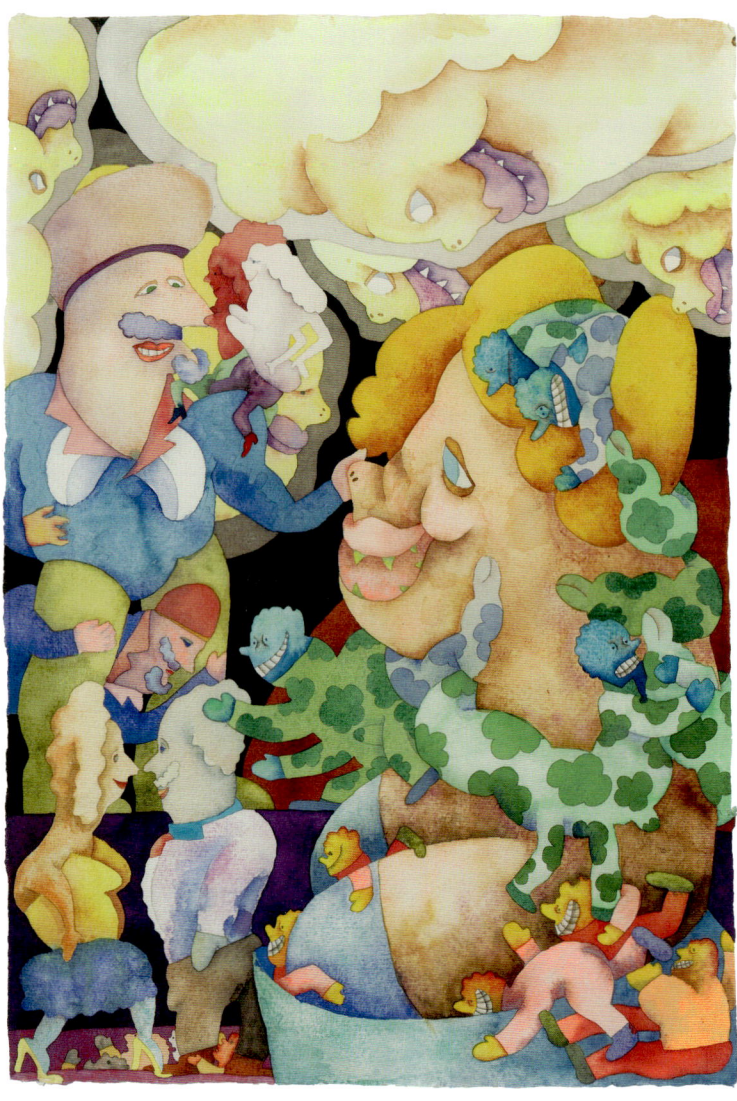

Cloud Burste

90
Gladys Nilsson

1969. Watercolor on board,
22 × 15 in.

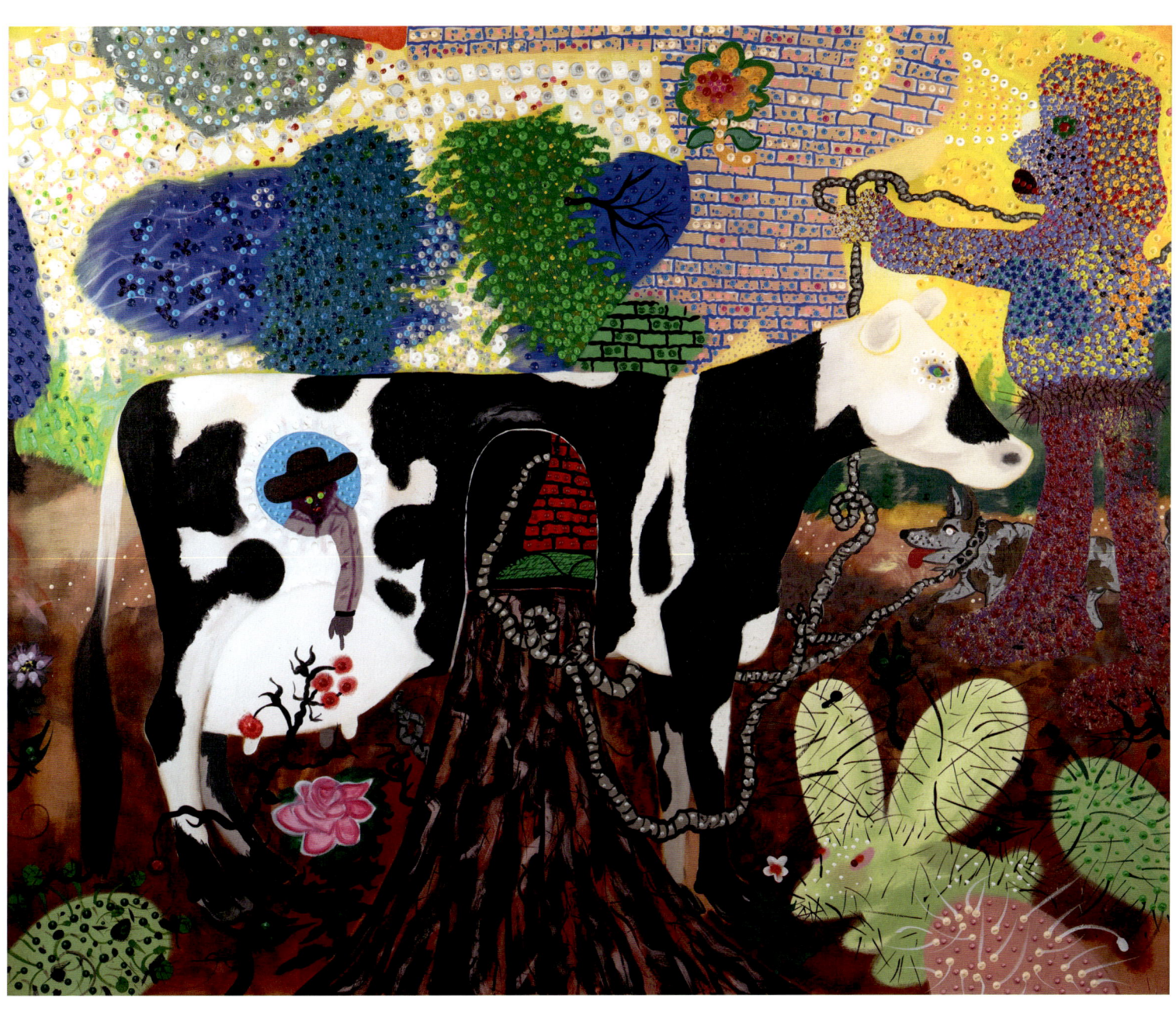

91
Roy De Forest
(1930–2007)

Trouble in the Bovine Quarters
1975. Acrylic on canvas, 60¼ × 72¼ in.

151

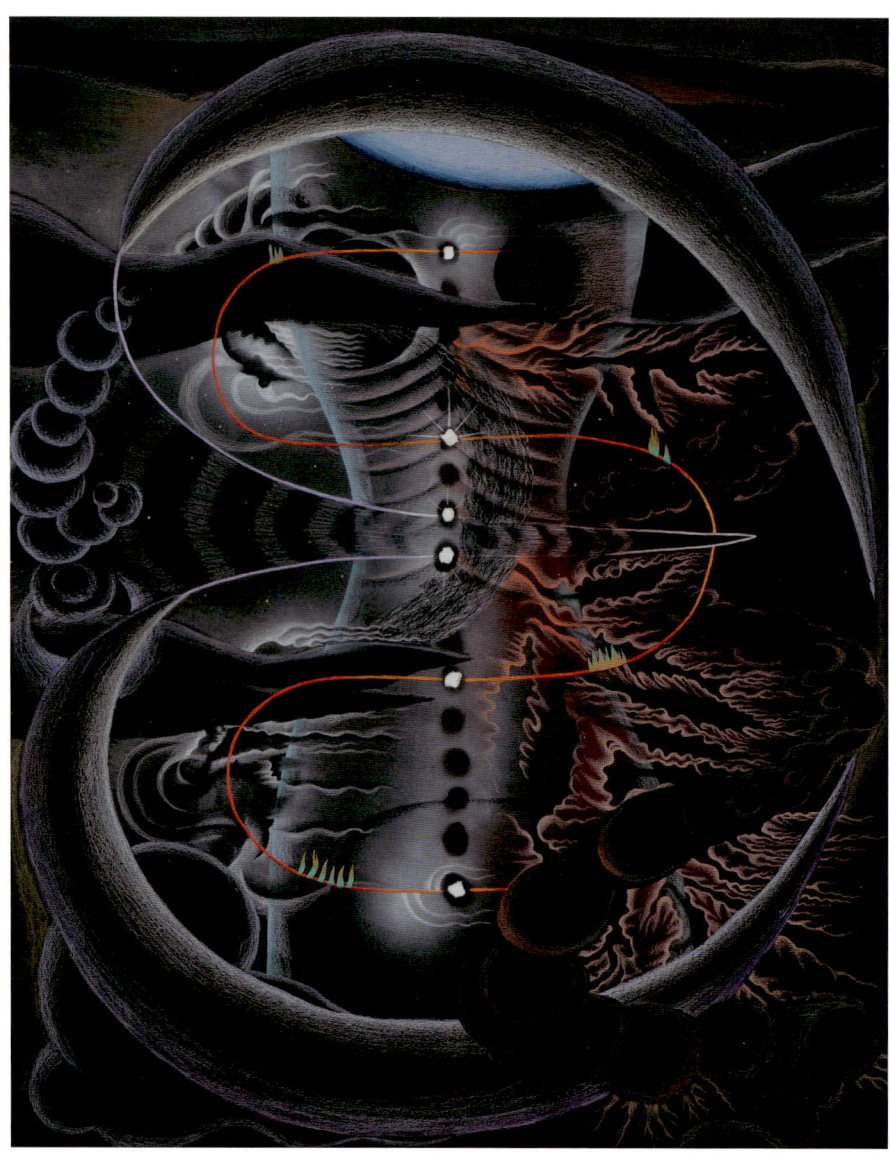

92
Marcy
Hermansader

Living with the Moon
1987. Colored pencil, acrylic, spray paint, and
pastel on board, 30 × 27 in.

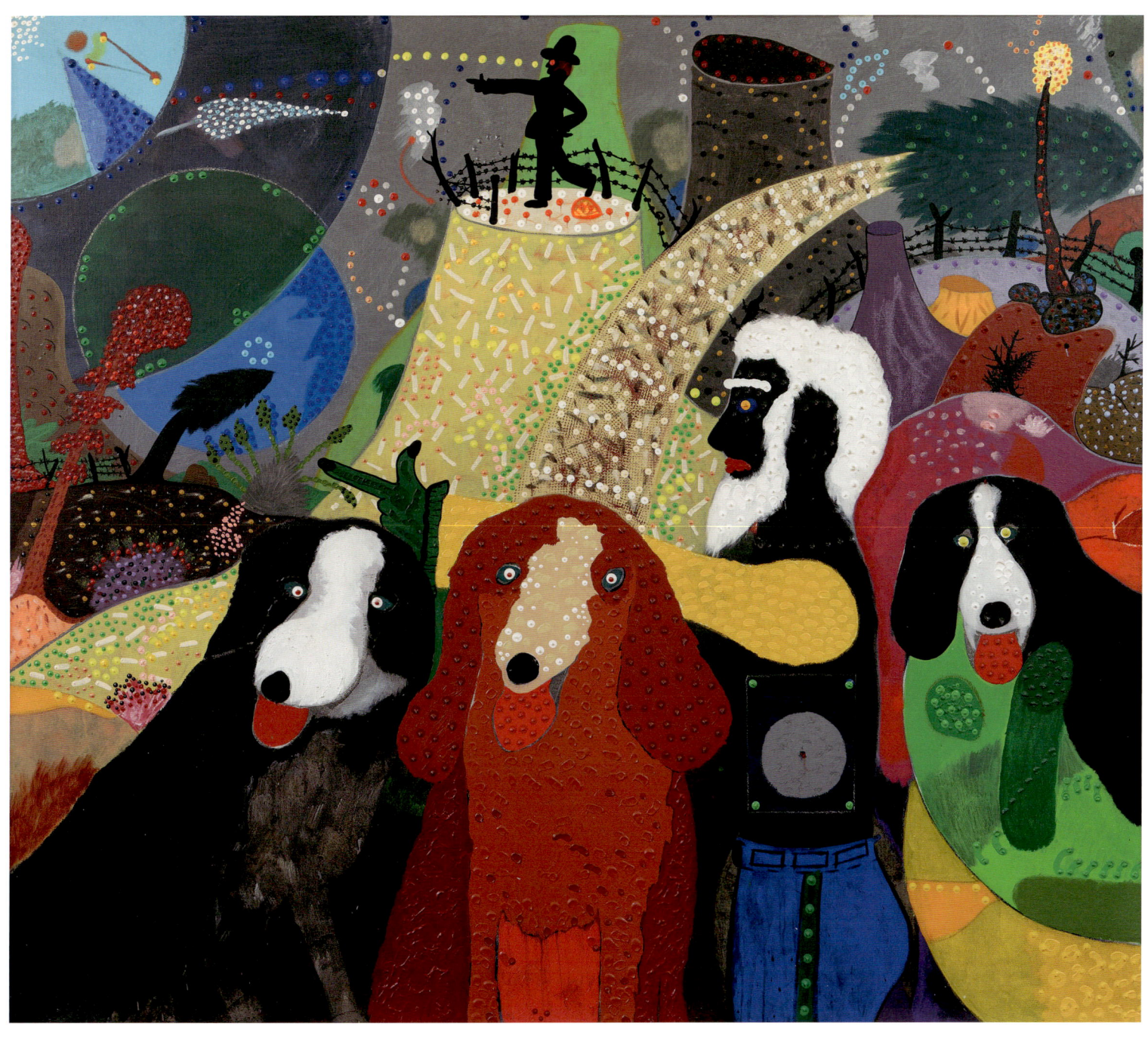

93
Roy De Forest

Watching for the Outriders
1976–77. Acrylic on canvas, 60 × 68 in.

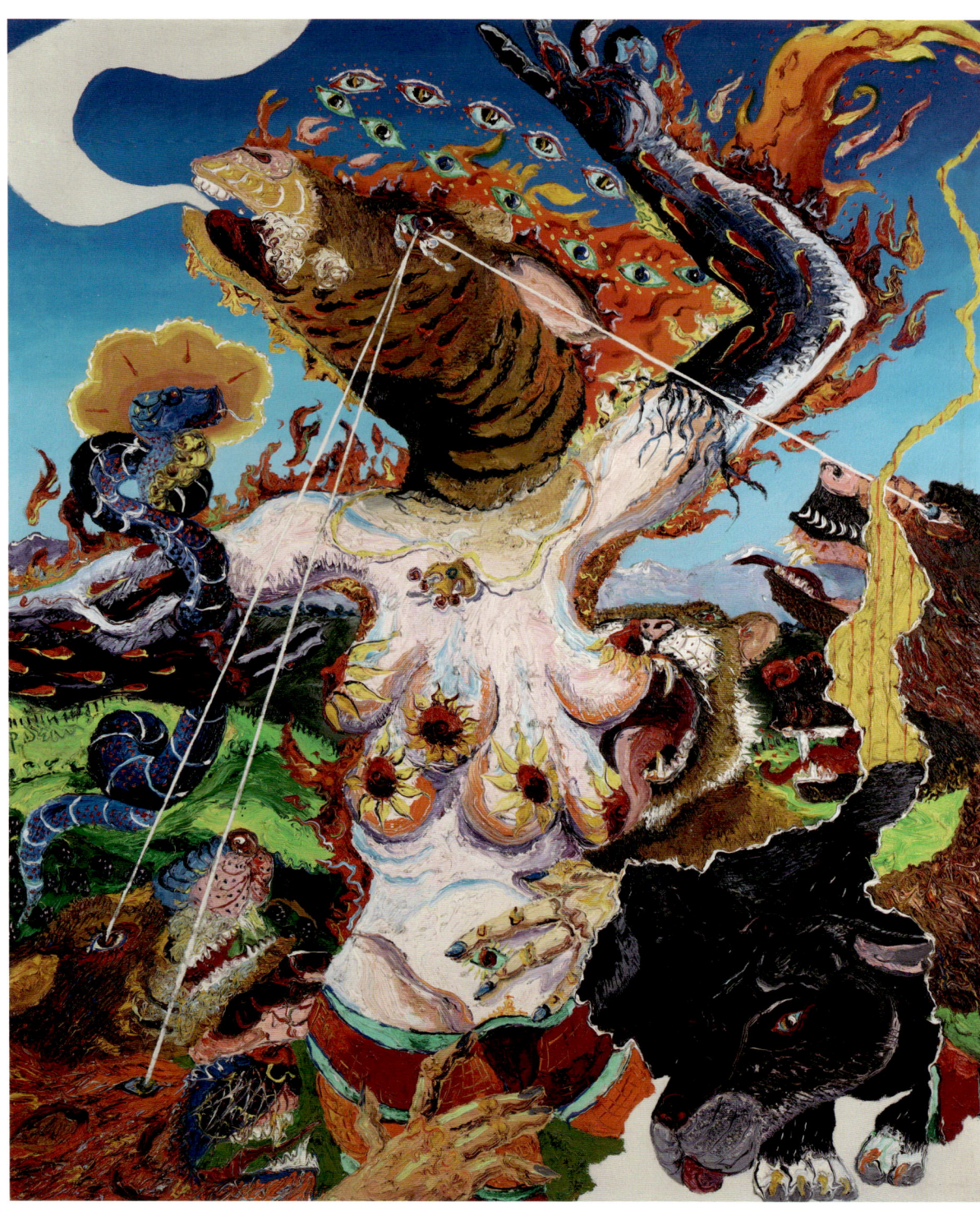

94
Peter Dean

Hounded
1977. Oil on canvas, 60 × 50 in.

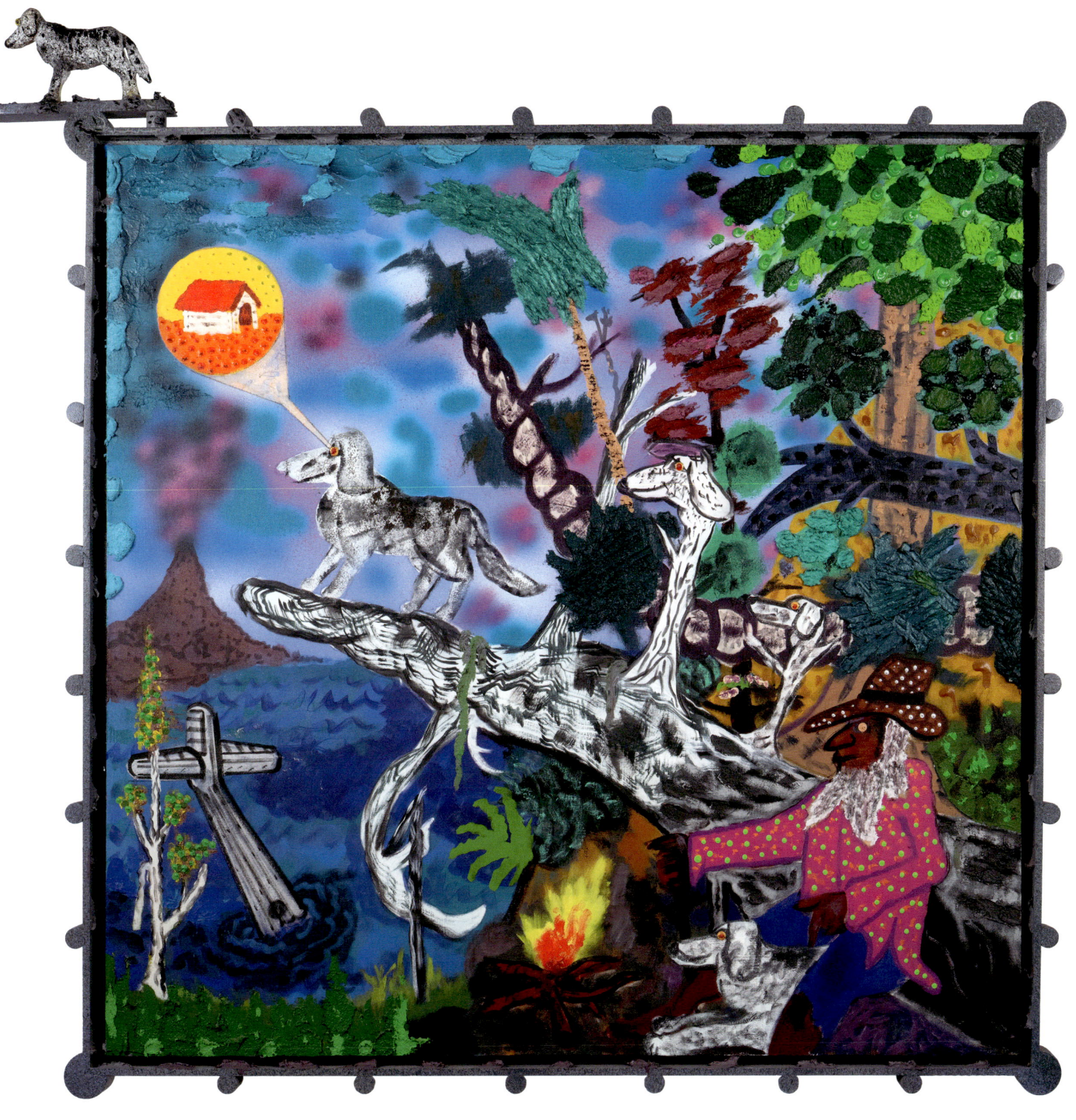

You Can't Go Home Again
1995. Acrylic on canvas, in artist's frame,
58 × 60 in.

95
Roy De Forest

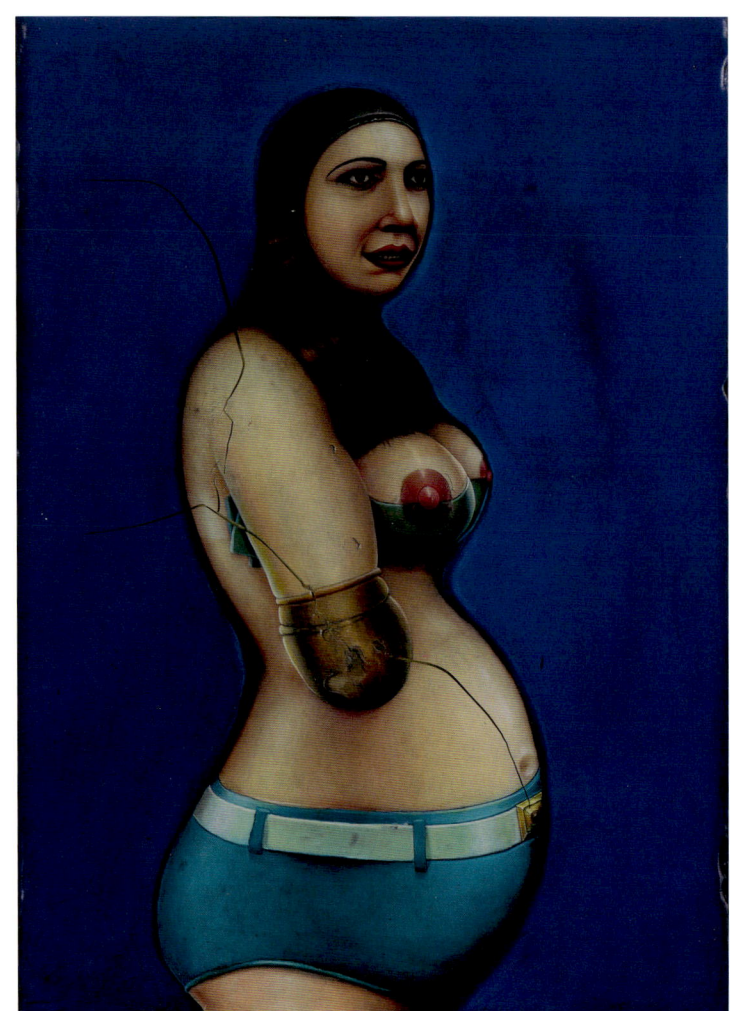

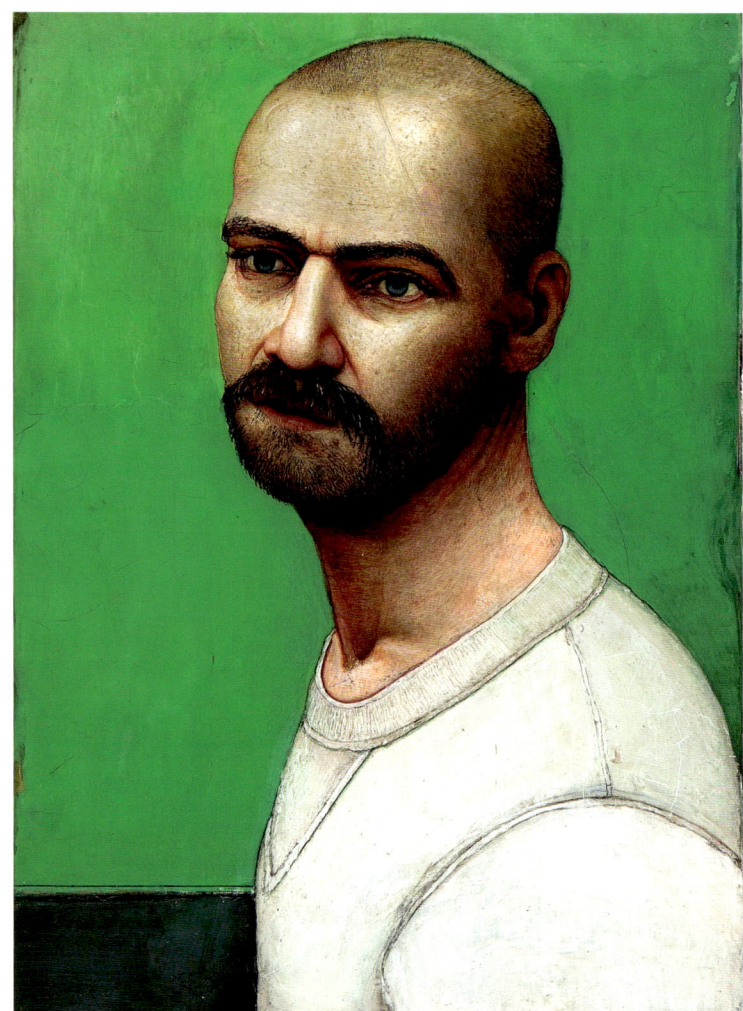

Woman on Blue Ground

96
Gregory Gillespie

1969. Mixed media, 15½ × 11½ in.,
artist's frame

Self-Portrait (Bald)

97
Gregory Gillespie

1971–72. Oil and Magna on wood,
15 × 10 in.

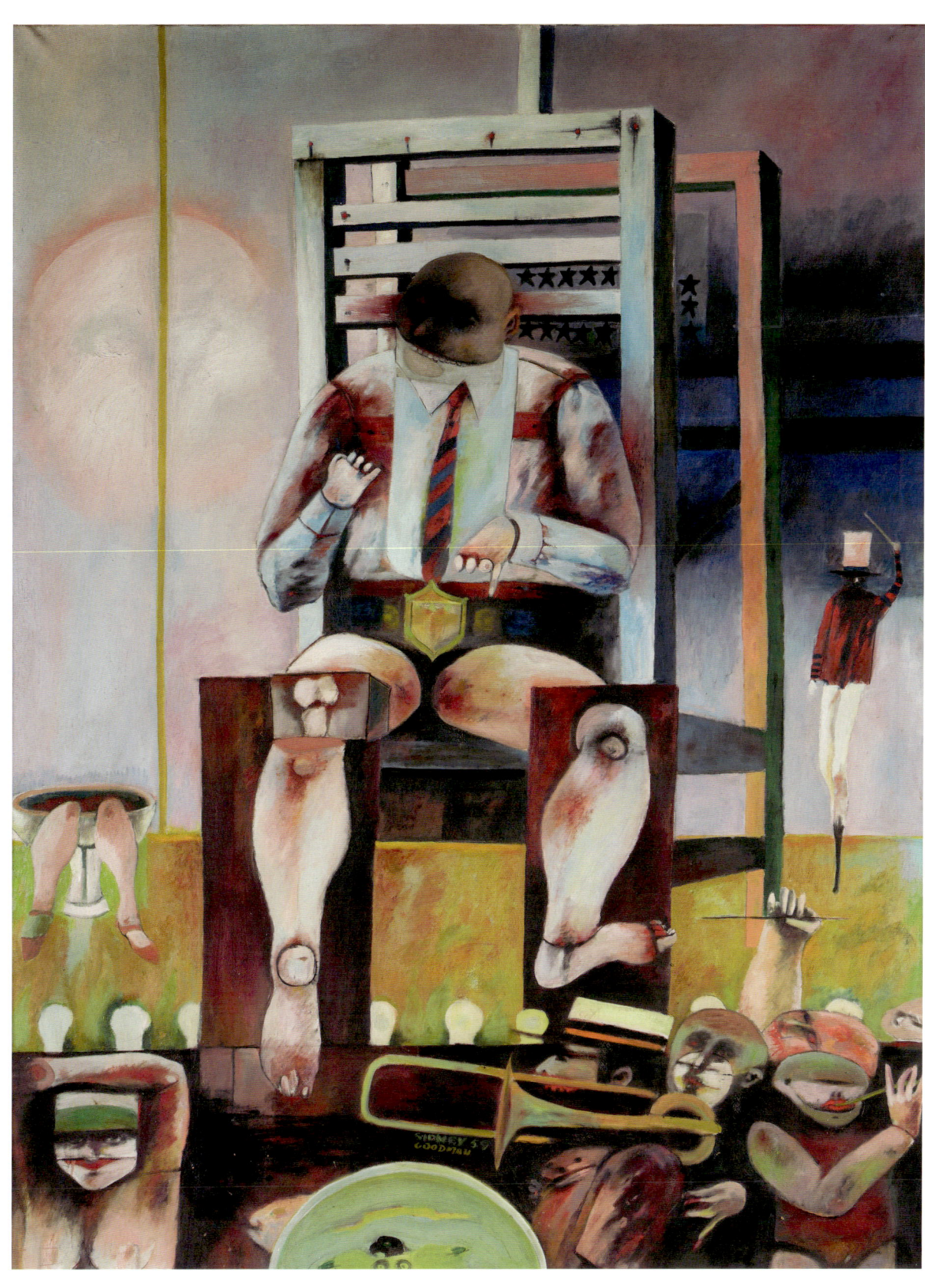

98
Sidney Goodman
(1936–2013)

Untitled (Electric Chair)
1959. Oil on canvas, 68 × 50 in.

157

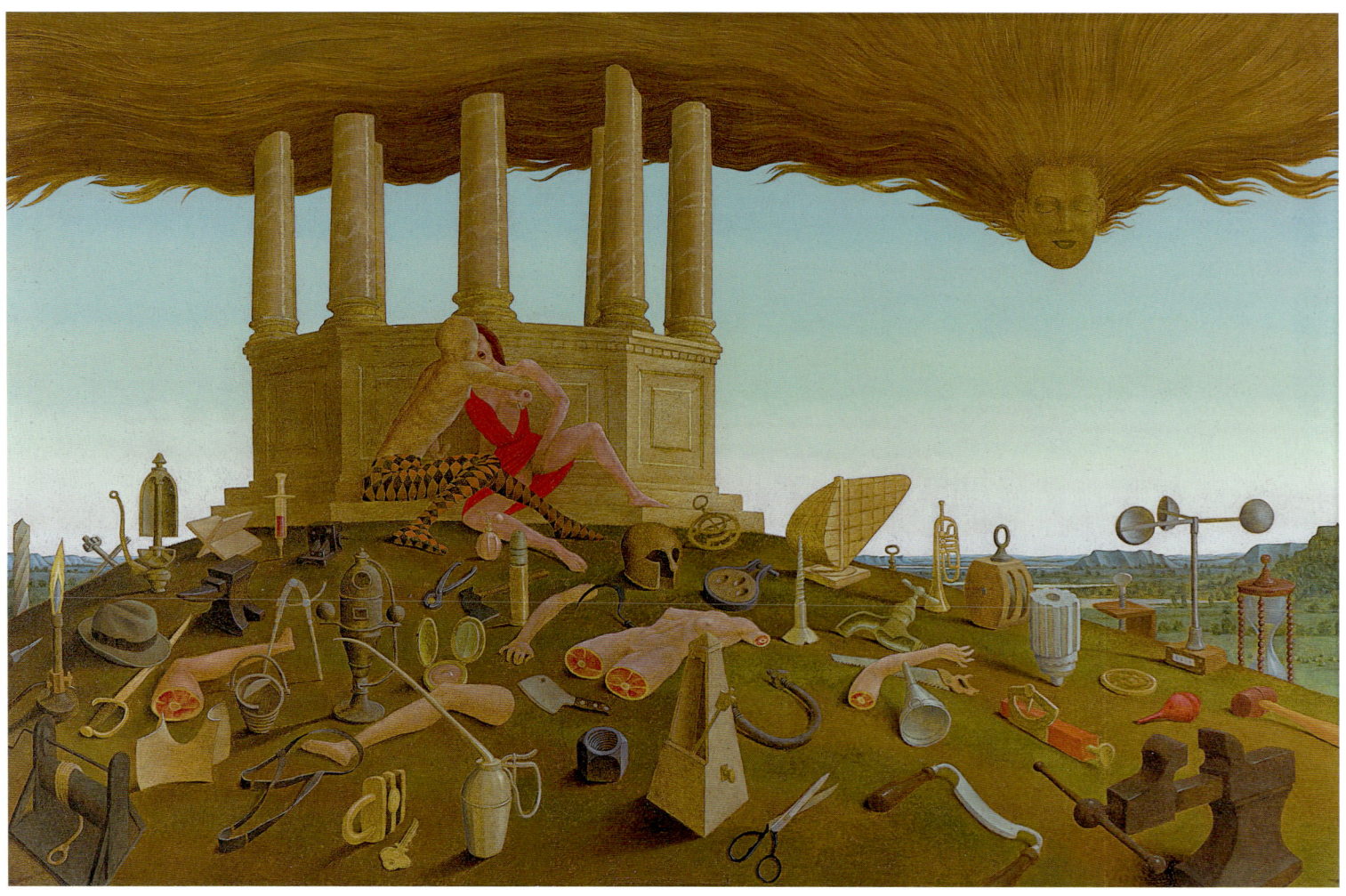

99
John Wilde

Work Reconsidered: Love After Murder
1989. Oil on wood, 13 × 20¼ in.

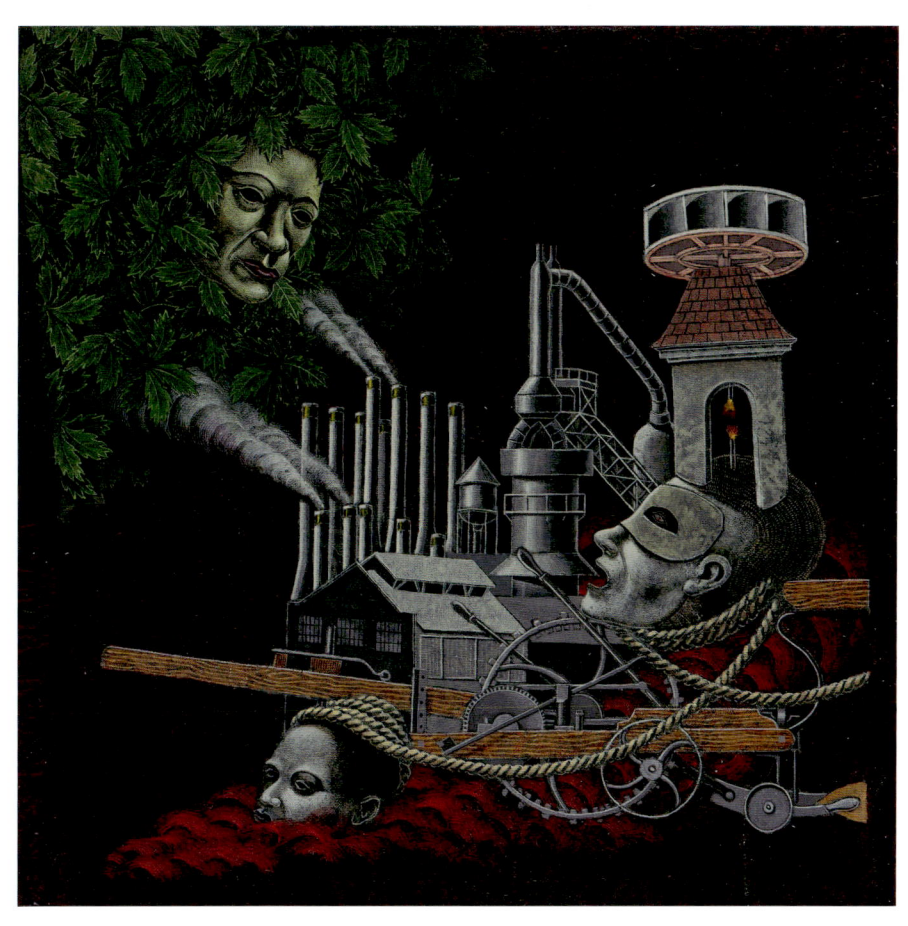

Untitled LR33

100

Eric Stotik

(b. 1963)

(Factory, machine, green man)
2006. Acrylic on cloth on panel,
7 × 7¼ in.

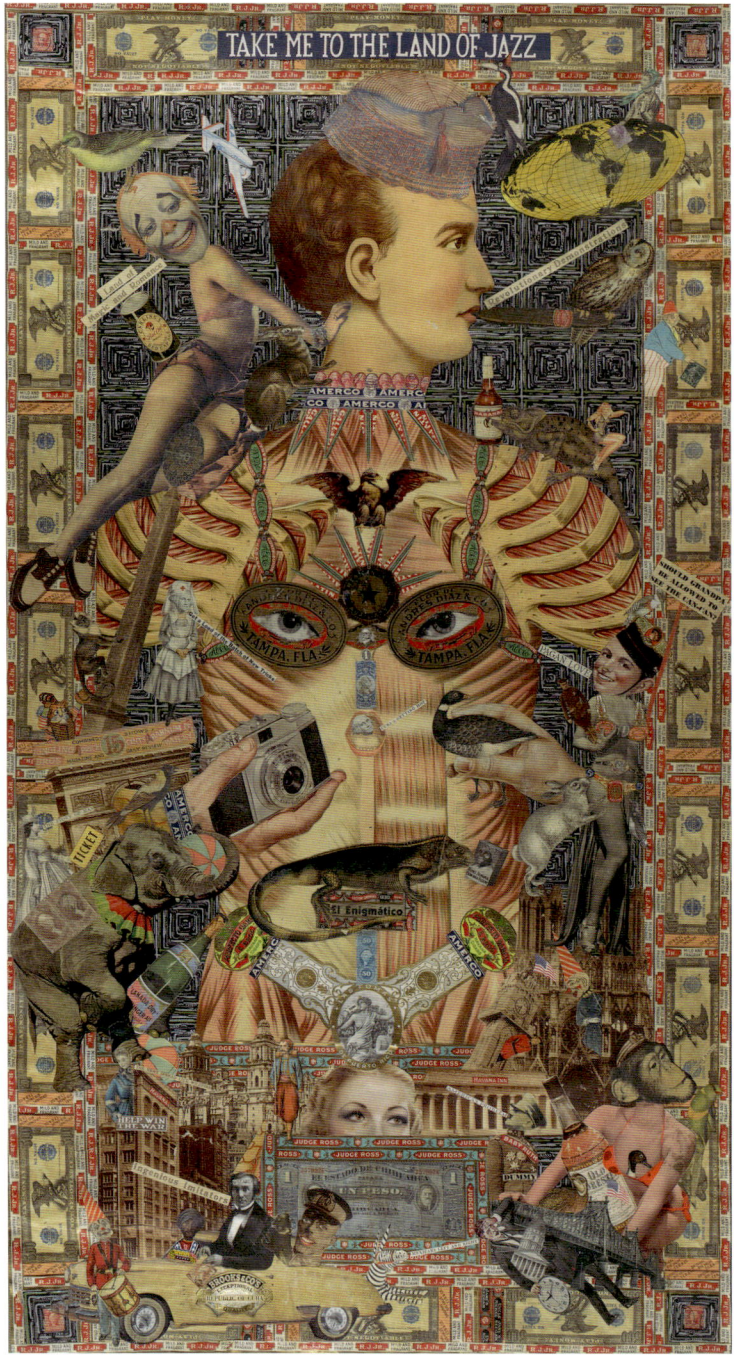

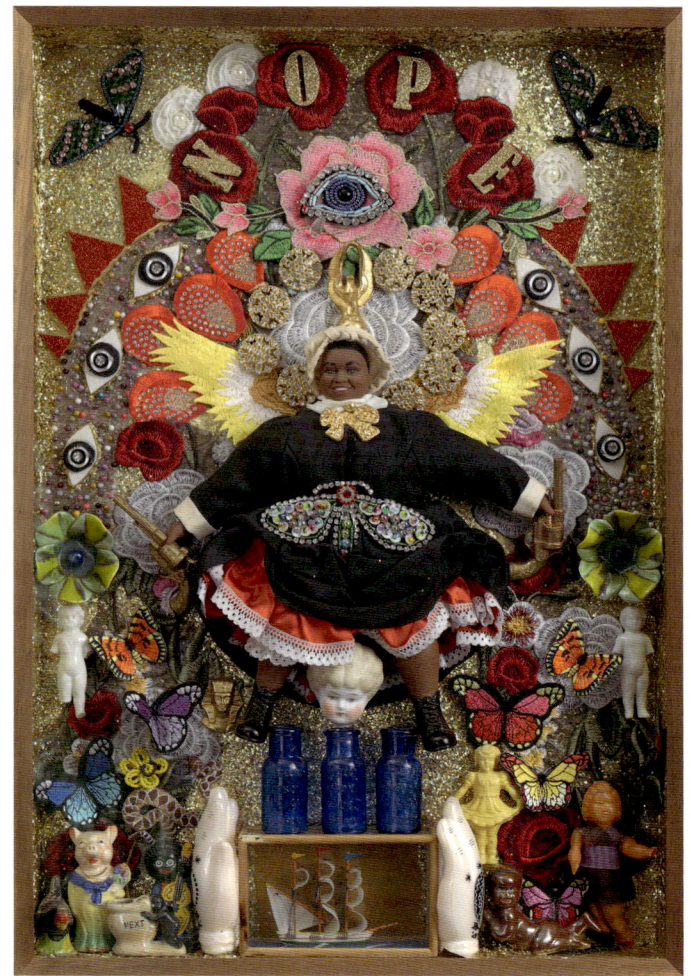

101
Felipe Jesus
Consalvos
(1891–1960)

Take Me to the Land of Jazz
c. 1920–50. Mixed-media collage,
51 × 27¼ in.

102
Vanessa German
(b. 1976)

Declaration of Independence
2020. Mixed-media assemblage,
27 × 17 × 4 in.

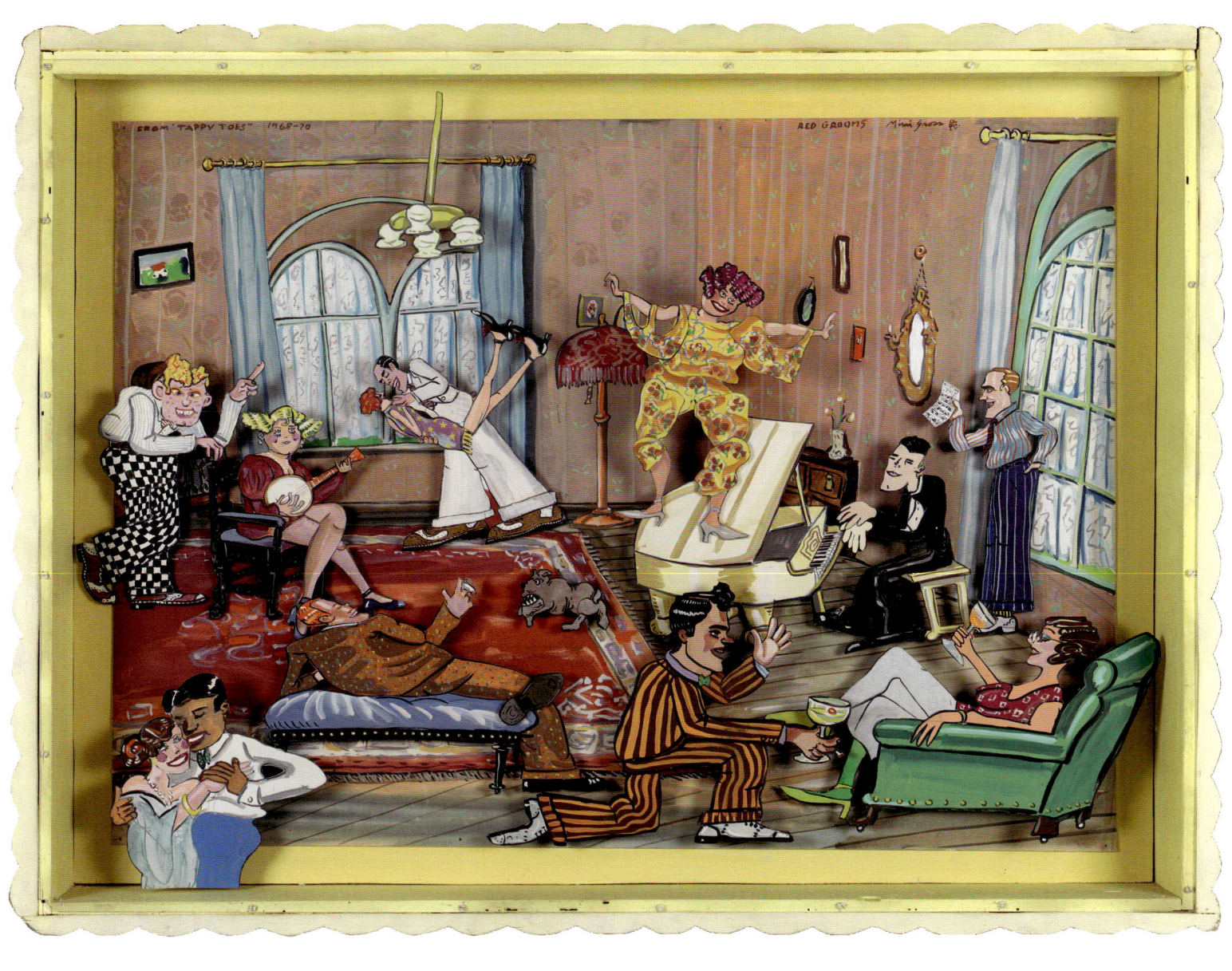

103
**Red Grooms
and Mimi Gross**

(Gross b. 1940)

Tappy Toes
1968–70. Acrylic on paper and wood,
35¾ × 46¼ × 5 in.

161

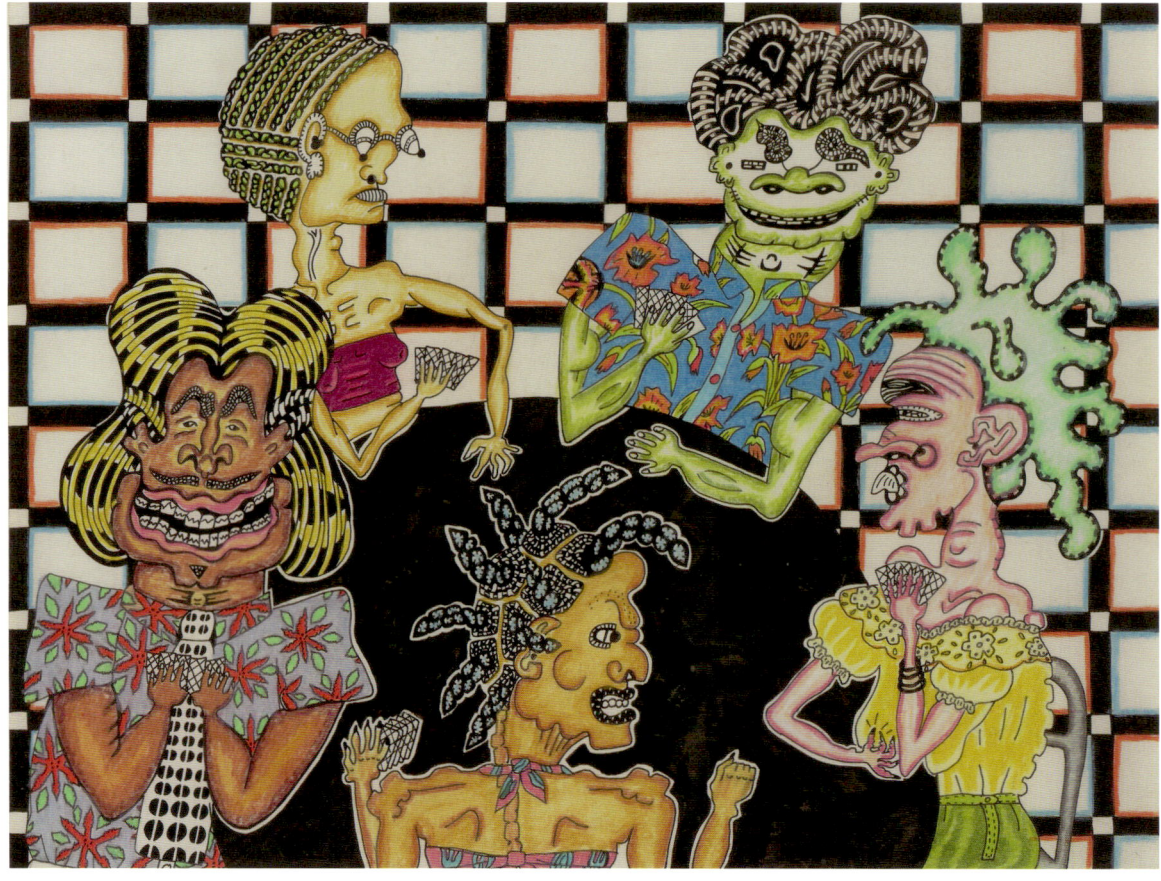

Imagists Playing Cards
Early to mid-1970s. Colored
pencil on paper,
11 × 14½ in.

104

Lorri Gunn

(b. 1942)

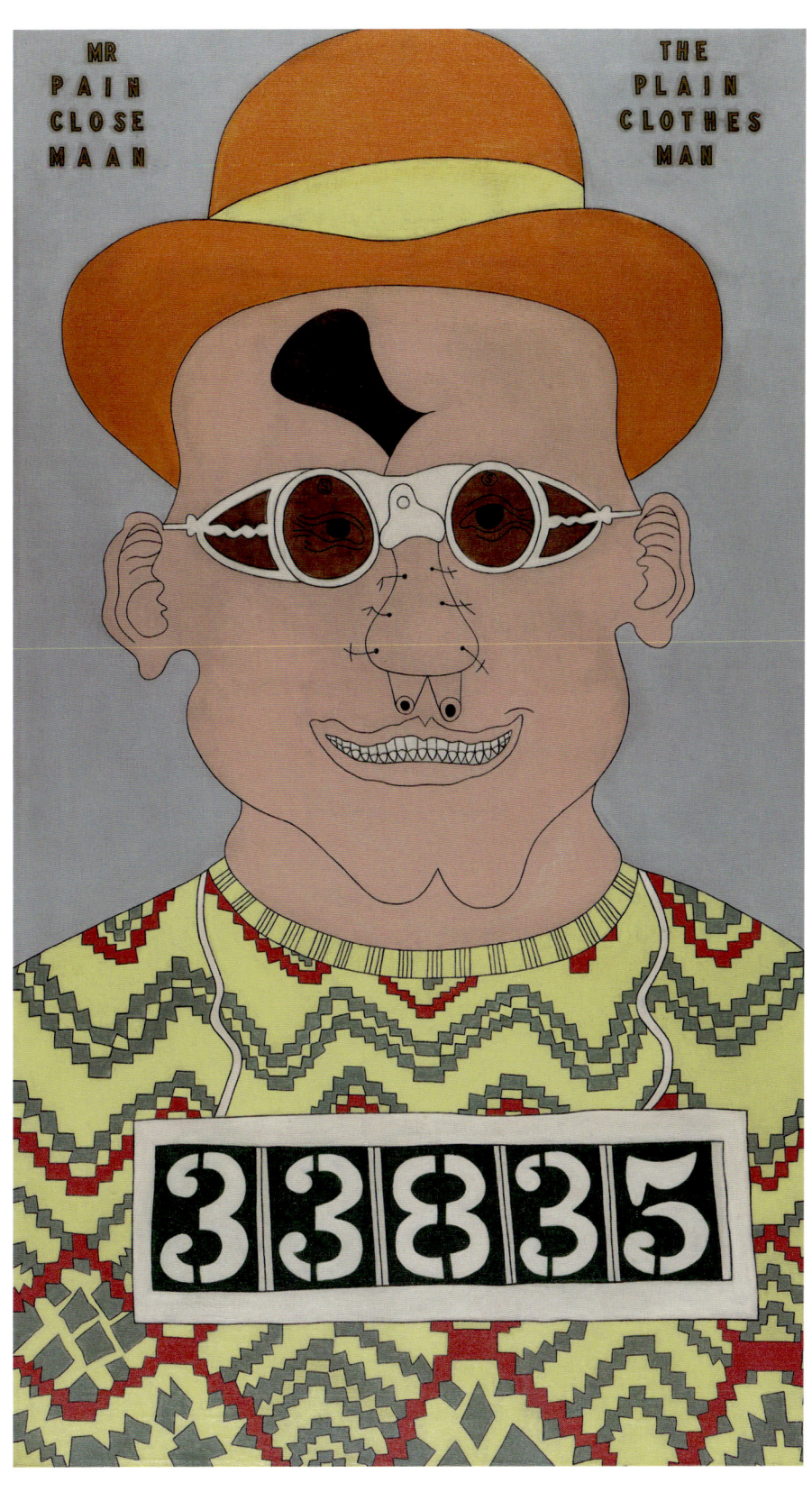

105
Karl Wirsum
(1939–2021)

Mr. Pain Close Maan the
Plain Clothes Man
1965. Oil and decals on canvas,
36⅝ × 21½ in.

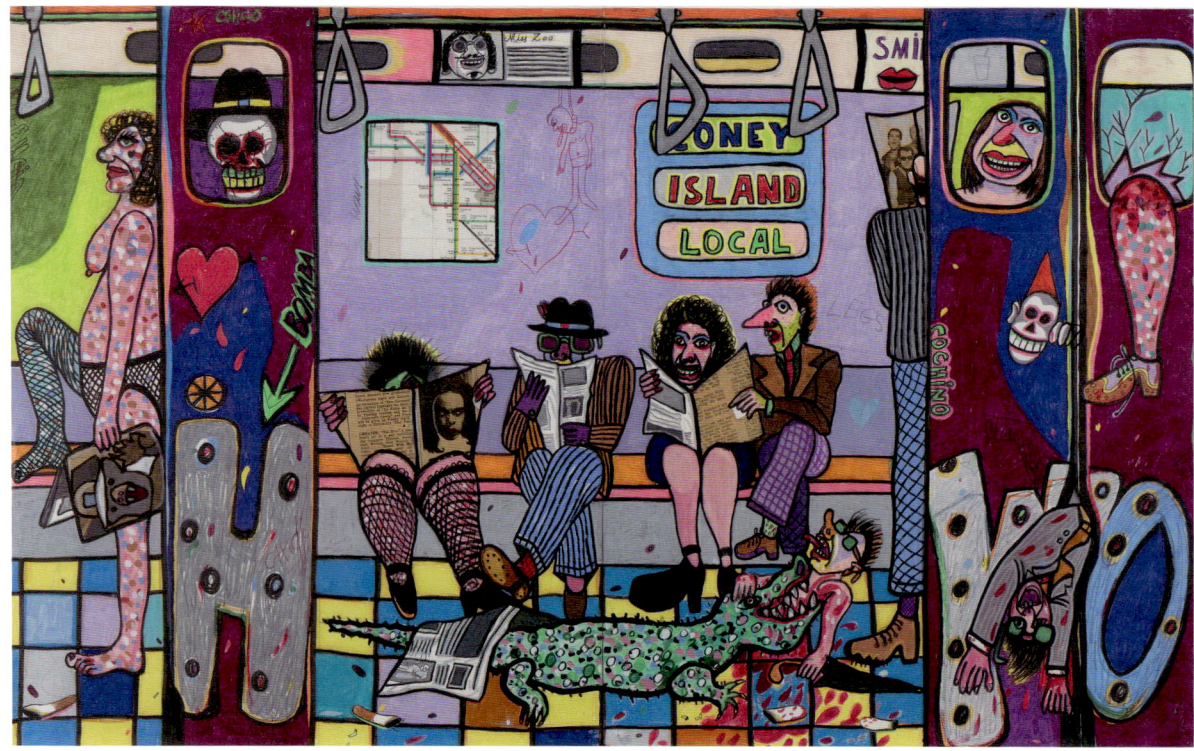

106
Luis Cruz
Azaceta

Coney Island Local
1975. Colored pencil, ink, and collage on paper,
24 × 38 in.

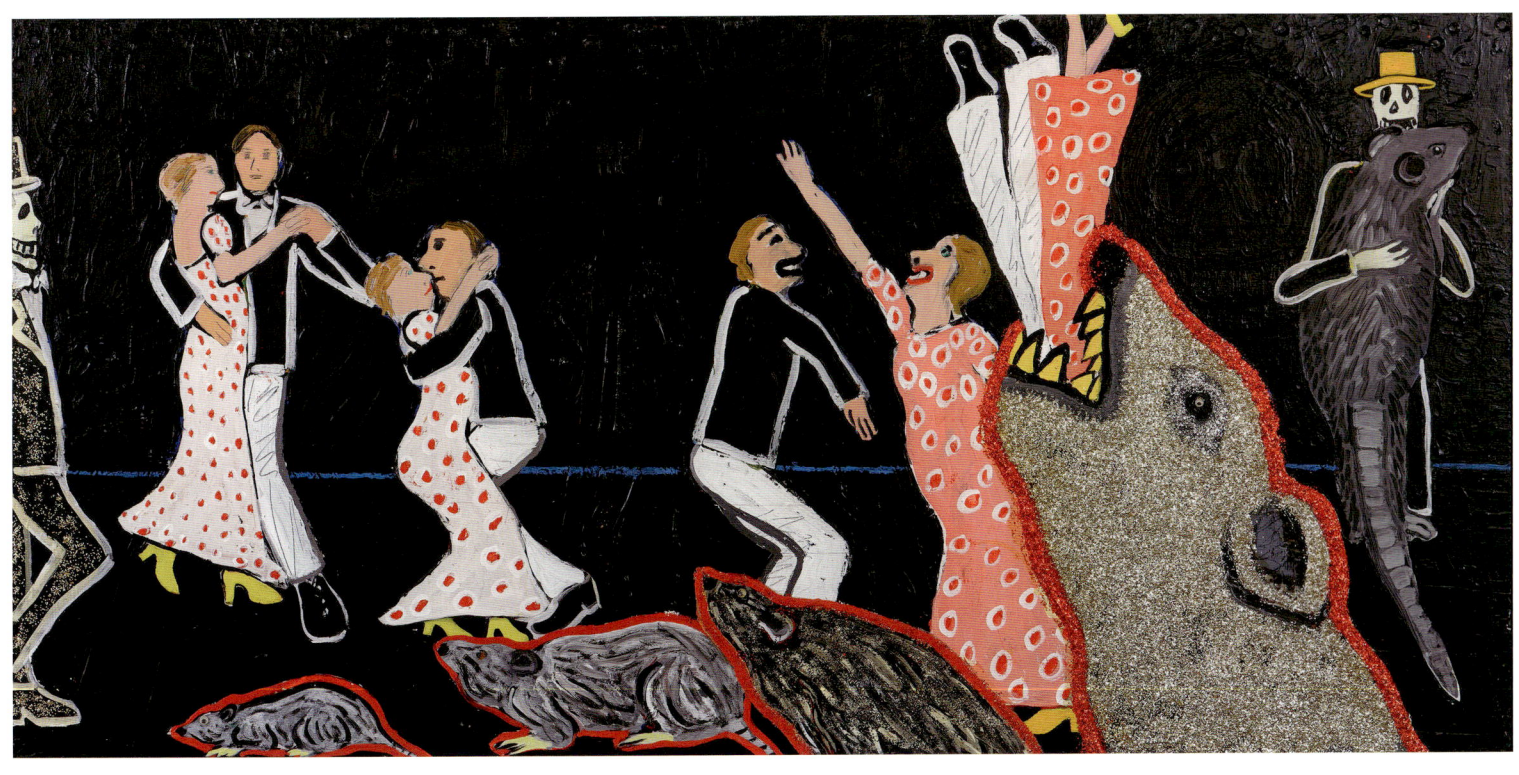

Joan Brown

The Last Dance
1973. Enamel, glitter, and plastic on
Masonite panel, 24 × 48½ in.

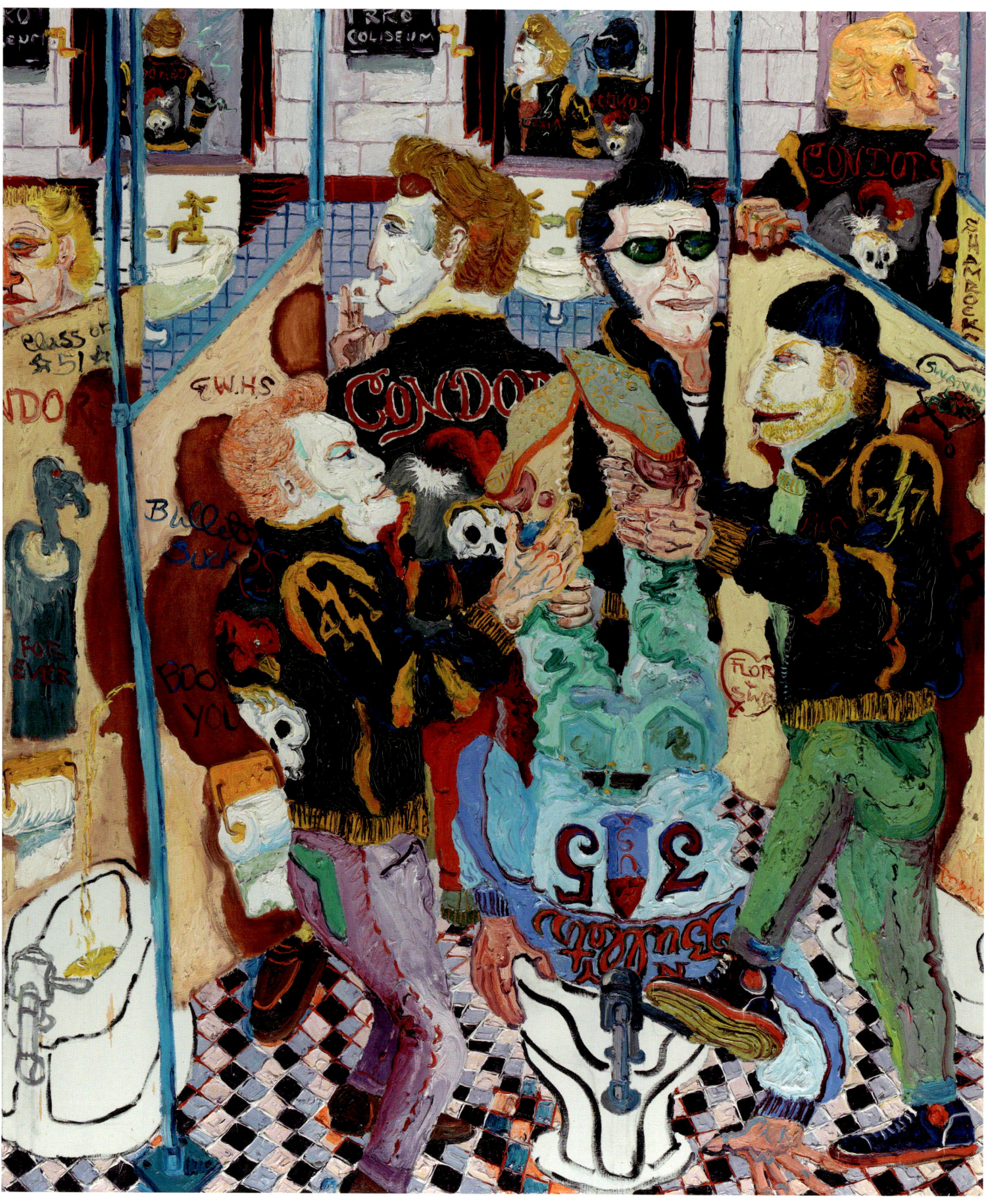

108

Peter Dean

Condor Flush

c. 1986. Oil on canvas, 80 × 64 in.

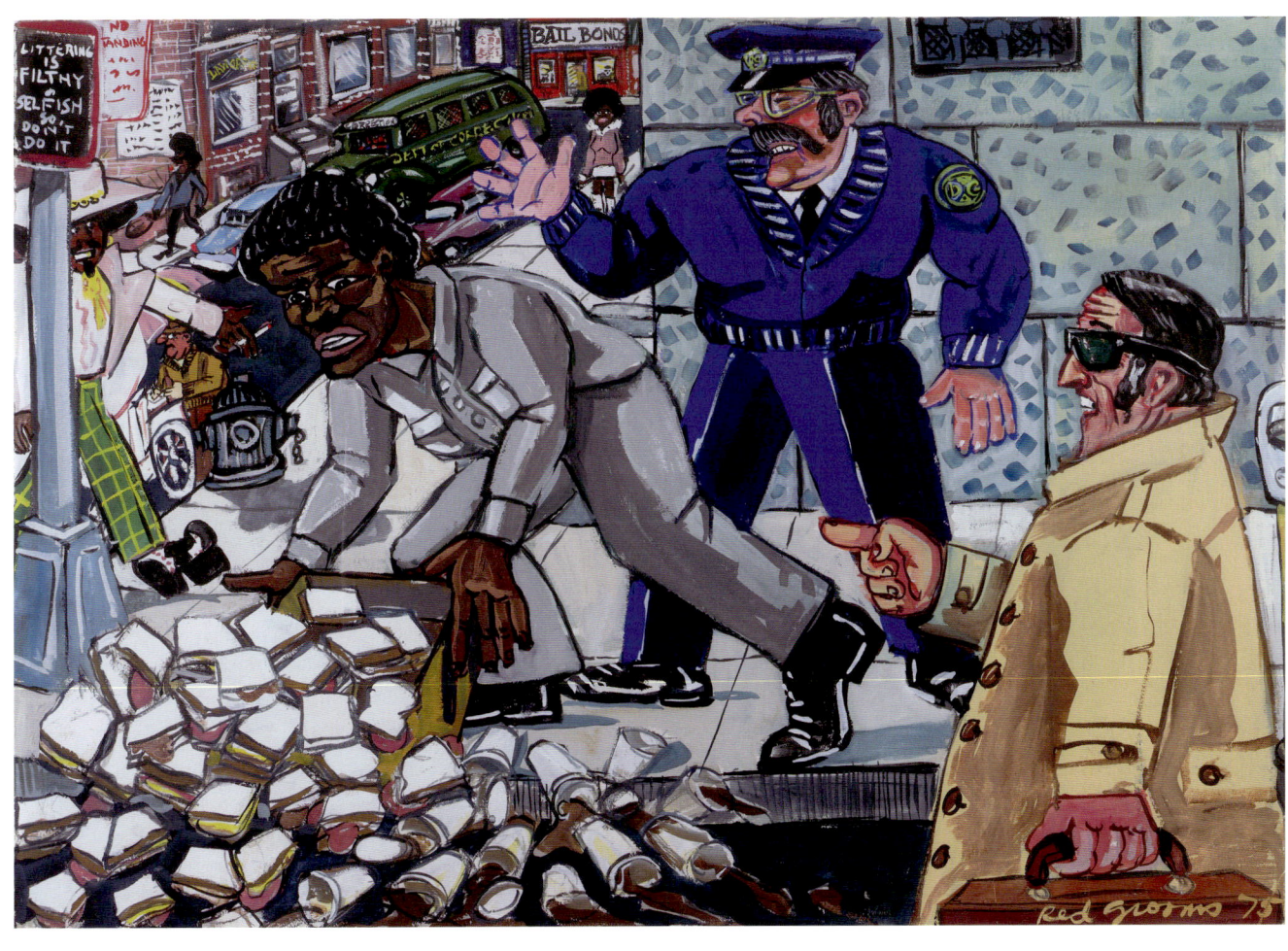

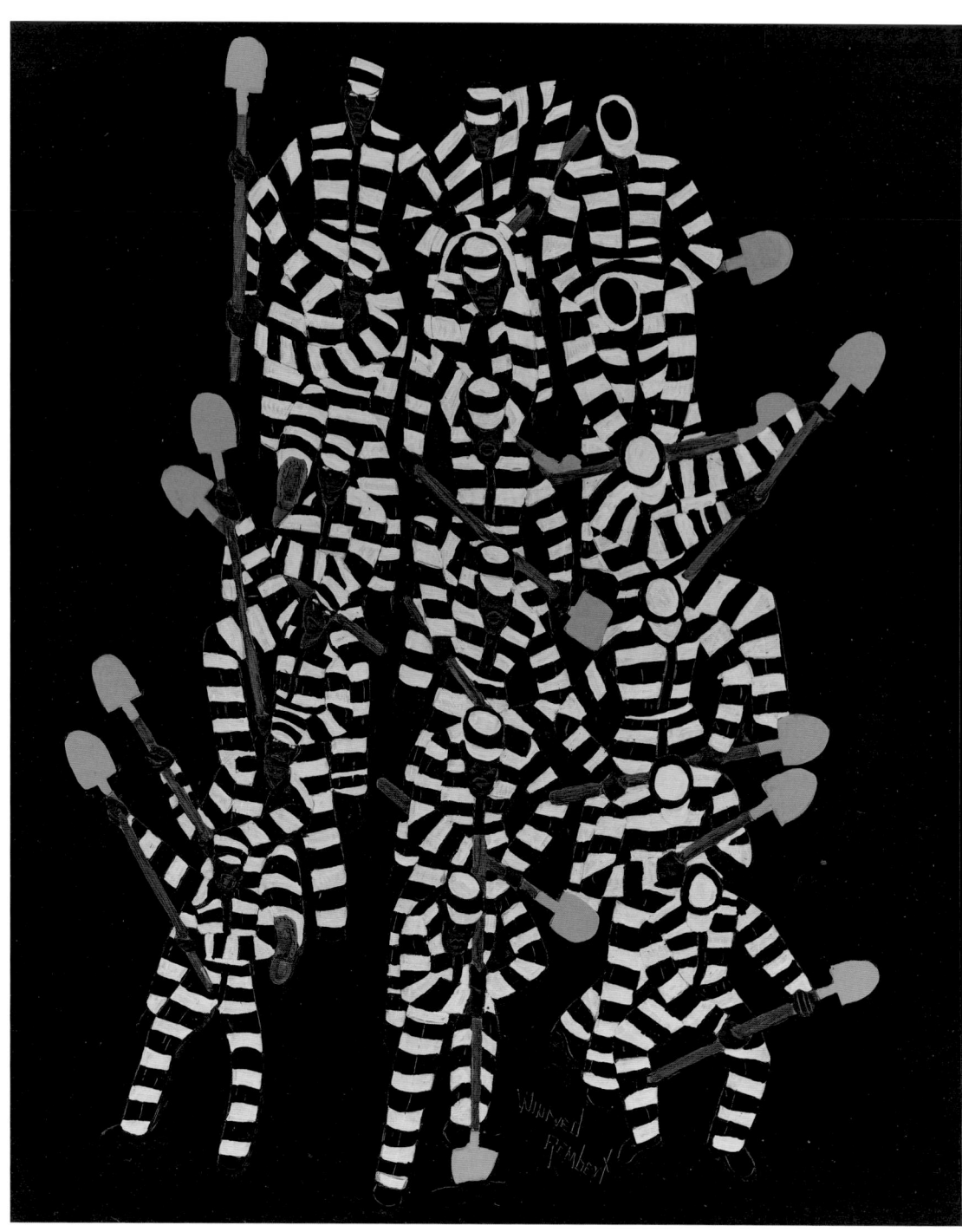

110
Winfred Rembert

Chain Gang
2005. Dye on tooled leather, 35¾ × 28¼ in.

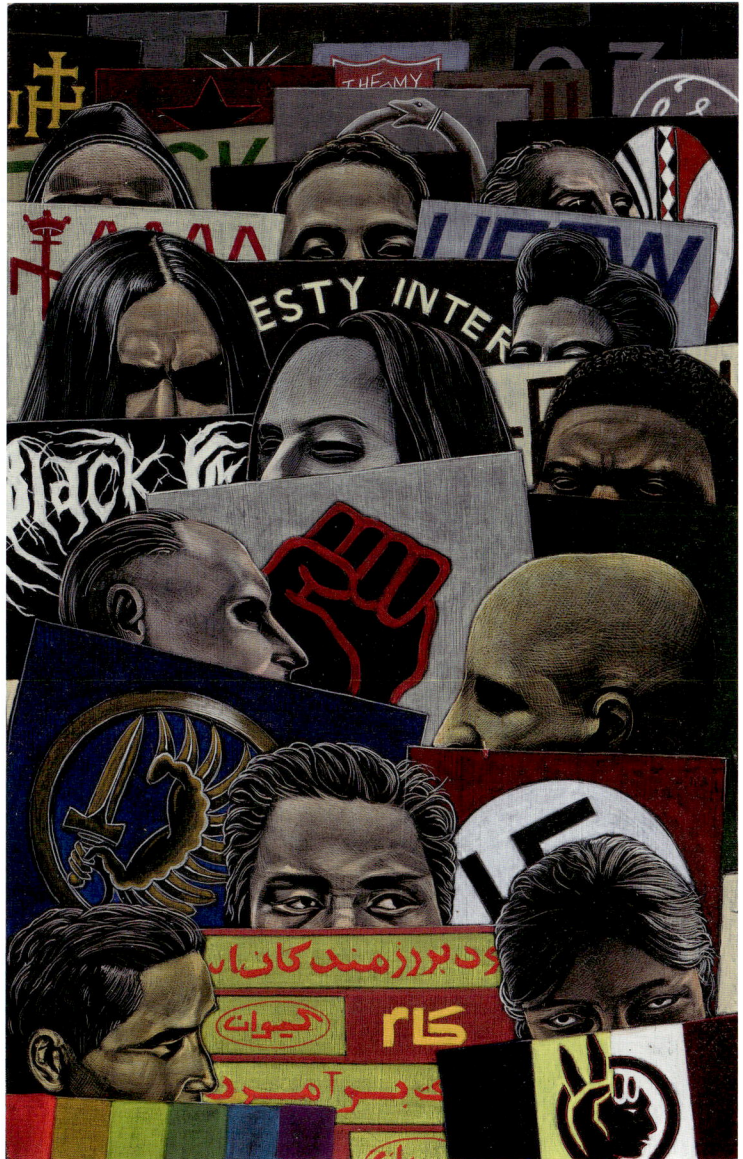

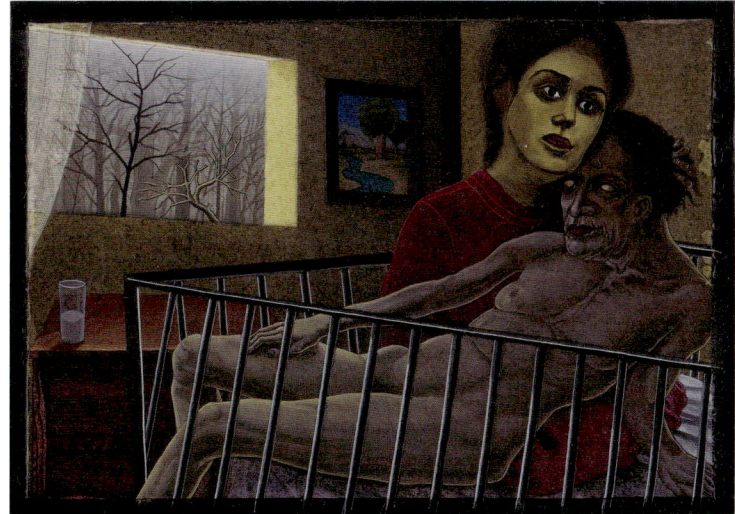

Untitled LR62 (Activists, posters)
2007. Acrylic on plywood,
9¾ × 6⅛ in.

111
Eric Stotik

Untitled
(Old man with woman in crib)
2008–2009. Acrylic on altered
book on foamcore, 5 × 7 in.

112
Eric Stotik

169

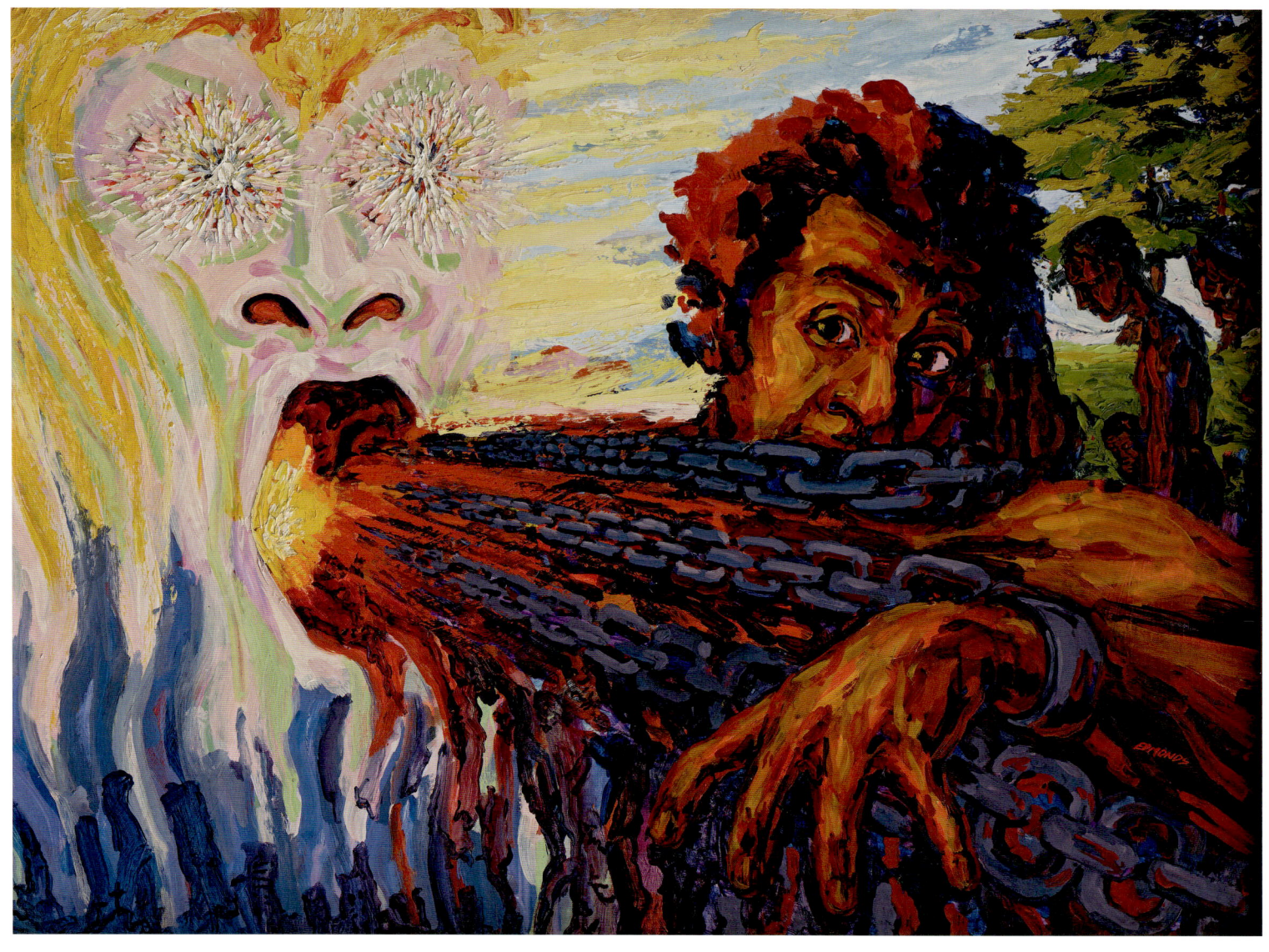

113
Walter Edmonds   *Sold into Bondage*
(1938–2011)   1974. Oil on board, 32 × 42 in.

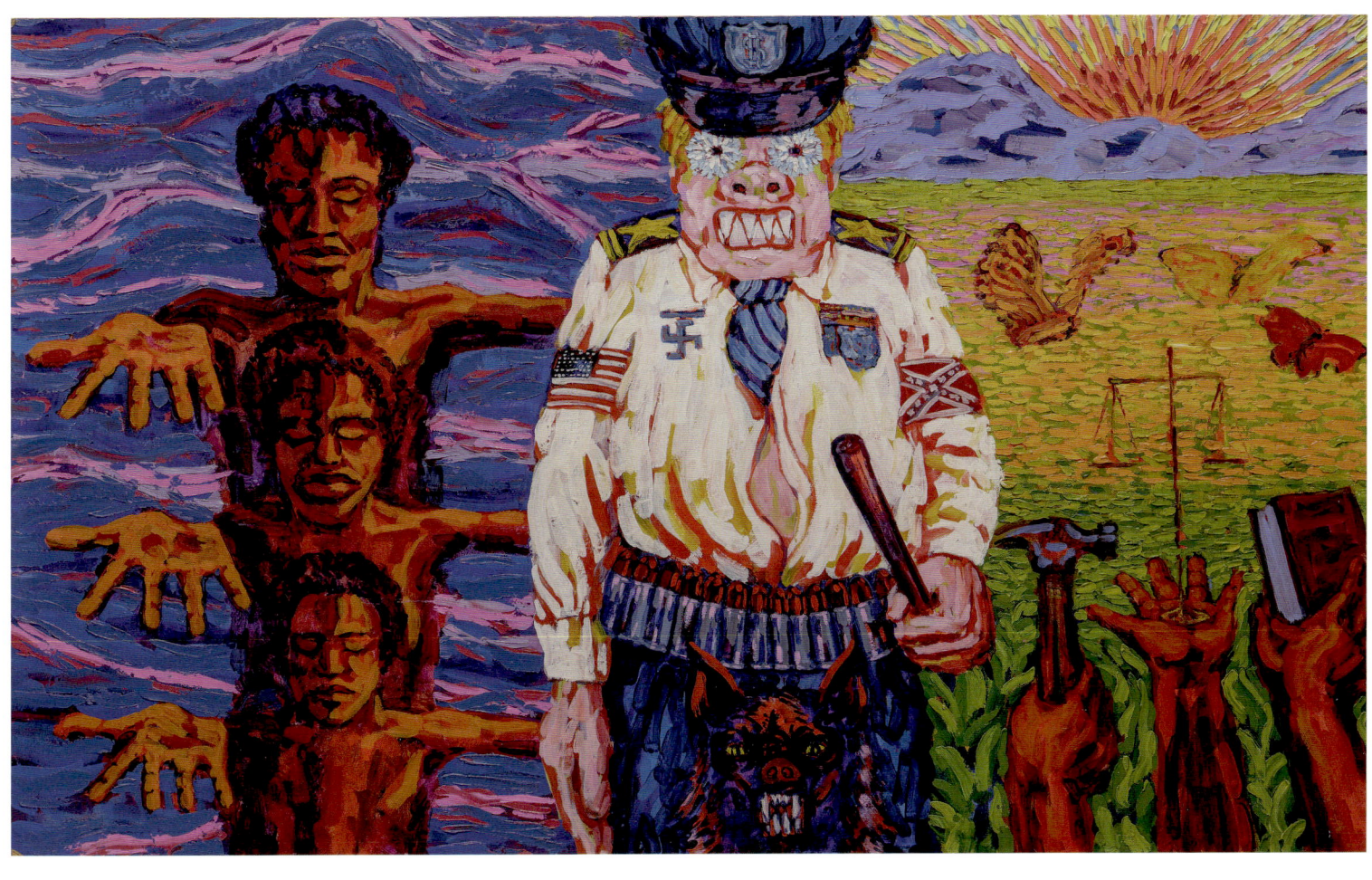

Walter Edmonds

So Jim Crow Pursued Us to Enslave Us
1974–75. Oil on board, 30 × 48 in.

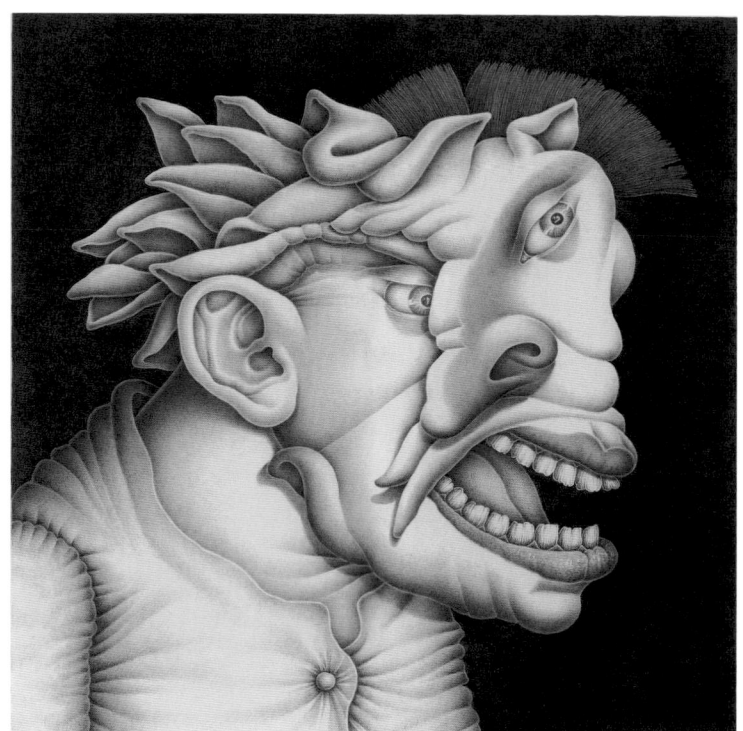

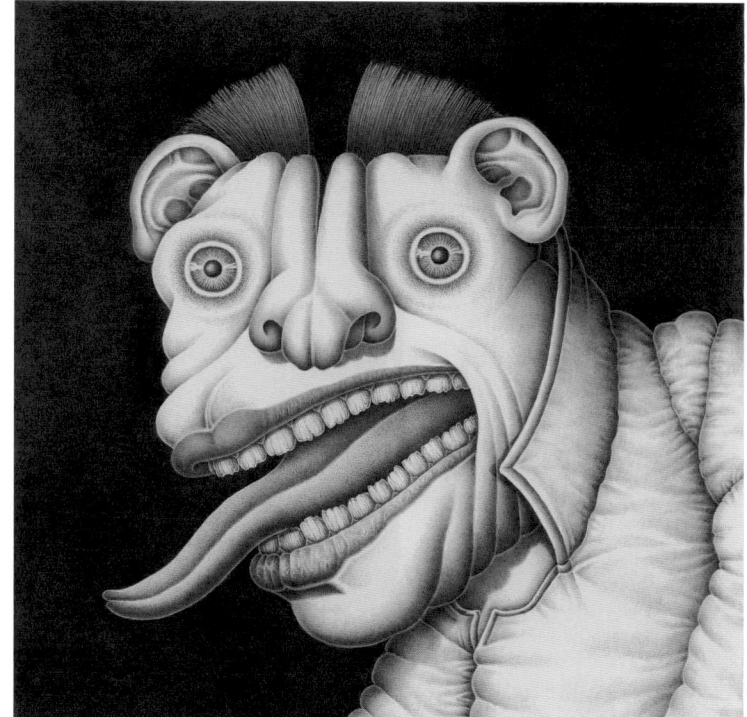

The Songs of War 9

115

Robert Lostutter

2021. Graphite on paper,
19¾ × 19¾ in.

The Songs of War 7

116

Robert Lostutter

2021. Graphite on paper,
19¾ × 19¾ in.

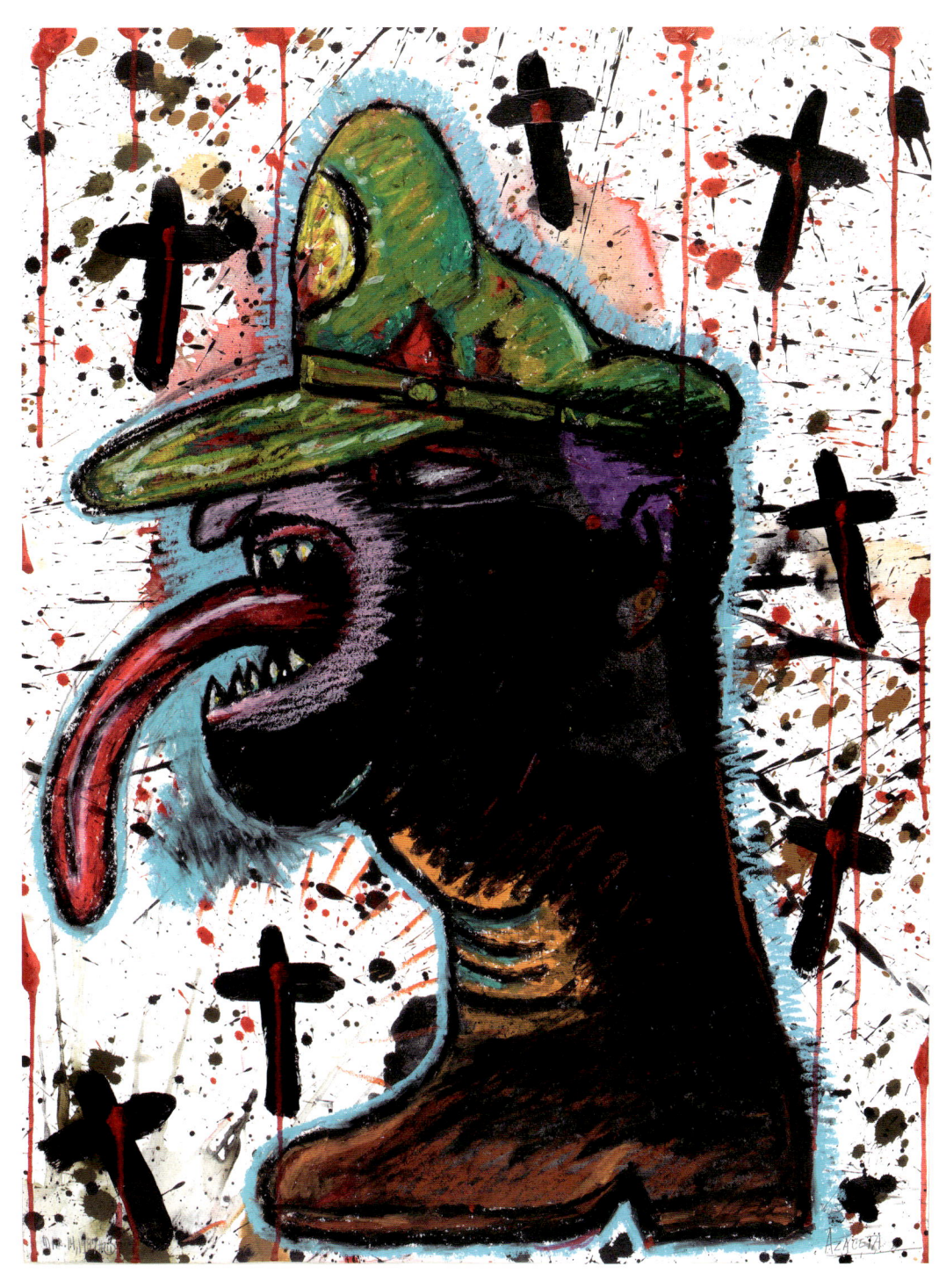

117
Luis Cruz Azaceta

Dictator's Head-Boot
1987. Acrylic and oil pastel on paper,
30 × 22 in.

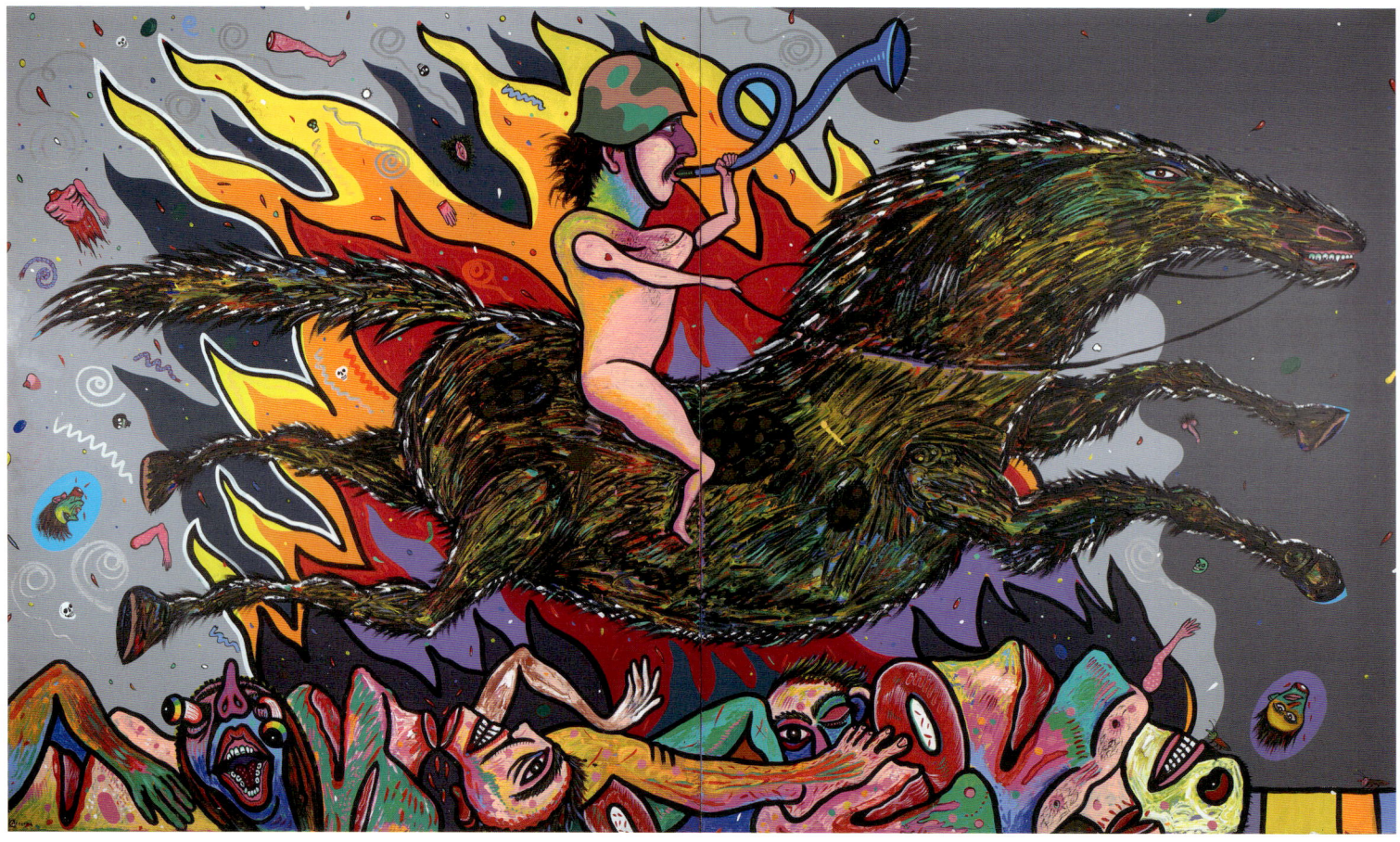

118

Luis Cruz
Azaceta

Self-Portrait: Apocalypse Now—or Later?
1981. Acrylic on canvas, 72 × 120 in.

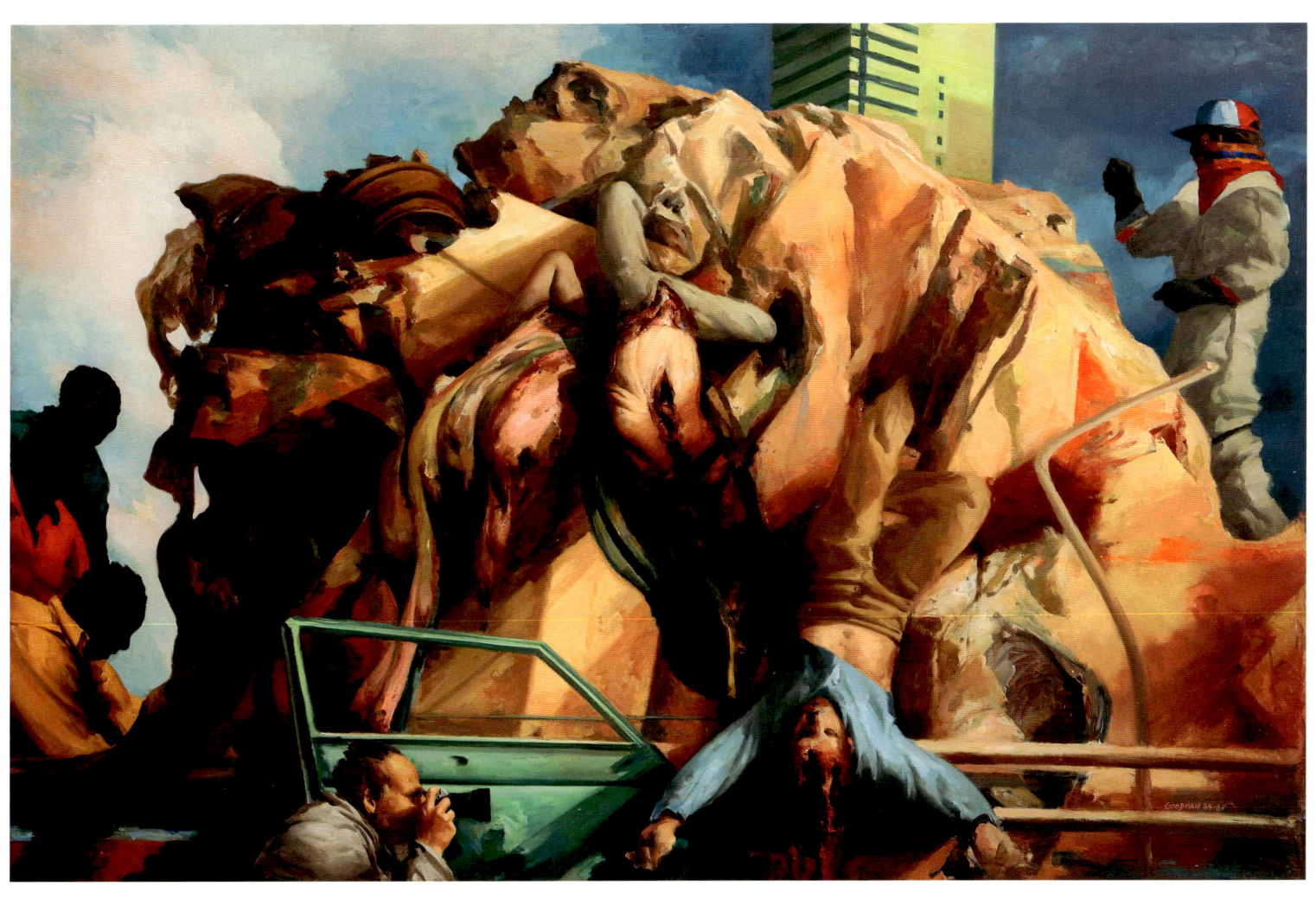

119
Sidney Goodman

A Waste
1984–86. Oil on canvas, 89 × 128⅝ in.

175

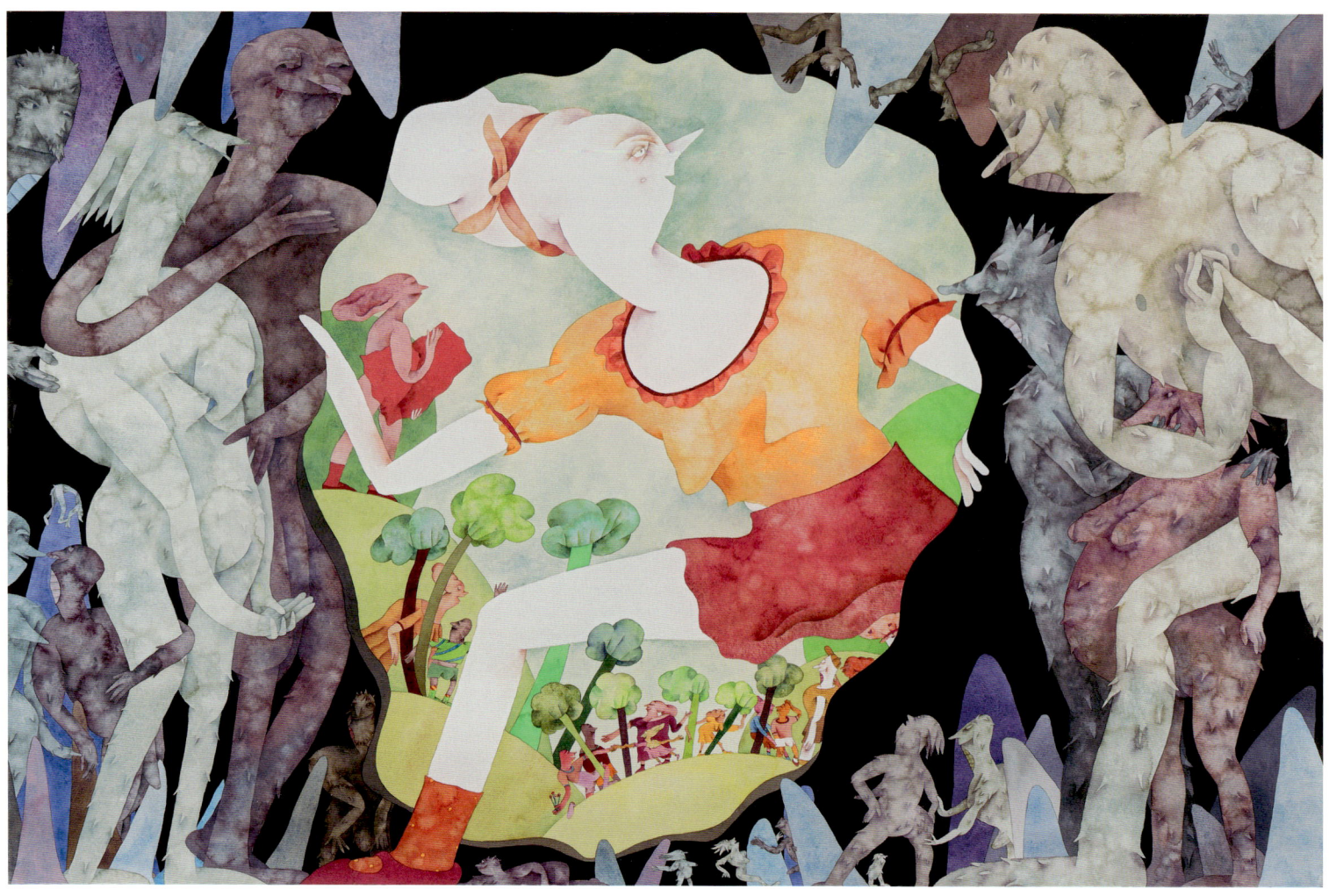

120
Gladys Nilsson

Checking Out the Other Side
1987. Watercolor on paper, 40 × 60 in.

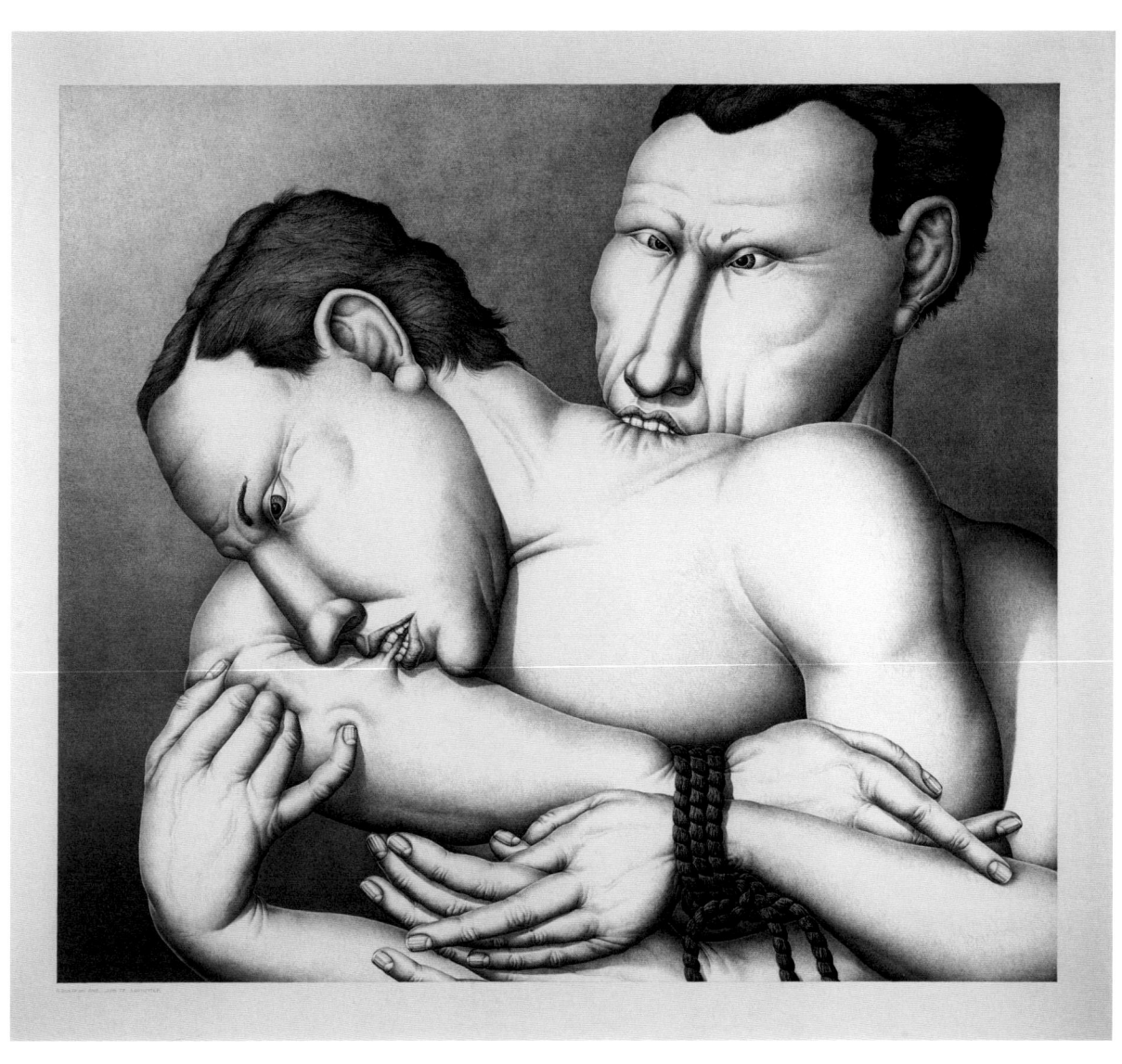

121
Robert Lostutter

A Sign of My Time
1977. Graphite on canvas, 44 × 48 in.

177

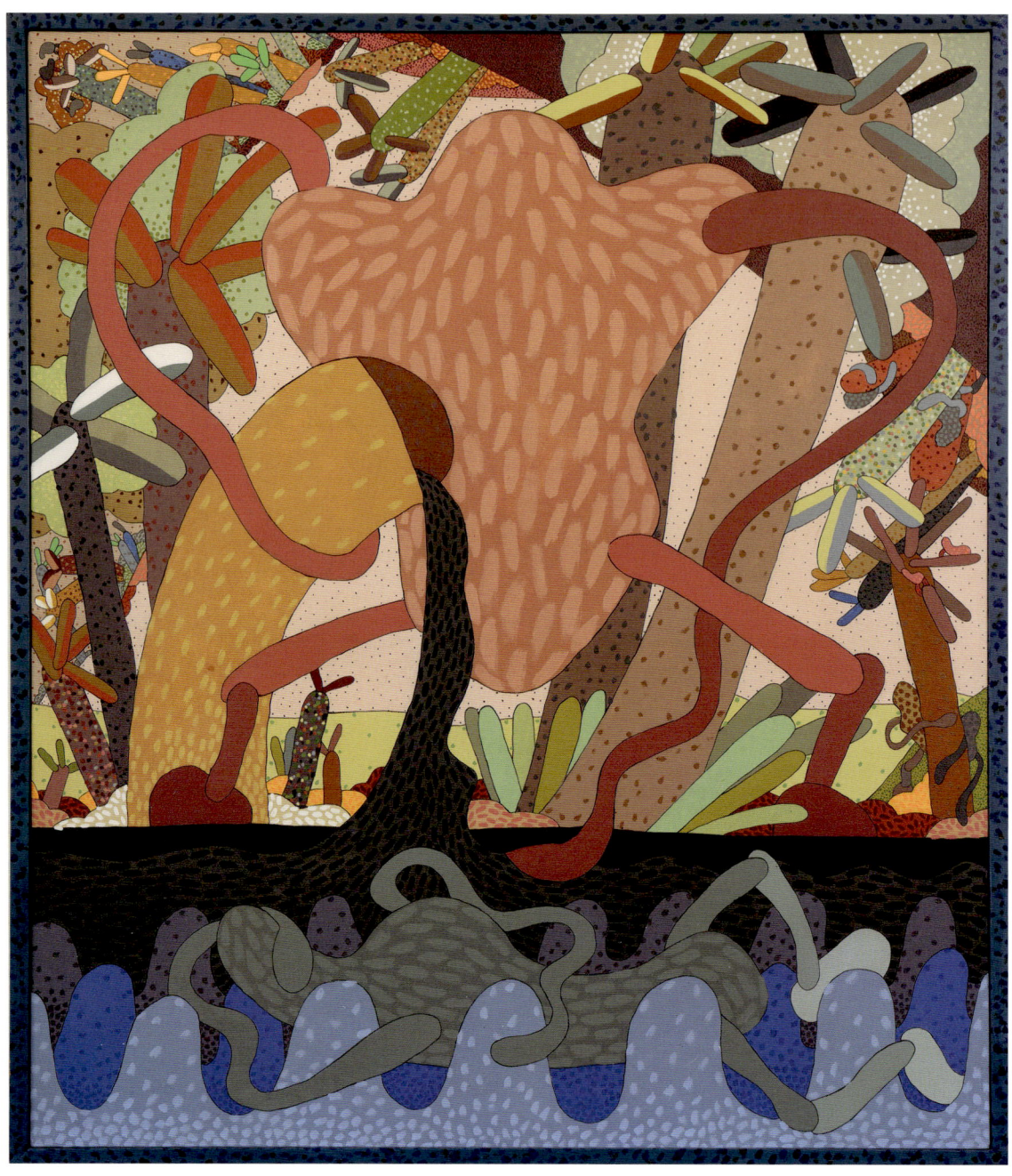

Drowners

122
Gladys Nilsson

1972–73. Acrylic on canvas, 43½ × 37½ in.,
artist's frame

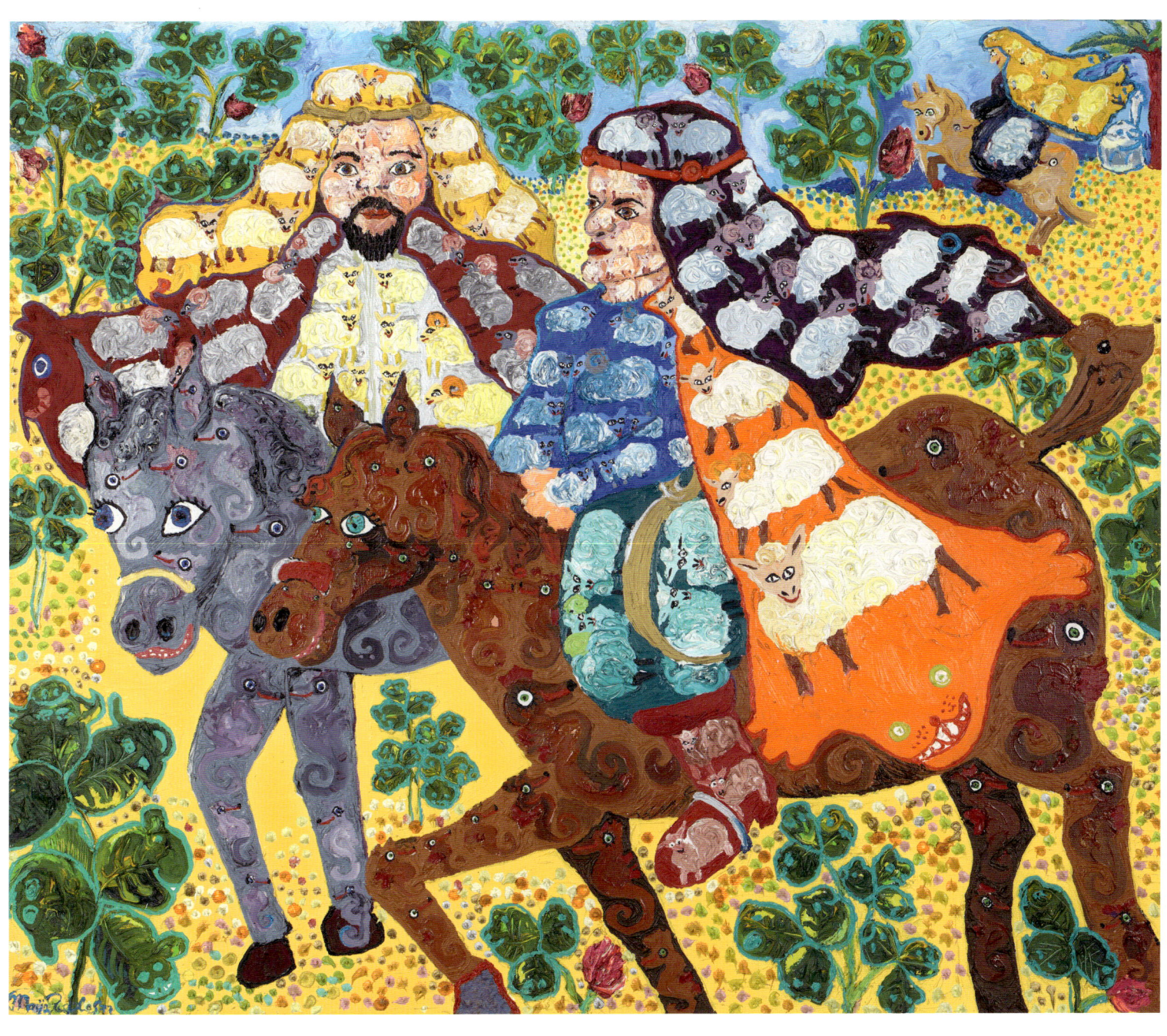

123
Maija Peeples-Bright (b. 1942)

Sheep Sheiks
1977. Acrylic and mixed media on canvas,
42 × 48 in.

179

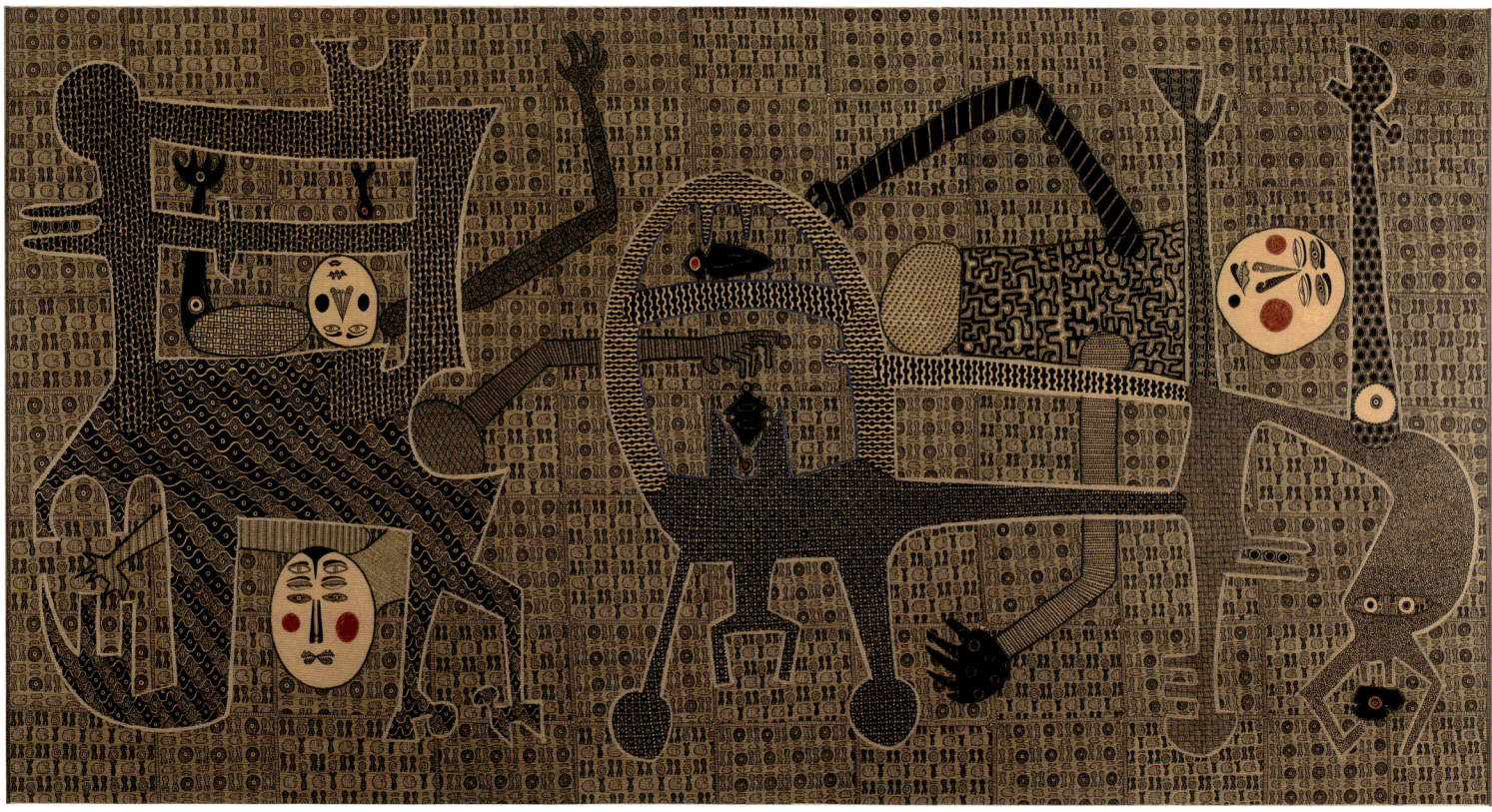

124
Evelyn Statsinger   *In the Penal Colony*
(1927–2016)   1949. Pen, ink, and crayon on paper, 31 × 58 in.

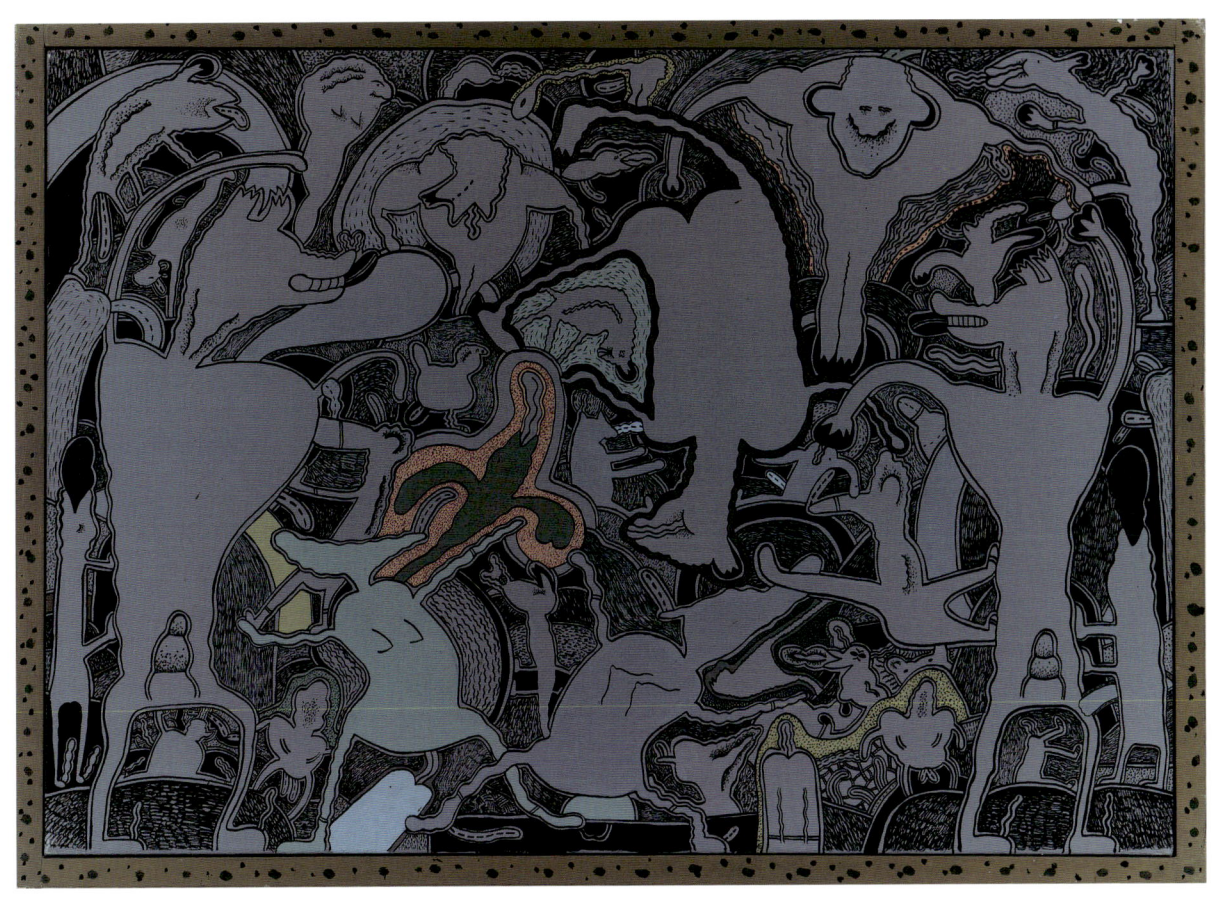

Gladys Nilsson

Semisighmetricall
1970. Acrylic on canvas, 20¼ × 28 in.,
artist's frame

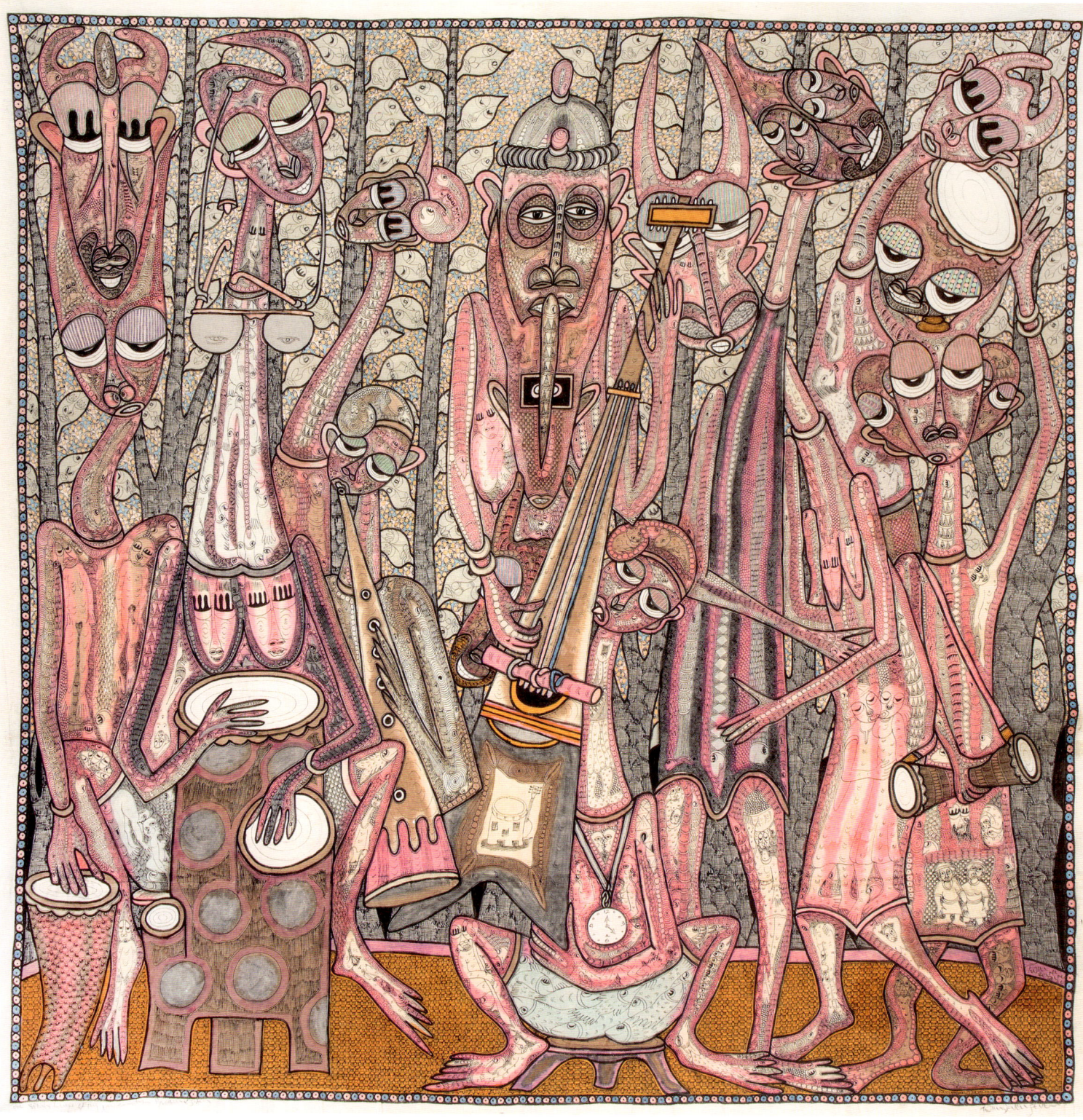

126
Twins
Seven-Seven
(1944–2011)

The Spirits of My Reincarnation
Brothers and Sisters
2006-7. Ink, batik, dye, watercolor,
acrylic, and oil on linen, 58 × 60 in.

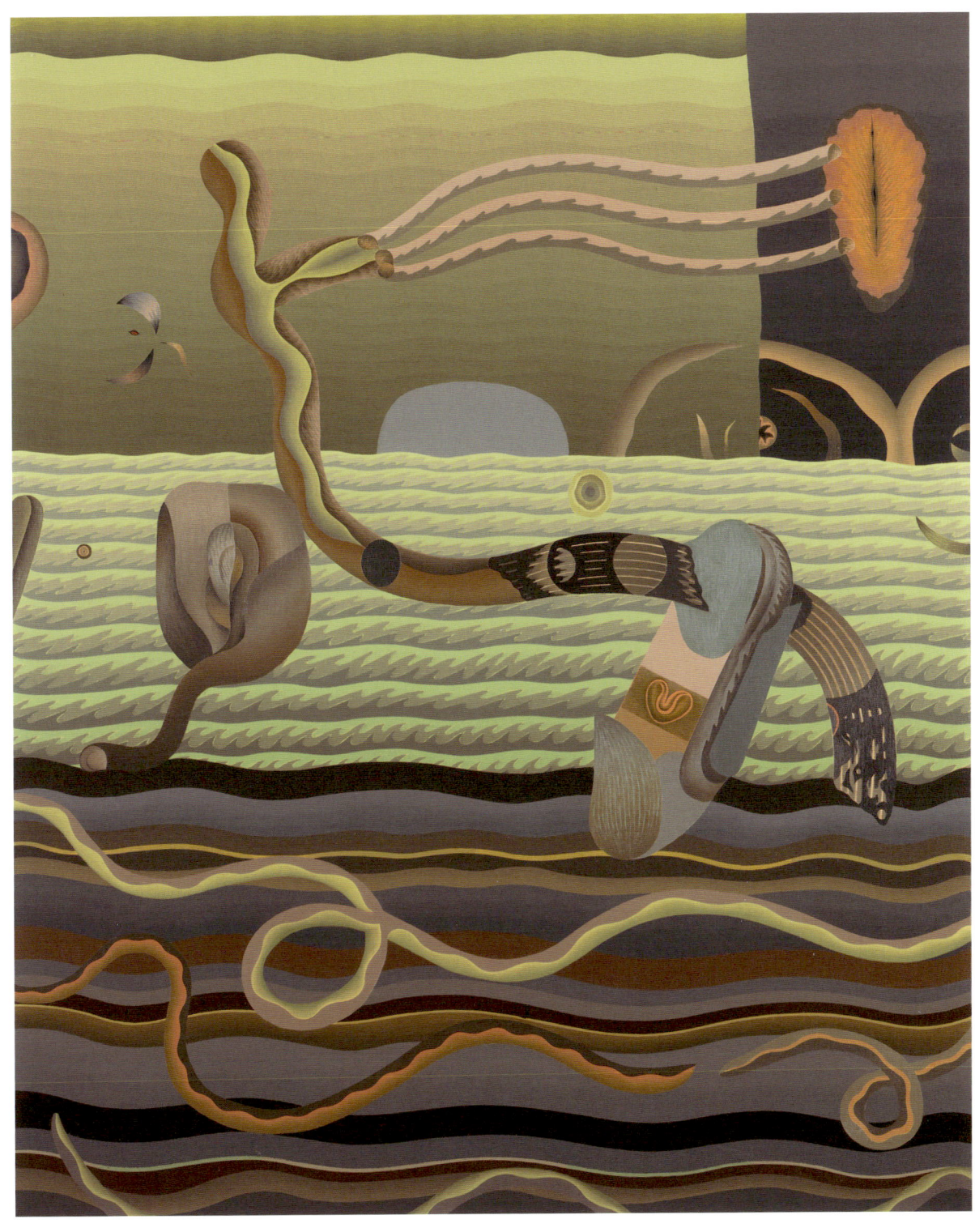

127
Evelyn Statsinger

Passing Creatures Near Movable Shores
1978. Oil on linen, 47⅞ × 38 in.

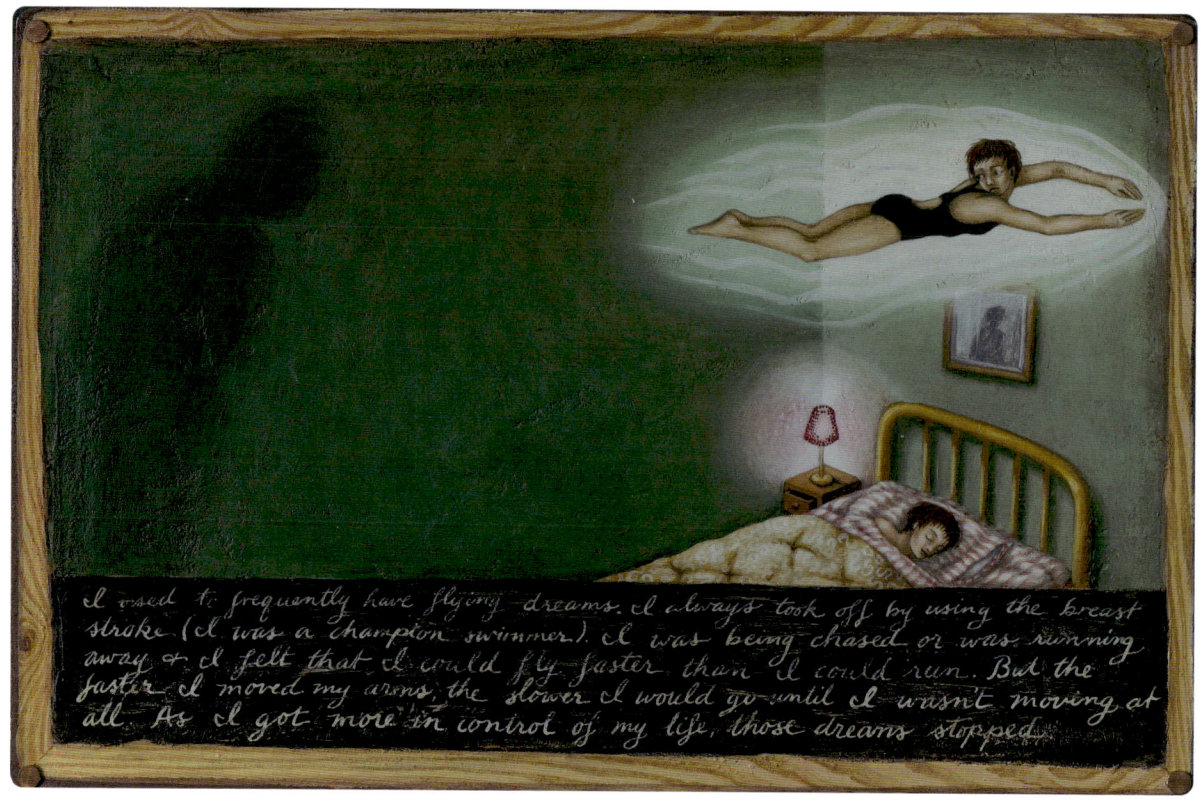

I used to frequently have flying dreams. I always took off by using the breast stroke (I was a champion swimmer). I was being chased or was running away & I felt that I could fly faster than I could run. But the faster I moved my arms, the slower I would go until I wasn't moving at all. As I got more in control of my life, those dreams stopped.

128
Tabitha Vevers
(b. 1957)

Flying Dream (Gillian)
2000. Oil on galvanized steel, 9 × 12 in.

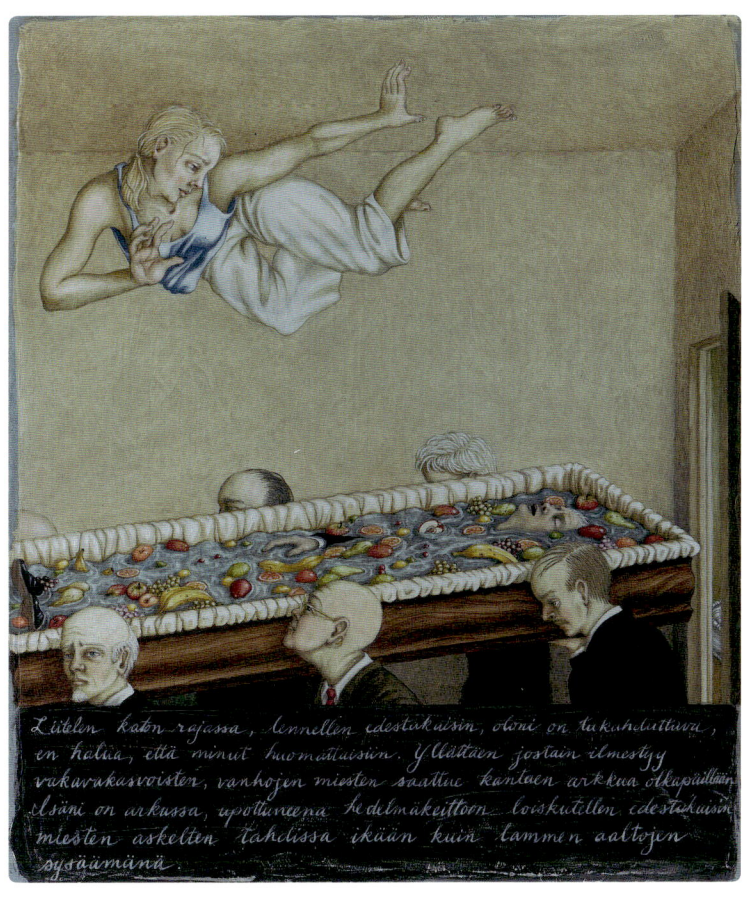

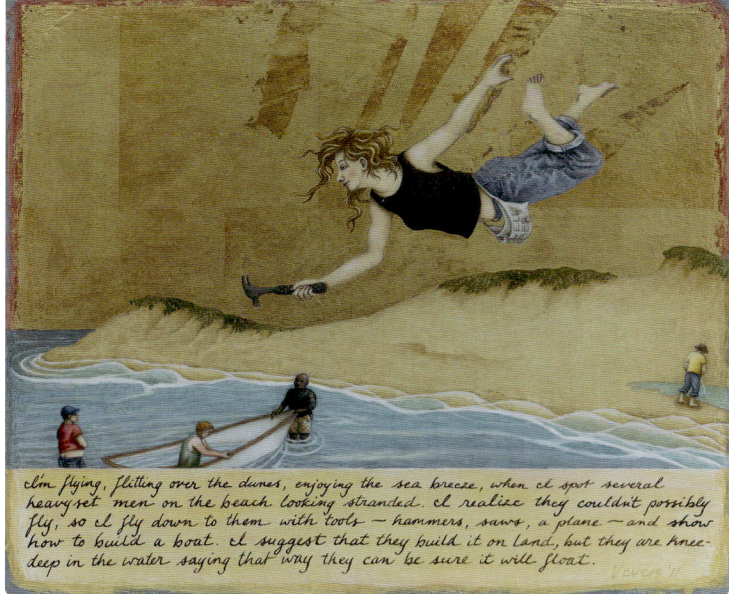

Liitelen katon rajassa, lennellen edestakaisin, oloni on lukauduttava,
en haluu, että minut huomattaisiin. Yllättäen jostain ilmestyy
vakavakasvoisten, vanhojen miesten saattue kantaen arkkua olkapäillään
Isäni on arkussa, upottuneena hedelmäkeittoon loiskutellen edestakaisin
miesten askelten tahdissa ikään kuin lammen aaltojen
sysäämänä.

I'm flying, flitting over the dunes, enjoying the sea breeze, when I spot several
heavyset men on the beach looking stranded. I realize they couldn't possibly
fly, so I fly down to them with tools — hammers, saws, a plane — and show
how to build a boat. I suggest that they build it on land, but they are knee-
deep in the water saying that way they can be sure it will float.

129
Tabitha Vevers

Flying Dream (Marja)
2003. Oil on galvanized steel,
12 × 10 in.

130
Tabitha Vevers

Flying Dream (In the Dunes II)
2011. Oil and gold leaf on
galvanized steel, 10 × 12 in.

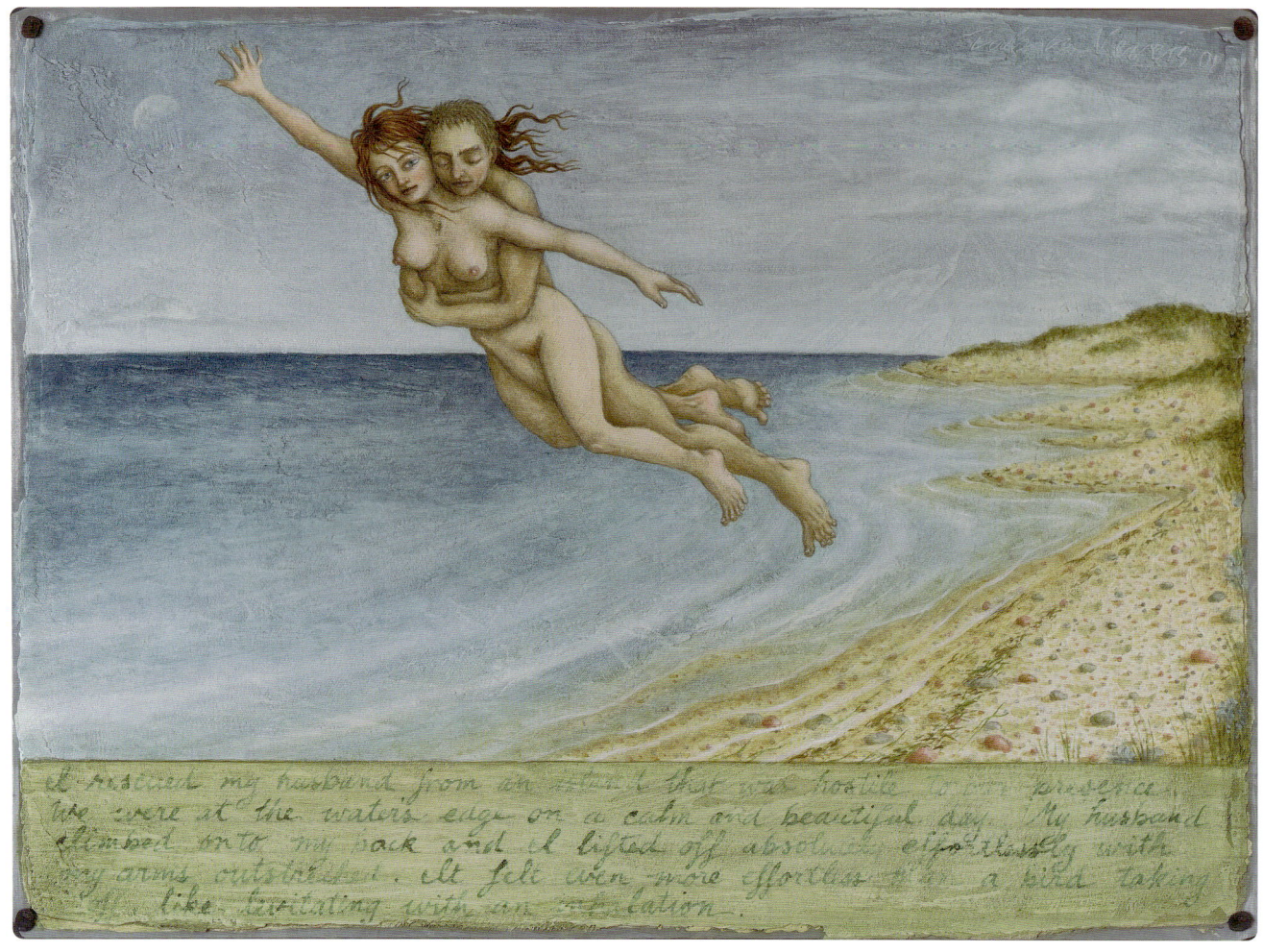

Flying Dream (The Rescue)
2001. Oil on galvanized steel,
9 × 12 in.

131
Tabitha Vevers

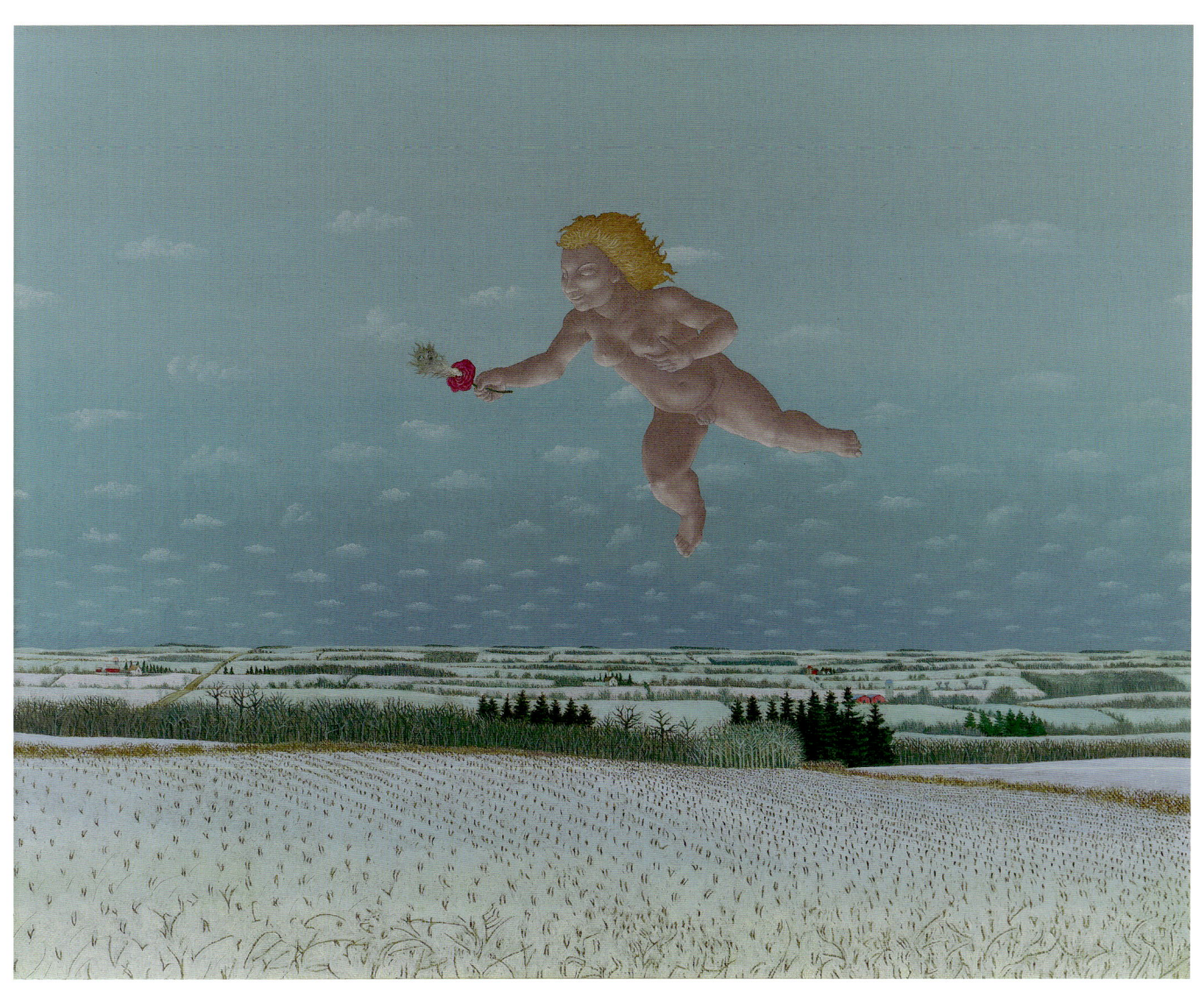

132
John Wilde

An Homage to Philipp Otto Runge
1987. Oil on linen, 16 × 20 in.

187

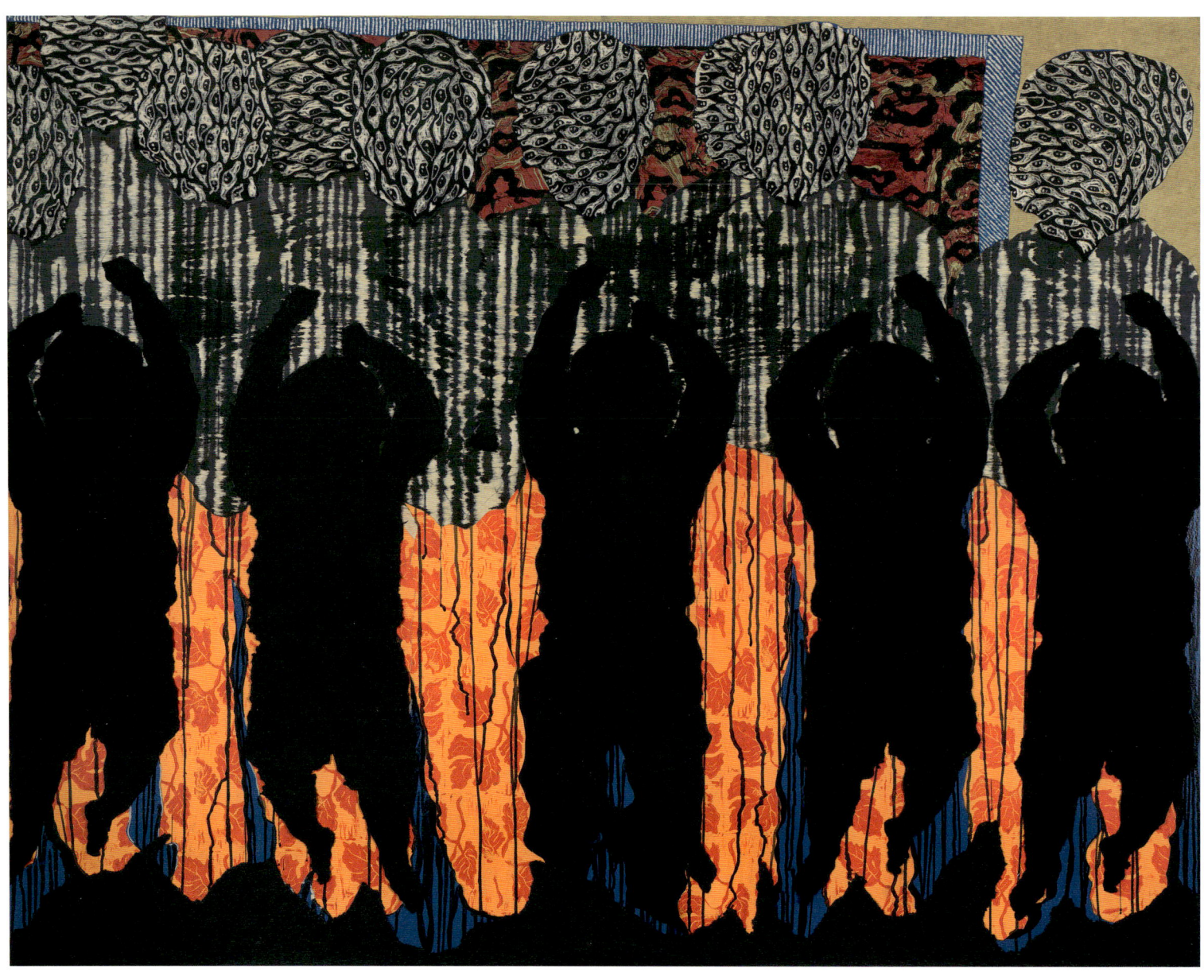

Bois Caiman

133
Didier William

2017. Collage and acrylic with carving on panel,
48 × 60 in.

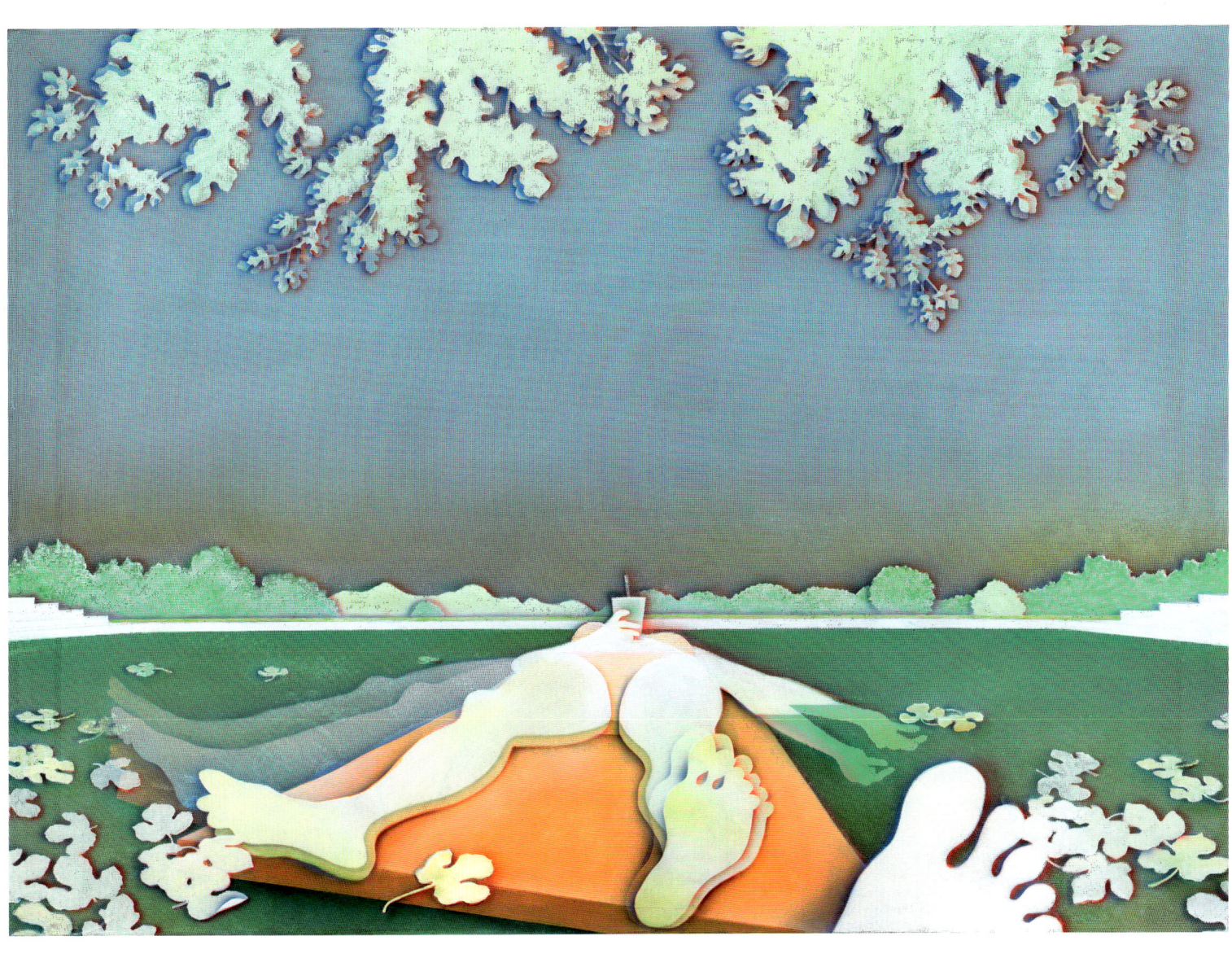

134
Alexi Worth
(b. 1964)

Tennessee
2013–16. Acrylic on nylon mesh, 42 × 56 in.

189

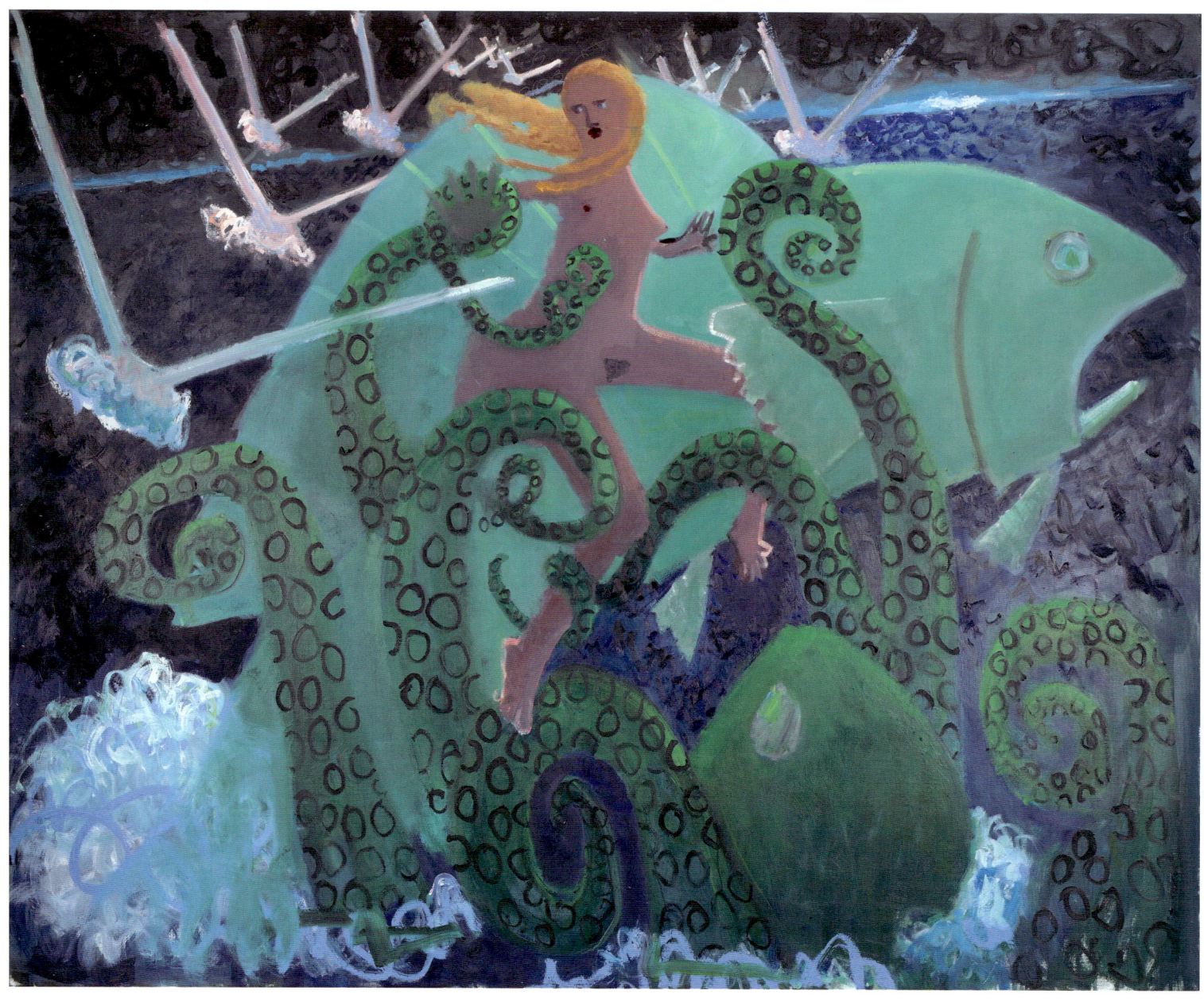

135

Kyle Staver

(b. 1953)

Octopus Ardor

2024. Oil on linen, 58 × 70 in.

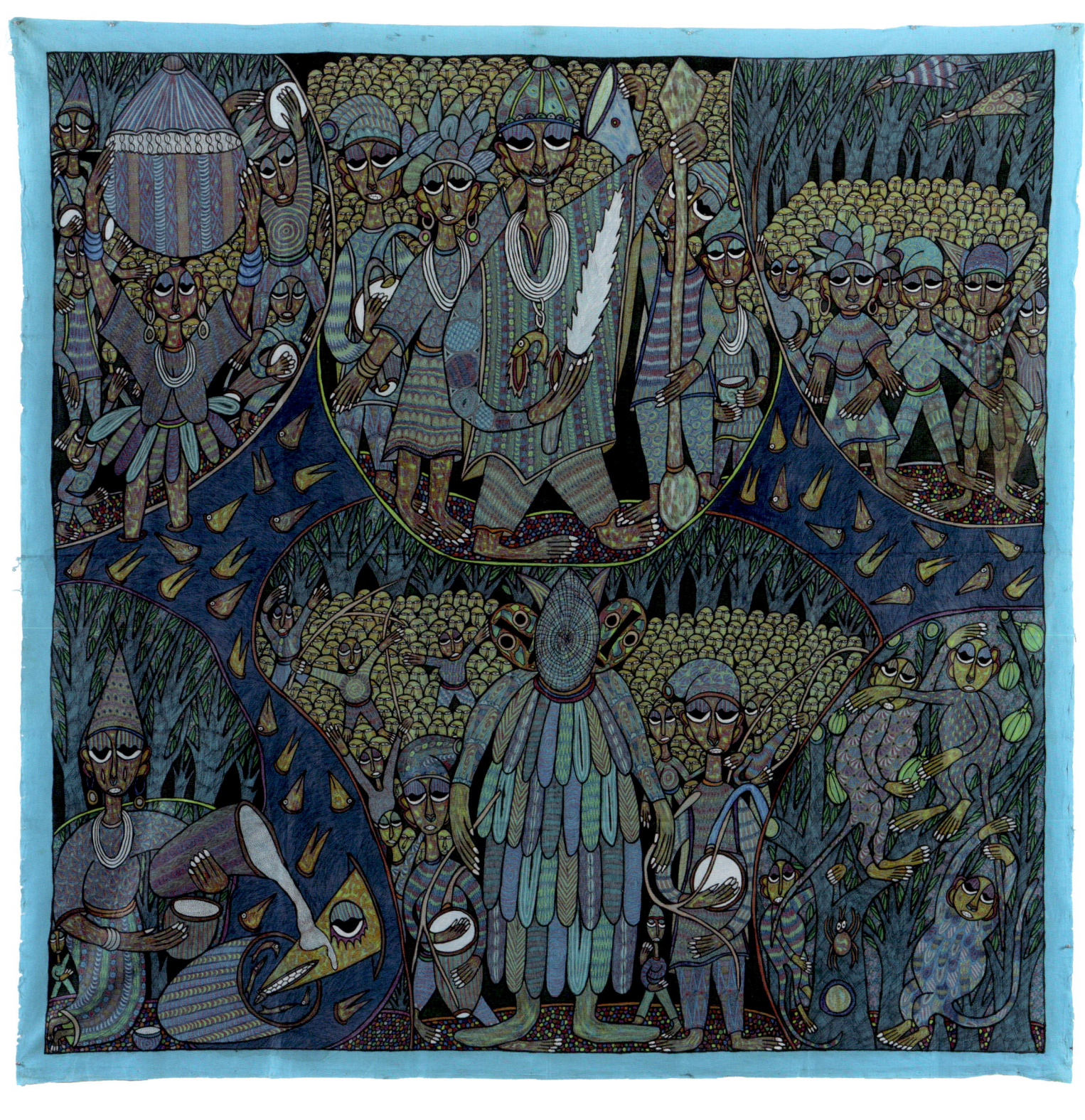

136
Twins
Seven-Seven

Oshun Whospers (Woshiper)
1988. Ink, watercolor, acrylic, and oil on
cloth, 89 × 89 in.

191

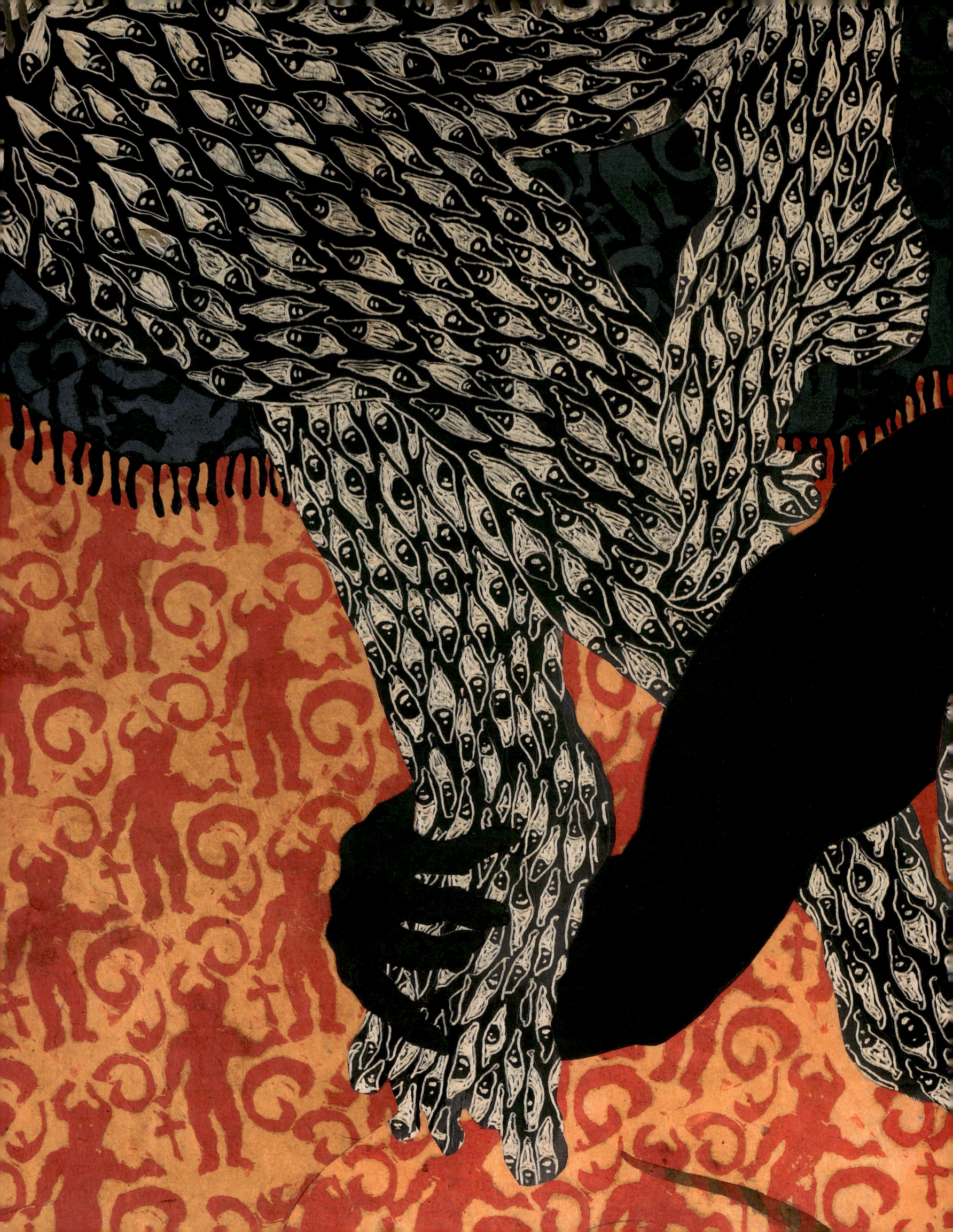

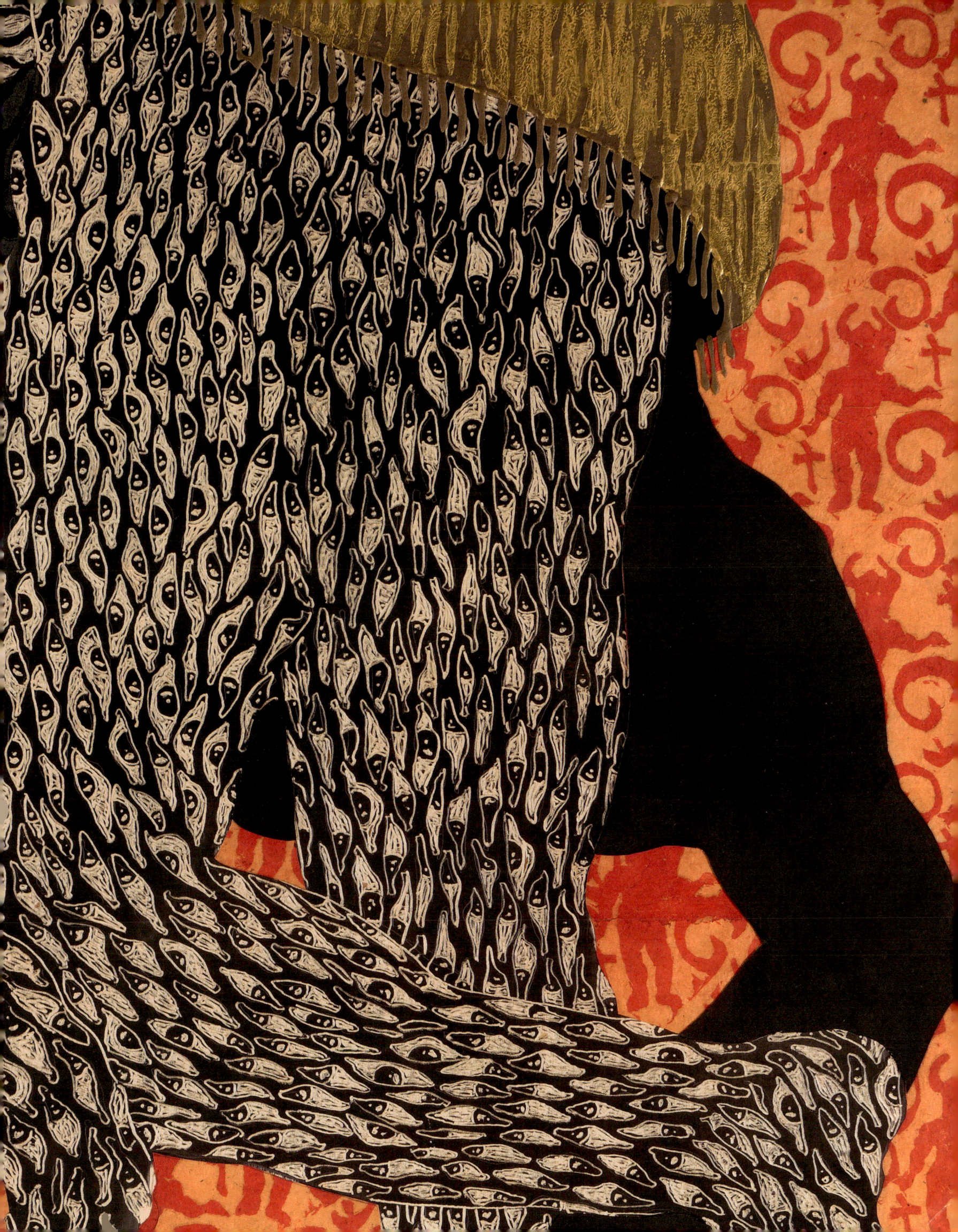

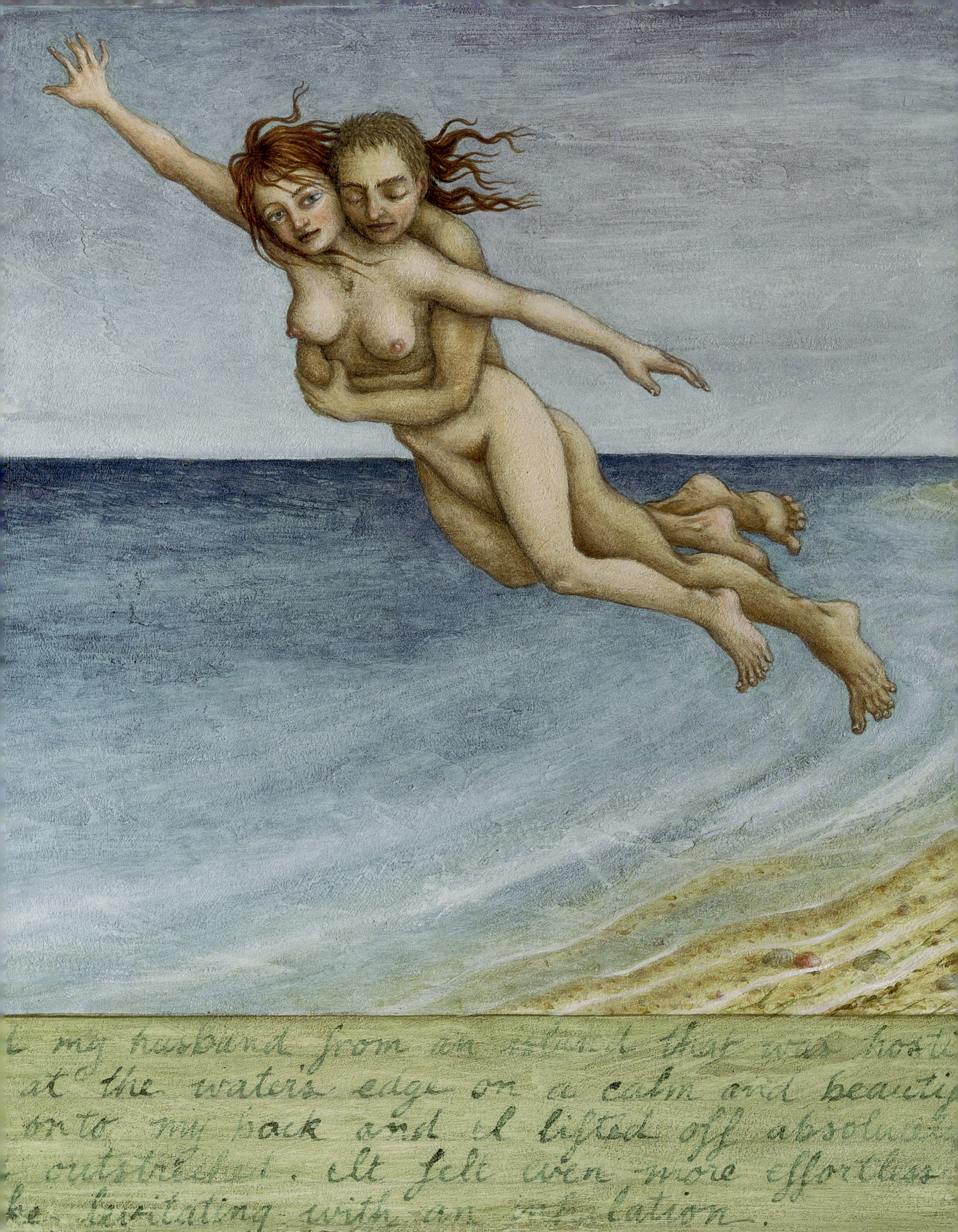

...t my husband from an island that was hostil...
at the water's edge on a calm and beautif...
onto my back and I lifted off absolut...
outstretched. It felt even more effortles...
be... levitating with an... lation.

Planned Bequest to the Pennsylvania Academy of the Fine Arts

Works already given to the Pennsylvania Academy of the Fine Arts are accompanied by accession numbers. Unless otherwise noted, the credit line is Robert and Frances Coulborn Kohler Collection.

Robert Amft
(American, 1916–2012)

Fritz, c. 1940
Enamel on canvas, 43¾ × 38 in.

Self-Portrait Fishing with Bill,
c. 1942
Oil on canvas, 30 × 23¼ in.

Mother and Father, c. 1943
Oil on wallpaper, 21¾ × 28¾ in.

Kids and Sign, 1944
Enamel on canvas, 18 × 24 in.

Big Bass, c. 1945
Oil on canvas, 41 × 33 in.

Compilation, 1950
Oil on canvas, 23¾ × 30 in.

Benny Andrews
(American, 1930–2006)

Self-Portrait at Jay Milder's Place,
1962
Gouache and ink on paper,
13½ × 10½ in.

Dew Drop Inn (The Thirties), 1972
Ink on paper, 18 × 12 in.

Robert Arneson
(American, 1930–1992)

Self-Portrait Drawing, 1978
Conté crayon on paper, 40 × 30 in.

Untitled (Double profile), 1978
Glazed ceramic, 16 × 14 × 4 in.

Try This, Jack (Self-Portrait), 1979
Conté and pastel on paper,
18¾ × 14¾ in.

Roy De Forest-Witness, 1980
Oil pastel, acrylic, and conté
crayon on paper, 51¹¹⁄₁₂ × 30 in.

Study for *Nasal Flat*, 1980
Pastel and acrylic on paper,
31½ × 27¾ in.

*Portrait of the Artist After Bacon
4*, 1981
Glazed ceramic, 15 × 13 × 4 in.

Head Skinned and Dyed, 1986
Bronze, ed. 3, 21½ × 31½ × ¾ in.

Reflections with Pink and Silver,
1990
Glazed ceramic and glass,
16 × 12 × 6 in.

Head Eater, 1991
Glazed ceramic, 15½ × 21½ in.

J. with Bloody Nose, 1991
Glazed ceramic, 15 × 12 × 7 in.

*Cookie Jar (How About a Little
Cookie?)*, 2002
Painted bronze, ed. 10,
15 × 13½ × 12½ in.

Roland Ayers
(American, 1932–2014)

Dream Boat, 1969–73
Ink on paper, 14 × 18 in.

Orgasm, 1969
Ink on paper, 11¼ × 11½ in.

Swing, 1972
Ink on paper, 7 × 5 in.

Untitled, 1972
Ink on paper, 11¾ × 16½ in.

Luis Cruz Azaceta
(Cuban-American, born 1943)

Coney Island Local, 1975
Colored pencil, ink, and collage on
paper, 24 × 38 in.

Ship of Fools, 1978
Colored pencil on paper, 18 × 24 in.

Self-Portrait with Phony Hat, 1980
Colored ink and pencils on paper,
22 × 30 in.
2013.20.2

*Self-Portrait: Apocalypse Now—or
Later?*, 1981
Acrylic on canvas, 72 × 120 in.
2015.29

Self-Portrait as Cockroach, 1981
Acrylic on canvas, 66 × 66 in.
2014.11

*Self-Portrait: Pistol and Other
Small Things*, 1981
Watercolor and colored pencils on
paper, 32 × 25 in.

*Self-Portrait Throwing the Devil
Out*, 1981
Ink and colored pencil on paper,
22 × 30 in.

Study for *The Journey*, 1986
Oil pastel on paper, 35½ × 44½ in.

Dictator's Head-Boot, 1987
Acrylic and oil pastel on paper,
30 × 22 in.
2015.40

James Barsness
(American, born 1954)

Young Woman in Twilight, 1991
Oil and gold leaf on canvas,
49½ × 40¾ in.

Citta del Collino, 2000
Ink and paper collage on canvas,
27¼ × 39 in.

Poker Night (Self-Portrait), 2002
Acrylic, ballpoint pen, collage, and
gold leaf on paper, 21 × 26 in.

My Playground, 2003
Acrylic, ink, and collage on canvas,
48 × 65¾ in.
2012.16.2

My Princess Dress, 2004
Acrylic and ink on paper mounted
on canvas, 49¾ × 67¾ in.

Engine, 2005
Acrylic, ink, and paper on canvas,
51¾ × 69 in.

Bifrost Bridge, 2005–6
Acrylic, ink, and paper on canvas,
51½ × 69½ in.

**Macena Barton
(American, 1901–1986)**

Untitled (Rosanna in pink), c. 1935
Oil on canvas, 48 × 38 in.

Self-Portrait, 1940s
Oil on canvas, 36 × 20 in.

Untitled (Outer space), 1962
Oil on canvas, 50 × 62 in.

**Joanna Beall
(American, 1935–1997)**

Portrait of HCW(esterman), 1963
Oil on canvas, 46 × 40 in.

**William Beckman
(American, born 1942)**

Self-Portrait, 1980
Oil on panel, 15¼ × 13¼ in.

Study for *Diana IV*, 1980
Pencil on paper, 30 × 28 in.
2013.10.1

Diana in Sweatshirt, 1983
Charcoal on paper, 29½ × 24½ in.

Diana #7, 1985
Oil on panel, 22¾ × 20 in.

Portrait of Gregory Gillespie, 1996
Oil on panel, 14 × 11½ in.

Deidra, 2003
Oil on panel, 22 × 19½ in.

Blue on Blue Self-Portrait, 2006
Oil on panel, 18⅛ × 15½ in.
2022.23

**Vera Berdich
(American, 1915–2003)**

Olympia (A Mechanical Doll),
c. 1960s
Oil on canvas with collage transfer,
48 × 36 in.

The Game (Diptych), 1965
Oil on canvas with collage transfer,
52 × 76 in.

Brain Box, 1973
Oil on canvas with collage transfer,
48 × 54 in.

**Joan Brown
(American, 1938–1990)**

Bob, Sultana, and Guard, 1961
Enamel on canvas, 72 × 72 in.

Rock & Roll Rat, 1967
Oil enamel on plywood,
31 × ½ × 11½ in.

A Mouse at Snug Harbor, 1969
Oil on canvas, 12 × 12 in.

Self-Portrait in Knit Hat, 1972
Enamel on canvas, 20 × 16 in.

Self-Portrait in Scarf Drinking Tea,
1972
Enamel on canvas, 20 × 15¾ in.

The Last Dance, 1973
Enamel, glitter, and plastic on
Masonite panel, 24 × 48½ in.

**Craig Calderwood
(American, born 1987)**

*Notes on ♀ and ♂ from My Eight-
Year-Old Self*, 2018
Paint and thread on upholstery
fabric, 46 × 51 in.

Double D's, 2019
Pen on paper, 11 × 14 in.

Ringworm Inspection, 2019
Pen on paper, 11 × 14 in.

*You Can Tell by the Beast Between
Her Legs*, 2019
Pen on paper, 11 × 14 in.

Christina's Revelations, 2022
Ink on paper, 15 × 13¼ in.

Meat Bees, 2023
Ink on paper, 18 × 14¼ in.

**Wynn (Elwyn) Chamberlain
(American, 1927–2014)**

The Introduction, c. early 1950s
Oil on panel, 10¾ × 12½ in.

**Robert Colescott
(American, 1925–2009)**

Twilight Time in the Islands, 1990
Acrylic on canvas, 16 × 14 in.

**Felipe Jesus Consalvos
(Cuban-American, 1891–1960)**

Take Me to the Land of Jazz,
c. 1920–50
Mixed-media collage, 51 × 27¼ in.

**Peter Dean
(American, 1934–1993)**

Studio Portrait, 1973
Oil on board, 12 × 13 in.

Me and Eye, 1974
Oil on canvas, 19¼ × 19¼ in.

Self-Portrait, 1975
Oil on canvas, 20 × 16 in.

Separation, 1975
Oil on panel, 15 × 15½ in.

*Crazy Dance at the Crack of Real-
ity*, 1976
Oil on canvas, 75 × 62 in.
2015.1.4

Hounded, 1977
Oil on canvas, 60 × 50 in.
2015.1.2

Wianno Double Halo, 1979
Oil on canvas, 50 × 60 in.

Wianno Sunset, 1979
Oil on canvas, 60 × 50 in.

*Exchange on Spring Street in the
Rain*, 1979–82
Acrylic on canvas, 81 × 68 in.
2018.46

Portrait of the Artist, 1981
Oil on canvas, 27 × 22 in.
2015.1.1

Portrait of a Winner, 1981
Oil on canvas, 30 × 22 in.

Condor Flush, c. 1986
Oil on canvas, 80 × 64 in.
2015.1.3

Hercules with Tiger Head, n.d.
(1970s)
Oil on canvas, 34 × 20 in.

Untitled (Self-portrait with two
masks), n.d. (mid-1970s)
Oil on Masonite, 15¾ × 10½ in.

Untitled (Self-portrait with unicorn),
n.d. (mid-1970s)
Oil on Masonite, 15½ × 9½ in.

**Roy De Forest
(American, 1930–2007)**

Untitled (Two birds), 1969
Pastel, crayon, and watercolor on
paper, 20½ × 29½ in.

Trouble in the Bovine Quarters,
1975
Acrylic on canvas, 60¼ × 72¼ in.

Untitled (Talking horse), 1976
Acrylic on canvas, 21 × 16¼ in.

Watching for the Outriders,
1976–77
Acrylic on canvas, 60 × 68 in.

Untitled, 1977
Pastel and pencil on paper,
20 × 26½ in., artist's frame

Savage Echoes, 1982–83
Acrylic on canvas, 74½ × 78 in.

You Can't Go Home Again, 1995
Acrylic on canvas, 58 × 60 in., artist's frame

Dog Bench # 1, 2001–3
Polychrome cast bronze and stain-
less steel, 48 × 68 × 35 in.

**Tommy Olof Elder
(American, born Sweden, 1951)**

*Gregory Gillespie, Frances Cohen
Gillespie, Jane Lund*, n.d. (c. 1985)
Photographs, 8½ × 11 in.

**Rafael Ferrer
(American, born Puerto
Rico, 1933)**

Encuentro, 1983
Oil on canvas, 80 × 60 in.
2006.26

La Espera (Waiting), 1983
Oil on canvas, 72 × 60 in.

Satisfaccion, 1983
Oil on canvas, 24 × 18 in.

El Bolero, 1983–84
Oil on canvas, 60 × 72 in.

S.P. (Self-portrait), 1986
Oil on panel, 13 × 9½ in.

Wayne, 1987
Oil on board, 21 × 17 in.

Monica, 1988
Oil on wood panel, 26 × 21¾ in.

Reading, 1988
Oil on panel, 12 × 9¼ in.

Self-Portrait, 1988
Aquatint etching state I, ed. 2/15,
15 × 11 in.

Untitled, 1988
Oil on wood panel, 24 × 18 in.

Sombrero de Palma, 1991
Oil on canvas, 24 × 18 in.

La Pintura: Descarga Del Monte,
1995
Oil on canvas, 96 × 72 in.

Smoke, 1998–99
Oil on canvas, 36 × 24 in.

**Walton Ford
(American, born 1960)**

Warning Sign, 1988
Acrylic on panel, 34 × 26 in.

**Robert Forman
(American, born 1948)**

Otilia, 1998
Silk thread on board, 16 × 24 in.,
artist's frame

*Les Demoiselles d'Avignon Revis-
ited*, 2007
Silk thread on board, 18 × 19 in.,
artist's frame

Dutch Wife, 2008
Silk thread on board, 32 × 20 in.,
artist's frame

Eileen Foti
(American, born 1963)

Les Femmes d'Afrique, 2007
Gouache on paper, 12 × 11 in.

Viola Frey
(American, 1933–2004)

Veiled Lady, Edith Sitwell, 1977
Glazed ceramic, 25½ × 10¼ × 8 in.

The Dinner, also Junk Eating, 1978–79
Glazed ceramic, 19 × 15 × 12 in.

Untitled (Yellow hat, red flower), from the series *Greedy Grandmother*, 1980
Oil and acrylic on canvas, 30 × 22 in.

Untitled (Kissing couple and dog in window), 1982
Oil on paper, 60 × 40 in.

Vanessa German
(American, born 1976)

Declaration of Independence, 2020
Mixed-media assemblage, 27 × 17 × 4 in.
Funds provided by Robert Kohler
2021.17

Frances Cohen Gillespie
(American, 1939–1998)

Nude Self-Portrait in Chair, c. 1972
Oil on panel, 48 × 57 in.
2015.28

Leila, 1972–73
Oil on panel, 72 × 48 in.

Gregory Gillespie
(American, 1936–2000)

Seated Couple, 1967
Oil on panel, 9 × 7 in.

Woman with Baby, 1968
Mixed media, 7½ × 6½ in.

Woman on Blue Ground, 1969
Mixed media, 15½ × 11½ in., artist's frame

Self-Portrait (Bald), 1971–72
Oil and Magna on wood, 15 × 10 in.

Beetle and Frog, 1972
Mixed media on Masonite, 8 × 12 in.

Visionary Landscape, 1974
Oil and Magna on paper on panel, 10 × 8¾ in.

Dark Painter (Portrait of a Renaissance Painter), 1982–83
Oil on panel, 23 × 20 in.

Wheel of Birth, 1983–90
Oil and alkyd on panel, 29½ × 18 in.
2010.19

The Kiss, 1984
Pencil on Mylar, 12⅜ × 9⅛ in.

Peg and Friend, 1984 and 1999
Oil on panel, 16 × 18 in.

Rita, 1985
Oil on panel, 19½ × 15¾ in.

The Kiss, 1987 and 1996
Oil and pencil on lithograph on panel, 21 × 17½ in., artist's frame

Manic Depression, c. 1987
Graphite on Mylar, 29¼ × 12¾ in.

Lydia and Her Demon, 1988
Oil and alkyd on panel, 17¼ × 14¼ in.

Julianna, 1991
Oil on panel, 16½ × 15 in.

Self-Portrait with Mother and Son, 1991–92
Oil on panel, 48 × 37¼ in.

William Beckman, 1993
Oil and alkyd on panel, 98 × 86 in.

Peggy, 1996
Oil on panel, 35½ × 24½ in.

Schizophrenic Saint Shrine, 1999
Oil on panel, 25⅜ × 33⅝ × 2 in.

Untitled (Notes and sketch), n.d. (1990s?)
Marker on paper, 12 × 9 in.

Juan González
(Cuban-American, 1945–1993)

Nacimiento (The Birth), 1979
Watercolor on paper on wood, 6⅛ × 6¾, tabernacle frame 15 × 15 × 10⅝ in.

Jardin Gris, 1989
Acrylic and tempera on canvas, 15¾ × 15¾ in.

Untitled (Black leather tulip), n.d. (early 1970s)
Pencil on embossed paper, 12 × 5¾ in.

Red Grooms
(American, born 1937)

Gauguin, 1963
Oil on canvas, 30 × 30 in.

No Gas, 1971
Lithographs, collage, ed. 46/75, 22 × 28 in.

Nervous City, 1971
Color lithograph on paper, 22 × 29¾ in.

P'town Bicycle (Arthur Cohen), 1971–74
Crayon on paper and acrylic on wood, 56½ × 49 in.

Harry Watley Gets Rabbit-itis, 1975
Gouache on paper, 30⅛ × 41⅞ in.

Jill, 1976
Watercolor and ink on paper, 14 × 11 in.

Portrait, Brittany, 1980
Watercolor on paper, 24 × 18 in.

Self-Portrait, Summer, 1986
Watercolor on paper, 10 × 14 in.

Red Grooms
(American, born 1937) and
Mimi Gross
(American, born 1940)

Tappy Toes, 1968–70
Acrylic on paper and wood, 35¾ × 46¼ × 5 in.

Lorri Gunn
(American, born 1942)

Imagists Playing Cards, early to mid-1970s
Colored pencil on paper, 11 × 14½ in.

Hairy Who (James Falconer, American, 1943–2022; Art Green, American, 1941–2025; Gladys Nilsson, American, born 1940; Jim Nutt, American, born 1938; Suellen Rocca, American, 1943–2020; and Karl Wirsum, American, 1939–2021)

The Portable Hairy Who!, 1966
Color offset lithographs on newsprint and coated paper (covers), bound volume, 11 × 7 in. (closed)

The Hairy Who Sideshow, 1967
Color offset lithographs, bound volume, 11 × 7 in. (closed)

Hairy Who, 1968
Color offset lithographs on coated paper, bound volume, 11 × 7 in. (closed)

Marcy Hermansader
(American, born 1951)

Seveso, 1981
Colored pencil and acrylic on paper, 30 × 44 in.

Alterations in the Blood, 1985
Colored pencil, acrylic, and fabric on paper, 30 × 18 in.

Living with the Moon, 1987
Colored pencil, acrylic, spray paint, and pastel on board, 30 × 27 in.

R. B. Kitaj
(American, 1932–2007)

Quentin, 1979
Charcoal and pastel on paper, 25¾ × 15¾ in.

Bather (Psychotic Boy), 1980
Pastel and charcoal on paper, 52¾ × 22½ in.

William Eckhardt Kohler
(American, born 1962)

Big John, 2002
Oil on canvas, 32 × 26 in.

The Forest (Dream Self-Portrait), 2003
Oil on canvas, 22 × 20 in.

Joyce Kozloff
(American, born 1942)

La Conquesta, 1999
Watercolor, plaster, and rope on cardboard globe, 12¾ in. dia.

Anne Kraus
(American, 1956–2003)

The Performer, c. late 1990s
Glazed whiteware and stand, 18½ × 15½ × 8½ in.

New Hope Shopping Land, 1999
Glazed whiteware, 34 × 33½ in.

Reception in NYC, 2000
Glazed earthenware, 10½ in. dia.

Rushing Towards the Next Train, 2000
Glazed earthenware, 10½ in. dia.

The Dormant Garden, 2001
Glazed whiteware, 36 × 32 in.

The Spiral Staircase, 2001
Glazed whiteware, 42 × 27 in.

Deborah Kravitz
(American, born 1951)

Self-Portrait with Piranha, 1972
Mixed-media collage on mat board, 13 × 7¾ in.

Spider Woman, 1972
Mixed-media collage on mat board, 10½ × 10 in.

Mother and Child in Front of Door, c. 1972
Acrylic on panel, 23 × 6¼ in.

Mother, Mirror, Child, c. 1973
Acrylic on panel, 22½ × 9½ in.

Vampire Embrace, 1974
Mixed-media collage on artist's board, 6⅝ × 7⅞ in.

Boy-Woman Dream, 1975
Mixed-media collage on mat board, 11¾ × 13 in.

Demon, 1975
Mixed-media collage on mat board, 10½ × 8½ in.

Woman, Drawing, Door, 1975
Oil on panel, 13½ × 8¼ in.

Clear and Painful Vision, c. 1975
Mixed-media collage on artist's board, 11¾ × 8½ in.

Mad Woman with Spider, c. 1975
Mixed-media collage on mat board,
11 × 8 in.

Girl Drawing II (Girl Drawing Door),
1978
Acrylic on panel, 14½ × 7 in.

The Children's Crucifixion, 1980
Acrylic on mat board, 21¼ × 16½ in.

The Dollmakers, 1980
Acrylic on mat board, 14¼ × 10¼ in.

An Incarnation, 1980
Acrylic on panel, 11¾ × 14½ in.

On the Edge of the Woods, 1980
Acrylic on panel, 5¼ × 7¾ in.

Rebirth of the Discarded Ones,
1980
Acrylic on panel, 10¼ × 7¼ in.

*Tree with Skull, Infant, Tentacled
Figure Sketch*, 1980
Charcoal and chalk on gray paper,
6¾ × 5 in.

The Path, 1981
Acrylic on panel, 5¼ × 7¾ in.

Ceremony, 1982
Acrylic on panel, 6⅛ × 7⅝ in.

*Circle of Lizards Around a Lizard
Child Dancing in a Flower*, preliminary drawing for a painting never
painted, 1982
Pencil and chalk on gray paper,
7 × 14½ in.

Lizard Person Sketch 1, 1982
Pencil on white paper, 4¼ × 7½ in.

Lizard Person Sketch 2, 1982
Pencil on white paper, irregular
shape

Sketch of a Lizard Person, 1982
Pencil on white paper, irregular
shape

Preliminary sketch for *The Ritual*,
1982
Pencil on white paper, 9 × 13 in.

Preliminary sketch for *The Ritual*,
1982
Pencil on gray paper, 10 × 10½ in.

Within the Lotus, 1983
Acrylic on panel, 8¼ × 8¼ in.

Self-Portrait, 1996
Pencil on panel, 14½ × 10¼ in.

At the End of the Day, 2003
Mixed media on paper, 7¾ × 9¾ in.

The Edge of Night, 2006
Acrylic on panel, 8 × 10 in.

Twilight Glowing Horizon, 2006
Acrylic on panel, 8 × 10 in.

**Gina Litherland
(American, born 1955)**

Four Seasons, 2006
Oil on Masonite, four panels, each
12 × 9 in.

Owl's Net, 2007
Oil on Masonite, 12 × 10 in.

Queen of an Uncharted Territory,
2008
Oil on Masonite, 30 × 10 in.

Lupercalia, 2011
Oil on Masonite, 24 × 30 in.

Wolf Alice (for Angela Carter), 2011
Oil on Masonite, 12 × 9 in.

Tea Leaf Reading, 2014
Oil on panel, 11¾ × 9⅛ in.

Housekeeping, 2015
Oil on panel, 30 × 15 in.

*My Braids of the Past (for Marosa
di Giogio)*, 2016
Oil on panel, 14 × 12 in.

Winter Solstice, 2017
Oil on panel, 9¼ × 7½ in.

Pistis Sophia, 2018
Oil on panel, 36 × 18 in.

**Robert Lostutter
(American, born 1939)**

Untitled (Two standing figures with
hoop), c. 1968
Watercolor on paper, 10¼ × 13 in.

Untitled (Woman in stockings),
1968
Watercolor on paper, 10½ × 13 in.

Untitled (Woman, smoking tower-
man), 1969
Watercolor on paper, 12 × 10¾ in.

Untitled (Woman stepping out of
frame), 1969
Watercolor on paper, 13¼ × 11¼ in.

Untitled (Woman with flower), 1969
Watercolor on paper, 8 × 8 in.

Untitled (Seated woman), 1970
Pencil on paper, 8¾ × 7½ in.

Untitled (Burning man), 1971
Watercolor and graphite on cardstock, 7¾ × 6¾ in.

Untitled (Man with mask, spikes),
1971
Oil on canvas, 46 × 35½ in.

Map to the Morning Dance 3, 1973
Oil on canvas, 66 × 43½ in.

A Sign of My Time, 1977
Graphite on canvas, 44 × 48 in.

Red-Throated Bee-Eater, 1978
Watercolor on paper, 12½ × 14 in.

*Little Blue Heron and Scarlet
Ibis in Late Afternoon*, 1986
Watercolor on paper, 8 × 34 in.

Red Masdevallia, 2004
Watercolor on paper, 35 × 43 in.

The Songs of War 7, 2021
Graphite on paper, 19¾ × 19¾ in.

The Songs of War 9, 2021
Graphite on paper, 19¾ × 19¾ in.

**Michael Lucero
(American, born 1953)**

Lady with Butterfly, 1991
Glazed ceramic, 14½ × 8 × 10½ in.

NYC Man, 1991
Glazed ceramic, 18 × 14 × 6½ in.

Untitled (Standing woman), 1991
Glazed ceramic, 9 × 5½ × 3¾ in.

Barking Dog, 1994
Glazed ceramic, 16½ × 18 × 9½ in.

Tea Pot Series (House), 2009
Glazed ceramic, 8¾ × 12½ × 5 in.

**Jane Lund
(American, born 1939)**

Party, c. late 1960s to early 1970s
Pastel on paper, 37 × 30 in.

Dominions of the Moon, 1970–73
Ink on paper, dimensions vary
2017.59.1–17

Act of Mercy, c. 1974–75
Lithograph, ed. 1/60, 9 × 6¾ in.

Ancient Rite, c. 1974–75
Pastel on paper, 34 × 29 in.

Barely Alive, c. 1974–75
Lithograph, ed. 8/60, 7½ × 8 in.

Dream Objects, c. 1974–75
Lithograph, ed. 1/60, 7 × 6 in.

The Elevator, c. 1974–75
Lithograph, ed. 11/69, 7½ × 6¼ in.

The Initiation, c. 1974–75
Lithograph, ed. 33/60, 8 × 6¾ in.

Party for Myself, c. 1974–75
Pastel on paper, 24 × 38 in.

The Priestess, 1975
Pastel on paper, 36¾ × 24¼ in.

Anniversary, c. 1975
Pastel on paper, 28 × 31 in.

Separate Realities, c. early 1970s?
Glazed terra cotta, 16 × 5½ × 5½ in.
and 9½ × 4 × 4 in.

Old Friend, c. early 1970s
Pastel on paper, 27½ × 33½ in.
(oval)

The Choice, c. mid- to late 1970s
Pastel on paper, 30 × 33 in.

Pregnant Woman, 1978
Pastel on paper, 28 × 22 in.

Domestic Scene, 1985
Lithograph, ed. 4/36, 8 × 6¾ in.

Home Front, 2014
Mixed media, plastic box,
8⅝ × 16 × 8 in.

*Artists of a Certain Age: Self-
Portrait with Jean-Étienne Liotard,
1702-1789*, 2016
Pastel on paper, 20 × 27 in.

**Charles Marsh
(American, born 1944)**

Untitled (Screw over landscape),
c. 1990
String, collage, and salvaged
frame, 18¾ × 23⅛ in.

Untitled (Street scene with plan-
ets), c. 1990
Sequins, fabric, collage on paper,
and frame, 27 × 20 in.

Imp, c. 1995
Feather, butterfly, test tube,
and mixed-media on board,
9 × 6¾ × 2 in.

Untitled (Fight, flee), c. 1995
Stamped metal and mixed
media on velvet on game board,
12¼ × 10½ × 1½ in.

Untitled (Woman holding fairy),
c. 1995
Collage, ink, acrylic, and
mixed-media on photograph,
23½ × 19½ in.

**Sam Messer
(American, born 1955)**

Jon in Yellow Chair, 1992
Oil on canvas, 28 × 22 in.

Jon in Red Chair, 1993
Oil on canvas, 20 × 16 in.

Untitled (Jon Serl eating), c. 1992
Pencil on paper, 11 × 17½ in.

Amerika, 2006
Oil on canvas, 14 × 17 in.

Josephine, 2006
Oil on canvas, 18 × 14 in.

New York Harbor, 2006
Oil on canvas, 17 × 13 in.

Surrounded by Paper, 2007
Oil on canvas, 77 × 62 in.

Birthday Portrait #51, 2007
Oil on canvas, 18 × 14 in.

Exfoliating Self-Portrait, 2011-12
Oil on canvas, 20 × 16 in.

Anne Minich
(American, born 1934)

AEGM at 35, c. late 1960s
Oil on canvas, 24 × 20 in.

Sunday's Lover, 1981
Graphite and colored pencil on
paper, 7¾ × 10⅜ in.

Imposition at Monadnock, 1988
and 2011
Graphite and colored pencil on
paper, wood frame with shells,
26¾ × 20 in.

*Christmas Eve 1993, for Maria and
Daniel*, 1993
Graphite and gold paint on artist's
board, 8 × 8 in.

Gender Issue: Damage, 1994
Graphite, watercolor, and collage
on paper, 11¾ × 13⅝ in.

Lost Colony, 1998
Graphite and metallic paint
on artist's board and paper,
11⅝ × 13⅞ in.

The Anglican and the Jew, 2001
Graphite, colored pencil, and
watercolor on paper, 10 × 10⅝ in.

Jesus and the Soul Boat, 2010
Oil and mixed-media on board,
10¾ × 15 in.

Feral Nun, 2012–13
Graphite on paper in mixed-media
frame (shells, metal), 34 × 19 in.

An Annunciation in NYC, 2016
Oil and mixed-media on birch ply,
32½ × 24⅝ in.

Diana Moore
(American, born 1946)

Bust Urn, 2000
Cast carbon steel,
10½ × 8½ × 4½ in.

Purse of Plenty, 2000
Cast carbon steel, ed. 2/3,
7½ × 9 × 7 in.

Seedy Purse, 2001
Cast carbon steel, ed. 1/8,
7¼ × 8 × 6¼ in.

Darrel Morris
(American, born 1960)

Baby Race, 1988
Embroidery and fabric appliqué,
9½ × 11 in.

*The Fate of Three-Legged
Chickens*, 1991
Embroidery and fabric appliqué,
8½ × 7⅜ in.

Allowed to Open the Door, 1992
Embroidery and fabric appliqué,
9 × 6⅛ in.

Target Practice, 1995
Embroidery and fabric appliqué,
7¼ × 6⅝ in.

Sam Overton, 1996
Embroidery and fabric appliqué,
9¾ × 15 in.

Wait…, 1999
Embroidery and fabric applique,
8 × 7½ in.

Hold the Baby, c. late 1990s–early
2000s
Embroidery and fabric appliqué,
4⅞ × 4⅛ in.

Playing Right Field, c. late 1990s–
early 2000s
Embroidery and fabric appliqué,
8¾ × 10½ in.

College, 2004
Mixed media on paper, 13 × 10½ in.

In Bed, 2004
Found fabric and thread on canvas, 7 × 6¾ in.

Study for *In Bed*, 2004
Mixed media on paper, 6 × 9¾ in.

Preacher, 2004
Mixed media on paper, 10 × 8 in.

Teaching Typing, 2004
Found fabric and thread on
canvas, 10 × 7½ in.

Decline, 2007
Embroidery and fabric appliqué,
8¾ × 12¾ in.

More Like Your Brother, 2013
Embroidery appliqué on fabric,
7⅜ × 7⅜ in.

Self-Portrait (at Age 22), 2013
Acrylic on canvas, 12 × 12 in.

Robert Neal
(American, 1916–1987)

Cheese and Butter Line, 1984
Oil on canvas, 36 × 30 in.
2021.13

Street People, 1986
Oil on canvas, 35 × 31 in.

Gladys Nilsson
(American, born 1940)

Walkers, 1966
Watercolor on paper, 16 × 11 in.

Havsies, 1968
Watercolor and gouache on paper,
22 × 15 in.

Archway Peckercysters, c. 1968
Watercolor on paper, 14¾ × 11¼ in.

Cloud Burste, 1969
Watercolor on board, 15 × 22 in.

Untitled (Mermaid), 1969
Pen and silver ink on black laid
paper, 9½ × 12½ in.

To Couples: DeKaled, 1969
Watercolor on paper, 22¼ × 30½ in.

Semisighmetricall, 1970
Acrylic on canvas, 20¼ × 28 in.,
artist's frame

Banded Below, 1971
Acrylic on canvas, 38 × 25¾ in.,
artist's frame

To in the Timber, 1972
Oil on canvas, 45½ × 37½ in.,
artist's frame

Drownders, c. 1972–73
Acrylic on canvas, 43½ × 37½ in.,
artist's frame

Hairdresser's Surprise, 1977
Watercolor on paper, 33 × 25½ in.

Drafty, 1978
Watercolor on paper, 30¼ × 22¼ in.

Checking Out the Other Side, 1987
Watercolor on paper, 40 × 60 in.

*Big School Picture: Little Paper
Mural*, 1992
Photoprint on paper, ed. 19/50,
18 × 21 in.

Cut Paper Lady, 1993
Watercolor on paper, 11⅛ × 7½ in.

Going, 1995
Watercolor, gouache, and collage
on paper, 5½ × 7½ in.

Sunni Gal, 1997
Acrylic and collage on canvas
embroidery hoop, 8 in. dia.

Gift Box, 1999
Watercolor and gouache on paper,
40¾ × 60 in.
2012.16.1

Uni-verse, 2001
Watercolor and gouache on paper,
14⅞ × 22 in.

Plant #2, 2010
Ink and graphite on paper collage,
11¾ × 11¾ in.

Irene Hardwicke Olivieri
(American, born 1959)

PaleoGirl with Ponytail, 2006
Bones from owl pellets on wooden
rising bowl, 25½ × 17 in.

Coaxing a Better Me, 2012
Oil on metal tabletop, 30 × 30 in.

Subterranean Family, 2013
Oil on wood, 35 × 30 in.

Chacho, Catalpa, El Capitan, 2015
Cat bones on wooden rising bowl,
31 × 16 in.

I'd Marry You in a Minute, 2019
Mixed media on wooden plate,
11 in. dia.

The Painter and Her Skeleton, 2019
Oil on wood, 31½ × 20 in.

Papachongo, 2024
Oil on wood, 26 × 18 in.

Ed Paschke
(American, 1939–2004)

Black Man, 1974
Graphite on paper, 22½ × 17 in.

Gleason, 1975
Graphite on paper, 29 × 23 in.

Jimmie, 1975
Graphite on paper, 22 × 13½ in.

Julius, 1975
Graphite on paper, 20¼ × 11½ in.

Tudor, 1976
Lithograph on paper, ed. 8/20,
28¾ × 23 in.

Maija Peeples-Bright
(American, born 1942)

*Several Smokles with Seal Skater
and Scabiosa*, c. 1977
Oil on canvas, 53 × 67 in.

Sheep Sheiks, 1977
Acrylic and mixed-media on canvas, 42 × 48 in.

Alex Queral
(American, born Cuba 1958)

Nutt Nose, 2003
Oil on carved phone book, 11 × 9 in.

*Rock & Roll Survivor (Keith Rich-
ards)*, 2006
Acrylic on carved phone book,
11 × 9 in.

*He Was Right About Bush (Michael
Moore)*, 2007
Acrylic on carved phone book,
11 × 9 in.

Inner Self, c. 2007
Acrylic on carved phone book,
11 × 9 in.

Soul Singer (James Brown), 2009
Acrylic on carved phone book,
11 × 9 in.

Alexander Graham Bell, c. 2010
Acrylic on carved phone book,
11 × 9 in.

Self-Portrait II, 2013
Acrylic on carved phone book,
11 × 9 in.

Christina Ramberg (American, 1946–1995)

Golden Madonna, 1970
Acrylic on Masonite, 12½ × 9¾ in.
in artist's original frame

False Bloom, 1971
Acrylic on Masonite, 17 × 12¾ in.
in artist's original frame

David Regan (American, born 1964)

Leda in the Mussel Teapot, 2004
Porcelain, 8 × 11½ × 9 in.

Winfred Rembert (American, 1945–2021)

T. J. the Tooler, 1998
Dye on tooled leather,
25¾ × 24¾ in.

Chain Gang, 2005
Dye on tooled leather,
35¾ × 28¼ in.

The Hungry Eye Cafe #2, 2006
Dye on tooled leather, 31½ × 24¼ in.

Sugar Cane, 2009
Dye on tooled leather, 52 × 29½ in.

Philip Sherrod (American, born 1935)

Untitled (Androgynous person), 1970
Oil on canvas, 39½ × 30 in.

Bar, Baby, and 6th Avenue, 1977
Oil on canvas, 54 × 46 in.

Cityscape Triptych, 1977
Left
Ari Bohack, Royal, Heinz Ketchup
Oil on canvas, 42½ × 41½ in.
Center
El Pic Pop, Sherrod of Four Cityscapes
Oil on canvas, 47¼ × 47¼ in.
Right
Heckers, Helena, and Sunnyside-Times Boat
Oil on canvas, 43¼ × 42½ in.

Julie Speed (American, born 1951)

Mr. Livingston's ID, 2000
Gouache and collage on paper,
17 × 18¼ in.
2011.13.1

Double-Header, 2001
Gouache and collage on paper,
16¼ × 11¼ in.
2011.13.2

9/11, 2001
Gouache, collage, and engraving on paper, 16¾ × 11½ in.
2012.16.3.2

Hellfire, 2002
Gouache and collage on paper,
17½ × 9 in.
2011.13.3

Yellow Leviticus, 2002
Etching and gouache on paper, ed. 43/50, 10½ × 11¼ in.
2012.16.3.1

The Dogmatists II, 2004–5
Oil on linen, 24¼ × 37⅛ in.
2011.5

Kyle Staver (American, born 1953)

Bad Dog, 2007
Linocut on paper, 33 × 36 in.

In the Mirror, 2007
Linocut on paper, 36 × 30 in.

Feeding the Cockatoo, 2009
Oil on canvas, 48 × 56 in.

Trapeze, 2012
Oil on canvas, 68 × 58 in.

Groupers, 2013
Oil on canvas, 70 × 58 in.

Untitled (Venus and Adonis), 2018
Ink, pastel, pencil, and watercolor on paper, 11 × 8½ in.

Dolphins, 2021
Oil on canvas, 70 × 68 in.

Valkyries, 2021
Aquatint etching, studio proof 1/2,
8 × 10 in.

Fortitude, 2023
Oil on panel, 7 × 5 in.

Octopus Ardor, 2024
Oil on linen, 70 × 58 in.

Eric Stotik (American, born 1963)

Untitled 6483359 (Boats and bodies), 1990
Acrylic on canvas on Masonite,
8 × 11 in.

Untitled ES024-195 (Squatting figure with baby), c. 2002
Ink on paper, 12¾ × 8 in.

Untitled LR66 (Interior, boy, woman), 2003
Acrylic on paper on foamcore,
5 × 7 in.

Untitled LR31 (Bats, prone man), 2006
Acrylic on jute on foamcore, 7 × 7 in.

Untitled LR33 (Factory, machine, green man), 2006
Acrylic on cloth on panel, 7 × 7¼ in.

Untitled LR37 (Woman, boat, buildings), 2006
Acrylic on jute on foamcore,
6 × 4 in.

Untitled LR62 (Activists, posters), 2007
Acrylic on plywood, 9¾ × 6⅛ in.

Untitled (Old man with woman in crib), 2008–9
Acrylic on altered book on foamcore, 5 × 7 in.

Untitled LR205 (Two male figures, abstractions), 2010
Acrylic on wood panel, 8 × 5 in.

Bob Thompson (American, 1937–1966)

Loren in the Cedar, 1960
Ink on paper, 16¾ × 14 in.
2011.14.1

High Night # 2, M. Bills, John, Red, Me, c. 1963
Ink on paper, 10¾ × 13⅞ in.

Artaud, 1964
Marker on paper, 19½ × 13¾ in.
2011.14.2

Tabitha Vevers (American, born 1957)

Noisy Dreams, 1990
Oil and wood on board, 21½ × 18 in., decorative frame

Flesh Memories: Heat, 1994
Oil and mixed-media on wood panel, 20 × 24 in.
2015.12.2

Still Running from Some Forgotten Thing, 1994
Engraved metal, mixed-media box,
3½ × 3 × 1 in.

Flesh Memories: Seeking Pink, 1996
Oil and mixed-media on wood panel, 30 × 40 in.
2015.12.1

Transient Anatomies: Hatch, 1996
Ink and oil on goatskin vellum,
9 × 8 in.
2015.3

Secular Icon: Caught in a Whirlpool, 1988
Oil and gold leaf on wood panel,
26 × 24 × 2½ in., artist's frame

Flying Dream (Gillian), 2000
Oil on steel, 7¾ × 11¾ in.

Flying Dream (The Rescue), 2001
Oil on galvanized steel, 9 × 12 in.

Flying Dream (Anonymous), 2003
Oil on galvanized steel, 12 × 9 in.

Flying Dream (Marja), 2003
Oil on galvanized steel, 12 × 10 in.

Flying Dream (The Restaurant), 2003
Oil on galvanized steel, 6¾ × 12 in.

Embrace (IV.06a), 2006
Oil and gold leaf on shell,
4¾ × 6⅞ in.

Rapture (II.06a), 2006
Oil and gold leaf on shell,
4½ × 6½ in.

Eden (Eveandadam VI.07a), 2007
Oil and gold leaf on ivorine,
9⅜ × 9⅞ in.

Eden: Marsupedonna, 2008
Oil and gold leaf on ivorine,
9⅝ × 8 in.

Eden (Expulsion), 2008–9
Oil and gold leaf on ivorine,
13⅜ × 14¼ in.

When We Talk of Rape IV, 2009
Oil and gold leaf on Mylar,
10⅞ × 14⅞ in.

Flying Dream (In the Dunes II), 2011
Oil and gold leaf on galvanized steel, 10 × 12 in.

Shiva (Fire and Ice), 2011
Oil and gold leaf on ivorine,
16 × 14 in.

Pearl Maker VII, 2013
Oil on clamshell in decorative box with fabric, 6¾ × 5¾ in.

Petrichor, 2021
Oil, mixed-media, and palladium leaf on panel, 24 × 12 in.

Mark Wagner (American, born 1971)

Big Fish Little Fish, 2008
Currency collage on panel,
16 × 12 in.

Noir, 2009
Currency collage on panel,
24 × 18 in.

Hand to Mouth / Are What You Eat What You Are, 2011
Currency collage on panel,
24 × 18 in.

Kara Walker (American, born 1969)

Resurrection Story Without Patrons, 2017
Etching with aquatint on paper, ed. 4/30, 39 × 49 in.

C. K. Wilde
(American, born 1972)

Emptiness: Portrait of Thich Quang Duc, 2006
Currency collage on panel, 24¾ × 24¾ in.
2016.23

John Wilde
(American, 1919–2006)

Myself with Long Hair, 1940
Graphite on paper, 20¾ × 18 in.

Untitled (Design for man with one eye closed), 1940–41
Pencil on paper, 18 × 13½ in.

Untitled (Man with one eye closed), 1941
Oil on Masonite, 24¼ × 18¼ in.

The Chair, 1968
Oil on canvas, 40 × 30 in.

H. and Death #2, 1968
Oil on panel, 6¾ × 8¼ in.

Family Portrait I, Inside, 1971
Oil on panel, 9¼ × 19¼ in.

From the Wood, What Shirley Found, 1977
Oil on board, 7¼ × 9¼ in.

Will and Joyce Wartman Floating in Marital Bliss, 1982
Oil on wood, 14½ × 20 in.

Wildeview, 1985
Lithograph, ed. 25/85, 17¾ × 35½ in.

An Homage to Philipp Otto Runge, 1987
Oil on linen, 16 × 20 in.

Work Reconsidered: Love After Murder, 1989
Oil on wood, 13 × 20¼ in.

Myself in 1944 Contemplating the Following 60 Years, 2004
Oil on panel, 24 × 40 in.

Didier William
(American, born Haiti, 1983)

Bois Caiman, 2017
Collage and acrylic with carving on panel, 48 × 60 in.

Karl Wirsum
(American, 1939–2021)

Untitled (Study for *Baseball Girl*), 1964
Ink and colored pencil on paper, 14 × 11 in.

Untitled (Study for *Mr. Pain Close Maan*), 1964
Graphite and colored pencil on paper, 14 × 11 in.

Untitled (Study for *Show Girl Series*), 1969
Ink on paper, 36 × 24 in.

Alexi Worth
(American, born 1964)

Study for *Arizona*, 3, 2010
Oil on Mylar, 12 × 18 in. (image)

Tennessee, 2013–16
Acrylic on nylon mesh, 42 × 56 in.

Woman Reading, 2016
Oil on Mylar, 10 × 22 in.

Bryce Zackery
(American, born 1984)

Orphan Angel, 2018
Jute rope, burlap, and acrylic on canvas, 30 × 40 × 2 in.
2020.31.2

Donations or Partial Gifts to PAFA by Robert and Frances Coulborn Kohler

Robert Barnes
(American, born 1934)

James Joyce, 1958
Oil on canvas, 96 × 72 in.
Partial gift of Robert Frumkin, with support from Robert and Frances Coulborn Kohler

Jack Beal
(American, 1931–2013)

The Roof, 1964–65
Oil on canvas, 96 × 120 in.
Gift of Robert and Frances Coulborn Kohler in honor of Dr. David R. Brigham, CEO and President of PAFA, 2010–20
2021.20

Sondra with Shell Sofa, 1967
Oil on canvas, 72 × 78 in.
Partial gift of Andrea Lea Landsman and Malcolm Holzman, with support from Robert and Frances Kohler
2017.39

Interior with Waders, 1968–79
Oil on canvas, 60 × 69 in.
Funds provided by Robert and Frances Coulborn Kohler
2016.34

Skowhegan Self-Portrait, 1980
Oil on canvas, 24 × 30 in.
Promised Gift of Robert Kohler

Sondra at Her Desk, n.d. (early 1980s)
Pastel on paperboard, 30½ × 40 in.
Collection of Robert and Frances Coulborn Kohler
2020.25

Sue Coe
(American, born England, 1951)

It Can Happen Here, 2016
Linocut on off-white wove paper, ed. 38/100, 10 × 8 in.
Gift of Robert Kohler
2023.4.1

Birth of Fascism, 2017
Linocut on heavy white wove paper, ed. 26/300, 10 × 7½ in.
Gift of Robert Kohler
2023.4.2

The Total Eclipse of Rationality, 2017
Linocut on thin white Rives paper, ed. 18/300, 11⅛ × 8½ in.
Gift of Robert Kohler
2023.4.4

Tweeter in Chief, 2017
Linocut on thin white Rives paper, ed. 15/300, 11 × 8½ in.
Gift of Robert Kohler
2023.4.3

Enemy of the People, 2019
Linocut on off-white Arches paper, ed. AP, 10¼ × 8½ in.
Gift of Robert Kohler
2023.4.5

Cardboard Coffins: 37,186 Dead, 2020
Linocut on white Rives paper, ed. 2/100, 10¼ × 8⅝ in.
Gift of Robert Kohler
2023.4.7

Dr. MAGA, 2020
Linocut on white Rives paper, ed. 18/100, 10¼ × 8½ in.
Gift of Robert Kohler
2023.4.6

Waiting for the Other Shoe to Drop, 2020
Linocut on Rives paper, ed. 2/100, 17 × 13½ in.
Gift of Robert Kohler
2023.4.8

Abort the Court, 2021
Linocut on lightweight white Rives paper, ed. 6/100, 10¼ × 8½ in.
Gift of Robert Kohler
2023.4.11

Democracy, 2021
Linocut on lightweight white Rives paper, ed. 1/100, 10¼ × 8½ in.
Gift of Robert Kohler
2023.4.10

Failed IQ, 2021
Linocut on lightweight white Rives paper, ed. 19/100, 10¼ × 8½ in.
Gift of Robert Kohler
2023.4.9

The Censor, 2022
Linocut on lightweight white Rives paper, ed. 6/100, 10⅜ × 8½ in.
Gift of Robert Kohler
2023.4.14

DeSanTrump, 2022
Linocut on lightweight white Rives paper, ed. 1/100, 10⅝ × 8⅞ in.
Gift of Robert Kohler
2023.4.13

Forced Birth, 2022
Linocut on white paper, ed. 2/35, 10¼ × 8½ in.
Gift of Robert Kohler
2023.4.15

Sinking Ship, 2022
Linocut on lightweight white Rives paper, ed. 1/100, 10⅜ × 8½ in.
Gift of Robert Kohler
2023.4.12

Warrington Colescott
(American, 1921–2018)

Raft of the Titanic, 1988
Etching and aquatint, ed. 16/25, 27½ × 43¼ in.
Promised Gift of Robert Kohler

James Garrett Faulkner
(American, 1933–2010)

The Loge and Small Niagara with Observation Stand for J.B. II, 1992
Collage on paper, 16¾ × 26¾ in.
Collection of Robert and Frances Coulborn Kohler
2016.24

Mary Frank
(American, born England 1933)

Skies in Blossom, 2014
Archival pigment print on bamboo paper, ed. 2/9, 16¼ × 21⅝ in.
Collection of Robert and Frances Coulborn Kohler
2020.31.1

Natalie Frank
(American, born 1980)

One Eye Two Eyes Three Eyes (Grimm's Fairy Tales I–II), 2014
Diptych; gouache, chalk pastel on paper, 30 × 22 in.
Robert and Frances Coulborn Kohler Collection
2016.9.4,5

Woman I, 2018
Linen pulp on cotton base sheet
with fabric, 28 × 22 in.
Collection of Robert and Frances
Coulborn Kohler
2021.24

**Linda Lewis Kramer
(American, born 1937)**

Plateboy Bunny Young, 1972
Colored pencil on paper, 29 × 23 in.
Funds provided by Robert and
Frances Coulborn Kohler
2016.9.6

Plateboy Bunny Middle Age, 1972
Colored pencil on paper, 29 × 23 in.
Funds provided by Robert and
Frances Coulborn Kohler
2016.9.7

Plateboy Bunny Old, 1972
Colored pencil on paper, 29 × 23 in.
Funds provided by Robert and
Frances Coulborn Kohler
2016.9.8

Plateboy Bunny Very Old, 1972
Colored pencil on paper, 29 × 23 in.
Funds provided by Robert and
Frances Coulborn Kohler
2016.9.9

The Prisoners of Love, 1982
Painted porcelain, 22 × 14 × 12 in.
Funds provided by Robert and
Frances Coulborn Kohler
2016.2

**Hilary Pecis
(American, born 1979)**

Untitled (Fall series #6), 2008
Ink, collage, and acrylic on panel,
36 × 24 in.
Promised gift of Robert and Frances Coulborn Kohler

Untitled (Fall series #7), 2008
Ink, collage, and acrylic on panel,
36 × 24 in.
Promised gift of Robert and Frances Coulborn Kohler

**Peter Saul
(American, born 1934)**

Politics, 1985
Color lithograph, ed. 3/10,
32¾ × 23½ in.
Promised Gift of Robert Kohler

**Evelyn Statsinger
(American, 1927–2016)**

In the Penal Colony, 1949
Pen, ink, and crayon on paper,
31 × 58 in.
Funds provided by Robert and
Frances Coulborn Kohler
2015.13

Passing Creatures Near Movable Shores, 1978
Oil on linen, 47⅞ × 38 in.
Funds provided by Robert and
Frances Coulborn Kohler
2014.43

**Twins Seven-Seven
(Nigerian, 1944–2011)**

Village Life Under Cocoa Tree,
2007
Mixed media on carved wood
panel, 48 × 96 × 1 in.
Gift of Robert Kohler
2023.27

**William T. Wiley
(American, 1937–2021)**

Spooky on the Line, 1979
Lithograph, ed. 24/100, 30 × 22 in.
Promised Gift of Robert Kohler

**Karl Wirsum
(American, 1939–2021)**

Mr. Pain Close Maan the Plain Clothes Man, 1965
Oil and decals on canvas,
36⅝ × 21½ in.
Museum purchase and funds provided by Robert and Frances Coulborn Kohler
2014.16

Mirror MIRROR (MERE) (ROAR) on the wall who is the FAIREST of THEM ALL!, 1970
Ballpoint pen and ink on paper,
17 × 14 in.
Funds provided by Robert and
Frances Coulborn Kohler
2013.36

Jimmy Jones Brother Jack, Jimmy Jones Junior, Tree Son, 1973–74
Acrylic, papier-mâché, light fixtures, soldering iron, wood, and fabric, dimensions variable
Funds provided by Robert and
Frances Coulborn Kohler and
museum purchase
2016.9.1a–h

Robert and Frances Coulborn Kohler Gifts to Woodmere

Unless otherwise noted, the credit line is Museum purchase with funds generously provided by Robert and Frances Kohler.

**Robert Asman
(American, born 1951)**

Untitled, n.d.
Toned gelatin silver print from
paper negative, 23¾ × 20 in.
2022.81.1

Untitled, n.d.
Toned gelatin silver print from
paper negative, 19¾ × 23 in.
2022.81.2

**Roland Ayers
(American, 1932–2014)**

Fleeing Goddess, 1959–60
Gouache on cardboard panel,
28 × 30 in.
2023.15

Emancipated Hero, 1963
Oil pastel and ink on paper, 10 × 7 in.
2021.13.4

Charlie Parker, 1968
Ink on paper, 5⅝ × 3¾ in.
2021.13.1

Untitled, 1968
Ink on paper, 6 × 4 in.
2023.29.3

Untitled, 1968
Ink on paper, 4 × 6 in.
2023.29.4

Untitled, 1969
Ink on paper, 6 × 4 in.
2023.29.6

H. Rap Brown, 1970
Ink on paper, 5¹⁄₁₆ in. dia.
2021.13.3

Bull Fish, 1971
Ink on paper, 4½ × 6½ in.
2021.13.2

The Prophet Garvey, 1972
Ink on paper, 7¹⁄₁₆ × 3½ in.
2023.29.7

Untitled, 1972
Ink on paper, 6 × 4 in.
2023.29.5

Untitled, 1973
Gouache on paper, 31 × 30 in.
2021.13.5

Rooftops, 1975
Ink on paper, 23 × 28¼ in.
2023.16

Astral Ribbon, 1976
Ink on paper, 10½ × 14 in.
2019.76.2

Earth Masses Moving, 1979–80
Ink on paper, 18 in. dia.
2021.13.6

Improvisation #8, Series 1, 1980
Ink on paper, 18 × 24 in.
2019.76.1

Untitled, 1984
Ink on paper, 7⅜ × 7½ in.
2021.13.8

Wind Jammer, 1984
Ink on paper, 9½ × 14½ in.
2021.13.9

Paul Robeson, 1987
Lithograph (artist's proof),
20 in. dia.
2021.13.7

An Old Blues Story, n.d.
Ink on paper, 4¼ × 6¾ in.
2023.29.2

**Susan S. Bank
(American, born 1938)**

Early Morning in el Campo, 2002
Gelatin silver print, 12¼ × 18¼ in.
2018.89.2

Pavos in Sala, 2002
Gelatin silver print, 18¼ × 12¼ in.
2018.89.1

**Henry Bermudez
(American, born Venezuela 1951)**

The RainMakers Dance, 2018
Acrylic paint with glitter on canvas,
72 × 106 in.
2022.5

Miss America, 2019
Acrylic paint with glitter on canvas,
50 × 72 in.
2024.15.2

Our Cousin from Europe Visiting America/Nuestra Prima Europea Visita America, 2020
Oil on canvas, 53 × 48 in.
2024.15.3

Coyote, 2021–22
Acrylic and fabric on paper, dimensions variable
2024.15.1

**Theresa Bernstein
(American, born Poland,
1890–2002)**

The Chess Players, 1926
Oil on canvas, 39½ × 50 in.
2022.71

George Biddle
(American, 1885–1973)

Portrait of Abraham Walkowitz, 1943
Oil on canvas laid to waxed canvas,
40 × 30 in.
2022.80

Brett Bigbee
(American, born 1954)

Portrait of Ann, 1997
Graphite on paper, 24½ × 20½ in.
Gift of Robert and Frances Kohler,
2024
2024.102

Samuel Joseph Brown
(American, 1907–1994)

Untitled, from the series *One World,* 1946
Silkscreen on board, 28½ × 22 in.
2023.29.1

Metamorphic Hands, 1971
Oil and turpentine wash on board,
40 × 30 in.
2024.93.2

Untitled (Classical Figures), 1974
Oil and turpentine wash on board,
40 × 30 in.
2024.93.1

Barbara Bullock
(American, born 1938)

Remembrance, 1985
Acrylic on canvas, 74 × 40 in.
Partial gift of the artist and
museum purchase with funds generously provided by Robert and
Frances Kohler, Osagie Imasogie,
and Jim Nixon, 2020
2020.38

Lizard Spirit, from the series
Child in the Land of the Spirits, 1997
Gouache collage on heavy watercolor paper, 51 × 23 in.
2023.47.2

Healing Feeling, 1998
Acrylic, matte medium and gold-
leaf on watercolor paper, 50 × 41 in.
2020.74

*Child Dreams of Snakes in the
Grass,* c. 2005
Gouache collage on heavy watercolor paper, 39 × 20 in.
2023.47.3

Used Furniture, from the series
Katrina, 2007
Acrylic paint and matte medium on
watercolor paper, 51 × 46½ in.
2023.47.1

Otherworldly 1 (portrait #13), 2022
Acrylic paint and matte medium on
watercolor paper, 23 × 16¼ × ¼ in.
2023.47.4

Selma Hortense Burke
(American, 1900–1995)

Embrace, c. 1970
Black marble, 20½ × 8½ × 10½ in.
Museum purchase with fund-
ing generously provided by Rob-
ert and Frances Kohler, Osagie
Imasogie, and Joseph & Pamela
Yohlin, 2021
2021.49

Felipe Jesus Consalvos
**(American, born Cuba,
1891–1960)**

Sisters Going to Nurse the Lepers,
1920–50
Collage, 13¾ × 16⅞ in.
Gift of Robert and Frances Kohler,
2009
2009.19.3

Joan Wadleigh Curran
(American, 1950–2023)

Fish, 1982
Gouache on paper, 24¼ × 29¾ in.
Gift of Robert and Frances Kohler,
2011
2011.69.2

Fish on a Plate, 1982
Gouache on paper, 20¼ × 29¾ in.
Gift of Robert and Frances Kohler,
2011
2011.69.1

Jessie Drew-Bear
**(American, born England,
1879–1962)**

Bathing, 1945
Oil on canvas, 34 × 44 in.
2024.39

Walter Edmonds
(American, 1938–2011)

Strange Fruit, 1973–75
Oil on canvas, 42 in. dia.
2023.21.2

Sold into Bondage, 1974
Oil on board, 32 × 42 in.
2023.21.1

*So Jim Crow Pursued Us to
Enslave Us,* 1974–75
Oil on board, 30 × 48 in.
2024.17

Martha Mayer Erlebacher
(American, 1937–2013)

In a Garden, 1976
Oil on canvas, 64 × 64 in.
Gift of Robert and Frances Kohler,
2006
2006.7

Study for *Reclining Nude,* 1977
Graphite and watercolor on paper,
16 × 16 in.
Gift of Robert and Frances Kohler,
2004
2004.15.2

Self-Portrait, 1989
Oil on canvas, 17 × 13 in.
Gift of Robert and Frances Kohler,
2004
2004.15.1

Varvàra Fern
(American, born Russia 1999)

Step into the Unknown, 2024
Resin, acrylic paint, 9 × 30 × 4½ in.
2024.23.2

Rafael Ferrer
**(American, born Puerto Rico
1933)**

Francisco, 1986
Oil on wood panel, 24 × 18 in.
Gift of Robert and Frances Kohler,
2017
2017.78

Ashley Flynn
(American, born 1985)

Dad in His Casket, 2010
Mixed media on board, 33 × 25⅛ in.
Gift of Robert and Frances Kohler,
2019
2019.14

*Somerset St, Kensington,
Philadelphia,* 2025
Mixed media, dimensions variable
2022.13

Frank Galuszka
(American, born 1947)

Devon Consoles Greta, 1982–83
Oil on canvas, 10 × 18 in.
Gift of Robert and Frances Kohler,
2009
2009.19.2

Friends, 1982–83
Oil on canvas, 12 × 13 in.
Gift of Robert and Francis Kohler,
1987
1987.12

Greta, 1983
Silverpoint on paper, 11⅜ × 15 in.
Gift of Robert and Frances Kohler,
2013
2013.40.2

Greta and Devon (In a Meadow),
1983
Oil on canvas, 14 × 18 in.
Gift of Robert and Frances Kohler,
2009
2009.19.1

Greta with Flowers, c. 1985
Oil on canvas, 26 × 32¼ in.
Gift of Robert and Frances Kohler,
2004
2004.15.4

Algebra, c. 1990
Oil, Wissahickon mica and wax on
canvas, 12 × 16 in.
Gift of Robert and Frances Kohler,
2013
2013.40.1

Sidney Goodman
(American, 1936–2013)

Untitled, 1958
Oil pastel on paper, 14¼ × 16½ in.
2019.40

Untitled (Electric Chair), 1959
Oil on canvas, 68 × 50 in.
2022.81.5

A Waste, 1984–86
Oil on canvas, 89 × 128⅝ in.
Gift of Robert and Frances Kohler,
by exchange, with additional funds
provided by the Charles Knox
Smith Art Acquisition and Conser-
vation Fund, 2004
2004.16

Still Life, n.d.
Oil on canvas, 36½ × 26½ in.
2022.81.6

Bernard Harmon
(American, 1935–1989)

Striped Dress, c. 1970
Oil on board, 42 × 36 in.
2024.48

Dara Haskins
(American, born 1992)

Embodied—Offering I Have, 2022
Oil and acrylic on canvas,
32 × 52 in.
2023.9.1

Marcy Hermansader
(American, born 1951)

Learning to Fly, 1981
Colored pencil, crayon, acrylic, and
collage on paper, 29¹³⁄₁₆ × 44¾ in.
Gift of Robert and Frances Kohler,
2019
2019.39

The Fire and Ice of Pain, 1987
Mixed media on paper, 23½ × 26 in.
2021.26

Frank Hyder
(American, born 1951)

The Dance, 1987
Oil on plywood, 15 × 19½ in.
Gift of Robert and Frances Kohler,
1990
1990.13.2

Untitled, from the series *Dream Box*, 1990
Acrylic on carved panel, 12 × 12 in.
Gift of Robert and Frances Kohler,
2004
2004.15.3

Ben Kamihira
(American, 1925–2004)

Figure Composition, n.d.
Oil on canvas, 44¼ × 38 in.
2023.72

Paul F. Keene Jr.
(American, 1920–2009)

Odysseus, 1949
Oil on linen canvas, 24 × 20 in.
2022.33

Ed Bing Lee
(American, born 1933)

Decorative Ring #1, 1967–68
Flax linen, 4 × 2 × 1 in.
2022.35.1

Decorative Ring #2, 1967–68
Flax linen, 1½ × 3 × 3 in.
2022.35.2

Decorative Ring #3, 1967–68
Flax linen with beads, 6½ × 3 × 1 in.
2022.35.3

Decorative Ring #4, 1967–68
Flax linen, 6½ × 1¼ × 1½ in.
2022.35.4

Decorative Ring #5, 1967–68
Flax linen, 7 × 1½ × 2½ in.
2022.35.5

Decorative Ring #6, 1967–68
Flax linen, 6½ × 1¾ × 2 in.
2022.35.6

Decorative Ring #7, 1967–68
Flax linen, 6½ × 2½ × 2½ in.
2022.35.7

Swan Ring, 1968
Flax linen, 6 × 4 × 3 in.
2022.35.8

David Lynch
(American, 1946–2025)

Cross and Skulls, 1973
Offset lithograph, 19 × 25 in.
2022.81.3

Untitled, 1973
Lithograph, 19 × 25 in.
2022.81.4

Dindga McCannon
(American, born 1947)

Sister Alone with Her Spirits, 2022
Etching with Chine Colle,
12¼ × 14¾ in.
Published with EFA Robert Blackburn Printmaking Workshop
Printed by Jazmine Catasus
2023.9.2

Caitlin McCormack
(American, born 1988)

Low Country Special, 2021
Crocheted cotton string, glue,
enamel paint, steel pins, and velvet
on wood, 14 × 25 × 12 in.
2025.21

Anne Minich
(American, born 1934)

Image of a Nursery Rhyme, 1992
Oil, graphite, and shell on wood,
21 × 45⅝ in.
2016.37.2

Event, 2002
Graphite and acrylic on rag paper,
28½ × 36 in.
2016.37.1

Ghosthitte, 2006
Oil on wood and stone,
15⅝ × 17¾ in.
2023.48.1

The Ghost Among Us, 2008
Oil on wood and found metal,
15³⁄₁₆ × 19¼ in.
2023.48.2

Boneboat, 2013
Oil on wood, bone, and metal shard,
10⅞ × 20⅞ in.
2016.8

Bridal Vestment I, 2016
Graphite on rag paper, 30 × 24 in.
2016.37.3

Bridal Vestment II, 2016
Graphite on rag paper, 30 × 24 in.
2016.37.4

Bone Boy, 2024
Oil on wood and found material,
12 × 12 in.
2024.62.1

Ode to Ellsworth Kelly, 2024
Oil on wood and found material,
12 × 12 in.
2024.62.2

124 Bluestone Road, 2024
Oil on wood and found material,
12 × 12 in.
2024.62.3

Anamaria and The Holy Three,
2024
Oil on wood and found material,
12 × 12 in.
2024.62.4

Care, 2024
Oil on wood and found material,
12 × 12 in.
2024.62.5

The Minimal Jesus Among Us, 2024
Oil on wood and found material,
12 × 12 in.
2024.62.6

Stage, 2024
Oil on wood and found material,
12 × 12 in.
2024.62.7

Drawing 101, 2024
Oil on wood and found material,
12 × 12 in.
2024.62.8

The Great Straddle, 2024
Oil on wood and found material,
12 × 12 in.
2024.62.9

Stop!, 2024
Oil on wood and found material,
12 × 12 in.
2024.62.10

Name? Mary, 2024
Oil on wood and found material,
12 × 12 in.
2024.62.11

City Year, 2024
Oil on wood and found material,
12 × 12 in.
2024.62.12

Alice Neel
(American, 1900–1984)

Geoffrey Hendricks and Brian,
1980
Screenprint, 33½ × 25½ in.
2023.27

Tina Newberry
(American, born 1954)

The Three Graces, 1987
Oil on Masonite, 22 × 11¾ in.
Gift of Robert and Frances Kohler,
1990
1990.13.1

The Rectangular Office, 2009
Oil on birch ply panel, 20 × 25½ in.
2019.30.1

Discussing the Probabilities of the Next Advance, 2018
Oil and paper on medium-density
fiberboard, 18 × 24 in.
2019.30.2

Albert Paley
(American, born 1944)

Brooch, 1971–72
Amethyst, oxidized sterling silver,
ivory, and pearl, 7½ × 2½ × 1½ in.
Museum purchase with funding
generously provided by Jessica
Berwind, Robert and Frances
Kohler and Nancy McKinney
McNeil, 2023
2023.32

Peter Paone
(American, born 1936)

Black Cat, n.d.
Lithograph (publisher's proof),
22 × 16½ in.
2022.81.7

Untitled, n.d.
Lithograph, 22 × 16½ in.
2022.81.8–10

Alex Queral
(American, born Cuba 1958)

Boy Is My Face Red, 2003
Acrylic on carved telephone book,
11 × 9 in.
Gift of Robert and Frances Kohler,
2014
2014.45.2

Layered Individual, 2003
Acrylic on carved telephone book,
11 × 9 in.
Gift of Robert and Frances Kohler,
2014
2014.45.5

Aviator, 2007
Acrylic on carved telephone book,
11 × 9 in.
Gift of Robert and Frances Kohler,
2014
2014.45.1

Hope (Barack Obama), 2008
Acrylic on carved telephone book,
11 × 9 in.
Gift of Robert and Frances Kohler,
2014
2014.45.3

Jack II (Nicholson), 2008
Acrylic on carved telephone book,
11 × 9 in.
Gift of Robert and Frances Kohler,
2014
2014.45.4

Self-Portrait II, 2014
Digital print on canvas, 48 × 36 in.
Gift of Robert and Frances Kohler,
2014
2014.70

Marta Sanchez
(American, born 1959)

90th Summer, 2020
Oil and enamel on metal, 48 × 48 in.
2024.87.1

Retablo for Stan, 2015
Oil and enamel on metal, 48 × 48 in.
2024.87.2

Retablo for Paul, 1989
Oil and enamel on copper,
18 × 24 in.
2024.87.3

Retablo for Lucinda, 1989
Oil and enamel on copper,
18 × 24 in.
2024.87.4

Retablo for My Brother, 2022
Oil and enamel on copper, 12 × 12 in.
2024.87.5

Judith Schaechter
(American, born 1961)

A Patient Lady, 2021
Stained glass in lightbox,
24⅛ × 23⁷⁄₁₆ in.
2025.11

Charles Searles
(American, 1937–2004)

Dancer #1, 1974
Oil on canvas, 70½ × 46½ in.
2025.25

Twins Seven-Seven
(Nigerian, 1944–2011)

The Smelling Ghost, 1966
Ink, watercolor, and oil on brown
paper, 39½ × 31½ in.
2019.21

The Anti-Bird Ghost, 1967/68
Pen and ink on paper, 39¼ × 25¼ in.
2020.64

Father Beast of the Jungle of Pil-grimage, 1968
Mixed media on panel, 23¾ × 24 in.
2024.14

Oshun Whospers (Woshiper), 1988
Ink, watercolor, acrylic, and oil on
cloth, 89 × 89 in.
2019.79

Untitled, 2004
Mixed media on paper,
13¾ × 16¾ in.
2021.4.3

*The Spirits of My Reincarnation
Brothers and Sisters*, 2006–7
Ink, batik, dye, watercolor, acrylic,
and oil on linen, 58 × 60 in.
2018.88

Untitled, 2010
Limited-edition giclée print on
paper, 21½ × 35 in.
2021.4.1

Untitled, n.d.
Limited-edition giclée print on
paper, 23½ × 39¼ in.
2021.4.2

Village Life Under Palm Tree, n.d.
Oil on wood, 48 × 96 in.
2023.68

Danny Simmons
(American, born 1953)

Hocus Pocus, 2017
Oil on canvas, 48 × 36 in.
2021.52

Olaf Skoogfors
(American, born Sweden,
1930–1975)

Brooch, c. 1962–63
Silver and crystal, 1¾ × 2½ × ¾ in.
2022.63

Christopher Smith
(American, born 1958)

A View from the Box, 2016
Glass fiber reinforced concrete,
28 × 54 in.
2017.20

Ellen Powell Tiberino
(American, 1937–1992)

Repose, c. 1960s/70s
Oil on canvas, 36 × 28 in.
2024.40

Andrew Turner
(American, 1944–2001)

The Bartender, n.d.
Acrylic on canvas board,
25 × 20½ in.
2023.38.3

Concert, n.d.
Acrylic on canvas board,
25½ × 33½ in.
2023.38.4

Sax on the Down Beat, n.d.
Acrylic on wood, 38 × 39½ in.
2023.38.2

Tennis Girls, n.d.
Acrylic on canvas board,
26½ × 32½ in.
2023.38.5

Trumpet, n.d.
Acrylic on canvas, 45 × 34½ in.
2023.38.1

Kukuli Velarde
(American, born Peru 1962)

A Mi Muerto (head severed), from
the series *Isichapuitu*, 1997–2005
Low fire white clay with oil paint
and markers, 22 × 15 × 10 in.
2023.17.5

The Bride, from the series
Isichapuitu, 1997–2005
Low fire white clay with glaze,
22 × 15 × 10 in.
2023.17.4

Mi Padre y Yo, from the series
Isichapuitu, 1997–2005
Low fire white clay with glaze and
oil paint, 22 × 15 × 18 in.
2023.17.3

Tallada, from the series *Isichapuitu*,
1997–2005
Low fire white clay with oil paint
and wax, 21 × 15 × 10 in.
2023.17.1

Yo Misma Soy, from the series
Isichapuitu, 1997–2005
Low fire clay with underglazes,
21 × 15 × 10 in.
2023.17.2

Didier William
(American, born 1983)

*Dancing, Pouring, Crackling,
Mourning*, 2015
Collage, acrylic, stain on panel,
60 × 48 in.
Gift of Robert and Frances Kohler,
2024
2024.54

John Winters
(American, 1904–1983)

Clown at Circus, 1943
Casein on canvas, 22 × 27 in.
2020.26.3

Wanamaker's Display Designs,
1948–73
Mixed media including watercolor,
gouache and pencil on paper and
paperboard, dimensions variable
2020.26.4-42

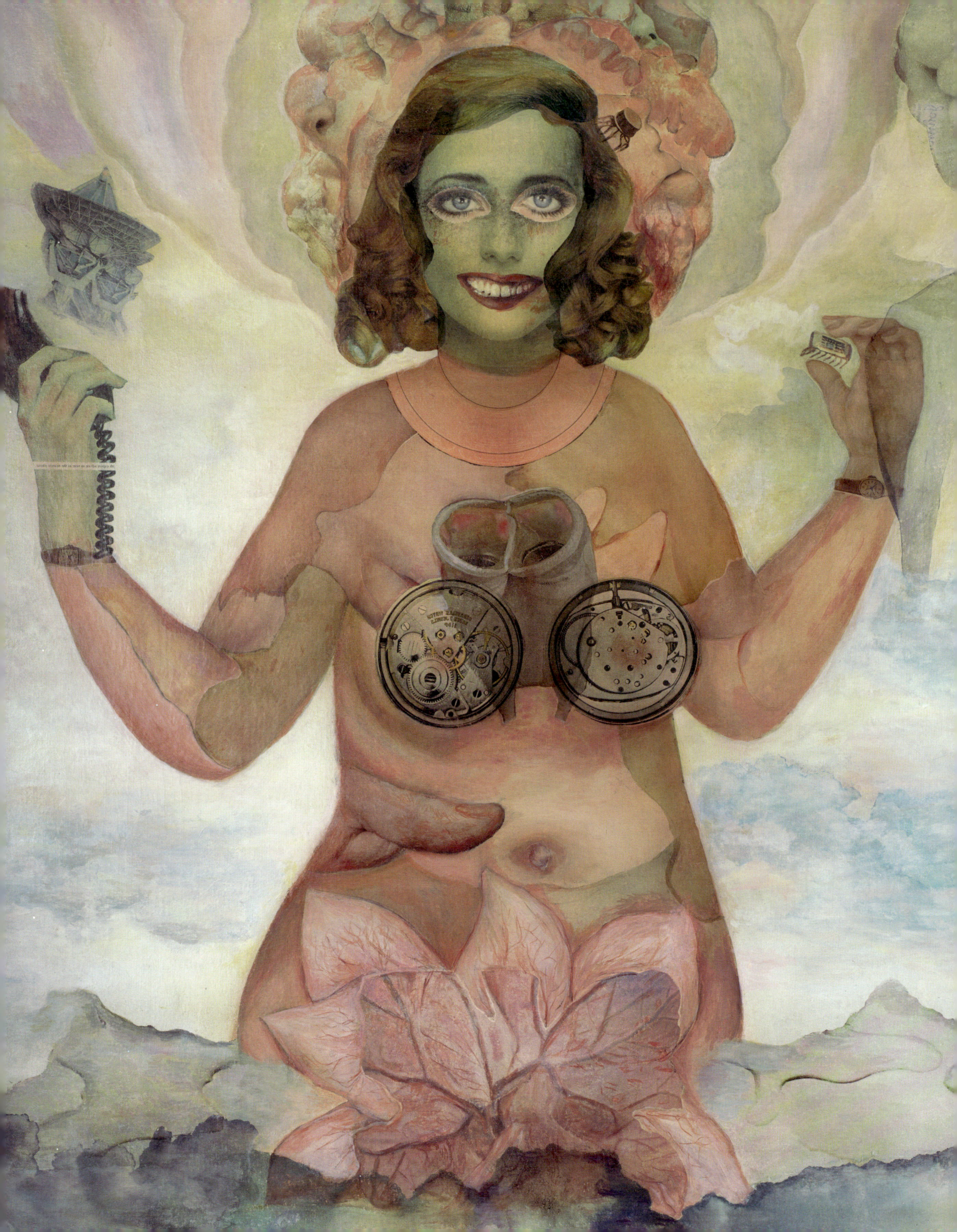

Robert Cozzolino is a Minneapolis-based independent curator, art historian, and critic who approaches curation collaboratively, in partnership with artists, colleagues, and broad communities. "Starting where you are" is critical to his practice—knowing the immediate context and deeper history of the place in which he works. Dr. Cozzolino is drawn to artists who express the full range of human experience, especially those who aspire to visually express the intangible. Although he has worked on topics from the nineteenth and twentieth centuries, he often collaborates with contemporary artists in examining history. He considers himself a curator of fluid time, not bound by the labels and bins imposed on the field. Among his over forty exhibitions are *Supernatural America: The Paranormal in American Art* (2021–22), *World War I and American Art* (2016–17), *Peter Blume: Nature and Metamorphosis* (2014–15), *David Lynch: The Unified Field* (2014), and *With Friends: Six Magic Realists, 1940–1965* (2005).

Robert E. Kohler trained as a chemist, but has long been informally devoted to books and creative literature. A happy accident in midlife led him to unite these separate threads in history of science and environmental history, fields he pursued as a scholar and teacher at the University of Pennsylvania from 1973 to his retirement in 2006. His passion for collecting contemporary art, which he shared with his wife, Frances, began as a secondary pursuit but developed into a mid- to late-life vocation and primary life's work. Frances was another creative shapeshifter: educated in classics and comparative literature, she discovered a gift and calling in history of science, as managing editor of the premier journal in the couple's shared field.

William R. Valerio is the Patricia Van Burgh Allison Director and CEO of Woodmere in Philadelphia. Over the last fifteen years, he has led a transformative revitalization of the institution's community engagement, collections, financial health, and cultural relevance. As the lead visionary behind the museum's exhibitions, he has deepened the scholarship and celebration of the art and artists of Philadelphia, through such major exhibitions as *A Grand Vision: Violet Oakley and the American Renaissance* (2017), *We Speak: Black Artists in Philadelphia, 1920s–1970s* (2015), and *Schofield: International Impressionist* (2014). Valerio holds a PhD in art history from Yale, an MBA from Wharton, an MA in art history from the University of Pennsylvania, and a BA cum laude from Williams College.

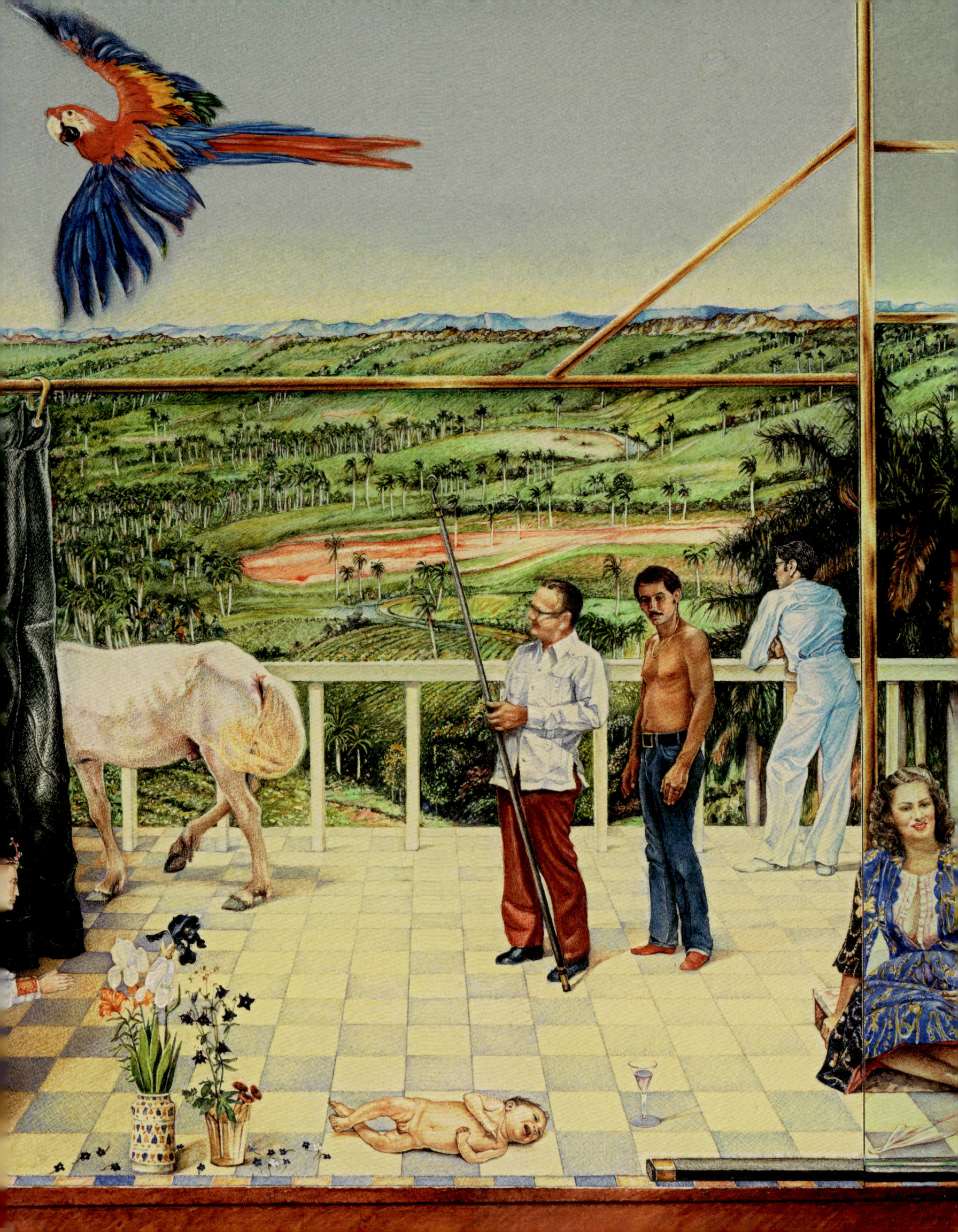

Acknowledgments

Robert Cozzolino

M y life and my curatorial work have been immeasurably enriched through Rob and Frances Kohler's friendship and support. It is a pleasure to give the Philadelphia community a sense of their adventurous taste, their dedication to artists, and their generosity to public museums. Rob and Frances entered my life as I was beginning my career as a curator. Our mutual interests, shared sense of humor and the absurd, and exuberant curiosity bonded us as collaborators. Curators need advocates, especially when they champion artists, subject matter, and eras that the field has written off or forgotten. We need those kindred spirits who understand the value of looking where others are not, reconsidering marginalized artists, raising up those who were ahead of their time—their ideas too radical for their contemporaries. Rob and Frances were foremost among the friends and colleagues who uplifted me in my critical formative years working at the Pennsylvania Academy of the Fine Arts (PAFA). Their support made me a better curator and gave PAFA a reputation as a courageous museum at the edge of the field.

My friend and colleague John Corbett introduced me to the Kohlers in February 2006. I had been at PAFA for a little over a year and had just opened an exhibition I organized, called *Art in Chicago: Resisting Regionalism, Transforming Modernism*. The show presented three generations of modern artists in Chicago and drew from PAFA's permanent collection, collectors in Chicago, artists, and two Philadelphia collections. John had connected me to some lenders, which was critical as the exhibition was organized from scratch in an extremely short period of five months. "Do you know Rob and Frances Kohler?" he asked one day. I told him no—and he said something like "you will get along famously" and "their collection will blow your mind." He brought them by after the exhibition opened and I gave them a tour. Afterward they invited me to visit their home, and indeed, my mind was blown.

And we did form an instant camaraderie that grew into a deep friendship. I think Rob was amazed that there was a curator in Philadelphia who knew and championed Chicago artists like Gladys Nilsson. The Kohlers had strayed from institutions and stayed away for several years, but their heads were turned when they saw PAFA devoting time and space to what was then considered a feral, meandering path in American art. That rough road less traveled in American art is what I found at their home. For instance, Gregory Gillespie, among my favorite artists and one off my colleagues' radars, was there represented in depth, including his most challenging imagery.

Rob and Frances introduced me to artists I had not known before, like Jane Lund, a close friend of Gregory and Frances Cohen Gillespie, and others, expanding my understanding of the intertwined communities of makers. I loved their support of artists who were willing to make themselves vulnerable in their work—to poke and prod at the trouble spots in their psyches and lives. In turn, they responded when I shared with them artists I felt they would understand right away, like Anne Minich, based in Philadelphia. Anne introduced herself to me at the opening event for PAFA's exhibition celebrating Linda Lee Alter's gift of her collection of art by women. After visiting Anne's home and studio, I called Rob to gush over the incredible range and invention of her work. Their own close friendship ensued, and the Kohlers became Anne's most dedicated patrons.

While Rob and Frances and I built trust together and they began to feel connected to PAFA, I believe a turning point came when they watched the process of Linda Lee Alter working with me and deciding to donate her collection to PAFA. Seeing Lee's relationship with PAFA and me, and hearing from Lee about why she felt that PAFA was a good home for her collection, convinced Rob and Frances to make their own plans. The collections are each personal and intimate, with distinctive points of view, and they complement one another. They guarantee that PAFA and Philadelphia will be destinations for artists and researchers curious about a wide range of figurative and representational art, particularly work made since 1970. The emphasis of so many artists in both collections on explorations of gender, sexuality, and identity make PAFA uniquely equipped to support projects that examine what it is to be human and to express lived experience in especially self-referential art. It is a legacy I hope future patrons will extend, following the artist-centered generosity the Kohlers have shown.

While this project celebrates the Kohlers' planned bequest of their collection to PAFA, it also gives us an opportunity to honor their longstanding and ongoing support of Woodmere Art Museum. They have, in particular, transformed the representation of Black artists in that collection, in collaboration with William Valerio, the museum's director. This is a critical part of Philadelphia's culture that Woodmere is dedicated to making visible.

My work on this project was made possible through the substantive support of the staff at both museums, named in the directors' foreword. I want to mention friends and colleagues who have been a great help over the years as I got to know Rob and Frances and through the process of realizing this project: George Adams, Alex Baker, David Brigham, Diane Burko, Cate Cooney, John Corbett, Derek Eller, Tory Folliard, Peggy Gillespie, Nancy Hoffman, Anna Marley, Richard Michelson, Richard Norton, John Ollman, Julien Robson, Barbara C. A. Santini, and Jodi Throckmorton. Barbara Katus, Jack Ramsdale, and Zoe Smith provided photography;

Nora Stewart helped clear permissions. At PAFA, Leah Graup and Jacob Stevens installed the exhibition and assisted with photography at Rob's home. Hoang Tran, Director of Archives, Library, and Collections kindly fielded my image and research requests.

Finally, I wish to thank the artists who answered my queries about their work in the Kohler collection, giving their time and valuable insight into their art over the years: Luis Cruz Azaceta, William Beckman, Henry Bermudez, Barbara Bullock, Craig Calderwood, Red Grooms, Mimi Gross, Lorri Gunn, Marcy Hermansader, Joyce Kozloff, Gina Litherland, Robert Lostutter, Jane Lund, Anne Minich, Gladys Nilsson, Maija Peeples-Bright, Tabitha Vevers, Didier William, and the late Karl Wirsum.

This publication is dedicated to the memory of Frances Coulborn Kohler.

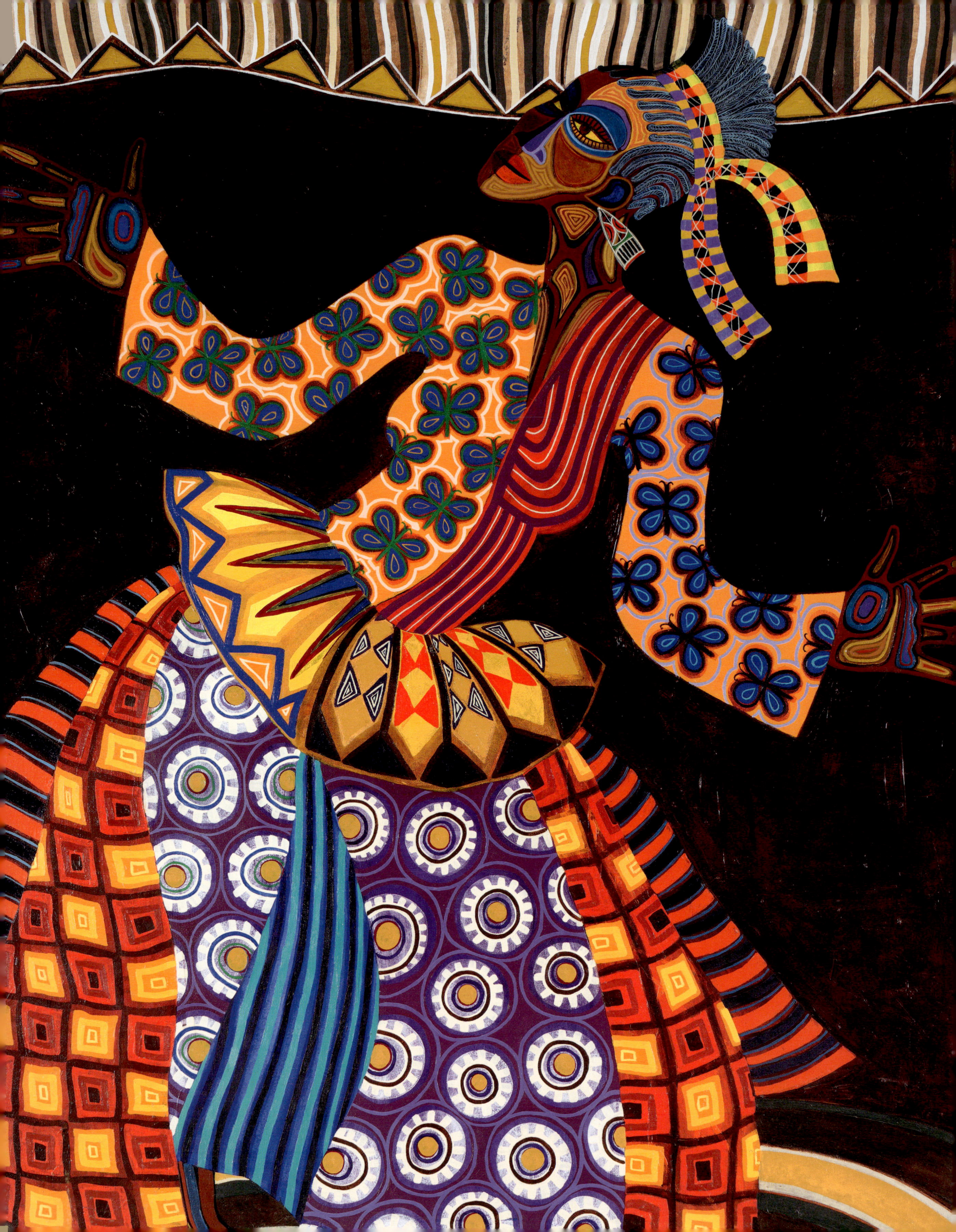

Index of Works Illustrated

Arneson, Robert
 Head Eater, 82
 Reflections with Pink and Silver, 28
 Roy De Forest–Witness, 85
 Self-Portrait Drawing, 21
 Study for *Nasal Flat*, 84
 Untitled (Double profile), 83
Ayers, Roland
 Orgasm, 65
 Swing, 126
 Untitled, 126
Azaceta, Luis Cruz
 Coney Island Local, 164
 Dictator's Head-Boot, 173
 Self-Portrait as Cockroach, 98
 Self-Portrait Throwing the Devil Out, 81
 Self-Portrait: Apocalypse Now—or Later?, 44, 49, 174
 Self-Portrait: Pistol and Other Small Things, 80
 Study for *The Journey*, 36
Barlow, Leslie
 Nicole and Seth and Their Daughter (and Daughter to Be), in the Kitchen, 61
Barsness, James
 Bifrost Bridge, 109
Barton, Macena
 Self-Portrait, 86
 Untitled (Outer space), 89
 Untitled (Rosanna in pink), 88
Beall, Joanna
 Portrait of HCW(esterman), 102
Beckman, William
 Diana #7, 27
 Diana in Sweatshirt, 112
 Self-Portrait, 77
 Study for *Diana IV*, 113

Berdich, Vera
 Olympia (A Mechanical Doll), 87, 206
Bermudez, Henry
 Miss America, 94
Brantley, Sherman James
 Brother James, 60
Brown, Joan
 The Last Dance, 165
 Self-Portrait in Knit Hat, 76
 Self-Portrait in Scarf Drinking Tea, 76
Bullock, Barbara
 Healing Feeling, 10, 16
 Remembrance, 62
Calderwood, Craig
 Meat Bees, 127
 Notes on ♀ and ♂ from My Eight-Year-Old Self, 58
 Ringworm Inspection, 119
 You Can Tell by the Beast Between Her Legs, 127
Consalvos, Felipe Jesus
 Take Me to the Land of Jazz, 160
Crosby, Njideka Akunyli
 I Always Face You, Even When It Seems Otherwise, 68
Curran, Joan Wadleigh
 Fish on a Plate, 12
Dean, Peter
 Condor Flush, 166
 Crazy Dance at the Crack of Reality, 36
 Hounded, 154
 Portrait of the Artist, 101
 Untitled (Self-portrait with two masks), 101
De Forest, Roy
 Savage Echoes, 28
 Trouble in the Bovine Quarters, 151
 Watching for the Outriders, 153
 You Can't Go Home Again, 155

Edmonds, Walter
    So Jim Crow Pursued Us to Enslave
        Us, 171
    Sold into Bondage, 16, 170
Erlebacher, Martha Mayer
    In a Garden, 115
    Study for *Reclining Nude*, 114
Ferrer, Rafael
    El Bolero, 144
    Encuentro, 27
    La Pintura: Descarga Del Monte, 32
    Sombrero de Palma, 142
Frey, Viola
    The Dinner, also Junk Eating, 29
    Untitled (Kissing couple and dog in
        window), 140
Galuszka, Frank
    Greta with Flowers, 111
German, Vanessa
    Declaration of Independence, 160
Gillespie, Frances Cohen
    Leila, 33
    Nude Self-Portrait in Chair, 75
Gillespie, Gregory
    Dark Painter (Portrait of a Renaissance
        Painter), 26
    Julianna, 110
    The Kiss, 129
    Lydia and Her Demon, 51
    Manic Depression, 129
    Rita, 26
    Seated Couple, 130
    Self-Portrait (Bald), 156
    Self-Portrait with Mother and Son, 93
    Wheel of Birth, 2, 116
    William Beckman, 74
    Woman on Blue Ground, 156
    Woman with Baby, 130
González, Juan
    Jardin Gris, 95
    Nacimiento (The Birth), 64, 208
Goodman, Sidney
    A Waste, 13, 175
    Untitled (Electric Chair), 157
Grooms, Red
    Harry Watley Gets Rabbit-itis, 167
    P'town Bicycle (Arthur Cohen), 99
    Self-Portrait, Summer, 37
Grooms, Red, and Mimi Gross
    Tappy Toes, 161
Gunn, Lorri
    Imagists Playing Cards, 162

Harmon, Bernard
    Striped Dress, 15
Hendricks, Barkley
    J. S. B. III, 60
Hermansader, Marcy
    Alterations in the Blood, 128
    Living with the Moon, 152
Hyder, Frank
    The Dance, 13
Keene, Jr., Paul F.
    Untitled, 143
Kitaj, R. B.
    Bather (Psychotic Boy), 131
    Quentin, 78
Kraus, Anne
    The Dormant Garden, 141
Kravitz, Deborah
    Ceremony, 138
    Girl Drawing II (Girl Drawing Door), 133
    Mother and Child in Front of Door, 133
    The Path, 25
    Rebirth of the Discarded Ones, 25
    Self-Portrait, 106
    Within the Lotus, 138
    Woman, Drawing, Door, 53
Lehrer, Riva
    Mike Ervin and Anna Stonum, 61
Litherland, Gina
    My Braids of the Past (for Marosa di
        Giogio), 124
    Pistis Sophia, 135
    Queen of an Uncharted Territory, 39
    Winter Solstice, 136
Lostutter, Robert
    A Sign of My Time, 31, 177
    Map to the Morning Dance 3, 121
    Red Masdevallia, 122
    Red-Throated Bee-Eater, 139
    The Songs of War 7, 172
    The Songs of War 9, 172
    Untitled (Burning man), 139
    Untitled (Two standing figures with
        hoop), 123
    Untitled (Woman in stockings), 123
Lund, Jane
    Ancient Rite, 24
    Anniversary, 24, 137
    Artists of a Certain Age: Self-Portrait
        with Jean-Étienne Liotard,
        1702-1789, 92
    Bob, Sultana, and Guard, 91
    The Choice, 132

Party for Myself, 18, 52
Pregnant Woman, 79
The Priestess, 117
Messer, Sam
   Jon in Yellow Chair, 100
   New York Harbor, 38
Minich, Anne
   AEGM at 35, 39
   The Anglican and the Jew, 118
   Bridal Vestment I, 15
   Bridal Vestment II, 15
   Christmas Eve 1993, for Maria and Daniel, 97
   Feral Nun, 47
   Hungry Jesus, 65
   Imposition at Monadnock, 96
   Sunday's Lover, 118
Morris, Darrel
   More Like Your Brother, 35
Neal, Robert
   Cheese and Butter Line, 103
   Street People, 56
Newberry, Tina
   The Three Graces, 14
Nilsson, Gladys
   Archway Peckercysters, 148
   Checking Out the Other Side, 46, 176
   Cloud Burste, 150
   Drownders, 4, 178
   Gift Box, 90
   Going, 30
   Hairdresser's Surprise, 125
   Semisighmetricall, 181
   To Couples: DeKaled, 149
Olivieri, Irene Hardwicke
   The Painter and Her Skeleton, 134
Paschke, Ed
   Gleason, 105
   Jimmie, 105
Peeples-Bright, Maija
   Sheep Sheiks, 179
Ramberg, Christina
   False Bloom, 120
Rembert, Winfred
   Chain Gang, 168
   Sugar Cane, 104
   T.J. the Tooler, 40
   The Hungry Eye Cafe #2, 6, 145
Searles, Charles
   Dancer #1, 147, 212
Sherrod, Philip
   Bar, Baby, and 6th Avenue, 38

Statsinger, Evelyn
   In the Penal Colony, 180
   Passing Creatures Near Movable Shores, 183
Staver, Kyle
   Dolphins, 40
   Octopus Ardor, 190
Stotik, Eric
   Untitled (Old man with woman in crib), 169
   Untitled LR33 (Factory, machine, green man), 159
   Untitled LR62 (Activists, posters), 169
Thompson, Bob
   Artaud, 32
Tooker, George
   Dark Angel, 54
Twins Seven-Seven
   Oshun Whospers (Woshiper), 191
   The Spirits of My Reincarnation Brothers and Sisters, 182
Vevers, Tabitha
   Eden (Eveandadam VI.07a), 66
   Eden: Marsupedonna, 34
   Flying Dream (Anonymous), 66
   Flying Dream (Gillian), 184
   Flying Dream (In the Dunes II), 185
   Flying Dream (Marja), 185
   Flying Dream (The Rescue), 186, 194
   Shiva (Fire and Ice), 66
Wilde, John
   An Homage to Philipp Otto Runge, 187
   The Chair, 35
   Family Portrait I, Inside, 108
   H. and Death #2, 35
   Myself in 1944 Contemplating the Following 60 Years, 107
   Myself with Long Hair, 106
   Work Reconsidered: Love After Murder, 72, 73, 158
Winters, John
   Untitled (Easter Eggs), 12
William, Didier
   Bois Caiman, 188
   Dancing, Pouring, Crackling, Mourning, 146, 192–193
Wirsum, Karl
   Mr. Pain Close Maan the Plain Clothes Man, 163
   Untitled (Study for Show Girl Series), 31
Worth, Alexi
   Tennessee, 189

Published by the Pennsylvania Academy of the Fine Arts and Woodmere Art Museum, Philadelphia, and distributed by the University of Pennsylvania Press.

This publication honors Robert and Frances Coulborn Kohler, the collection they formed, the artists they have supported, and their generosity to Philadelphia and beyond. It was produced in conjunction with the exhibition *Bodies and Souls*, at PAFA and at Woodmere, curated by Robert Cozzolino with the support of colleagues from each museum. The exhibition ran concurrently from March 13 to July 12, 2026, at PAFA and March 7 to June 7, 2026, at Woodmere. The essays in this volume were hand-written and are the original thoughts of sentient organic beings.

Pennsylvania Academy of the Fine Arts
128 N. Broad Street
Philadelphia, PA 19103
pafa.org

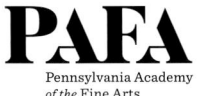

Pennsylvania Academy
of the Fine Arts

Woodmere Art Museum
9201 Germantown Ave
Philadelphia, PA 19118
woodmereartmuseum.org

WOODMERE

Distributed by the University of
Pennsylvania Press
pennpress.org

Published 2026

ISBN 979-8-9931280-1-6
Library of Congress Control Number:
2025949540

This paper meets the requirements of ANSI/NISO Z39.48-1992 (Permanence of Paper).

Produced by Marquand Books, Seattle
marquandbooks.com

Edited by Gretchen Dykstra and
    Melissa Duffes
Designed by Ryan Polich
Typeset in Forma DJR, Miller Text, and
    VC Henrietta by Brynn Warriner
Proofread by Nick Allison, with assistance
    from Irene Elias
Color management by I/O Color, Seattle
Printed and bound in Italy by
    Printer Trento S.p.A.

Section opener credits
front cover: Gladys Nilsson, detail of *Checking Out the Other Side*, 1987
back cover: Charles Searles, *Dancer #1*, 1974
Page 2: Gregory Gillespie, *Wheel of Birth*, 1983–90
Page 4: Gladys Nilsson, *Drownders*, c. 1972–73
Page 6: Winfred Rembert, *The Hungry Eye Cafe #2*, 2006
Page 10: Barbara Bullock, *Healing Feeling*, 1998
Page 18: Jane Lund, *Party for Myself*, c. 1974–75
Page 44: Luis Cruz Azaceta, *Self-Portrait: Apocalypse Now—or Later?* 1981
Pages 72–73: John Wilde, *Work Reconsidered: Love After Murder*, 1989
Pages 192–193: Didier William, *Dancing, Pouring, Crackling, Mourning*, 2015
Page 194: Tabitha Vevers, *Flying Dream (The Rescue)*, 2001
Page 206: Vera Berdich, *Olympia (A Mechanical Doll)*, c. 1960s
Page 208: Juan González, *Nacimiento (The Birth)*, 1979
Page 212: Charles Searles, *Dancer #1*, 1974

Photography credits
Robert Cozzolino: Kohler figs. 1, 34; **Daniel Dennehy:** Cozzolino fig. 16; **Rick Echelmeyer:** Valerio figs. 1–10; plates 22, 42, 45, 46, 59, 83, 113, 114, 119, and 136; Cozzolino fig. 14; **Michael and Carolina Ellenbogen:** plates 89, 91, and 95; **Robert Chase Heishman:** plate 73; **Barbara Katus:** Kohler figs. 11, 18, 26, 28; Cozzolino figs. 7, 9–11, 21; plates 2, 18, 26, 32, 44, 47, 94, 97, 103, 105, 108, 117, 124, 127; **Jack Ramsdale:** Kohler figs. 4–6, 8–10, 12–15, 17, 21–24, 27, 29–31, 33; Cozzolino figs. 2a,b, 4–6, 8, 15a,b, 17–20; plates 3–7, 9–14, 20, 21, 23–25, 27–30, 33–41, 43, 48–53, 55–58, 60–72, 74–82, 84–88, 90, 92, 93, 96, 99, 100, 104, 106, 107, 109–112, 115, 116, 120, 122, 125, 128–132; **Zoe Smith:** Kohler figs. 2, 19, 20, 25, 32 plates 1, 8, 15–17, 19, 54, 101, 102, 118, 121, 123, 133–135.

Image credits
In reproducing images contained in this publication, every effort has been made to identify rights holders and obtain permissions for use. Errors or omissions in credit citations have been either unavoidable or unintentional. In those instances where rights holders could not be located, notwithstanding good faith efforts, the authors and publisher welcome any information that would allow them to correct future reprints.
Valerio essay: figs. 2, 9, 6–7, 10 courtesy of and © the artists; **Kohler essay:** figs. 3–6, 11, 15, 16, 19, 20, 21, 22, 25, 27, 29, 30–32, courtesy of and © the artists; fig. 34, courtesy of Robert Cozzolino; **Cozzolino essay:** figs. 1–3, 5–6, 8, 9, 12–14, 16, 18–20 courtesy of and © the artists; fig. 10 © Barkley L. Hendricks. Courtesy of the Estate of Barkley L. Hendricks and Jack Shainman Gallery, New York; fig. 11 Courtesy of Stanek Gallery, authorized representative of James Sherman Brantley artwork; fig. 15a-b Copyright Juan Gonzalez, courtesy Nancy Hoffman Gallery; fig. 7, © Estate of George Tooker. Courtesy of DC Moore Gallery, New York; **Plates:** 6, 68, Estate of R. B. Kitaj, courtesy of PIANO NOBILE, London; 31, © 2025 Dumbarton Arts, LLC / Licensed by VAGA at Artists Rights Society (ARS), NY; 34–35, © Marc Paschke/Ed Paschke Estate; 52, Courtesy the Estate of Christina Ramberg and Corbett vs. Dempsey, Chicago; 7–9, 18, 20, 22, 24–30, 32, 36, 40, 48–51, 53–58, 61–63, 69–79, 81–84, 86, 88–90, 92–94, 100, 103–104, 106, 108, 109, 111–118, 120–123, 125, 128–131, 133–135, courtesy of and © the artists; Robert Arneson works © 2025 Estate of Robert Arneson / Licensed by VAGA at Artists Rights Society (ARS), NY; William Beckman additionally courtesy of Forum Gallery New York; Joan Brown, © 2025 Estate of Joan Brown; Craig Calderwood images additionally courtesy of George Adams Gallery; Roy De Forest, © 2025 Estate of Roy De Forest / Licensed by VAGA at Artists Rights Society (ARS), NY; Viola Frey, © 2025 Artists' Legacy Foundation / Artists Rights Society (ARS), NY; Vanessa German courtesy of the artist and Olney Gleason; Gregory Gillespie images courtesy of The Gregory Gillespie Revocable Trust; Lorri Gunn and Karl Wirsum images, Courtesy of Lorri Gunn Wirsum; John Wilde images Courtesy of the Shirley Wilde Trust.

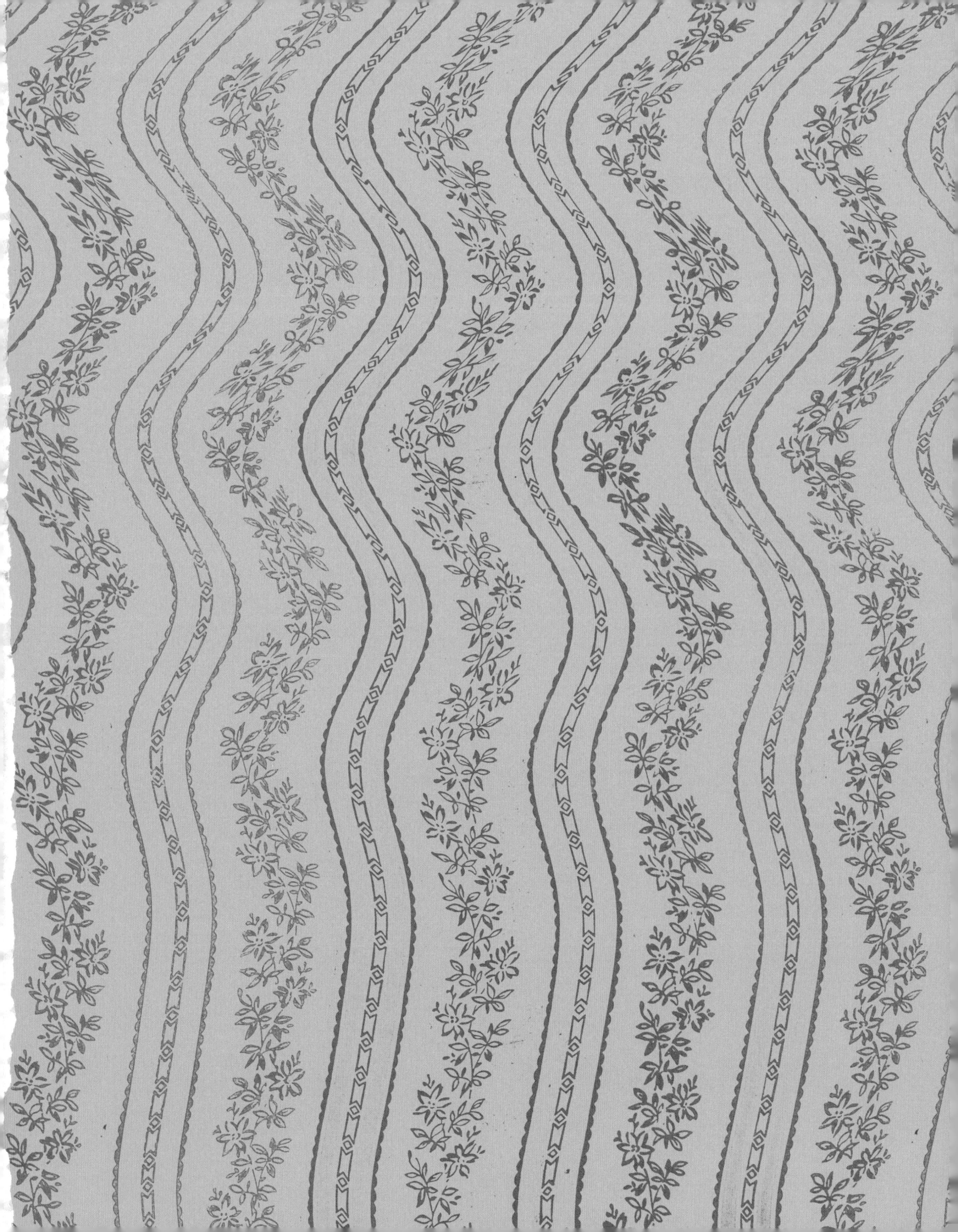

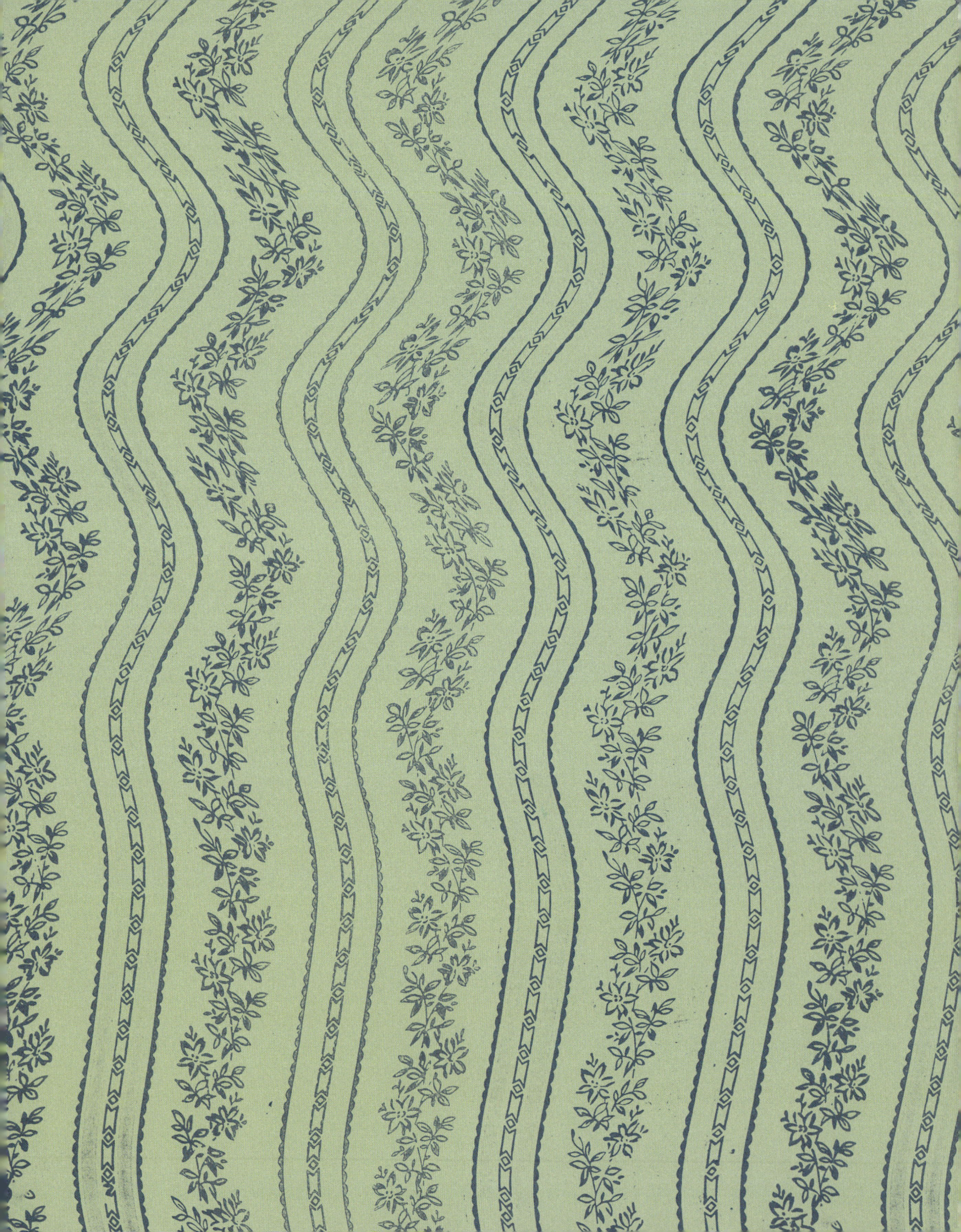